NONVERBAL COMMUNICATION

NONVERBAL COMMUNICATION

SECOND EDITION

Loretta A. Malandro *Malandro Associates, Inc.*

Larry L. Barker *Auburn University*

Deborah Ann Barker

Random House New York

Second Edition

98765432

LIBRARY OF CONGRESS
Library of Congress Cataloging-in-Publication Data

Malandro, Loretta A.
      Nonverbal communication / Loretta A. Malandro, Larry L. Barker,
   Deborah Ann Barker.—2nd ed.
         p.   cm.
      Includes bibliographies and index.
      ISBN 0-394-36526-7
      1. Nonverbal communication.   I. Barker, Larry Lee, 1941–
II. Barker, Deborah Ann.   III. Title.
P99.5.M34 1988
001.56—dc 19   88-10285
                                                        CIP

Manufactured in the United States of America

Book Design by Glen Edelstein
Cover Design by Sandra Josephson

CHAPTER OPENING PHOTO CREDITS: *Chapter 1:* Joel Gordon; *Chapter 2:* Jean-Claude LeJeune; *Chapter 3:* F. B. Grunzweig/Photo Researchers; *Chapter 4:* Peter Southwick/Stock, Boston; *Chapter 5:* Joseph Schuyler/Stock, Boston; *Chapter 6:* Robert V. Eckert, Jr./EKM-Nepenthe; *Chapter 7:* Chuck Fishman/Woodfin Camp & Associates; *Chapter 8:* Hazel Hankin; *Chapter 9:* Carolyn Hine/The Picture Cube; *Chapter 10:* Michael Weisbrot and Family; *Chapter 11:* Mark Chester/Photo Researchers.

COVER CREDIT: Max Burchartz, Lotte (Eye), c. 1928. Silver gelatine print, 33.5 × 44.1 cm. Museum Folkswang, Fotografische Sammlung, Essen, Germany.

PREFACE

"We cannot *not* communicate!" This often quoted axiom is a foundation of the nonverbal communication theory and research that is surveyed in the second edition of *Nonverbal Communication.* Our goal, however, has been not only to present a complete, detailed discussion of research and theory but also to make it understandable, interesting, and readable to students. During many years of teaching nonverbal communication, the three authors of this text have discovered that students want much more than what has been offered in traditional textbooks. Our students want books that are enjoyable to read and that are stimulating both intellectually and emotionally. *Nonverbal Communication* attempts to address the need for a comprehensive, thorough survey of theory and research that conveys to students the great excitement of this area of study.

Like the first edition, the second edition of *Nonverbal Communication* aims for a comprehensive survey of the field. The text covers such topics as taste, smell, dance, and the use of time, in addition to major nonverbal factors such as body types, movements and gestures, clothing, facial expression, and voice. At the same time, we have aimed for in-depth coverage, discussing each content area, where possible, in terms of functions, perceptions, characteristics, and effects. The text, like the first edition, is student centered. A wide variety of examples, quotations, and illustrations clarifies concepts and relates them to students' lives. Chapter summaries help students review, and extensive references provide students with sources for further study.

Professors examining the second edition will be pleased to see that it has been substantially updated to reflect the considerable growth of theory and research in nonverbal communication. Our goal has been to make this revised edition the most current survey available in the field. The graphic design, illustrations, and examples have also been revised and updated to maintain student interest and accessibility, while making the second edition more consistent with the academic approach common to most college classrooms.

We would like to express our deep appreciation to several people who helped bring this book to completion. First, we gratefully acknowledge several students, friends, and colleagues who helped author or coauthor individual chapters in the first edition of this text. In each case these individuals conducted the initial research and wrote original chapter drafts. Thanks to Tally Anderson (Chapter 4); Renee Edwards (Chapter 7); Frances Sayers (Chapter 9); Kathy Shumaker (Chapter 1); and Kittie Watson (Chapters 1 and 5). Also, thanks to Sondi Feldmaier who contributed the section on "Dance" in Chapter 11.

Second, although a single thank you could never be enough, we also would like to express our appreciation to Sylvia Lippold. Sylvia's tireless efforts as our research assistant allowed the second edition to progress in the timely way that it did. So we would like to say here, "Sylvia, you were marvelous!"

Our reviewers for the second edition offered valuable insights and recommendations. Our special thanks to Mark E. Comadena, Illinois State University; Lynne Webb, University of Florida; Paul D. Krivonos, California State University, Northridge; Carol Ann Valentine, Arizona State University; Gordon R. Owen, New Mexico State University; John Wanzenried, University of Nebraska at Omaha; Janis Andersen, San Diego State University; Peter Andersen, San Diego State University; Richard Cheatham, Southwest Texas State University; and Tom Steinfatt, Clarkson University.

Finally, thanks to all our students in nonverbal communication classes over the past ten years who provided the basis for many of the examples and illustrations included in the text.

L.A.M., *Tempe, Arizona*
L.L.B., *Auburn, Alabama*
D.R.B., *Auburn, Alabama*

CONTENTS

NONVERBAL COMMUNICATION

CHAPTER 1

INTRODUCTION TO NONVERBAL COMMUNICATION

From a man's face, I can read his character; if I can see him walk, I know his thoughts.

Petronius, *Satyricon,* 1–65 A.D.

For Sally, Sam's behavior was just a bit confusing, especially today of all days. They were lunching at their favorite restaurant by the bay . . . were talking about their fabulous evening the night before . . . and yet Sam was acting differently in several ways. As they talked, Sally noticed that Sam's gaze kept wandering, as if he were in another place and time. Although he was usually the life of the party— always smiling, laughing, and teasing everyone around—he now sat quietly and laughed nervously as they talked about his upcoming interview at 3 P.M. Despite the confidence he had exhibited the night before, while talking about the new executive position, Sally noticed that Sam was now fidgeting with the cuffs of his new custom-tailored suit. And he had already kicked her twice under the table as he shifted from side to side.

The preceding example illustrates a variety of nonverbal messages that we communicate when we are experiencing stress. Even though Sam was usually outgoing, fun, and witty, he became more quiet, nervous, and tense under stress. In addition, although he was usually candid and confident, his conversation with Sally was now both strained and hesitant.

Like Sam, we all act differently at various times, depending on the situation. Although we may not all possess Sam's outgoing personality, we do exhibit behavioral changes that are equally extreme. By examining how Sam's nonverbal messages influenced his interactions, you may begin to see the role that nonverbal communication plays in everyday life. In addition, you may begin to learn the importance of nonverbal awareness, or the ability to observe, interpret, and influence (positively) nonverbal behavior.

In our example above, Sam's gaze behavior was an immediate clue that something was distracting his attention. In this instance, that "something" was his pending interview, despite the confidence that he had demonstrated the night before. Additionally, Sam's body language suggested that something was wrong— or at least that he was feeling insecure. Had she known more about the messages that nonverbal behavior sends, Sally might have been less confused and more capable of assessing the situation. In turn, increased awareness might have allowed her to help Sam feel more comfortable and secure.

Another nonverbal factor that influenced this situation was that Sam was already dressed for the interview, despite the fact that the meeting was not to take place until 3 P.M. Just as clothing affects the perceptions of other people, so, too, does it affect our own psychological state of mind. Although Sally may have believed she was encouraging Sam by inviting him to have lunch on the day of his interview, she may actually have heightened his anxiety level by asking him to wear his new suit so that she might see it. Once again, sensitivity and nonverbal awareness could have helped Sally to support Sam better on the day he needed her most.

Finally, the environment in which they chose to meet was a rather formal one—perhaps another contributing factor to Sam's increased level of stress. Although the restaurant, indeed, was Sam and Sally's favorite, it also happened to be the "in place" where corporate executives in the city often met for lunch. Thus, the fact that the room was filled with people holding positions to which Sam aspired also influenced his communication behavior. In turn, his behavior affected Sally's perceptions and mood negatively.

As you can see, nonverbal communication significantly affects the behaviors of others and the outcomes of many communication events. Characteristics such as your voice, body movements, gestures, spatial distancing, and touch relay important information that is often universally understood. For this reason, it is vital for you to understand what you and others communicate nonverbally.

The following pages provide a perspective through which you can view information and research efforts related to nonverbal communication. The chapters that follow will assist you in creating a general understanding of just what nonverbal communication is and how it plays an important role in your everyday life.

A PERSPECTIVE ON NONVERBAL COMMUNICATION

Does anybody really know when nonverbal communication (as a discipline) originated? Harrison and Wiemann (1983) trace interest in nonverbal communication to the early Greeks (400–600 B.C.). Other authors of texts on this subject (e.g., Weitz, 1979) trace the origins to the elocutionary period in which language was rudimentary and gestures were emphasized. Darwin (1872), because of his work in explaining the relationship between animal and human behavior, is also mentioned by some authors as the father of nonverbal communication as a field of study. As you can see, although there is disagreement regarding the exact time at which the (disciplined) study of nonverbal communication began, a consensus does exist regarding its importance to our understanding of the overall communication process.

Nonverbal behavior, experiences, and communication are with you literally all of the time. Television, radio, motion pictures, records, magazines, newspapers, public speeches, private conversations, classroom interactions, and solitary daydreams all have nonverbal dimensions that affect you significantly. The ability to identify specific nonverbal behaviors that communicate effectively (or even miscommunicate) can assist you in improving your communication skills.

What Is Nonverbal Communication?

Although our primary emphasis will not be on the origins of or early research pioneers in nonverbal communication, we need to address the issue of what nonverbal communication *is*.

Most authors of nonverbal communication texts choose to define communication first and then address the nonverbal component separately. We will follow this lead. For our purposes, **communication** will be viewed as the dynamic and irreversible process by which we exchange and interpret messages within a given situation or context. To help you better understand our definition, let's look at its individual components. For us, communication is "dynamic" because it is constantly in motion and changing. It is "irreversible" in that nothing we say or do can ever be completely retracted. To illustrate, think of the last time that you said or did something out of anger—only to realize that you had made a mistake the minute you began to talk. Unfortunately, in circumstances such as this, even an apology cannot completely erase the scars. For this reason, we must always strive to be responsible communicators. (Note: Memories of positive interactions can also never be taken away. This is fortunate, for positive memories often overshadow any negative events that have occurred.)

To continue an elaboration of our definition, we describe communication as a "process" because it is a specific, continuous series of actions directed toward some end. In this instance, that end is the "exchange and interpretation of messages." It is at this point that we have reached the very heart of our definition. For us, communication involves the sending and receiving of some message, whether that message is verbal or nonverbal in nature. However, in order for "communication" to take place—and to be defined as something more than simple "behavior"—the sender's message must actually be interpreted by the receiver in some way. Thus, the inclusion of the "interpretation" component allows us to separate human behavior from human communication. Additionally, it previews the limits that we will set on our definition of "nonverbal communication," still to come.

The final component of our definition involves the importance of the situation or context to communication. We have included this component because of its contribution to our understanding of any communication event. Without knowledge of the complete situation about which someone is talking, messages cannot be accurately exchanged and interpreted. Likewise without a context in which to place a given message, meanings may be misconstrued and misinterpreted as well. For example, if Sara has shared information about Danielle with you without bothering to explain Danielle's entire situation, you may unwittingly misinterpret Sara's message and make inaccurate inferences about Danielle as a person. Likewise, if you overhear only a portion of a conversation between Ken and Anna about Danielle, any "reality" that you assign to her plight may also be inaccurate.

To this point, we have presented our current definition of "communication." (Like most definitions, ours will change as we acquire more knowledge.) However, it should be pointed out that considerable academic debate exists concerning which definition of communication is the most useful and valid. One primary debate concerns whether communication necessarily involves two or more people. For example, some communication scholars argue that "talking to oneself" is *not* a form of communication.

In an effort not to be drawn into controversies such as this, we have provided a broad-based definition of communication that allows for the study of all possible forms of verbal and nonverbal communication. In addition, it should allow for the study of any events that may influence human beings. In short, we have elected to use a broad definition of communication in an attempt to bring together the greatest number of approaches, variables, and ideas to improve our understanding of nonverbal objects, events, behaviors, and processes. Let us now turn our attention to the question, "What is nonverbal communication?"

If someone asked you to define "nonverbal communication" at this point in your reading, how would you answer the question? Perhaps some of the following definitions would come to mind:

- Nonverbal communication is communication without words.
- Nonverbal communication can be viewed as occurring whenever an individual communicates without the use of sounds.
- Nonverbal communication is anything someone does to which someone else assigns meaning.
- Nonverbal communication is the study of facial expressions, touch, time, gestures, smell, eye behavior, and so on.

To some extent, each of these definitions would be valid. As a matter of fact, if you were to research the topic, you would more than likely find some component of your definition in at least one nonverbal communication textbook. The point we are making is that people conceive of nonverbal communication in a number of ways, just as they do when attempting to define "communication." A psychologist's orientation toward nonverbal communication is different from that of a sociologist. Likewise, an interpersonal communication student's view of nonverbal communication is different from that of an organizational or mass communication student.

As a new student of nonverbal communication, you may or may not be aware of—or care about—the controversy surrounding the meaning of this term. However, as a scholar, it is important that you possess a clear and workable definition of it. After all, you will probably agree that it is more difficult to learn about something that has never been clearly defined for you.

For our purposes, then, **nonverbal communication** will be defined as the process by which nonverbal behaviors are used, either singly or in combination with verbal behaviors, in the exchange and interpretation of messages within a given situation or context. As you can see, we have chosen to elaborate on our earlier, more general definition of "communication" in order to describe nonverbal communication specifically. The primary difference is that, here, we draw a distinction between verbal and nonverbal behaviors (and hence verbal and nonverbal communication).

To better comprehend this distinction, try to think of communication as a type of matrix (see Figure 1.1). At the top are the distinctions between verbal (symbolic) and nonverbal (nonsymbolic) behaviors. In turn, these may be divided into vocal and nonvocal behaviors. The result is a matrix consisting of four potential sets of communication behaviors: (1) verbal/vocal behaviors, (2) verbal/nonvocal behaviors, (3) nonverbal/vocal behaviors, and (4) nonverbal/nonvocal behaviors. At this point, it may be useful to provide an explanation and illustration of each.

The first block diagrammed in our communication matrix is that of **verbal/vocal behaviors.** These include the actual words or symbols that we choose when communicating with others. For example, when spoken aloud, the actual words in the sentence, "I'm thrilled," comprise the verbal/vocal component of communication. However, you should note that this component does not include the way in which the sentence is spoken. As such, verbal/vocal behaviors are not generally included in the study of nonverbal communication.

Verbal/nonvocal behaviors, on the other hand, are included in some discussions, although we do not address them comprehensively, since they have much in common with verbal/vocal behaviors. Like those behaviors, described in the

	Verbal (symbolic)	Nonverbal (nonsymbolic)
Vocal	Verbal/vocal behavior	Nonverbal/vocal behavior
Nonvocal	Verbal/nonvocal behavior	Nonverbal/nonvocal behavior

FIGURE 1.1   **A matrix of verbal versus nonverbal behaviors**

paragraph above, verbal/nonvocal behaviors utilize a structured system of symbols. In addition, they often employ their own formal laws or rules of grammar. Two examples are American Sign Language, which is used by the deaf, and the numerous examples of sign language ceremoniously used by American Indian tribes. Additionally, all written messages represent forms of potential verbal/nonvocal communication.

The third component of our communication matrix houses **nonverbal/vocal behaviors.** These include all cues in oral and written speech other than the actual content itself. For example, they include characteristics of the voice as well as rate, loudness, softness, and speed of speech. Additionally, they include "how" any one given sentence is expressed. To illustrate, return for a moment to the sentence, "I'm thrilled!" exemplified above. This sentence may be stated in any number of ways: sarcastically, sincerely, or exasperatedly. It can also be used in any number of situations. The way in which something is said (as opposed to the content of what is said) represents the nonverbal/vocal component. As such, it is the first which we classify as purely "nonverbal."

The fourth and final component of our communication matrix is that represented by **nonverbal/nonvocal behaviors.** This component includes all of those behaviors which are used to communicate a message—other than through the voice. For example, your body shape, size and posture communicate messages about you, as do the clothing you wear and the way you wear your hair. The gestures you use when talking, your facial expressions and your use of space also fall into this domain. Touching behaviors are categorized here, as well. Perhaps it is this category of behaviors which is most often addressed in nonverbal communication texts. As such, it will provide a primary basis for our discussions.

To this point, we have defined both "communication" and "nonverbal communication" as we perceive them. In addition, we have distinguished among four different types of communication behavior. Although it would be easy to stop here and to think that you understand the nature of our subject, you need to be aware of other complexities and issues involved. This is particularly true since you have elected to examine nonverbal communication as a specialized area of study.

As you will see in the following section, nonverbal communication has been approached in many ways. As a result, several important dimensions of the concept have emerged. Five highly salient dimensions of verbal versus nonverbal communication that have been examined—and that help us to illustrate the complexity of studying human communication—are addressed in the following paragraphs. We hope that our discussion will clear up any misunderstandings that may still exist regarding their relationships. At the very least, we hope that it will clarify their primary differences.

Dimensions of Verbal versus Nonverbal Communication

With increased interest in the study of nonverbal communication, a controversy concerning how nonverbal communication should be defined has arisen. Present definitions range from early "beyond words" definitions like that of Ruesch and Kees (1956), in which nonverbal communication is defined as all communication other than the spoken word, to more specific definitions such as that proposed by Burgoon and Saine (1978):

> Nonverbal communication is those attributes or actions of humans other than the use of words themselves which have socially shared meaning, are intentionally sent or interpreted as intentional and are consciously received and have the potential for feedback from the receiver. (p. 9)

Definitions such as this one—as well as our own—often present a limited picture of the many and varied dimensions of nonverbal communication. By examining characteristics that distinguish verbal from nonverbal communication, we hope to provide you with a clearer understanding of nonverbal communication. Based on our own and other authors' distinctions, the following dimensions of verbal and nonverbal communication will be discussed: (1) structure versus nonstructure, (2) linguistic versus nonlinguistic, (3) continuous versus discontinuous, (4) learned versus innate, and (5) left- versus right-hemispheric processing.

Structure versus nonstructure.   Verbal communication is highly structured and has formal laws or rules of grammar. In every language (French, German, Spanish, etc.), these rules help us consistently make sense out of what other people are saying. Foreigners, when learning a new languge, often misuse appropriate language structures (for example, they might say "Love I you!" and "See you, very nice, was it"). On the other hand, with nonverbal communication there is little or no formal structure with which to guide communication. Most nonverbal communication occurs unconsciously without a predictable sequence of events. Because there are no formal rules, we must be careful to look at all the available cues to interpret nonverbal messages correctly. Without a pattern, the same nonverbal behavior can mean different things at different times. For example, people can cry when they are sad, excited, happy, or for no reason at all.

Linguistic versus nonlinguistic.   Since there is no specific structure for nonverbal communication, there are few assigned symbols in the system. In some cultures, nodding your head indicates agreement, whereas in others it indicates disagreement. Although some researchers have attempted to assign specific meaning to particular facial movements (Birdwhistell, 1970), there exists no documented nonverbal language system. Some theorists would say that the only exception to this is the universal sign language of the deaf. Even the deaf, however, have unique nonverbal symbols with no assigned meanings. This is not the case in verbal communication. Verbal communication is a system of symbols to which we arbitrarily assign meanings.

Continuous versus discontinuous.   Nonverbal communication is continuous, whereas verbal communication is based on disconnected units. There is no way

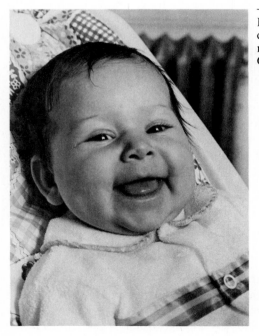

People are born with some nonverbal communication instincts. For example, no one teaches babies to smile. (Julie O'Neil/The Picture Cube)

to stop communicating nonverbally unless you leave the room, and even then your intrapersonal processes (communication within and to oneself) keep on going. Even without other people present, our bodies, emotions, and minds send continuous verbal and nonverbal messages that we must process during our waking hours. As long as your body, face, and presence are perceived by another individual or yourself, the potential for nonverbal communication exists. However, words and symbols have definite beginning and ending points. Nonverbal messages linger on. After a heated discussion, there may be no further words exchanged, yet cold stares, angry glances, and stiff body positions suggest that the disagreement is far from resolved—at least nonverbally.

Learned versus innate.   Although you learn much about nonverbal communication through observation and reinforcement, you are seldom taught to communicate nonverbally. No one teaches a child to smile; however, when infants are happy, they do smile to indicate contentment. We believe that individuals are born with basic nonverbal instincts. On the other hand, it is obvious that verbal communication is learned. Although most people are born with the ability to make sounds, they do not speak a "language" or know how to communicate with others until they are taught how to say words, make sentences out of groups of words, and attach meaning to them. Our innate abilities to communicate nonverbally can best be explained by watching tourists in a foreign country. Initially, tourists eagerly attempt to look up words and phrases in a dictionary. Eventually, however, many tourists revert to nonverbal symbols to find food, rest rooms, and motels.

Left- versus right-hemispheric processing.   A final characteristic involves the neurophysiological approach to nonverbal communication. This approach explains that most nonverbal stimuli, such as those involving spatial, pictorial, and gestalt tasks, are processed in the right hemisphere of the brain. Conversely, the majority of verbal stimuli, often involving analytical and reasoning tasks, are processed in the left hemisphere (Andersen, Garrison, and Andersen, 1979). Although neurophysiological research is continuing, the results currently acknowledge the differences that exist between the processing of verbal and nonverbal stimuli. It also is important, however, to understand the implications involved. Processing differences for verbal and nonverbal messages also suggest differences in the ability to exchange and interpret messages. It is possible that some individuals may not use the correct hemisphere at appropriate times and, therefore, may confuse a given message and its corresponding meaning.

   The foregoing has been a brief discussion of five dimensions of verbal and nonverbal communication. These dimensions do not constitute an exhaustive list. Rather, they are included to aid you in understanding the potential differences between verbal and nonverbal communication. Given an understanding of these differences—and our working definition of nonverbal communication—we now turn to a more complete discussion of a related matter. The following section examines three variables that influence the potential of nonverbal communication: context, potential for a behavioral response, and motivation of behavior.

Variables that Determine the Potential for Nonverbal Communication

Context.   Biting your nails while you are alone in your bedroom may or may not indicate anxiety. In most cases, you are probably unaware that you are biting your nails and the action may simply be a behavior that has become a habit. However, if your teacher observed you biting your nails during an exam, then the behavior could be interpreted as an expression of nervousness about the test. Although you may bite your nails in either context, the action of biting your nails is interpreted differently in a context that has the potential to communicate to others. Since different situations elicit unique responses, when observing another's nonverbal cues, it is very important that you keep in mind the context of the behaviors.

Potential for a behavioral response.   Whenever the potential for a response exists, the potential for nonverbal communication also exists. For example, a seven-year-old boy, Tommy, just bought a triple-dip ice cream cone from a park vendor. Just as he was about to take his first lick he tripped and the three dips fell to the ground. Immediately, tears welled up in his eyes and began to roll down his little cheeks. At first, you may not label this event as a possible form of nonverbal communication, but it is. In this case several nonverbal messages were transmitted simultaneously. As soon as the ice cream fell to the ground, the potential for a response existed. Intrapersonally, Tommy's crying provided feedback to himself and to others about his emotional state. These nonverbal behaviors also had the potential of causing others to respond. In this case, Tommy's mother saw what happened and bought Tommy more ice cream, but this time in a cup.

Motivation of behavior.   The third variable that influences the potential for nonverbal communication is the motivation of a behavior. Messages can be sent intentionally or unintentionally. In the example above, Tommy sent both intentional and unintentional messages. Intentionally, Tommy may have held three fingers up to reinforce that he wanted three scoops of ice cream. He repeated his oral message nonverbally to make sure the vendor understood what he wanted. On the other hand, Tommy unintentionally dropped the ice cream and unintentionally began to cry. Little Tommy did not want to communicate his clumsiness or his sadness to others.

It is important for you to understand the importance of intentionality in distinguishing and identifying different purposes of nonverbal behavior. McKay's (1972) discussion of goal-directed and non-goal-directed behavior helps to

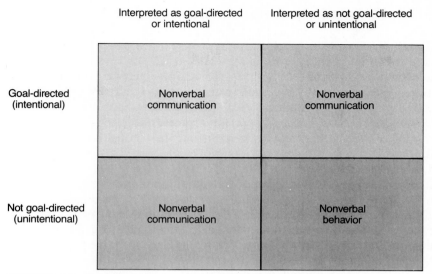

	Interpreted as goal-directed or intentional	Interpreted as not goal-directed or unintentional
Goal-directed (intentional)	Nonverbal communication	Nonverbal communication
Not goal-directed (unintentional)	Nonverbal communication	Nonverbal behavior

FIGURE 1.2   **Intentionality in nonverbal behavior and nonverbal communication**

explain degrees of intentionality during nonverbal communication. (See Figure 1.2.)

McKay presents four dimensions of nonverbal communication. The first is concerned with behaviors that are goal-directed (intentional) and interpreted as goal-directed (intentional). For example, during an introduction two business professionals usually shake hands with each other. This ritual, or greeting, is interpreted by both persons as purposeful because handshaking serves as a polite way of establishing relationships. Intentional messages are exchanged between the two professionals.

Other nonverbal behaviors occur unintentionally but are perceived as intentional. For example, John accidentally bumped into a young woman at a local bar. Immediately, she turned around and said, "Watch where you're going!" The woman thought John had bumped into her on purpose. Likewise, if a person forgets to call to reconfirm an airline reservation, an airline company usually cancels the reservations. The lack of a response causes the booking agent to interpret the message intentionally. At times, previous interactions influence the ways that unintentional messages are interpreted. To illustrate, Sally and Doug had an argument about spending too much money on long-distance calls, so when Doug didn't call for two weeks, Sally thought he was just trying to prove his point. Doug, however, had started dating someone else and did not want to continue calling or dating Sally.

A third form of nonverbal behavior is communicated intentionally but is not interpreted as intentional by the receiver. At times such as these, we often attach inaccurate meanings to the nonverbal messages received. For example, a group of girls with negative self-concepts decided to go to the beach during spring vacation. While en route, several carloads of guys passed them, waving and honking. The girls didn't wave back, but each time the group waved, the girls pulled over to see if something was wrong with their car. Later, when they stopped for gas, one of the drivers of the cars that had honked was also getting gas at the same filling station. Concerned about their safety, one of the girls asked the driver if he had seen something wrong with their car. He looked puzzled and said, "We were just saying hello. . . . " In this case, the girls interpreted the guys' message incorrectly. Instead of realizing that the guys were flirting, they thought something was wrong with their car. Nevertheless, an intentional message was sent, but it was perceived in an unintended way.

A fourth nonverbal behavior is communicated unintentionally and is perceived as unintentional. For instance, think of a time when you have caught yourself staring off into space for a few minutes. There was probably no reason for this lapse of concentration. In this context, your gaze was not intentional and probably would not be perceived as intentional by anyone else. Since the behavior was not perceived by anyone else or yourself as intentional, it would not be classified by McKay as a form of nonverbal communication.

In summary, then, it can be said that there are four dimensions of intentionality regarding nonverbal behavior: intentional and perceived as intentional; intentional but not perceived as intentional; unintentional but perceived as intentional; and unintentional and perceived as unintentional. From these four dimensions, you can see that only three sets of behaviors may be viewed as instances in which (nonverbal) communication has occurred: those which involve perceptions of intentionality on the part of the one or more persons involved.

Functions of Nonverbal Communication

Just as nonverbal communication may be viewed along a number of important dimensions, so it may be classified according to the functions which it can perform. As you will see in several of the chapters to follow, nonverbal communication serves six primary functions: complementing verbal messages, substituting for verbal messages, accenting verbal messages, contradicting verbal messages, repeating verbal messages, and regulating verbal messages. Each of these functions will be examined more completely in the following pages.

Complementing.   If you hug a child while saying that you are proud of his or her report card, the hug serves to complement or add to the meaning of your verbal message. Nonverbal cues—such as tone of voice, facial expression, gestures, or distance between people—often serve to complement the verbal message and add to, clarify, or reinforce the meaning. The term "complement" indicates that the behavior alone would not communicate the intended message. A complementing nonverbal message changes the meaning of the verbal message by adding additional insights or information. Recently, a new teacher asked his sixth-graders to "sit down and listen" to their daily assignments. After waiting for a moment, he repeated his request. Finally, after only a handful of students responded appropriately, he raised his voice and hit his fist on the desk. At that point, after he had reinforced and clarified his message, the students sat down and looked to their teacher attentively.

Contradicting.   At other times our nonverbal messages contradict our verbal messages. Think of a time when you have had a "forced" or artificial smile on your face. Verbally, when expressing gratitude for an unwanted present you received, you may have forced an expression of happiness. At times it is difficult to manifest consistent verbal and nonverbal behaviors, and contradictions, when perceived by others, create confusion. Others tend to believe your nonverbal messages rather than your verbal messages when there are contradictions.

Repeating.   A nonverbal restatement of the verbal message is known as "repeating." Repetition differs from complementing in that the former of the two functions can stand alone without the verbal message. Repetition is used in order to emphasize or clarify the verbal message. Think back to the last sporting event you attended. Because of spectator noise you may have found yourself holding up two fingers to tell the hot-dog vendor how many you wanted, while at the same

How might the nonverbal communication between this parent and child affect the verbal communication? (Steve Takatsuno/The Picture Cube)

time asking for them verbally. You could have screamed to repeat "two, please," but instead you decided to repeat the message nonverbally.

Regulating.   Regulation often serves to coordinate the verbal dialogue between people. It can occur in the form of a head nod (which a speaker might use to indicate to a group member that it is his or her turn to speak), a drop in one's vocal tone to suggest the end of a thought, or a touch of a person's arm to let him or her know you have something to say. The next time you listen to a friend talk, observe how you nod your head as he or she speaks and how you let each other know who should speak next. These nonverbal messages serve to regulate the flow of communication interactions.

Substituting.   Substitution occurs when a nonverbal message is transmitted in place of a verbal message. For instance, substitution is used when barriers to verbal communication exist in the environment. A noisy school cafeteria might prompt you to wave at a friend instead of screaming to get his or her attention. Substitution is also used for emphasis. Picture yourself in a group of friends when your girlfriend or boyfriend decides to tell the group about your most embarrassing experience! Instead of verbally expressing your objection, you may use a substitute for words by glaring into his or her eyes until your message that you do not want the experience repeated comes through loud and clear.

Accenting.   The primary function of accenting is to emphasize a particular point in a verbal message. Although some accenting might be considered a form of complementing, the distinction lies in the placement of the nonverbal behavior. For instance, a well-skilled public speaker might pause before or after an important point in a speech. The pause would serve to highlight or accent the point that the speaker is about to make. At other times, touch is used to accent or emphasize a point. After a marital argument, Jane's husband expressed his regret and told her he loved her while holding her close and kissing her cheek.

Meaning and Nonverbal Communication

Such popular books as Julius Fast's *Body Language* (1970) have left the impression with many people that nonverbal behaviors and communication have particular indisputable meanings associated with them. This text will help provide some insight into common "stereotypes" that people have concerning particular nonverbal events, behaviors, and actions. These stereotypes, however, cannot be accepted as categorically true without understanding the "total" situation and interaction. Perhaps the most useful way to approach the meaning of nonverbal communication is through the use of some rather broad "metaphors" suggested by Albert Mehrabian (1981). The following section is developed, with some adaptation, from Mehrabian's discussion of the metaphors in the recent edition of his book, *Silent Messages.*

The approach metaphor.   The **approach metaphor** is concerned with what Mehrabian (1981) refers to as immediate behaviors. In simple terms, the approach metaphor suggests that you approach or locate yourself near something or someone you like and avoid or create distance between yourself and something or someone you dislike. Mehrabian contends that the approach metaphor manifests itself as early as infancy. Children, for example, will reach for or crawl toward bright, colorful objects that they find interesting or attractive. Conversely, children will not seek objects that do not initiate interest in them or that they find aversive. Along these lines, parents attempt to encourage interests in some areas and to discourage interest in others. For example, although children are almost instinctively attracted to candy, parents warn their children to avoid strangers with candy.

The approach metaphor need not be limited entirely to nonverbal behavior; examples of the approach metaphor are clearly found in verbal communication. For example, the use of the adjective "this" as opposed to "that" is a demonstration of the difference between immediate and nonimmediate verbal language. "This" tends to suggest a psychological or physical degree of closeness that is not implied in the adjective "that."

The willingness to approach or be close to someone or something does not occur only in a physical sense. Think about someone you feel close to. Chances are that you think this person is easy to talk to and that you have a good idea of how this person feels about certain issues. This implies a "mental closeness" that does not require physical proximity to attain. Watch the behaviors of others sitting on benches in the parks, on public transportation, or in cars. Different messages are communicated when two people sit on opposite ends of a park bench, when a person moves to find an empty seat on a bus, or when a couple sits side by side in a drive-in theater.

There are several specific nonverbal behaviors that result from the approach-avoidance metaphor: You sit closer to someone with whom you feel positive; you are more willing to touch a person whom you approach and you are more willing to be touched by that person; in a conversation with someone you like you tend to communicate in a face-to-face position as opposed to a side-by-side position in which eye contact is more limited.

The arousal-activity metaphor.   We live in an environment that is rich in stimuli, an environment that we often take for granted because we have become accustomed to certain stimuli and events, such as neon lights in a large city or the smell of fresh, clean air in the country. However, certain unique, exciting, and outstanding environments or elements within a particular environment may create an emotional reaction in you. As a result of your reaction to a particular environment, you may change or modify your behavior. It is this quality of change that results from the environment that Mehrabian describes as the **arousal-activity metaphor.** In simple terms, you are aroused by your environment and react to that arousal in either a positive or negative manner. For example, you visit a major metropolis. The environment of the city might negatively arouse you, or it might positively excite you. If you are accustomed to a large city and find it to be exciting, you may react negatively to a rural environment when you visit the country. Or think for a moment about the arousal experiences in different types of restaurants. Fast-food establishments with bright colors, hard seats, loud music or no music, and fast service encourage you to eat and run. In contrast, the finer restaurants encourage you to linger and enjoy the cuisine by using secluded seating, dim lighting, comfortable surroundings, soft music, and leisurely but "professional" service. People have different reactions to the same environment. For example, a child may feel high levels of arousal at the suggestion of McDonald's and get fidgety and bored during a two- to three-hour meal.

Arousal level, according to Mehrabian, is measured in three areas: the amount of change in your facial and vocal expressions, the rate at which you speak, and the volume of your speech. An example of a highly aroused person is one who is speaking with a great deal of variation in voice (pitch and tone), who is revealing emotions through facial expressions, and who is speaking loudly and rapidly. It is not unusual to see high levels of arousal at football games, pep rallys, rock concerts, and amusement parks.

The power metaphor.   The **power metaphor** is viewed as a dominance-submission dimension of communication. In other words, behaviors that give an individual dominance in a situation will result in that person's being perceived as powerful. When you visualize a powerful person, what image comes to mind? Do you think of a small, tense, watchful individual or someone who is large, relaxed, and confident? It's obvious that power and "bigness" are often associated. As a result of this association, another dimension of power is fearlessness. Obviously, if you are stronger and larger than the people around you, you have less to fear from them than they have to fear from you. Of course, there are some behaviors that are culturally specific or even situationally specific. For example, powerful people are "allowed" to engage in greater eye-contact behavior than less powerful people. Think of a time as a child when you were in a staring contest with another child. You did not want to be the first one to blink or look away. Either of these behaviors would have suggested that the other child was more powerful or braver than you. In some contexts, staring is not a sign of power. Staring at someone in a crowded elevator or at someone who is handicapped, for instance, is a sign of rudeness, not of power.

CLASSES OF NONVERBAL COMMUNICATION

Scholars and practitioners have identified and categorized literally hundreds of objects, behaviors, vocal characteristics, and events as forms of nonverbal communication. As we noted previously, many of these nonverbal behaviors may not technically involve intentional communication, but all have the potential to impart meaning to a receiver. The following section will identify the specific classes of nonverbal behavior and communication discussed in this text. Each class discussed relates to a chapter in the text. The description serves not only as a definition of the specific class of nonverbal communication or behavior but also as a preview of the chapters to come.

Body Types, Shapes, and Sizes

Almost everyone wants to be considered attractive. Your attractiveness can be viewed from three different perspectives. The first is how attractive others perceive you to be. The second is how attractive you perceive yourself to be. The third is how attractive you think you are to others. Each of these perceptions of your attractiveness is an important element in the development of your personality. The perception you have of your attractiveness is probably one of the most important variables in your self-concept. Your perceived attractiveness affects not only your personality but also your behavior patterns. When you are confident of your looks, you are more likely to behave in a manner that reflects feelings of confidence.

The image you have of your body is an important dimension of your perception of your attractiveness. A lack of awareness or an inaccurate image of one's body can result in body depersonalization, distortion, and/or the establishment of extreme physical boundaries around yourself. In addition to body awareness, the shape of your body can be related to certain personality characteristics. Your shape probably falls into one of the following categories: **ectomorphic,** a slender and fragile body type; **mesomorphic,** a muscular and firm body type; or **endomorphic,** a heavy and rounded body type.

Many other dimensions of your body influence your attractiveness, such as your hair color, height, and skin color. Depending upon your individual physical characteristics, your feelings about yourself can range from contentment to dissatisfaction.

Clothing and Personal Artifacts

The style in which you dress directly influences how others perceive you. In our culture, clothing is no longer primarily associated with the functions of protection and modesty. In today's society, clothing supplies information about yourself. Others' perceptions about how you dress may result in the formation of opinions about your social status, age, and socioeconomic level. Clothing is a powerful form of nonverbal communication that people often use to stereotype others, not only in terms of demographic characteristics but also in terms of inferred personality traits.

What type of jewelry do you wear? Do you smoke a pipe? Are you one of the many men who wear a beard? The artifacts you do or do not adorn yourself with

Clothing and artifacts may indicate something about the person. What inferences might you make about the people in this picture from their clothing and objects? (Steve Takatsuno/The Picture Cube)

supply an observer with clues about you. Many of the objects you wear transmit both intentional and unintentional messages. A diamond ring on the fourth finger of the left hand usually indicates that a woman is engaged or married; consequently, many single women avoid wearing diamonds on that finger so that they will not be falsely categorized. By the same token, some single women *will* wear an "engagement" or "wedding" ring just so that they will be falsely categorized and thus will be able to avoid "come-ons" from members of the opposite sex. In order to communicate more effectively, it is important to be aware of the messages your clothing and artifacts transmit to others, as well as what messages you receive from the dress of others.

Body Movement and Gestures

The study of **kinesics** (body movement, gestures, and posture) has been a major concern of researchers in psychology, communication, and many other areas of academic endeavor. Your behaviors serve very specific functions in either complementing your verbal messages or substituting for them. Researchers have divided body movements into five categories: emblems, illustrators, regulators, affect displays, and adaptors. These categories of movement will be defined in a later chapter.

Beyond the classification of nonverbal behavior, the study of posture and its relation to immediacy, status, gender differences, locomotion, and emotion is an important concern. For example, are you aware of the differences in your posture when you are with a person you like and when you are with a person you don't particularly like? Do you lean toward the person you like, move in closer, and allow him or her to get closer to you? Often our posture reveals our attitudes toward people. Even gender differences reveal important information. Do you smile a great deal, cock your head, and look down with your eyes? If you do, you may be exhibiting submissive nonverbal behaviors. It's important that you realize that your behaviors will often affect the response of others. For example, submissive behaviors may encourage others to treat you as a subordinate.

Facial Expression and Eye Behavior

Facial expressions have many universal meanings throughout the world. There are, however, certain facial expressions that tend to be culturally specific. It is not easy to manipulate facial expressions, although there are people who have learned the skill of facial management and control. Facial management usually is used for one of four reasons: (1) to intensify a true emotion, (2) to deintensify a true emotion, (3) to neutralize a true emotion, or (4) to mask a true emotion. Detection of facial manipulation is difficult to the untrained eye, but not impossible. The trained eye can distinguish sincere and natural facial behaviors from manipulated expressions.

Because of its importance to the communication process, eye behavior is studied independently from facial behaviors. Eye behavior can serve in four capacities: (1) to establish and define relationships, (2) to control channels of communication, (3) to display emotion, and (4) to reduce distractions.

Eye behavior is even more difficult to manipulate than facial expression because much of eye behavior is involuntary. Differences in a person's sex, culture, and personality, as well as the context of the situation, also affect the use of eye movement in the communication process.

Environment

Learning about the communication potential of their environment enables people to predict what types of behavior and emotion to expect in specific situations. How you perceive your environment influences how long you will remain there, what type of interactions will occur, and whether interaction will occur again in that environment. As mentioned earlier, fast-food restaurants are decorated with semihard seats, bright lights, and plastic decoration—an interior not conducive to lingering conversations. The logic behind this interior design is that the restaurant makes more money when there is a fast turnover of customers. Consequently, the management does not want you to stay any longer than is absolutely necessary to complete your meal. Better yet, in many cases they encourage you to order your meal "to go."

The environment can be viewed in two dimensions. The first dimension is that of **macrospace,** or space that is fixed and generally out of the control of the individual. A school building and a town square are both examples of macrospaces. The second dimension of the environment is that of **microspace,** the immediate environment around an individual that he or she can control or change. Examples of microspaces are seating arrangements, table size, lighting, and room color. All the elements within one's microspace help to determine the attractiveness of the surroundings. The type of interaction that takes place within an environment, the degree of intimacy during the interaction, and the behavior involved in the interaction are all influenced by the perceived attractiveness of that environment. This is illustrated by the elaborate "honeymoon suites" with their heart-shaped bathtubs in the honeymoon haven of the Poconos, as contrasted with a traditional motel room with its standard bathtub built for persons under 5 feet tall.

Personal Space, Territory, and Crowding

The study of proxemics, or space, is critical. Proxemic messages are communicated through the use and misuse of space. There are two types of space that deserve attention. The first type is called **human territory** and is defined as the continuous association of a person or group with a certain place. Human territory can be classified on the basis of four criteria: (1) the size of the territory, (2) the importance of the territory to the "owner," (3) the type of interaction occurring within the territory, and (4) the body territory. Territory categorized by size can range from a "spot," a small territory, to a "nucleus," a territory large enough for several people to occupy. Based on its importance to the owner, territory can be divided into primary and secondary territories and can be further divided into public, temporary, and home territories. Interactional territory has to do with the number and status of people interacting in a place. Finally, body territory is concerned with personal space and one's actual body.

One of the most important aspects in the study of territory is how people react when someone else invades or encroaches on their designated territory. Encroachment usually takes one of three forms: (1) violation of one's designated territory, (2) invasion of one's designated territory, or (3) the contamination of one's designated territory.

In addition to the type of space called human territory, there is a second type of space referred to as **personal space.** Personal space is the expanding or contracting "bubble" that surrounds and travels with an individual. The size of this imaginary bubble varies as a function of the situation; the intimacy of the relationship; and the individual's age, sex, status, and culture.

Another area in the investigation of space is concerned with what happens when there is a lack of space. "Crowding," for instance, is a psychological experience that occurs when a person becomes aware of spatial restrictions. The importance of crowding becomes apparent when people are forced to live "on top of one another," as many must today in our large cities. Crowding can produce certain negative behaviors and may cause people to develop defense mechanisms. The potential dangers involved with overcrowding in cities generally result from these negative reactions.

Touching Behavior

People touch for many different reasons, in many different ways, and in many different places. Research indicates that all human beings need and want some form of tactile stimulation. However, the intensity and the frequency of touch that one is willing to give and accept are often determined, at least in part, by one's culture, sex, age, status, and personality.

One method of studying the effects of touch on humans is to examine touching behavior in animals and how it relates to their growth and development. Research indicates that animals need a certain degree of touch in order to grow and develop in a normal and healthy manner. Not surprisingly, similar findings for human development have also been discovered. Touch serves a variety of functions in society. Five functional categories of touch include functional-professional, social-polite, friendship-warmth, love-intimacy, and sexual arousal.

Cultures tend to have specific norms concerning the appropriateness of the amount and type of touch. North Americans, for instance, are one of the least touch-oriented cultures in the world. If you have ever traveled to a Latin American country, you may have noticed that their willingness to touch and to be touched is perhaps stronger than that with which you may be comfortable. Conversely, Latin Americans tend to find North Americans somewhat aloof because of their reluctance to touch.

The process of touch can transmit various specific messages. A tactile message may communicate an emotion or an interpersonal attitude. For example, you may grab someone with whom you are angry or stroke someone you love. One particular category of physical touch is **body contact/tie signs.** Body contact/tie signs supply information on bonds existing between two people. Examples of body contact/tie signs are a handshake, a kiss, a caress, or an embrace. Each of these touching behaviors indicates a particular bond that exists between the two people engaging in the behavior.

Voice Characteristics and Qualities

Verbal communication will not be effective if your receiver cannot understand what you are saying. A lack of verbal understanding may result from the speaker's mumbling, speaking too softly, or various other negative vocal behaviors. **Paralinguistics,** the study of all cues in oral speech other than the content of the words spoken, addresses these problems as well as other vocal behaviors.

Vocal behaviors have a greater influence on the way you are perceived than you might realize. The *way* you say what you say may be more important than the *content* of the message. The manner in which you use your voice influences the expression of feeling within the message, the receiver's perception of your socioeconomic status, and the receiver's judgment of your personality. Do you speak quickly, slowly, loudly, or softly? Your ability to persuade others is influenced by your vocal behaviors. In addition, **vocalics,** or vocal behaviors, serve to regulate conversations and assist in detecting verbal deception in communication. One of the most effective vocal behaviors is no sound at all—the pause. A pause in a conversation or a speech can be used to emphasize a point or to give the audience a chance to process what has just been said.

Taste and Smell

People in the United States are obsessed with "smelling good." The money Americans spend on products such as perfume, deodorant, toothpaste, and mouthwash reaches billions of dollars annually. Smelling good, however, is not universally agreed upon. Often a pleasant aroma in one society is offensive in another. For example, there are certain cultures in which people, for religious reasons, bathe infrequently. Consequently, natural body odors in these cultures are accepted and probably not noticed. However, if they were to travel to the "sweet-smelling" United States and continue to bathe on an irregular basis, they might offend others by their odor. Conversely, if you were to travel to their country covered with six different scents, your body smell might be equally offensive to them.

The study of smell, however, goes beyond the mere pleasantness or unpleasantness of a scent. **Olfactics** has proven to be useful in the field of medicine in helping to diagnose certain medical problems. Moreover, the fact that certain smells are often associated with particular environments aids in describing other environments. For example, when describing your Italian friend's home, you might say it always smells like pasta or spaghetti sauce.

Another dimension of smell is the role it plays in the taste process. Although the tongue is the principal organ involved in the tasting process, the sense of smell also plays a part in helping you taste certain foods. As you are probably aware, when you have a cold, often food does not taste as good as it usually does. Or you may not be able to taste it at all. Part of the reason for your diminished sense of taste is the fact that your nose is clogged and is blocking some of the aroma that you traditionally associate with particular foods.

Culture and Time

In today's world, the necessity to be cross-culturally aware is increasing daily. We encounter people from various cultures in all aspects of our lives. As a result of this cultural diversity, we must realize and accept the fact that each culture has its own unique norms regarding proper nonverbal behavior. Acceptance of these various cultures' norms will aid in effective **cross-cultural communication.**

One of the most important cultural differences is the perception and treatment of time. An example of this difference can be found in the attitude toward arrival time throughout the world. In some cultures, arriving "on time" is viewed as impolite rather than proper behavior. Two types of time that can be studied universally are our psychological time orientation and our biological time system.

Perception of time is not the only nonverbal behavior about which cultures differ. Certain body movements and facial expressions differ from culture to culture. Examples are to be found in types of greetings, kissing behaviors, and cultural dances.

SUMMARY

This chapter defines and presents a general overview of nonverbal communication. To begin, however, one must have some understanding of communication overall. To aid in increasing your understanding, the following definition of "communication" is offered: *Communication is the dynamic, irreversible process by which we exchange and interpret messages within a given situation or context.* From here it is easy to create a useful definition of "nonverbal communication." For us, it is best defined as *the process by which nonverbal behaviors are used, either singly or in combination with verbal behaviors, in the exchange and interpretation of messages, within a given situation or context.*

In order to distinguish nonverbal from verbal communication more clearly, it seems useful to differentiate verbal from nonverbal behaviors. One excellent way you can remember these differences is to recall the distinctions between verbal/vocal behaviors, verbal/nonvocal behaviors, nonverbal/vocal behaviors, and nonverbal/nonvocal behaviors.

Despite some agreement on the boundaries of nonverbal communication, different approaches to its study have caused considerable controversy. One method of understanding the issues more clearly is through an examination of additional differences between verbal and nonverbal communication. Five such distinguishing characteristics include (1) structure versus nonstructure, (2) linguistic versus nonlinguistic, (3) continuous versus discontinuous, (4) learned versus innate, and (5) left- versus right-hemispheric processing. Three variables that help to determine the communicative potential of nonverbal behaviors are (1) communication contexts, (2) motivations of behaviors, and (3) potential for behavioral responses.

Nonverbal communication functions to complement verbal messages, substitute for verbal messages, accent verbal messages, regulate interactions, repeat verbal messages, or contradict verbal and nonverbal messages. Nonverbal behaviors also give meaning to our message exchanges through three broad metaphors. The approach metaphor is concerned with degrees of liking or disliking of people or things. The arousal-activity metaphor deals with positive and negative responses to aspects of the environment. Finally, the power metaphor refers to the degree of dominance or submission suggested through displays of nonverbal communication.

Theorists and practitioners of nonverbal communication have identified and categorized hundreds of objects, behaviors, vocal characteristics, and events as nonverbal communication. The following chapters of this text preview the major categories of nonverbal communication. These chapters cover such topics as body types, shapes, and sizes; clothing and personal artifacts; body movement and gestures; facial expression and eye behavior; environment; personal space, territory, and crowding; touching behavior; voice characteristics and qualities; taste and smell; and culture and time.

As you can see, the subject of nonverbal communication is extremely broad and ranges from such specific and isolated behaviors as yawning to larger categories such as the voice. This text attempts to provide an understanding of the major areas of nonverbal behavior that have communication potential. Since major categories are presented, specific areas such as mime, music, learning, dance, and sign language are touched on only briefly. It is our hope that this text will provide a partial understanding of nonverbal phenomena and the role nonverbal communication plays in your daily life.

References

Andersen, P. A., Garrison, J. P., & Andersen, J. F. (1979) Defining nonverbal communication: A neurophysiological explanation of nonverbal information processing. *Human Communication Research, 6* (1), 74–89.

Birdwhistell, R. L. (1970) *Kinesics and context.* Philadelphia: University of Pennsylvania Press.

Burgoon, J., & Saine, T. (1978) *The unspoken dialogue.* Boston: Houghton-Mifflin.

Darwin, C. (1872) *The expression of emotions in man and animals.* London: John Murray (Reprint [1965], Chicago: University of Chicago Press.)

Fast, J. (1970) *Body language.* New York: Evans.

Harrison, R. P., & Wiemann, J. M. (1983) The nonverbal domain: Implications for theory, research, and practice. In J. M. Wiemann & R. P. Harrison (Eds.), *Nonverbal interaction.* Beverly Hills, Calif.: Sage, pp. 271–285.

McKay, D. M. (1972) Formal analysis of communicative processes. In R. A. Hinde (Ed.), *Nonverbal communication.* New York: Cambridge University Press.

Mehrabian, A. (1981) *Silent messages,* 2nd ed. Belmont, Calif.: Wadsworth.

Ruesch, J., & Kees, W. (1956) *Nonverbal communication: Notes on the visual perception of human relations.* Berkeley, Calif.: University of California Press.

Weitz, S. (1979) *Nonverbal communication: Readings with commentary,* 2nd ed. New York: Oxford University Press.

CHAPTER 2

BODY TYPES, SHAPES, AND SIZES

*Why not be oneself? That is the whole secret of a
successful appearance. If one is a greyhound,
why try to look like a Pekingese?*

Edith Sitwell, "Why I Look as I Do," *Sunday
Graphic,* December 4, 1955

Sandi had been competitive in beauty pageants almost as long as she could remember. By the age of five, she had won her first pageant—even though she had hated the way her mother had fixed her hair. By the age of 15, she was a poised professional who could present herself successfully to large and often critical audiences.

However, the audience which was watching her now was the most difficult one she had ever addressed. The myriad of faces that watched her now and hung breathlessly to each word were not the faces of seven captivated judges, but those of seven young women taking part in a therapy session. As she spoke, their eyes widened and filled with tears, for they all shared a common bond. Each of them, like Sandi, was attempting to battle the torturous problems of bulimia.

Anorexia nervosa and bulimia are only two of many problems that plague American society today. However, they are two significant problems of particular interest to nonverbal experts, since each disorder can stem, either directly or indirectly, from a preoccupation with one's body concept. Although time and space limitations preclude in-depth treatment of eating disorders, we will briefly discuss this topic later in the chapter. Before doing so, however, we now turn to a discussion of several additional ways that humans have manipulated their bodies in order to conform to society's views of attractiveness. As you will see in each instance, the primary goal is a subtle (or not-so-subtle) form of nonverbal communication.

AN HISTORICAL PERSPECTIVE

The human body has been twisted, pulled, and pushed into a myriad of shapes for the sake of beauty and in order to be perceived as a visual symbol of group identification. The human body has been distorted by men and women in many cases in order to communicate a particular message to others, as the following examples attest.

The practice of binding the foot at infancy to inhibit growth lasted nearly a thousand years in China. The Chinese Golden Lily Foot, as it is referred to, was based on experience in horticulture, in which certain branches of a plant are sacrificed in order to feed others. It was believed that the dislocated bones in a woman's foot would produce hypertrophy of her sexual parts. The result of the foot binding was the mutilation of muscles and bones, which made walking an excruciatingly painful experience. The smallness of a woman's foot was also used to communicate wealth: The shoe of the bride-to-be was placed in the window of her family's home.

Have you ever wondered how Scarlett O'Hara, in *Gone with the Wind,* managed to have a 17-inch waistline? During this period, nature was assisted with the whalebone corset, which was strapped around a woman's waist. The beauty-conscious woman slept in the corset at night in addition to wearing it during the day. (This explains why there were many "swooning" beauties.) Waist constriction of this type (the result was referred to as the wasp waist) was also practiced by men as far back as ancient Greece and in traditional tribes, as among the Papuans.

The Mayans of Mexico filed their teeth into points and placed jewels in them. Decorative body scars and tattoos were also common throughout history. In fact, anthropologists claim that no part of the body is safe from tattooing. History records that people have tattooed their lips, gums, and genitals—even the tip of the tongue. Everything but the eyeball has been tattooed.

Females of central Africa's Saras-Djinges tribe, at the age of four, had their lips stretched with wooden disks. Eventually their lips could reach 14 inches in diameter, looking like soup plates. Barely able to talk, these women could consume only liquids.

Reshaping the head has been another popular pastime. During childhood, the Congo's Mangbettu females had their heads tightly bound to produce an elongated shape. The Mayans, on the other hand, tied boards to their children's heads to flatten them. When the powdered wig was popular in France, girls' heads were laced to form ridges upon which the wig could rest. In the Burmese culture, brass or iron rings—each about one inch thick—were placed around girls' necks. With the help of the rings, the young girls' necks were stretched up to 14 inches in length.

What are people willing to do today in order to be perceived as attractive, beautiful, or handsome? One of the most dramatic techniques for reshaping the body was ushered in during the 1960s: liquid silicone. This treatment was hailed as a salvation to the underendowed woman. Unfortunately, although breasts did grow in size with the injection of the silicone, so did the problems. The silicone began to solidify and to travel through the body, creating lumps in places that are not supposed to have any. Also, the use of plastic surgery to "remake" all parts of the body has skyrocketed during the last decade, especially among men. Both face and body lifts all across the human anatomy are being used to help fight the downward pull of gravity. And although Americans are not binding their feet, they have put spiked heels on them in order to raise themselves anywhere from 3 to 8 inches off the ground. The abnormal arch into which the foot is thus forced causes a painless type of crippling and may result in foot problems later on.

Whether in ancient Egypt or contemporary America, the body, in all its various shapes and forms, is used to communicate important messages. The purpose of this chapter is to explore how the body communicates specific messages with regard to (1) attractiveness; (2) body image and appearance; and (3) body types, shapes, and sizes.

ATTRACTIVENESS

To what specific parts of the body are men and women attracted? In a study by Maier and Lavrakas (1984), the favorite male physique reported was the "V look"—or a medium-wide upper trunk, broad arms, a medium-thin lower trunk, and thin legs. The most disliked physique was the "pear shape," or a physique with a thin upper trunk and wide lower trunk. These findings regarding male subjects' preferences were almost identical to those of a 1975 study by Lavrakas focusing on females' preferences. However, unlike females, whose preferences were found to be influenced by a level of conservatism (Lavrakas, 1975), males' preferences were found to be more affected by their attitudes toward women. More specifically, men who were discovered to have more negative attitudes toward women favored the muscular, V shape over a more moderate, idealized physique. Additionally, men with rigid personalities also favored the more traditional V shape.

With the wealth of research available on attraction, it is important to determine what effect, if any, varying degrees of attractiveness or unattractiveness have in a communication context. Specifically, how does being attractive or unattractive affect interpersonal contacts with others? In searching for these answers, a series of questions must be asked. First, what are the characteristics of the "beautiful people"? Do these people actually possess the socially desirable attributes that we ascribe to them? Second, how are attractive persons perceived by others? Third, what effect does being attractive or unattractive have on the individual and on others? Does a negative body concept, for instance, affect the self-concept of an individual? These questions will be explored in the following pages.

Characteristics of Attractive People

Attractive women seem to receive differential treatment when compared with their less attractive counterparts. Attractive women receive higher grades in both high school and college courses (Murphy, Nelson and Cheap, 1981; Singer and

Attractive people may be stereotyped in both positive and negative ways. (G. Gorman/Sygma)

Lamb, 1966); are more successful in changing attitudes, especially when their arguments are cogent (Puckett, Petty, Cacioppo, and Fischer, 1983); are given lighter sentences in court hearings (Sigall, 1974); and are ten times more likely to marry than unattractive females (Udry and Eckland, 1984). But are attractive people more likable or more socially skilled than individuals of lesser attractiveness? In other words, do attractive individuals actually possess the behavioral characteristics that enable them to interact effectively with others?

In an article entitled "Good Looking People are Likeable Too," researchers William Goldman and Phillip Lewis (1977) provide some interesting data on the actual characteristics (rather than the perceptions) of attractive individuals. One hundred and twenty students were divided into male-female pairs. Each pair talked for five minutes and was then asked to rate one another on scales for social ease, anxiety, and likability. The three scales were combined for an overall rating, and outside observers rated each student's physical attractiveness. Findings revealed that for both men and women, attractive students were consistently considered more socially skillful and more likable than less attractive ones. The final question, which remains unanswered, is "Are attractive people more socially skilled because they are treated more favorably all their lives?"

Consider yourself and the varying degrees of attractiveness that you have experienced throughout your life. Were you an attractive child, an ugly teenager, a college beauty? Most people experience an "ugly" phase in their lives, often during their teenage years. During these various phases of your life, do you remember how people responded to you? If you have had a significant life experience such as having your nose reshaped or losing 20 pounds, chances are that the response to this bodily change was very dramatic. Some people, for example, report that after a dramatic weight loss they are surprised by the fact that people seem to increase eye contact with them and maintain it for longer periods of time.

Probably the most potent communicative value of "attractiveness," then, rests with the perception of others. For instance, attractive persons are readily stereotyped both in negative and positive ways.

Perceptions of Attractive People

Attractive and successful male movie stars such as John Travolta, Tom Cruise, Mark Harmon, and Matthew Broderick report having faced crises in their careers because of others' perceptions of their attractiveness. Like their beautiful female counterparts, they too are often perceived as being "nothing more than just another gorgeous face." As Alain Delon, the quintessential French lover, bitterly observed, "For years I've fought to make people stop believing I am just a pretty boy with a beautiful face."

According to researchers, however, attractive persons are perceived stereotypically to possess more socially desirable characteristics as well. For example, they are rated higher on perceived popularity, sociability, and sexuality—as well as on success, persuasiveness, and overall happiness (Berscheid and Walster, 1972). As a result of this particular stereotype, physically attractive individuals often experience more success in their interactions with others (Adams, 1977). Additionally, they are predicted to have more fulfilling lives, happier marriages, and more prestigious occupations (Dion, Berscheid, and Walster, 1972).

The perception of mismatched couples (i.e., an attractive partner and an unattractive partner) has been of interest to researchers Bar-Tal and Saxe (1976). They report that evaluations of males may change dramatically if they are married to someone who is very different in physical attractiveness. Among other things, unattractive men with attractive women were perceived as making more money, as being more successful in their occupations, and as being more intelligent than attractive men with attractive partners. Very likely the unattractive man was assumed to have had something special to offer for an attractive woman to marry him. In contrast, however, the ratings of an unattractive woman with a handsome man did not increase significantly. This research suggests that people perceive the unattractive partner as attempting to balance the scales on the financial or emotional side. It is somewhat as the advertising slogan claims: "Avis tries harder."

Although some mismatching such as that described above does occur in dating situations, similarity is generally the name of the (dating) game. As Folkes (1982) has verified, taking steps to date more often is correlated with similarity in physical attractiveness. To support this hypothesis, Folkes examined the steps taken by members of a Los Angeles dating service to meet and date one another. Results of the study revealed that the differences in attractiveness between any two given people decreased from a person's initial expression of interest in meeting up through the first date. (Steps which were examined included (1) contemplated phone contact only, (2) actual contact by phone to set up a date, (3) completion of the initial date, and (4) attempts to set up and execute a second date.) Additionally, Folkes discovered that similarity in attractiveness was a greater determinant of early dating patterns than either occupational status or age (pp. 635–636). She concluded that perceived similarity in attractiveness can and does determine—at the outset—the formation of dating relationships.

The Effects on Behavior

How persuasive are people who are not physically attractive? Do unattractive people develop poor self-images which, in turn, affect their dating habits and marital plans? In what ways does level of attractiveness affect our abilities to interact? Researchers continue to conduct studies about how attractiveness affects interpersonal relationships and the development of self-esteem. Their findings indicate that an individual's degree of attractiveness does affect (1) persuasiveness, (2) courtship and marriage choices, and (3) interaction behavior.

Persuasion and manipulation.   Over the past twenty years, persuasion experts have conducted a number of studies assessing the relationship between attractiveness and persuasion. Not surprisingly, they have found a strong relationship. One such study, conducted by Puckett, Petty, Cacioppo, and Fischer (1983), examined the impact of both age and attractiveness on persuasion. To determine the effects of these variables, the authors asked 220 college students to read essays containing either cogent or invalid arguments attributed to either young or old, socially attractive or unattractive authors. Results of their study showed that attractive authors were rated as more persuasive than unattractive authors when the arguments of the essay were strong. However, when the arguments of the essay were weak, attractive authors were criticized more and rated as less persuasive than unattractive authors. Puckett and his associates concluded that, although attractiveness can positively enhance the overall communication process, judgments and attitudes about attractive people are typically more extreme than judgments and attitudes regarding unattractive individuals (p. 342).

In addition to research focusing on the relationship between attractiveness and persuasion, there have also been studies addressing the extent to which physical attractiveness is related to higher grades in school or college. For example, in an early study, Singer (1964) documented a positive relationship between higher grade-point average in college, birth order, and level of attractiveness. (Firstborns generally have higher grades than children who were born second.) Singer's research has been supported in a number of recent studies, such as that of Murphy, Nelson, and Cheap (1981). In their study, Murphy and his colleagues asked college students to rate pictures of both male and female high school students on level of attractiveness, academic achievement, and sociability. Results of this study revealed that, in situations in which we know little about specific individuals, females are perceived to be more socially skilled and academically inclined than males. Additionally, attractive persons are more positively evaluated than those people who are judged to be less attractive. Interestingly enough, when Murphy examined the actual academic performance of the individuals whose pictures were evaluated, he found a similar relationship between appearance and actual grade-point average. Specifically, he found that females generally receive higher grades than males of equal ability when ability is measured by standardized achievement tests (p. 106).

Does the attractiveness of an individual affect our system of justice? Specifically, do attractive defendants receive lighter sentences? Some researchers answer yes and report that unattractive defendants are more likely to receive longer sentences. In a study using simulated jurors, a photograph and summary sheet of facts was given to each juror. They were then asked to determine the guilt or innocence of a female defendant in a college cheating case. Although evaluations of the male jurors were influenced by the physical attractiveness of the fictitious female, the effect on female jurors was not as pronounced. Researcher Efran (1974) reported that the "physically attractive defendants were judged with less certainty and given less severe recommended punishments."

Consider how the "good guys" and the "bad guys" are depicted on television. They are markedly different in terms of attractiveness. The bad guys always seem to have obvious facial scars and are clad in dark clothing. The good guys, our heroes, are usually clean-shaven and good-looking, and they wear colors other than black. Most horror films depict the ominous creature, human or animal, as an "ugly" entity. It may be that we subconsciously label an attractive person as "good" and an unattractive person as "bad." As you can see in either case, attractiveness affects the degree to which an individual can persuade or manipulate others.

Courtship and marriage choices.   Does physical attractiveness also affect our decisions regarding whom we will date and marry? Past findings lean toward an affirmative response: physical attractiveness *is* a highly significant factor. For example, Walster, Aronson, Abrahams, and Rohmann (1966) found that physical attractiveness is a very important determinant of how much a date will be liked by his or her partner. Likewise, Dion, Berscheid, and Walster (1972) discovered that physically attractive people are judged to have more desirable personalities than those individuals who are seen as being less attractive. Additionally, attractive people are predicted to have happier marriages, better jobs, and more satisfying lives.

Attractiveness also affects our marriage decisions, as indicated in a recent landmark study by Udry and Eckland (1984). Studying the *actual* marital and socioeconomic status of 1,346 people fifteen years after they had graduated from high school, Udry and Eckland found that, indeed, females whose high school pictures were rated high in attractiveness married more often and married highly educated men with high income levels. Additionally, these researchers found that the timing of marriage is affected by attractiveness for both males and females. Specifically, they discovered that attractive males and females married earlier than those individuals judged to be less attractive. By age twenty, only 13 percent of the least attractive males had married, while 30 percent of the highly attractive males had married. Likewise, 66 percent of the highly attractive females had married by age twenty while only 38 percent of the least attractive females had married.

As you can see, physical attractiveness can affect courtship and marriage, although other important factors also come into play. To demonstrate this point—as well as others about nonverbal communication—we conduct a four-hour "blindfold" experiment once each term. Before the experiment begins, students are blindfolded securely and then allowed to interact freely for the four hours allotted. In every experiment we have conducted, some interesting "pairings" have taken place. For example, at one "blindfold," a very conservative young woman who had previously remarked that she detested men with long hair talked for two hours to a male student with very long hair and, in fact, made a date with him for the following evening. At the conclusion of the four hours, she and the other participants sat in a circle and removed their blindfolds. The room went silent, and they looked at one another in a state of shock. We are unsure about how the female student described above reacted, but as one male student later wrote, "When I was blindfolded, I thought that every woman I talked to was beautiful. Then when I had my eyes back, Barb, who I thought was tall, lean, and sensual, turned out to be five feet two, chubby, and less sensual than I perceived her to be." Another participant wrote, "I was bitterly shocked and disappointed to find that I and others judge people so much on their physical appearance.

Beauty may only be skin-deep, but you have to have it to attract someone and show them you're beautiful all the way through."*

Attractiveness appears to be a very potent variable, both in courtship behavior and marriage preferences. Being attractive or unattractive also affects how people behave in various settings toward the attractive or unattractive person.

Interaction behavior.   Darren, thirteen years old, decided to lose 25 pounds because he was tired of being left out of games and sports. He was called names and it was especially difficult for him to make new friends. Being unattractive at any age changes the way people perceive you and, ultimately, the way they treat you, as Darren found out. Schools provide the testing ground for the differential treatment of attractive and unattractive children. An unattractive child is seen as a chronic problem, for example, while the same misbehavior by an attractive child is dismissed as only a temporary problem.

According to Algozzine (1976), teachers interact less frequently and less positively with the unattractive elementary school child. Peers also react unfavorably to the unattractive child. With the unattractive individual, the nonverbal responses include behaviors of avoidance (e.g., reduced eye contact, greater distance from the person) as well as the verbal response of singling out the "misfit" through name calling or other forms of ridicule.

The attractive individual usually receives an approach response that involves nonverbal signs of interest. A recent study was conducted to determine if males exhibit different kinds of kinesic behaviors when they interact with attractive females. A subject and a female confederate (previously rated as "attractive") were told that the study was on first impressions. Findings showed that males with a low self-concept looked more at the attractive females, while males with high self-concepts looked more at both the attractive and unattractive female confederates (Fugita, Agle, Newman, and Walfish, 1977). (The findings of this study replicated a 1975 experiment conducted by Kleck and Rubenstein.)

Another interesting phenomenon involving attractiveness is the double standard of aging as it applies to men and women. Susan Sontag (1972) explains that according to social convention, aging progressively enhances a man but progressively destroys a woman. A woman is never totally accepted as she is. Her face is a "canvas upon which she paints a revised, corrected portrait of herself." Conversely, men need only have a clean face. Advertising capitalizes on the plight of women, as in the Oil of Olay ad that asks, "Is it a little scary competing with all those fresh-faced young girls out of college?" Probably thousands of middle-aged women have responded with a resounding yes.

The quest for attractiveness has been a theme of both historical and contemporary cultures. In Elizabethan England, hair was dyed red or saffron as a compliment to the queen. Beauties swallowed a combination of gravel, tallow, and

---

* Malandro and Barker recorded this and other similar personal feedback from students who participated in the blindfold experiments during the period 1972 to 1976. These records are unpublished.

Both adults and children tend to avoid unattractive children. (Barbara Alper)

ashes in an effort to make their skins pale. In medieval England, elaborate head-dresses required plucking the hair on the forehead and neck. Women used a mirror to aid them and did their plucking in public, an activity considered much less shocking than applying makeup (*Redbook,* 1978).

Since the stakes for being attractive are so high, it is understandable why people are willing to do just about anything to reap the benefits. After all, being attractive affects not only the way people perceive you but also the way they respond to you. However, as you will see in the following section, other factors affect the individual ways in which we interact with others. These factors include our personal body image and the resulting messages our body sends.

BODY IMAGE AND APPEARANCE

To most people, the body is unknown and alien. As Tennessee Williams observed in *Orpheus Descending,* all of us are sentenced to solitary confinement within our own respective bodies. And yet, throughout our lives, we use and abuse them, depending on the degree to which we are body-aware and body-satisfied. Unfortunately, in those instances when we are least aware and satisfied, our self-concepts and resulting communication behaviors suffer the most.

To help you explore your own personal levels of body awareness and satisfaction—and, we hope, to help maximize your positive perceptions of both—we now turn to a more complete discussion of each respective topic. We hope that when you complete this section, you will have a better grasp of the role that both variables play in your life. In addition, we hope that a more complete understanding will help you to improve your nonverbal communication with others.

Body Awareness

When was the last time you saw yourself unexpectedly in a mirror, photograph, or on film? Did you immediately recognize yourself? Or, for a moment, did you feel as if you were looking at an unknown individual? This experience of nonrecognition underscores the fact that most people simply do not know their own bodies. As a result, many people experience (1) **body distortion,** (2) **body depersonalization,** and (3) **skewed body boundaries.**

Body distortion.   In a classic investigation by Traub and Orbach (1964), subjects were put in front of a special mirror that had been cleverly designed to distort the image systematically. When they were shown how to manipulate the controls for the mirror, the subjects experienced great difficulty in converting the distorted reflection back to the true image. This suggests that people have trouble "remembering" what they actually look like. In a classroom experiment that replicated an earlier study by Wolff (1943), one of the authors asked her students to identify their hands from photographs taken during a nonverbal communication class. Although a number of students were able to make the correct identification from among the twenty-five to thirty pictures, several others were not able to tell their hands from those of the others. Look at your hands. Could you recognize them in a series of 100 photographs (the number of pictures used by Wolff)? You might be able to do so if someone told you that there was a picture of your hands among the photographs. But if you were not forewarned, chances are you would not recognize your own hands.

People also experience difficulty in accurately visualizing the size of certain body parts, especially when asked to judge the extent to which they are overweight. To support this hypothesis, Collins, McCabe, Jupp, and Sutton (1983) asked sixty-eight females who were undergoing weight-reduction counseling to judge the extent to which they were obese, using video-image representations of body size. All of the women judged themselves to be more overweight than they actually were. Those women who made the greatest number of errors in estimation were those who were more obese. After therapy, each woman was able to make a more realistic estimate of her body size. Therapy dropouts, however, saw themselves as significantly more overweight than those who completed the program (p. 507).

When provided with the opportunity to examine our bodies closely, we do so through a complex set of selective filters, seeing what we want to see. Unlike the women described in the paragraph above, we may also repress thoughts about areas of our bodies that could be improved. For example, a man with a potbelly may instead focus on his broad shoulders, while a woman with large hips may see only her 36-inch bust. Not knowing or being aware of your body may be traced, in part, to the fact that body curiosity is socially discouraged. A male who spends a great deal of time in front of a mirror is often ridiculed, while the same behavior in a female is more readily accepted. Yet for both males and females, a careful study of the front and back of the body is reserved for special groups of people such as artists and doctors. Since body curiosity is socially discouraged, it is understandable that both men and women suffer from a lack of knowledge about their own bodies.

It is interesting to note that people who are depressed are less satisfied with their bodies and see themselves as less physically attractive than people who are not depressed. To document this hypothesis, Noles, Cash, and Winstead (1985) asked 224 college men and women to complete tests measuring body image and personal depression. As the researchers hypothesized, depressed subjects distorted their body image negatively, while nondepressed subjects produced positive distortions. As Noles and his colleagues also postulated, the depressed group expressed less satisfaction with their body parts. Additionally, they expressed less satisfaction with their physical appearance overall (p. 92).

Body depersonalization.   Body depersonalization occurs when a person feels that he or she is surrendering his or her body to another person or persons. In some cases, it may be the fear of this surrender that keeps people from seeking medical or dental help. The average person, even after recognizing the need for medical help, will often delay and put off indefinitely setting up an appointment. This avoidance phenomenon occurs even with physicians and other well-educated persons who have technical knowledge and know that they should not delay. When people finally decide to submit their bodies to medical examination, they will then be probed and will essentially surrender the anatomy of their bodies. During a prolonged stay in the hospital, one's body actually becomes "public property": it seems to belong to the hospital establishment. This feeling of body depersonalization has been reported in other institutions such as prisons or the military (Fisher, 1973).

How does body depersonalization affect our behavior? The most dramatic effect occurs in our attempt to avoid body depersonalization. Through a variety of strategies such as eating spicy foods, smoking, dancing, exercising, engaging in sports, suntanning, and resorting to plastic surgery, we try to experience body sensations. Consider your level of physical activity. If you are a student, an avid television watcher, and/or office professional, your body sits for hours, rarely moving, and becomes a passive and alien object. The absence of physical stimulation and activity over a period of time may result in an increasing depersonalization of the body. Body security and the recognition of the physical boundaries of the body constitute another important area of body awareness.

Body boundaries.   Boundaries in general are extremely important to people. We spend great amounts of money and energy in erecting defensive boundaries such as forts, fences, and shelters. We build **body armor** in the form of clothing and use olfactory screens such as perfume or cologne. Military and police uniforms are similarly used with the addition of chest decorations, leather gloves, boots, hats, and helmets. In an early study, Kernaleguen (1968) found that college women who are most insecure about their **body boundaries** are likely to take the lead in wearing the newest clothing fashions in order to reinforce the boundaries by making them more visually vivid through the use of attention-getting clothing.

The car we drive is another example of a body boundary. When we get behind the wheel of a car, our body image actually expands to the "skin" of the car. We become the car, and the car becomes our new boundary. Seat belts provide an excellent example. Despite the fact that statistics prove we have a much better chance of surviving an accident unscathed if we are wearing seat belts, many people still refuse to fasten theirs. Seat belts may conflict with drivers' images of themselves. Neen (1976) speculates:

> You get in your Wildcat or Cougar; your body image expands. You feel speedy and omnipotent and then all of a sudden there's that seatbelt tugging at you, rubbing you around the waist, reminding you of your real and natural boundaries. The easiest way to deal with the conflict is by simply not buckling up. (pp. 94–95)

Body security, or the lack of it, may be reflected in various forms of body armor. Clothing, as already mentioned, is one form of body armor. A second type is the use of the body itself, such as crossing the arms in front of the chest. Sometimes these behaviors are used as a means of creating boundaries, and, as a result, body security.

The following section explores how body distortion, body depersonalization, and body boundaries relate to the degree to which people feel satisfied with their bodies.

Body Satisfaction

Are your satisfied with your body? If you are male and answer yes, then you share the feelings of the majority of men in a 1985 study. If you are female and answer yes, you are definitely in the minority! In a study by Fallon and Rozin (1985) 248 male and 227 female undergraduates were asked to indicate their current and ideal body shapes and the body shape that they felt would be most attractive to the opposite sex. For men, the three body shapes were almost identical. For women, their current body shape was perceived to be heavier than their perceptions of the most attractive figure. In turn, their perception of the "most attractive" body shape was heavier than that of the "ideal" figure—two perceptions which may explain why 90 percent of those who suffer from anorexia or bulimia are females (Bemis, 1978). Interestingly enough, when asked to predict the body shape preferred by the *opposite* sex, both males and females were wrong! Results of the study revealed that men think women like a heavier body type than women report liking and that women think men like women thinner than men report liking. As Fallon and Rozin argue, men's misperceptions serve to keep them more satisfied with their body shapes. However, women's misperceptions place pressure on them to lose weight (p. 102).

Aside from influencing your health and well-being (this relationship will be examined later in the chapter), the image that you have of your body affects your self-concept as well. In fact, body satisfaction, or the degree to which you are or are not satisfied with parts or processes of the body (also called body cathexis), plays a vital role in the development of your self-concept (Richards and Hawthorne, 1971). In the following section, we will examine more closely the relationship between body concept and satisfaction. Of particular importance is the relationship of both to the development of self-concept.

Body concept.   The term **body concept** refers to your perception of the attractiveness and the abilities of your body, which has developed through (1) your interactions with others, (2) your role in a specific cultural and social environment, and (3) your personal experiences. As stated earlier, there is evidence to suggest that your body concept is related to your self-concept (the feelings that you have about your social and psychological self). From a *Psychology Today* questionnaire on body image, Berscheid, Walster, and Bohrnstedt (1973a) found that only 11 percent of the respondents with a below-average body image had an above-average level of self-esteem. This suggests a relationship between one's feelings about one's body and one's feelings about oneself as a person.

An effect of the parental body attitude on children's body concept was reported in an early study by Arnaud (1955). He found that children raised in a family in which one of the parents had some serious body defect were unusually anxious about their own bodies. Whether you like your body or not may also be related to whether or not your parents like your body. According to investigators Jourard and Secord (1955), a poor body concept may in part be the result of negative feedback received from parents who considered their child's body to be unattractive. This conclusion from their early classic study was later supported by that of Berscheid, Walster, and Bohrnstedt (1973a), who reported that an overwhelming majority of their respondents who had a below-average body image were also frequently teased as children by their peers and parents about their appearance. Said one respondent: "My mother had a few pet names for me such as 'prune face' and 'garbage disposal.' These comments had more of an influence on me than anything my peers had to say."

Researchers Jourard and Secord (1955) reported that males were most satisfied when they were somewhat larger in body size than normal. Females, on the other hand, were satisfied when their bodies were smaller than normal and when their busts were larger than average. Berscheid, Walster, and Bohrnstedt (1973a) conclude: "A woman's self-esteem relates to her feeling pretty and slim; a man's self-esteem relates to being handsome and having a muscular chest."

As we have argued, feelings of inadequacies and a below-average body concept affect one's self-concept and ultimately one's behavior. Another area of concern is the structure of the body and what it communicates about the person.

Body structure.   Have you ever wanted to cry but held it in because other people were present? The process of "holding in" an emotion is not just a figurative expression; it is a reality. We tense our muscles, for example, in an effort to stop or hold in a particular emotion. If this tensing becomes habitual, then muscle patterns become fixed and, in turn, sustain an attitude. In other words, your mind shapes your body, and your body reshapes your mind (Gross, 1976).

Psychoanalyst Alexander Lowen, in studying depression and the body, points out the connection between **body structure** and the depressed state. "The degree of depression," explains Lowen, "is a measure of how much the person has lost his self-awareness as a bodily person. When the body dies, the person dies." When a person feels "alive," the body is also alive. Lowen (1967) explains this in more detail:

> If the body is relatively unalive, a person's impressions and responses are diminished. The more alive the body is, the more vividly does he perceive reality and the more actively does he respond to it. We have all experienced the fact that when we feel particularly good and alive, we perceive the world more sharply. In states of depression, the world appears colorless. (p. 5)

"The body never lies," claim Kurtz and Prestera (1970), authors of *The Body Reveals*. Healthy persons have a natural flow of expression. For example, in feeling sadness, we usually exhibit a trembling jaw, tears, or even sobbing. To block this emotion, we would tense the jaw, chest, diaphragm, stomach, and some muscles of the face and throat. This blocking or holding action halts the emotion and sets the muscles in the body. Could it be that a person whose shoulders are slumped forward is carrying the weight of the world? Or that the person with a sunken chest feels as if he or she has no energy left for life? Analyzing the body as a communicative message about a person's psychological and emotional world is the concern of many therapeutic approaches.

The manipulation of the body to relieve suffering is the concern of osteopaths and chiropractors. Gestalt therapy and psychodrama focus on the reality of body statements, although they do not involve actual physical work on the body. There

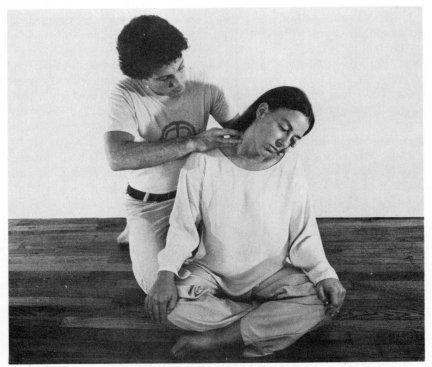

Some forms of therapy involve physically manipulating the body. (Baldwin/Watriss/Woodfin Camp & Associates)

are specific body-oriented approaches that involve physically manipulating the body so as to release muscle rigidity and areas of holding and tension. One such approach is structural integration, referred to as "rolfing" and developed by Ida Rolf. Both Reichian therapy and bioenergetics are also grounded in psychoanalytic theory and were pioneered by Wilhelm Reich and Alexander Lowen. Judith Aston, in collaboration with Dr. Rolf, developed an approach called "patterning" along the same theoretical perspective as rolfing. At the heart of each of these therapeutic approaches is the concept that the body is always communicating messages about the individual.

BODY MESSAGES

Attractiveness, body awareness, and body satisfaction communicate important information about an individual. Other messages of the body are communicated through body shape, height, weight, nudity, skin color, and hair. Before reading the next section, take the self-description test provided below. Completing this test and the corresponding reading will give you some information about yourself and about the theory and research in this area. In the following pages, you will have the opportunity to score your test and interpret some of the findings.

Instructions: Circle three (3) words for each of the following statements. If the words do not fit you exactly, select the words that seem to fit most closely the way you are. Select any three words from among the twelve choices offered.*

1. Most of the time I feel:

calm	relaxed	complacent	contented
anxious	confident	reticent	impetuous
cheerful	tense	energetic	self-conscious

2. When I study or work, I seem to be:

efficient	sluggish	precise	placid
enthusiastic	competitive	determined	meticulous
reflective	leisurely	thoughtful	cooperative

3. Socially, I am:

outgoing	considerate	argumentative	gentle-tempered
affable	awkward	shy	hot-tempered
tolerant	affected	talkative	soft-tempered

4. I am rather:

active	forgiving	sympathetic	introspective
warm	courageous	serious	cool
domineering	suspicious	soft-hearted	enterprising

5. Other people consider me rather:

generous	optimistic	sensitive	dominant
adventurous	affectionate	kind	detached
withdrawn	reckless	cautious	dependent

Instructions: Circle one (1) word for each of the following statements. If the words do not fit you exactly, select the word that seems to fit most closely the way you are.

6. I consider myself to be rather:

assertive	relaxed	tense

7. I consider myself to be rather:

hot-tempered	cool	warm

8. I consider myself to be rather:

withdrawn	sociable	active

9. I consider myself to be rather:

confident	tactful	kind

10. I consider myself to be rather:

dependent	dominant	detached

11. I consider myself to be rather:

enterprising	affable	anxious

---

*Self-Description Test, from J. B. Cortes and F. M. Gatti, "Physique and Self-Description of Temperament," *Journal of Consulting Psychology,* 1965, vol. 29, p. 434. Copyright © 1965 by the American Psychological Association. Adapted by permission of the publisher and author.

Body Shape

What would you do if you walked into a department store at Christmastime and saw a skinny man in a Santa Claus outfit? Or a very muscular man in Santa Claus clothes wearing tight pants? Chances are you would say, "That's not Santa Claus; after all, everyone knows that Santa is fat and jolly!" To most people Santa has an easily identifiable body shape (fat) and a very definite temperament (jolly). His body type would be referred to as endomorphic and his temperament as viscerotonic.

Researchers, philosophers, and writers have for some time suggested that there is a relationship between body type and temperament. As early as 1925, Ernst Kretschmer, a professor of psychiatry and neurology, made the first known comprehensive effort to record differences in body type. In his book *Physique and Character: An Investigation of the Nature of Constitution and of the Theory of Temperament,* Kretschmer claimed that individuals who share morphological similarities could be classified into three groups. The first group exhibited the asthenic or skinny, bony, and narrow body, the second group the athletic or muscular body, and the third group the pyknic or fat body.

Researchers are not the only group to suggest that there is a relationship between **body shape** and temperament. Shakespeare, with his uncanny insight into human character, revealed his perception of body shape and temperament in his well-known play *Julius Caesar:*

Caesar:	Let me have men about me that are fat; Sleek-headed men, such as sleep o'nights.
	Yond Cassius has a lean and hungry look; He thinks too much; such men are dangerous.
Anthony:	Fear him not, Caesar; he is not dangerous. He is a noble Roman and well given.
Caesar:	Would he were fatter! . . .

William Sheldon (1940, 1942, 1954) studied body types and temperaments. He suggested that a given body type or shape corresponded to a particular temperament. The following table illustrates the relationships hypothesized.

TABLE 2.1   **Sheldon's System**

Body type	Psychological type
Endomorph (oval-shaped body; heavy, large abdomen)	**Viscerotonic** (slow, sociable, emotional, forgiving, relaxed)
Mesomorph (triangular body shape, muscular, hard, firm, upright body quality)	**Somatotonic** (confident, energetic, dominant, enterprising, hot-tempered)
Ectomorph (fragile physique; flatness of chest; poorly muscled limbs)	**Cerebrotonic** (tense, awkward, meticulous, tactful, detached)

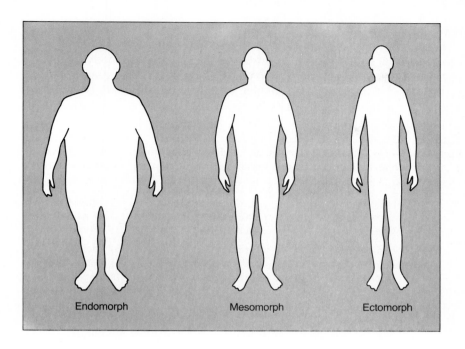

Endomorph   Mesomorph   Ectomorph

According to Sheldon, if you have an endomorphic physique, you probably also have a viscerotonic temperament, and so on down the line. However, Sheldon's method of measuring body type and temperament has been criticized. First, he committed a major experimental error by rating both the body builds and temperaments of his subjects himself. It was suspected that this subjective approach resulted in experimenter bias and influenced the ratings. Second, there have been reports of mathematical errors in Sheldon's computations. Although this criticism provides a sound basis for not accepting the findings of Sheldon's work as conclusive, the relationship Sheldon was investigating should not be rejected on this basis alone. As we shall see in a moment, other researchers have supported his hypotheses.

Before going any further, however, let's return to the self-description test that you filled out a bit earlier. This test has been used in numerous studies concerning the relationship between body types and temperament characteristics. The following description indicates how to score your test. Score your test now and compare it to the discussion of the psychological types.

On the following page, you will find the key for the self-description test. The number "1," "2," or "3" precedes each word. Count the number of words you have selected that have the number "1" in front of them. Follow this procedure for words that have a "2" or a "3" code in front of them. The total number of words you have chosen to describe yourself should add up to 21.

Your temperament score is based on the number of adjectives you chose from the endomorphic (#1 words), mesomorphic (#2 words), or ectomorphic (#3 words) category. For example, if you had a score of 4 in the endomorphic category, 12 in the mesomorphic category, and 5 in the ectomorphic category, your temperament score would be 4/12/5. This would suggest, according to Sheldon, that you have a mesomorphic physique and a somatotonic temperament.

Several major questions can be explored in the research on body types and temperaments. First, what are the perceived psychological characteristics of each body type? Second, what are the actual characteristics of each body type? Third, do the actual characteristics correlate with the corresponding psychological type?

Example: **Mike selected the words "relaxed," "contented," and "cheerful" to describe himself. Both "relaxed" and "contented" are number-one words (i.e., words that are preceded with the number one in the key) while "cheerful" is a number-two word. So far his score is 2/1/0.**

---

1. (1) calm
    (3) anxious
    (2) cheerful

    (1) relaxed
    (2) confident
    (3) tense

    (1) complacent
    (3) reticent
    (2) energetic

    (1) contented
    (2) impetuous
    (3) self-conscious

2. (2) efficient
    (2) enthusiastic
    (3) reflective

    (2) sluggish
    (2) competetive
    (1) leisurely

    (2) precise
    (2) determined
    (3) thoughtful

    (3) placid
    (3) meticulous
    (1) cooperative

3. (2) outgoing
    (1) affable
    (1) tolerant

    (3) considerate
    (3) awkward
    (1) affected

    (2) argumentative
    (3) shy
    (2) talkative

    (2) gentle-tempered
    (2) hot-tempered
    (1) soft-tempered

4. (2) active
    (1) warm
    (2) domineering

    (1) forgiving
    (2) courageous
    (3) suspicious

    (1) sympathetic
    (3) serious
    (1) soft-hearted

    (3) introspective
    (3) cool
    (2) enterprising

5. (1) generous
    (2) adventurous
    (3) withdrawn

    (2) optimistic
    (a) affectionate
    (2) reckless

    (3) sensitive
    (1) kind
    (3) cautious

    (2) dominant
    (3) detached
    (1) dependent

6. (2) assertive
    (1) relaxed
    (3) tense

7. (2) hot-tempered
    (3) cool
    (1) warm

8. (3) withdrawn
    (1) sociable
    (2) active

9. (2) confident
    (1) tactful
    (3) kind

10. (1) dependent
    (2) dominant
    (3) detached

11. (2) enterprising
    (1) affable
    (3) anxious

Your Score

TOTAL #1 WORDS	TOTAL #2 WORDS	TOTAL #3 WORDS	= 21

Perceived characteristics of body types.   Although there are no conclusive results on the correlation between body type and temperament, research findings do suggest that there is a correlation between body type and *perceived* psychological characteristics. For example, in an earlier study, Wells and Siegel (1961) showed 120 adult subjects silhouette drawings of an endomorph, a mesomorph, and an ectomorph. Their results underscored the perceived correlation between body types and psychological characteristics. The subjects rated the endomorph as more old-fashioned, lazier, weaker, more talkative, older, shorter (silhouettes were the same height), more warmhearted and sympathetic, more good-natured and agreeable, more dependent on others, and more trusting of others. They perceived the mesomorph as stronger, more adventurous, more masculine, more mature, more self-reliant, younger, and taller. They saw the ectomorph as more ambitious, thinner, younger, more suspicious of others, more tense and nervous, more inclined to be difficult, less masculine, more pessimistic, and quieter. A study by Strongman and Hart (1968) reports similar findings, as does a research report by David Lester (1982). However, one question raised by these studies is as follows: Do these "perceived characteristics" accurately reflect the actual psychological characteristics hypothesized for each body type?

Actual characteristics of body types.   Studies either replicating or partially replicating Sheldon's original ideas have examined body types in relation to (1) the need for achievement, and (2) prediction of behavior. Perhaps a different relationship would have been uncovered if the study had used female subjects. Beller (1977), in her book *Fat and Thin,* argues that fat women are not only cuddly, jovial, and loving, but sexier too. Endomorphic women, Beller claims, are more responsive to erotic stimulation and have greater sexual appetites. In one survey conducted in a Chicago hospital, "fat women outscored their thin sisters by a factor of almost two to one" in terms of excitability.

In comparing 100 delinquent boys (ages 16½ to 18½) who had been convicted in court with 100 nondelinquent boys of the same age, Cortes and Gatti (1965) examined the need for achievement. Each boy looked at pictures of persons in ordinary but ambiguous situations and was asked to write a story about each picture. The researchers found that the nondelinquent boys had a significant and positive association between the mesomorphic (muscular) body build and the need for achievement. On the other hand, ectomorphs demonstrated less need for achievement. In support of their earlier hypotheses, the researchers found that 80 percent of the mesomorphs were above average in the need for achievement, while 81 percent of the endomorphs were below average. The delinquent boys had the same associations, but at a lower level of significance.

Although the results of numerous studies indicate that there may be a correlation between body build and temperament, we cannot conclude that one's body causes or determines one's temperament. A possible explanation for the relationship between body types and temperaments may be based on the stereotyped perceptions. People clearly associate body builds with personality traits. Whether these stereotypes are accurate or not, they do exist. As a result, people expect a person with a "muscular" body type to be more dominant. Stereotyping about body builds serves to perpetuate self-fulfilling myths about people. If we perceive someone as a leader and treat that person as such, we tend to make the person a leader. By forcing people to fit our definitions of them based on body builds, we may create the corresponding psychological characteristics in them. In other words, people fulfill the role in which we picture them.

Whether we are talking about the perceived characteristics of body types or the actual correlation between the body type and temperament, one conclusion is inescapable: The shape of the body communicates.

Body Weight

People who are happy with their body weight are most satisfied with their bodies. Of the respondents to the *Psychology Today* questionnaire, almost half of the women and one-third of the men were very dissatisfied with their weight (Berscheid, Walster, and Bohrnstedt, 1973b). The great concern that society places on a trim figure is reflected in an article appropriately titled "Plump and Loving It" (*Cosmopolitan,* 1977):

> . . . how many women of ample girth appreciate their own sensuous figures? Very few. Invariably you find them plaintively condemning themselves because they haven't been able to whittle their womanly proportions down to fashion model size two.

Women tend to be especially concerned with body weight, so much so that cultural pressures on women to be thin have been linked specifically to serious eating disorders such as anorexia nervosa (Garner, Garfinkel, Schwartz, and Thompson, 1980). To document the shift in the last twenty years toward a thinner ideal shape for American women—and, hence, one possible link to the increase in cases of anorexia nervosa—Garner and his colleagues examined height, weight, and measurement data of *Playboy* magazine playmates over the past twenty years as well as the same data for both contestants and winners of the Miss America Pageant (1959 through 1978). In addition, they examined six popular magazines for articles about dieting and weight loss (for the same period listed above). Results of their study indicated that, over the past ten years, a shift toward a thinner, "ideal" female figure could indeed be documented. Results from both the *Playboy* centerfolds and Miss America contestants confirmed and quantified the trend. Additionally, their study of six popular magazines revealed corroborating evidence: the yearly average of dieting articles numbered 17.1 during the first decade which they examined; during the second decade, the average increased to 29.6.

As you can see, although women are pressured by society to conform to an "ideal" body type, such conformity can be linked to an increased number of eating disorders. The problem is that anorexia nervosa, in which the distaste for food and refusal to eat lead to excessive weight loss, can eventually result in death. Even chronic dieting can lead to problems such as irritability, poor concentration, anxiety, depression, apathy, mood shifts, fatigue, and social isolation (Garner, Garfinkel, Schwartz, and Thompson, 1980, p. 490). Such problems are most commonly found in adolescent and college-age females from about ten to twenty-five years of age. Because of its widespread nature, it may be of help to know the general symptoms of anorexia nervosa. Although difficult to define because they vary, they include the following:

Starvation, which results in excessive weight loss.

Amenorrhea, or total loss of menstruation.

Eating binges, which result in self-induced vomiting.

Obsession with food, in which the victim will spend hours making elaborate meals but will not eat them.

Hyperactivity, in which the individual feels as if she has unlimited energy.

Continual constipation, which causes the victim to become virtually addicted to laxatives and enemas.

Abnormality of body image and perception, in which the victim thinks she is unattractive and has no ability to recognize hunger and fatigue.

Body Height

For some time, police departments have had minimum height requirements of 5 feet 9 inches or 5 feet 11 inches, thereby excluding more than half of the country's men and nearly all of its women from police work. In response to equal-employment-opportunity legislation, lawsuits, and justice department guidelines that denied federal money to departments with minimum-height standards, many departments have eliminated the height requirement. Police departments were put to the test of demonstrating that height is an "operational necessity for designated job categories."

Although changes in guidelines have eliminated height requirements in many police departments today, studies show that attitudes toward short police officers have changed very little. As Lester and Sheehan (1980) report in their survey of twenty-nine supervisors, short patrolmen are believed to receive more complaints from citizens, to cause more frequent disciplinary problems, to issue more vehicle summonses and arrests, to cause poor morale, to initiate the greatest number of internal department complaints, and to be involved in more accidents than average or taller patrolmen. Tall patrolmen, on the other hand, are believed to cause the least number of disciplinary problems. Occupying the middle position, patrolmen of average height are believed to receive more letters of commendation, to give more warnings for vehicular violations, to get along better with their co-workers, to receive more job-related injuries, and to be chosen as the patrolmen most preferred to help members of the supervisors' families (Lester and Sheehan, 1980, p. 462).

If average to tall men are perceived more positively, in what ways does height affect communication behavior? According to Gillis and Avis (1980), women overwhelmingly choose males taller than themselves for husbands. Likewise, evidence exists that taller man develop relationships with more attractive women than do shorter men (Feingold, 1982). In short, both status and power are associated with people of taller stature.

Many fashionable European women in the late 1800s and early 1900s carried parasols. (Bobbi Carey/The Picture Cube)

Skin Color

During the 1800s, fashionable women everywhere protected their delicate complexions with sunbonnets that tied under the chin. The parasol also came in as a protector from the sun. Originating in the Orient as a mark of high rank, the parasol was copied by the Greeks from the Chinese, and the Romans copied it from the Greeks. Marie de Medicis brought the sunshade to France, and soon there were parasols for the sun and parapluies (umbrellas) for the rain. It was not until post-World War I days that it became fashionable for rich, successful people to be slightly suntanned. And since most people wanted to appear successful, the parasol went out and tanned skin came in.

Perhaps the most common method sought for changing skin color is by tanning (or in some cases, burning) the skin. The degree of tanning has communicated different messages over a period of time. When we lived in a largely agricultural society, a deep tan indicated long hours of working in the fields. Even Rhett Butler looked with disgust at the leathery hands of Scarlett O'Hara. During that time, a lily-white complexion indicated that the individual belonged to the wealthy, leisurely class of society.

No more—tan is beautiful—and so are sunglasses, which ultimately replaced the parasol. However, technically sunglasses are named incorrectly, since their original use was to block out movie lights and not the sun. Sunglasses became popular when movie stars began to wear them. At that time, they became a symbol of Hollywood glamour, although actors wore sunglasses because their eyes hurt from the early movie lights (called "klieg lights"). In fact, many actors developed a painful condition known as "klieg eyes," which resulted from excessive exposure to klieg lights.

The current popular trend is to obtain a tan despite the medical research that suggests that dangers are involved. Once again, in an attempt to be perceived as "beautiful" and/or "wealthy," people have demonstrated that they are willing to risk many things, including their health, in order to communicate a specific message.

Nudity

What does the human body communicate in its natural and uncovered state? The difference between being nude and being naked is that the term "nude" refers to acceptable instances of undress. Being naked, on the other hand, is considered somewhat vulgar and usually refers to instances of improper undress. Society accepts nudes in art, but naked men and women are considered shocking. According to this definition, then, the occasionally popular college pastime of streaking would be referred to as "running naked."

Clothing may not be a biological need, according to some anthropologists. On a voyage around the tip of South America, Charles Darwin observed that a native woman, wearing a loin cloth and suckling a baby, was unaffected by a sleet storm or the sleet clinging to her body. It is also reported that women who tend reindeer herds in northeast Siberia are able to sit around in circles on the ground in sub-zero weather, threading needles and sewing with bare hands. If clothing is not a biological necessity, then perhaps there is an even stronger case for its use as a communicative tool.

Hair

Much as height, weight, and skin color influence our own and others' perceptions, so too does the length, color, presence, and absence of hair have several functions. First, our hair acts as a body defense, insulating and protecting it from outside elements. Second, hair serves as a human waste-disposal system, allowing us to rid the body of poisons and excess waste. Finally (and perhaps most related to the study of nonverbal communication), hair provides a means of individual, self-expression.

Research on body and facial hair has been limited in a number of ways, particularly with regard to the relationship between personality characteristics and hair length and color. More plentiful research is available on perceptions related to hair as well as on the effect of hair on behavior. In order to give you a more complete understanding of each of these areas, we now turn to a more comprehensive discussion of each.

Characteristics of individuals.   Do blondes have more fun? Nobody really knows the answer to this question, but one study examined hair color in relation to preferences in sports. In a sample of single men under thirty-five in which 85 percent were brunettes, 11 percent were blondes, and 4 percent were redheads, the researchers reported the following sport preferences. Blonde men correlated with an affinity for aerobic sports such as skiing, ice-skating, tennis, and hiking. Redheads were above average in involvement with hunting and target shooting. The only definite preferences for brunettes were roller-skating, bowling, and backpacking. The researchers summarized their findings as follows:

> Do blonde men have more fun? We weren't particularly serious about this subject initially. What we have learned, however, is that there are distinctions to be made in behavior patterns that are related to basic hair color. If we have any conclusion, it is that differences are inherent to one's roots . . . ethnic, not hair. ("Do Blondes Have More Fun?" 1976)

Although we cannot conclude that hair color is related to specific behavioral or personality preferences, there is evidence to suggest that people "perceive" some differences to exist.

Perceptions of individuals.   Literature is complete with references to the attributes of hair color such as "the red devil," "the golden angel," or "the black temptress." Hair communicates messages through (1) color, (2) length, (3) hairstyle and gestures, and (4) the presence or absence of facial hair.

HAIR COLOR.   Blonde hair has been the mark of both the princess and the whore. In ancient Rome there were few natural blondes, so the state decided to make blonde hair a badge of sin. The wicked "ladies of the evening" were licensed, taxed, and required by law to wear yellow wigs or to dye their hair blonde as a mark of their profession. Messalina, the third wife of Emperor Claudius, threw a wrench in the works when she began wearing a blonde wig. Soon many other women in Rome, aside from the "ladies of the evening," began wearing blonde wigs. The Roman men were distraught and complained that they no longer could tell a lady from a prostitute by the color of her hair. Many centuries later, the German poet Goethe warned of the fair-haired beauty:

Beware of her fair hair for she excels
All women in the magic of her locks;
And when she winds them around a young man's neck,
She will not ever let him free again.

The "dumb-blonde" image has been another common, but unfortunate, association for women who have blonde hair. Perhaps the "dumb-blonde" image was a spin-off from the frenetic post-World War I period when the most frivolous of the flappers were also the most likely to experiment with the new platinum-blonde bleaches. Anita Loos summarized the image of blondes in the title of her 1925 book, *Gentlemen Prefer Blondes, But Gentlemen Marry Brunettes.* From 1925 until now, the perception of blondes has remained fairly consistent.

Although Americans have seen blondes positively for some time, blondes have produced quite a stir internationally with regard to reputation. In Japan, black hair is beautiful. When the Japanese encountered Europeans for the first time, they called them "red devils" because of their light hair. Even today a blonde foreigner may elicit sentiments of pity. The Brothers Grimm (1897), on the other hand, praised the blonde maiden: "Rapunzel was the most beautiful child under the sun. . . . Rapunzel had splendid long hair, as fine as spun gold."

Redheads also have communicated various messages throughout the centuries. During the fifteenth century, redheads were sometimes burned at the stake as witches. In the twentieth century, Ira Gershwin offered a different perception of the redhead in his lyrics from *Porgy and Bess:* "A redheaded woman makes a choo-choo jump its track, a redheaded woman, she can make it jump right back."* *Glamour* magazine summarized perceptions associated with hair color in this way: Red is tempestuous, brown is wholesome, black is siren-y, and blondes have more fun.

HAIR LENGTH.   Credibility may be related to the length of your hair, claim researchers Andersen, Jensen, and King (1972). Subjects in two different classes were asked to rate the credibility of a speaker who wore a different hairstyle when appearing before each class. For the first group, the confederate had his hair combed so it stood out from his head 1½ inches and appeared quite long. This style was similar to that of many of the students in the class. For the second group, the confederate combed his hair flat so that it appeared short. The findings revealed that the short-haired speaker was rated significantly higher on credibility dimensions of competence and dynamism (Andersen, Jensen, and King, 1972). One possible explanation for these findings is that males with long hair are perceived to be less serious and less mature when compared to males with short hair.

What about no hair at all? A New York psychiatrist claims that a "shaved head makes the whole body phallic." The advice for a man who's getting a little wispy

---

* Copyright © 1935 by Gershwin Publishing Corp. Copyright renewed, assigned to Chappell & Co., Inc. International copyright secured. All rights reserved. Used by permission.

and wants to be a sex object might be to "go for broke," either by shaving off all his hair or getting a thick new crop from a wig or transplant (LaBarre, 1976).

HAIRSTYLE AND GESTURES.   You already know that hair talks, but what do hairstyles say? *Glamour* magazine (1978) tells its readers that:

> . . . long hair says young, and bouffant says matronly . . . who's straightened up her hair has straightened up the mess that's inside; blonde hair says "gee, I'd like to have more fun," and dark roots says, "Oh, what the hell." (*Glamour,* 1978, p. 28)

How many women over thirty do you see with hair that falls past their shoulders? Probably not too many, since women tend to believe the myth that long hair should go short after the traumatic age of thirty is reached, perhaps as a symbolic sign that "youth" is over.

Besides hairstyles, there are hair gestures—symbolic movements that are used to communicate a particular message. Letting the hair down, expecially in one swoop, may be interpreted as both a symbol of abandonment and a striptease. There are also **preening behaviors** that are generally used in the presence of a person of the opposite sex, such as running your fingers through your hair, playing with your hair, or pushing it out of your eyes. These preening gestures provide an invitation for the other person to do likewise—in other words, to play with your hair. How about curling your hair around your finger or nibbling the ends? According to Waters, those gestures are a type of security blanket that goes back to when we were "little primates clinging to our mother's fur." Even if you play with your hair habitually, with no intention of communicating anything to anyone, your behavior may be mistaken for a sexual invitation (*Glamour,* 1978, p. 28).

FACIAL HAIR.   Since ancient times, male facial and body hair has been a symbol of fertility, virility, strength, and—most of all—power. The supposition that "a hairy man is a strong man" has been believed by many people over the ages. Ancient Greeks and Romans had a tradition of offering their hair to the gods, thereby symbolically giving some of their own fertility and strength while hoping for some of the gods' in return. Ancient Britons defied Caesar's armies by wearing long, drooping mustaches dyed green and blue. King Clovis, who reigned between 481 and 511, describes how his people chose their kings from the hairiest of their warriors. A king who lacked courage lost not only his throne but his hair also.

The shaving of both beards and head hair has been used as a means of punishment. One poor Spartan, convicted of cowardice in war, was reputed to have been made to wear half a mustache. Defeated enemies suffered a similar humiliation by having their heads and facial hair shaved.

Beards have communicated many different messages. Over 5000 years ago, fastidious men had their beards dyed, oiled, and scented. They also had them pleated, curled, frizzled, or starched. Persian gentlemen of high rank sometimes had their beards powdered with gold dust or laced with gold thread. This custom was not a mere episode in costume history but endured for fifteen centuries. Beards were also used to designate social class in the Roman army, thus providing information about the chain of command. The ancient Egyptians, on the other hand, considered the beard to be unclean. This may in part explain why the Egyptians perceived the bearded Byzantines as savages.

More recent perceptions of men with facial hair were discussed in a study by Pellegrini (1973), in which photos were taken of eight men who were either (1) fully bearded, (2) with only a goatee, (3) with a mustache, or (4) clean-shaven. One hundred and twenty-eight students reviewed these photos and judged the men at various stages in the process of accumulating facial hair. The results showed that the more hair the men had, the more they were judged to be masculine, mature, good-looking, self-confident, dominant, courageous, liberal, nonconformist, and industrious.

In an earlier study by Freedman (1969), a group of undergraduate students were asked how they felt about beardedness. None of the male students wore a beard. The majority of both men and women used adjectives of youthfulness to describe the clean-shaven men. Women described bearded men as masculine, sophisticated, and mature. This description accounted for 55 percent of the adjectives used. Of the men, 22 percent described bearded men as independent, while another 20 percent described them as extroverted. Additional interviews with women revealed that a beard heightens sexual magnetism by making the man appear more masculine and as a result making the women feel more feminine toward him. Although people will generally stand closer to beardless men, many bearded men themselves report that they are less tense with clean-shaven male strangers than with bearded ones. Freedman explains the social perception of beards in this way: "Beards may be more appealing to women and perhaps help love to blossom. They give men status in the eyes of other men and may increase social distance between two men."

Freedman also reports on a study by Parker in which students were asked to rate a picture of an elderly unbearded man and a young, serious-looking bearded man. The catch was that the same man was used in both pictures with a beard "drawn on" in one picture. The younger bearded man was perceived as having superior status with regard to masculinity, maturity, self-confidence, and dominance. In another comparison of a bearded man and a clean-shaven man, both were shown with an elderly women. The clean-shaven man was seen as young and troubled. With the addition of the beard, the man was perceived as being in control of the situation.

Hair and beards are perceived to communicate definite, although varying, messages. There is also evidence to indicate that they also affect the behavior of others.

Effects on behavior.   In the music industry, almost anything goes when it comes to clothing, hair, and beards. In fact, many members of the entertainment business have served as role models in these and other areas of nonverbal communication. In the sixties, Elvis Presley, Jimi Hendrix, Cher, the Beatles, and the Rolling Stones influenced hair length and style. Short hair and short sideburns became a thing of the past as entertainers began to wear their hair longer. In the seventies, James Brown, James Taylor, Joan Baez, Paul McCartney, and Rod Stewart hit the scene. These trend setters continued to favor long hair and to encourage a more free, unstyled, natural look. In the eighties, however, Americans began to favor shorter hair, and new hair colors were suddenly in. Entertainers who have influenced hairstyles in the eighties include The Police, Michael Jackson, Cyndi Lauper, Tom Cruise, Madonna, and Don Johnson (of *Miami Vice* fame). In fact, Don Johnson has been credited with single-handedly bringing the "five-o'clock shadow" into vogue.

Longer hair and beards have not always had a positive effect on others, however. As a placement officer at Stanford University succinctly stated:

> "The length of a male's hair is directly proportionate to the job opportunities he can find. . . . In other words, the longer the hair, the fewer the jobs."

As for women, long hair may have a negative effect in the workplace. Long hair is sexy hair unless it is pulled back or up and may create prejudices. Waters explains:

> Anything that smacks of sexuality engenders resentment among women, and the men think you're incompetent. Also, you're playing into their prejudices. Men are always afraid that women will try to use their sexuality to get ahead; sexual hair feeds their fears. (*Glamour*, 1978).

Hair, according to philosophers, poets, and researchers, affects not only the perception but also the behavior of others.

SUMMARY

The body, in all its various possible shapes and sizes, communicates powerful messages to others. One of the most dramatic ways in which the body communicates is through the degree of attractiveness. Both men and women have suffered untold pain for the privilege of being perceived as "handsome" or "beautiful." Reshaping the body to fit standards of beauty is recorded in both historical and contemporary fashion.

Available research in the area of attractiveness can be classified into three categories: (1) the personality characteristics of the attractive individual, (2) others' perceptions of attractive individuals, and (3) the effect of attractiveness on the behavior of others. The research available on the characteristics of attractive individuals is limited, although there is some evidence to suggest that attractive persons are more socially skillful and more likable than less attractive persons.

A great deal of research, however, has been conducted on how others perceive the attractive or unattractive individual. Attractive individuals are rated higher on a wide range of socially desirable evaluations such as success, personality, popularity, sociability, sexuality, persuasiveness, credibility, intelligence, and often happiness. When compared to unattractive individuals, attractive persons are also perceived to have more fulfilling lives, happier marriages, and more prestigious occupations.

Since attractive individuals are perceived to have more socially desirable characteristics, what effect, if any, do these perceptions have on behavior? Research findings reveal that attractiveness has a definite effect on behavior in relation to (1) persuasion and manipulation, (2) courtship and marriage choices, and (3) interaction behavior. Attractiveness correlates with greater persuasiveness in the classroom and in the courtroom. Marriage and courtship decisions are also based, in part, on the attractiveness of the partner. People interact and react differently to an individual based on that person's attractiveness. Teachers, for instance, interact less frequently and less positively with an unattractive student. The perceptions of the attractive individual and the effect of attractiveness on the behavior of others communicate important messages.

Body image and appearance are also potent nonverbal communicators. Body-image research focuses on body awareness and body satisfaction with regard to how these factors affect the development of body-concept and self-concept. The degree to which individuals are aware of their bodies will affect whether they experience body distortion, depersonalization, or insecurity about the actual physical boundaries of the body. Awareness and acceptance of the reality of one's body usually produces a state referred to as body satisfaction. The extent to which you are satisfied with your body may be related to events that occurred earlier in your life, such as being called "four eyes" by peers.

Feelings of inadequacy and body dissatisfaction affect one's self-concept and, subsequently, one's communication behavior. Also, many therapeutic approaches are directed toward adjusting the structure of the body to release pent-up emotions. The basis for these therapeutic approaches is that the body is always communicating messages about the psychological and physiological self.

Other messages of the body are communicated by body shape, type, weight, height, skin color, nudity, and body and facial hair. The most abundant research in these areas focuses on the perceptions of body shape, weight, and height. For example, people have very definite ideas about the personality characteristics of a heavy-set person. Perceptions may not, and in many cases do not, correspond with the actual attributes of an individual. The communication process, however, is dramatically affected by these perceptions.

The human body, with or without the adornment of clothing and artifacts, continually communicates nonverbal messages. Although the body serves many other purposes, research indicates that it functions as a major communicator about an individual's personality characteristics, attitudes, and self-concept.

References

Adams, G. R. (1977) Physical attractiveness research: Toward a developmental social psychology of beauty. *Human Development, 20,* 217–239.

Algozzine, R. (1976) What teachers perceive—children receive? *Communication Quarterly, 24,* 41–47.

Andersen, P. A., Jensen, T. A., & King, L. B. (April 1972) The effects of homophilious hair and dress styles on credibility and comprehension. Paper presented at the meeting of the International Communication Association.

Arnaud, S. H. (1955) Some psychological characteristics of children with multiple sclerosis. *Psychosomatic Medicine, 46,* 130–138.

Bar-Tal, D., & Saxe, L. (1976) Perceptions of similarity and dissimilarity of attractive couples and individuals. *Journal of Personality and Social Psychology, 33,* 772–781.

Beller, A. S. (1977). Fat and thin: A natural history of obesity. New York: Farrar, Straus and Giroux.

Beller, A. S. (October 24, 1977) Fat's where it's at. *Time,* p. 45.

Bemis, K. M. (1978) Current approaches to the etiology and treatment of anorexia. *Psychological Bulletin, 85,* 593–617.

Berscheid, E., & Walster, E. (1972) Beauty and the beast. *Psychology Today, 5,* 42–46, 75.

Berscheid, E., Walster, E., & Borhnstedt, G. (November 1973a) Body image. *Psychology Today,* p. 121.

Berscheid, E., Walster, E., & Borhnstedt, G. (November 1973b) The happy American body: A survey report. *Psychology Today,* pp. 119, 131.

Collins, J. K., McCabe, M. P., Jupp, J. J., & Sutton, J. E. (1983) Body percept change in obese females after weight reduction therapy. *Journal of Clinical Psychology, 39,* 507–511.

Cortes, J. B., & Gatti, F. M. (1965) Physique and self-description of temperament. *Journal of Consulting Psychology, 29,* 434.

Cosmopolitan. (October 1977) Plump and loving it.

Dion, K., Berscheid, E., & Walster, E. (1972) What is beautiful is good. *Journal of Personality and Social Psychology, 24,* 285–290.

Do blondes have more fun? (October 1976) *The OGI Times, 1* (3).

Efran, M. G. (1974) The effect of physical appearance on the judgment of guilt, interpersonal attraction and severity of recommended punishment in a simulated jury task. *Journal of Experimental Research in Personality, 8,* 45–54.

Fallon, A. E., & Rozin, P. (1985) Sex differences in perceptions of desirable body shape. *Journal of Abnormal Psychology, 94* (1), 102–105.

Feingold, A. (1982) Do taller men have prettier girlfriends? *Psychological Reports, 50,* 810.

Fisher, S. (1973) *Body consciousness.* Englewood Cliffs, N.J.: Prentice-Hall.

Folkes, V. S. (1982) Forming relationships and the matching hypothesis. *Personality and Social Psychology Bulletin, 8* (4), 631–636.

Freedman, D. G. (1969) The survival value of the beard. *Psychology Today, 3,* 36–39.

Fugita, S. S., Agle, T. A., Newman, I., & Walfish, N. (1977) Attractiveness, self-concept and a methodological note about gaze behavior. *Personality and Social Psychology Bulletin, 3,* 240–243.

Garner, D. M., Garfinkel, P. E., Schwartz, D., & Thompson, M. (1980) Cultural expectations of thinness in women. *Psychological Reports, 47,* 483–491.

Gillis, J. S., & Avis, W. E. (1980) The male-taller norm in mate selection. *Personality and Social Psychology Bulletin, 6,* 396–401.

Glamour. February 1978. What your hair says about you. pp. 27–28.

Goldman, W., & Lewis, P. (July 1977) Good looking people are likeable too! *Psychology Today,* p. 27.

Grimm, J. L. K. (1961) *Grimm's fairy tales.* London: Hamlyn Publishing Group.

Gross, A. (October 1976) How your mind shapes your body and how your body reshapes your mind. *Mademoiselle,* pp. 194–198.

Hensley, W. E. (1983) Gender, self-esteem and height. *Perceptual and Motor Skills, 56,* 235–238.

Jourard, S. M., & Secord, P. T. (1955) Body cathexis and personality. *British Journal of Psychology, 46,* 130–138.

Kernaleguen, A. P. (1968) Creativity level, perceptual style and peer perception of attitudes toward clothing. Unpublished doctoral dissertation, Utah State University. Cited in Fisher, S. (1973) *Body consciousness.* Englewood Cliffs, N.J.: Prentice-Hall.

Kleck, R. E., & Rubenstein, C. (1975) Physical attractiveness, perceived attitude similarity, and interpersonal attraction in an opposite-sex encounter. *Journal of Personality and Social Psychology, 31,* 107–114.

Kretschmer, E. (1925) *Physique and character.* New York: Cooper Square.

Kurtz, R., & Prestera, H. P. (1970) *The body reveals.* New York: Harper & Row.

LaBarre, H. (August 1976) Men and hair. *Cosmopolitan,* pp. 2, 144–147, 153.

Lavrakas, P. J. (1975) Female preference for male physiques. *Journal of Research in Personality, 9,* 324–334.

Lester, D. (1982) Ectomorphy and personality. *Psychological Reports, 51,* 1182.

Lester, D., & Sheehan, D. (1980) Attitudes of supervisors toward short police officers. *Psychological Reports, 47,* 462.

Lowen, A. (1967) *Betrayal of the body.* New York: Macmillan.

Maier, R. A., & Lavrakas, P. J. (1984) Attitudes toward women, personality rigidity, and idealized physique preferences in males. *Sex Roles, 11,* 425–433.

Murphy, M. J., Nelson, D. A., & Cheap, T. L. (1981) Rated and actual performance of high school students as a function of sex and attractiveness. *Psychological Reports, 48,* 103–106.

Neen, J. J. (December 1976) Auto man. *Road and Track,* pp. 94–95.

Noles, S. W., Cash, T. F., & Winstead, B. A. (1985) Body image, physical attractiveness, and depression. *Journal of Consulting and Clinical Psychology, 53* (1), 88–94.

Pellegrini, R. (1973) The virtues of hairiness. *Psychology Today, 6,* p. 14.

Puckett, J. M., Petty, R. E., Cacioppo, J. T., & Fischer, D. L. (1983) The relative impact of age and attractiveness stereotypes on persuasion. *Journal of Gerontology, 38* (3), 340–343.

Redbook. (Winter 1978) Long-ago faces. *Redbook's Be Beautiful,* p. 38.

Richards, E. A., & Hawthorne, R. E. (1971) Values, body cathexis, and clothing of male university students. *Journal of Home Economics, 63* (3), 190–194.

Sheldon, W. H. (1940) *The varieties of the human physique.* New York: Harper & Brothers.

Sheldon, W. H. (1942) *The varieties of temperament.* New York: Hafner.

Sheldon, W. H. (1954) *Atlas of man: A guide for somatotyping the adult male at all ages.* New York: Harper & Brothers.

Sigall, H. (1974) Psychologist proves good looks helpful. Associated Press release.

Singer, J. E. (1964) The use of manipulative strategies: Machiavellianism and attractiveness. *Sociometry, 27,* 128–151.

Singer, J. E., & Lamb, P. F. (1966) Social concern, body size, and birth order. *Journal of Social Psychology, 68,* 143–151.

Sontag, S. (September 23, 1972) The double standard of aging. *Saturday Review,* pp. 29–38.

Strongman, K. T., & Hart, C. J. (1968) Stereotyped reactions to body build. *Psychological Reports, 8,* 77–78.

Traub, A. C., & Orbach, J. (1964) Psychophysical studies of body image, I: The adjustable body-distorting mirror. *Archives of General Psychiatry, 2,* 53–56.

Udry, J. R., & Eckland, B. K. (1984) Benefits of being attractive: Differential pay-offs for men and women. *Psychological Reports, 54,* 47–56.

Walster, E. V., Aronson, V., Abrahams, D., & Rohmann, L. (1966) Importance of physical attractiveness in dating behavior. *Journal of Personality and Social Psychology, 4,* 508–516.

Wells, W., & Siegel, B. (1961) Stereotyped somatotypes. *Psychological Reports, 8,* 77–78.

Wolff, W. (1943) *The expression of personality.* New York: Harper & Row.

CHAPTER 3

CLOTHING AND PERSONAL ARTIFACTS

The same dress is indecent ten years before its time, daring one year before its time, chic, being defined as contemporary seductiveness, in its time, dowdy three years after its time, hideous twenty years after its time, amusing thirty years after its time, romantic 100 years after its time and beautiful 150 years after its time.

James Laver, 1966

As she entered the courtroom, all eyes locked on her. She was dressed in a coat at least two sizes too large. The collar was grotesquely broad and the sleeves so widely cuffed that they made her manacled hands look small and helpless. Her long hair hung listlessly on her shoulders and appeared deliberately lank. As she moved, her coat parted and one could catch a glimpse of the clothing that literally hung on her body. The neckline of her blouse sagged away from her thin neck, making it appear even thinner. The bow in her blouse was limp and tied low and, as it were, pulled the corners of her mouth down with it. Her skirt, simple and modest, fell slightly below her knees. She appeared to be a frail and vulnerable young woman, perhaps one who had suffered a great deal in the short span of her life.

The drama depicted in the paragraph above was not taken from a classic piece of literature. Rather it is a historical account of one of the most classic cases to be reviewed in a U.S. courtroom. In this very realistic scene, the actress was carefully dressed, and the audience's reaction was carefully calculated to produce the desired response. The producer and director was F. Lee Bailey, one of America's most flamboyant attorneys. The actress, Patty Hearst, was America's alleged kidnapped fugitive. The case of Patty Hearst, the daughter of a wealthy newspaper owner, is now a classic one. She allegedly had traded her position in upper-class society to become "a bank robber." However, whether she was guilty or not, it was up to Bailey to prove Patty's innocence. As her defense attorney, Bailey dressed Patty in much the same way that one would dress a Barbie doll. But in this case Patty was not dressed for the sake of fashion; she was dressed to save her life.

Whether or not you are familiar with this case, you probably are aware that clothing affects the impressions of others—especially a jury who is determining the outcome of a case. The guy with hair below his ears and a beard, who adamantly insists that he will not cut his hair or shave for anyone, will probably be quick to reverse his decision if he is brought to trial for possession of cocaine. Why? He simply does not want his clothing to communicate what he is verbally denying—that he was in possession of the drug. If his clothing communicates one message nonverbally and he verbally communicates another, such an inconsistency might turn the jurors against him. And so it is with most of us. Because we believe that others' perceptions of us are, to a large extent, based on our personal appearance, particularly the clothing we wear, we are careful to select clothing that conveys the image we wish to project.

The effects of dress on ourselves and others is obviously not limited to the courtroom. Our clothing has a communicative value that permeates all realms of society—the boardroom, conference room, classroom, and bedroom. To explore the communicative value of dress, several questions must be asked. What is the function of clothing in society? How are messages of dress communicated? What are the effects of dress on human behavior? These questions will be discussed in the sections that follow.

FUNCTIONS OF DRESS

"It is impossible to wear clothes without transmitting social signals," claims human behaviorist Desmond Morris (1977). "Every costume tells a story, often a very subtle one, about its wearer" (p. 213). And that includes those people who claim they pay no attention to their clothing with regard to its communicative value. People make quite specific comments about their social roles and, as Morris observes, "their attitudes toward the culture in which they live" (p. 213).

Comfort-protection

According to Morris, clothing serves three functions: **comfort/protection, modesty,** and **cultural display.** Comfort obviously fulfills the utilitarian purpose for wearing clothes. Early human beings evolved in a warm climate, and the body, through its complex physiological processes, regulated its own temperature, thereby making clothing unnecessary. As people began exploring the brutally hot deserts and the icy cold regions of the earth, Morris explains, their bodies proved to be inadequate in adjusting to the changes. At this point the protective function of clothing evolved. Protective clothing, however, created many problems, among which were body odor and disease. Clothing reduced skin ventilation, interfered with removal of sweat from the skin, and provided a perfect haven for small parasites. Fortunately, we know today how to cope with such problems. If human beings needed clothing only to fulfill the comfort and protection function, then there would be little need for costumes, a wide variety of colors and fabrics, or variations in styles. The fact that we do indulge in clothing beyond mere comfort and protection suggests yet another function—modesty.

Modesty

The modesty function of clothing is an attempt to conceal parts of the body. The full frontal exposure of the human body can deny the sexual display only by covering the genital area. "It is not surprising therefore," comments Morris, "to find that the loincloth is culturally the most widespread of all garments. In any social situation demanding costume shedding, it is the last clothing barrier to fall" (p. 215). The one-piece bikini provides a good example, since wearers are willing to forgo the tops but cling, as it were, to the bottoms. Consider your own behavior for a moment. If you were playing strip poker, which article of clothing would you remove last? It would be both comical and absurd to see a group of people playing strip poker with the lower parts of their bodies uncovered and their shirts still on.

History provides us with rich examples of extreme cases of modesty. In the seventeenth century in Armenia, a wife did not remove her veil until she had put her husband to bed and extinguished all lights. Since the wife also rose before her husband, it might be years before he ever caught a glimpse of her. (At this point we will avoid speculation as to whose advantage this was.) But society has deviated from these extremes of modesty by degrees over time. In Hollywood, naked navels were banned before 1930, and it was not until 1960 that topless females were allowed to appear on screen. The 1970s marked the era of full body exposure in magazines for both males and females. With the 1980s came complete body exposure in movies and films.

Cultural Display

The final function of clothing is that of cultural display, as illustrated in the following example. Dagny picks up her date, Mike, for the evening. Dagny is wearing a simple cotton dress and high-heeled shoes, while Mike is dressed in a similar casual fashion in his corduroy pants and long-sleeved cotton shirt. They go to a favorite restaurant to have a relaxing and intimate dinner. There they are greeted by the host, who informs them that they cannot be admitted because Mike is not wearing a necktie. In this case, the necktie serves no other function than that of a cultural badge. It is Mike's admission ticket to the restaurant.

Sometimes the use of clothing as a **cultural badge** is carried to absurd extremes. One of the authors went to the Key Club in New York with three friends. Everyone was dressed casually. One of the men in our group was wearing a short-sleeved suit jacket, and the other man was wearing a sports jacket. Upon entering the club, a big, burly man pulled us aside and explained that long-sleeved jackets were required for men. Rather than take the subway home to change, our friend was given a white jacket. This was fine, except that the sleeves fell 6 inches past his hands, the shoulders hovered conspicuously beyond the frame of his body, and the length of the jacket was appropriate only if he wanted to wear it as a dress. This attire, however, was considered acceptable for this "fancy" club, even though it appeared both comical and absurd to wear such ill-fitting clothing.

The use of clothing as a cultural badge can be traced back through history. In earlier centuries, costumes were dictated by law to separate social classes. For example, in the fifteenth century no one under the rank of lord was permitted to wear a tunic that covered the buttocks or to wear shoes with points longer than 2 inches. If a knight were caught wearing attire above his station, he would be subject to a fine and/or confiscation of the forbidden articles of clothing. A woman who dressed above her social class in Renaissance Germany might find her neck locked in a heavy wooden collar for punishment. In early New England, a woman was forbidden to wear a silk scarf unless her husband was worth at least $1000. The use of clothing as a cultural badge ranks as clothing's most ancient function, preceding even its protective and modesty roles (Morris, 1977, pp. 216–217).

Early research reported by Aiken (1963) suggests that display and decoration are the most important functions of clothing, followed by comfort, interest, conformity, and economy. This concern over clothing for aesthetic purposes was revealed in a study of 500 high school students. Specific uses of clothing were measured by eight Likert scales consisting of eleven statements each. The functions of clothing that were measured were the aesthetic, approval, attention, comfort, dependence, interest, management, and modesty functions. The statements were rated by the subjects on a scale of one to five. Among other findings, the

Clothing often reflects cultural traditions and values. (Carolyn Brown)

researchers found that high school girls had higher mean scores on each aspect of clothing when compared with high school boys. A possible explanation for this finding is that girls are brought up to place more value on their appearance than boys are. However, aesthetics in dress ranked as the first and most important use of clothing by *both* high school boys and girls. Beyond this point, boys were more concerned with management of clothing than with the remaining uses (Kuehne and Creekmore, 1971).

Gordon, Tengler, and Infante (1982) summarize the current symbolism of clothing as follows:

1. Clothing is instrumental in the perpetuation of traditions and religious ceremonies.
2. It also is used for self-beautification, real or imagined.
3. Cultural values regarding sexual identity and practice also are fostered through dress codes.
4. In addition, authority and roles are differentiated through dress.
5. Finally, clothing is used in the display of and acquisition of status.

As you can see, our current use of clothing as a part of our ceremonial attire suggests that clothes, indeed, communicate. The messages clothing sends about the wearer will be explored in the following section.

COMMUNICATION COMPONENTS
OF DRESS

How are messages of dress communicated? The process is not a simple one. To transmit a message about dress involves several components of communication working together. Let's take a look at Linda and Kent and analyze the communication process with regard to Linda's clothing. Linda wants to ask Kent out for Friday night, but she is a little uncertain if he has really noticed her. She decides to buy a new leather miniskirt and short leather boots. Linda is confident that she can communicate her interest in Kent through her clothes. In order to understand this process, it is important to look at the individual components. Linda is the **source,** the point at which the **message** has originated. Since this chapter is on dress, we will often refer to the source as the wearer. The message in this case is the nonverbal stimulus that serves to evoke meaning in the receiver. Linda's miniskirt and boots are the specific nonverbal stimuli, and Kent is the intended **receiver.** The **channel** is the means by which a message is conveyed from the source to the receiver. Linda is engaged in face-to-face interaction with Kent, and the channel is visual. The receiver, Kent, is the person who ultimately acquires the sources's message. In many cases we will refer to the receiver as the observer. The process seems pretty direct and simple so far. Obviously, Linda should have no difficulty in getting her message across. Right? Wrong!

Two important components of this process are **encoding** and **decoding.** Since Linda is interested in Kent, she must be careful to encode her message properly. Because of varied experiences and backgrounds, we cannot transmit *meanings* to other people; we can only transmit *messages.* Effective communication depends on proper encoding. If the message that is created does not represent the meaning Linda intends or if it stimulates different meanings in Kent, the exchange will not produce the desired outcome.

The decoding process works in a similar manner. Kent must process the message from Linda and compare it with previous messages and experiences to discover what she means. If Kent has a very different background and different experiences from those of Linda, or if he allows his own biases to enter the decoding process, the exchange will not produce the desired outcome. Since proper encoding and decoding are essential to communication, the transmission of messages becomes a more complicated process.

The final component of a communication system is **feedback.** Generally speaking, feedback tells the source (Linda) how the receiver (Kent) has understood the message. If Kent sees Linda in class and deliberately sits next to her when his usual behavior is to sit alone, Linda has received feedback of Kent's interest in her. An illustration of these communication components can be visualized as is shown in Figure 3.1

How would this model apply, for example, to the Patty Hearst case described in the introduction? In this instance Patty was the source, the message was the nonverbal stimulus of her clothing, and the receivers were the judge and jury. However, there is another dimension of Patty's communication that must be considered—that of **intentionality.** Did F. Lee Bailey dress Patty in such a way so as

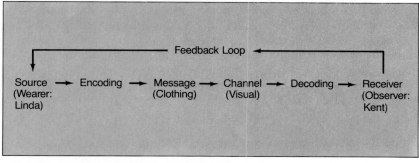

Feedback Loop

Source → Encoding → Message → Channel → Decoding → Receiver
(Wearer: (Clothing)   (Visual)   (Observer:
Linda)   Kent)

FIGURE 3.1 **A communication model**

to communicate a deliberate message? Do you dress with the deliberate intention of communicating a specific message?

Intentionality and Unintentionality of Messages

Most nonverbal messages of dress are unintentionally communicated and unintentionally received. Specifically, there are four possibilities with regard to the intentionality of messages.

1. The wearer *intentionally* sends a message that is *intentionally* received.

   For example, physicians dress in clean, stark white coats in order to communicate messages of credibility and cleanliness to their patients. In turn, patients look for signs of these variables in order to calm any fears they might have—as well as to discriminate doctors from other related staff members. In this instance, the physician is intentionally sending a message that his or her office is a sterile, secure place to be. In turn, patients intentionally look for (i.e., receive) those messages in order to assure themselves that their complaint will indeed be relieved.

2. The wearer *unintentionally* sends a message that is *intentionally* received.

   For example, Cheryl is interviewing for a job as vice-president of sales in a large corporation. She is interviewed by a panel of two males and one female. She has deliberately selected her clothing for the meeting, but she has paid little attention to her jewelry. She is wearing a large diamond wedding ring and a watch studded with diamonds. Her interviewers are looking for additional information about her. They presume she is married and in a middle to upper income bracket. In this case Cheryl unintentionally communicated a message with her jewelry that was intentionally received by the panel.

3. The wearer *intentionally* sends a message that is *unintentionally* received.

   For example, Dick is teaching at a university for the first time. Because he is so young, people often mistake him for a student. He grows a beard and avoids wearing jeans in an effort to communicate his higher-status position. Other professors and students unconsciously or unintentionally react to this change. They know that something is different, but they cannot specifically identify what it is.

4. The wearer *unintentionally* sends a message that is *unintentionally* received.

   For example, Mike gets dressed for class in his everyday clothing—jeans and a T-shirt. Both the other students in his class and the instructor unconsciously react to his dress. No intentional messages have been sent or received.

Now let's address the intentionality of messages with respect to Patty Hearst. F. Lee Bailey intentionally wanted to communicate that Patty was not capable of being a bank-robbing radical. Most likely the receivers of this message, the judge and the jury, were unintentionally receiving this message. This process would fit in Box 3 of Figure 3.2.

The purpose of studying the effects of dress on human communication is to reduce the number of messages in Box 4. Messages that are unintentionally sent and unintentionally received result in communication of which we are unaware. Some popular writers such as John T. Molloy (1975, 1977) suggest that the best possible world would be one in which we intentionally send a message that is unintentionally received (Box 3 of Figure 3.2). Perhaps Molloy and others consider the unconscious response to a message to be much like subliminal persuasion. However, we propose that effective communication is conscious communication in which both the sender and receiver are consciously aware of the

---

FIGURE 3.2   **Display of communication possibilities with intentional and unintentional messages**

	Intentionally sent	Unintentionally sent
Intentionally received	1	2
Unintentionally received	3	4

messages (Box 1 of Figure 3.2). It is our purpose in writing about the research and information on clothing to increase your understanding and awareness of the communicative value of dress. In so doing, we hope to increase the likelihood that the messages you send and receive about clothing will fall into Box 1—intentionally sent and intentionally received. In an effort to achieve this goal, we will examine the communication effects of dress and **artifacts.**

The clothing we wear is usually accompanied by artifacts, things used to serve an ornamental function, which in turn modify our appearance. Such artifacts include glasses, watches, jewelry, tattoos, masks, badges, and any other objects used for the purpose of ornamentation. Researchers have studied the relation of clothing and artifacts relative to (1) the characteristics of the source-wearer, (2) the perceptions of the receiver-observer, and (3) the effects on the observer and wearer. It is to these three areas of concern that we now turn.

PERSONALITY CORRELATES OF DRESS

Research that has focused on the characteristics of the wearer has been most concerned with the relationship between clothing, personality, and demographic variables. For example, do people with a high clothing awareness usually have higher incomes and educational levels than those of people with lower clothing awareness? What type of person wears a small design pattern on his or her clothing? Much of this research is based on the premise that one's self-image is expressed in the selection of clothing and artifacts. To the extent that certain types of clothing are related to certain personality traits, clothing may communicate the self-image or ideal image of the wearer.

Examine your wardrobe and check out the type of clothing you wear. Do you wear bright colors, pastels, large designs, or small designs? Are your clothes unusual or fashionable? "Dressing habits [also] might indicate the mental health of a person," according to Rosencranz (1976). "People who wear very bizarre, strange things might have some kind of problem," says Rosencranz (p. 3). As you read the following studies, consider how your personality and social characteristics relate to the clothing you wear.

Two personality variables which have been linked to our choice of clothing are the degrees to which people are dogmatic and exhibit Machiavellian (i.e., manipulative) tendencies. For example, in 1979 Pinaire-Reed demonstrated the existence of a significant relationship between predisposition to fashion and dogmatism. Likewise, although the correlation was not significant, Pinaire-Reed discovered a slight relationship between predisposition toward fashion and the use of Machiavellian tactics. To support these observations, the researcher asked 202 female undergraduates to assess their willingness to spend time, energy, and money on fashionable clothing and to complete two questionnaires measuring the degree to which they displayed dogmatic tendencies and the extent to which they "endorsed flattery, lying or deception" (i.e., the degree to which they tended to use Machiavellian tactics). Results of her study revealed the relationships addressed above.

Another set of studies that has emerged over the years has addressed the relationships between clothing consciousness and key personality variables. For example, Rosencranz examined the characteristics of married women who were high in clothing awareness in an early study in 1962. The findings are not startling and most likely confirm what you would guess to be the case. Married women who were very aware of the clothing they wore were in the upper social classes, belonged to many organizations, had attained a higher level of education, had higher incomes, had higher verbal intelligence, and were, for the most part, married to white-collar workers (pp. 18–22). Since few people would disagree that clothing communicates status, it follows that women who have a high clothing awareness identify with the classes of society that consider appearance to be of the utmost importance.

In a more recent study, Solomon and Schopler (1982) also examined the relationship between self-consciousness and clothing—this time focusing on the relationships for both men and women. As predicted, for both males and females who were highly conscious of their appearance and behavior, the relationship between public self-consciousness and clothing interest was highly significant. However, intriguing results emerged when Solomon and Schopler examined differences in clothing attitudes for males and females. Although females were found to be much more aware of and interested in clothing than males, in general, the relationships between self-consciousness and attitudes toward clothing were found to be radically stronger for males (p. 513). For example, in contrast with publicly self-conscious women who did not seem to strongly agree, publicly self-conscious men agreed strongly with the following statements:

1. When I get dressed in the morning, my decision concerning what to wear is influenced by situations in which I expect to find myself.
2. I often experience a psychological lift when I buy new clothes.
3. I feel self-conscious if I find myself dressed inappropriately for some occasion.
4. What I wear influences others' impressions of me. (Solomon and Schopler, p. 512)

Both males and females who were publicly self-conscious agreed that clothing influenced their moods, that making an effort to dress in the latest styles was important, and that what other people wore influenced their impressions. Solomon and Schopler concluded that the sex differences which emerged may have been a function of the fact that for women, clothing is much like "a second skin." As a result, its effect on self-concept may be more superficial than for men. Men, on the other hand, "are freer to determine [their] own level of clothing interest" (p. 514). Consequently, men who are publicly self-conscious may capitalize more than females on "the strategic utility of clothing for self-presentation, reflexive self-evaluation, and for subsequently increasing the value of the self as a social commodity on the interpersonal marketplace" (p. 514).

A final example of research which has addressed the relationships between clothing consciousness and personality is that of Rosenfeld and Plax in 1977.

However, in addition to clothing-consciousness, these researchers examined the relationships among personality variables and three other dimensions of clothing as well: exhibitionism, practicality, and interest in design. To complete the study, Rosenfeld and Plax administered to subjects a series of personality tests and a series of questions concerning the four dimensions of clothing listed above. Subjects' responses to the personality tests were then matched with their responses about the four dimensions of clothing.

Results of the study revealed that males who scored high on the dimension of exhibitionism were aggressive and confident but had a low self-concept in relation to their familial interactions. On the other hand, females who scored high were radical, detached from interpersonal relationships, and had a high opinion of their own self-worth. Males who were guarded about self-revelation and who had a low self-concept in relation to their familial relations scored low on this dimension. Females who scored low were timid, sincere, and accepting of others.

Who are the people who are more interested in practicality in clothing than in beauty? The Rosenfeld/Plax study indicated that males who felt this way about clothing were inhibited and rebellious and had a low motivation to make friends and that females who had this attitude were clever, enthusiastic, and confident. Males who scored low on this dimension were success-oriented, mature, and forceful. And females who scored low were self-centered, independent, and detached.

Of the males who responded that they would love to be a "clothes designer," characteristics such as cooperative, impulsive, and conforming were correlated. Females who answered in the same way were irrational, uncritical, and expressive. Males who preferred not to be a clothes designer were adventurous, egotistical, and dissatisfied. Females who expressed no interest in being a clothes designer were efficient, clear-thinking, and easily disorganized under pressure (Rosenfeld and Plax, pp. 24–31).

As you can see, all clothing has communicative value. Even those individuals who claim that they are uninterested in clothing are saying by the way they dress, something definite about themselves and the culture in which they live. In short, conformity—or the lack thereof—also makes a statement about a person. Generally, research has shown that conformity in dress is related to an individual's desire to be accepted and liked, two additional personality variables. Although such relationships between clothing and characteristics of the wearer will continue to be explored in the future, additional and more sophisticated discoveries are currently in the making. In the meantime, try to answer the following question for yourself: What statement does your wardrobe make about you and the culture in which you live?

PERCEPTION OF DRESS

In addition to the messages clothing sends concerning our respective personalities, the fashions we don play a major role in how others respond to us. As we implied in our opening illustration, F. Lee Bailey was most concerned with how the jurors in the Patty Hearst trial would perceive his wealthy and infamous defendant. In an attempt to play down her wealth, Bailey dressed Patty in typical middle-class fashion—in clothes that the jurors themselves or their families might wear. In doing so, he hoped to raise the level of perceived similarity between Patty and the jury, or the degree to which they would see Patty as like them in attitudes, values, and background. Ultimately, Patty's appearance, specifically her clothing, made a statement about her . . . and allowed her clever and famous lawyer to win his case. Her clothing contributed to her success because it created and sustained a stereotype with which the jurors could empathize. It is to the topic of stereotypes which are communicated by clothing that we now wish to turn.

Stereotypes

The accuracy with which people can judge others by their clothing depends on what is being judged. Greater accuracy is found in judging sex, age, nationality, socioeconomic status, identification with a specific group, occupational status, and official status. Lesser accuracy is found in judging personality, moods, values, and attitudes.

The research that is concerned with how others "perceive" clothing and artifacts is abundant. Many times these perceptions reinforce the stereotypes that we hold, such as "guys never make passes at girls who wear glasses." The following review of this area will be concerned mainly with an examination of clothing, although we will also take a look at the studies on artifacts such as glasses and makeup at the end of this section.

Dress Codes

Even if researchers could not identify conclusive relationships between clothing preference and the characteristics of the wearer, it is doubtful that companies would drop their dress codes for their executives. Why? Most companies know that although clothes may not make the person, they do affect the perception of the person. In other words, it's the appearance that counts.

Thomas J. Watson, Sr., chairman of the board of IBM, decided several years ago that IBM representatives and executives were to wear white shirts, dark suits, and stiff collars. Of course, this formal dress code has changed. Today representatives and executives at IBM are no longer required to wear the stiff collars. However, their dark suits and white shirts live on (Anderson, 1977, pp. 43–45). The IBM uniform is a symbol of conservatism and trustworthiness and, most importantly, of a well-established, highly regarded company.

IBM is not alone in this dress-code madness, however. Allied Stores, one of the largest department store chains in the United States, has a firmly written dress code that governs executive personnel. May Company, J. C. Penney Company, and Sears use similar dress codes. Men are instructed that a coat, shirt, and tie must harmonize. Major executives wear suits and dress even more conservatively. According to this policy, if you are not at the top, you may wear a conservative sports jacket. Jeans as well as neck jewelry for men are out. Women, apparently under fewer restraints, are generally asked to dress to complement the department in which they work. Tiffany and Company, on the other hand, is more restrictive with its female employees. Women are told to wear their skirts slightly above or below the knee. When wearing a pantsuit, the pant legs must cover the tops of the shoes but must not touch the floor. Tops must cover the bottom of the hips, and see-through blouses, tight-fitting tops, and decolletage are not permitted (Anderson, pp. 43–45). These major companies are just a few examples of the silent messages that clothes do communicate. But exactly what do they say? The following studies have attempted to come to grips with this question.

Social Impressions

In a 1983 study conducted by Harris and others, five different styles of women's clothing were rated by both male and female subjects. The five styles, which were modeled by the same women each time, included: (1) a formal suit or skirt, blouse, and jacket suitable for professional wear; (2) a formal pantsuit with blouse and jacket; (3) a casual skirt worn with a blouse, shirt, or sweater and with sandals or casual shoes; (4) casual pants with a blouse, shirt, or sweater and with sandals or casual shoes; and (5) blue jeans and a T-shirt with sneakers or sandals. Subjects were asked "to imagine seeing the model walking down the street at 5:30 P.M. on a Friday" and to rate her on eight different dimensions or perceived characteristics. The results clearly indicated that the model was seen as "most happy, successful, feminine, interesting, attractive, intelligent, and desirable as a friend" when she wore a formal suit. She was viewed as the least so when she wore blue jeans and a T-shirt. Additionally, Harris and her research team found that the formal pants suit was ranked to be second most positive, and the casual skirt outfit was ranked as second most negative. However, as the researchers predicted, the model was perceived to be more active when wearing pants as opposed to a skirt.

The results of this study would seem to suggest that "women who wish to be viewed as successful might be well advised to wear the dress styles suggested for women executives" (Harris et al., 1983). However, as both Harris and other researchers have noted, when additional personal information concerning an individual is taken into account, that information mediates our social impressions. More specifically, when the people in question know one another, clothing is not as influential in the overall perceptual process.

In a class assignment, the authors clearly saw this latter principle demonstrated. Our students were asked to dress in a manner that was opposite, or clearly different, from their normal dress behavior on campus. After conducting this experiment for an eight-hour period, the students unanimously reported that their friends tended to react less than anyone else to their change in clothing. This response, or lack of a response, suggests two possibilities. The first is that once impressions are formed, a change in clothing behavior is not observed as critical or even important since information about the person comes from many less superficial areas. The second is that when a person we know behaves differently, such as by wearing "strange" clothing, we tend to make allowances for it. Knapp (1978) concludes the "changes in clothing of a family member or a close friend may indicate a temporary change of mood, but it is likely that we will not perceive any basic changes in values, attitudes, or personality traits unless the clothing change becomes permanent for that individual (p. 178).

Popularity and perceived success are also related to the clothing and decorations we wear, whether in London, Paris, New York, or Papua, New Guinea. However, the relationship between success and clothing may be more salient with regard to women's perceptions of men rather than with men's perceptions of women. As Wilder (1982) has argued:

> Because [the human female, like many other animals] carries, bears and nurses her children and each child requires a tremendous investment of time and energy, [she] will do all she can to ensure their survival. Choosing a husband who will be able to help supply food for them has proved to be her best strategy for reproductive success—women thus have evolved a preference for traits that characterize a good provider. (p. 1051)

One such determinant of a man's ability "to provide" (i.e., his status) is the clothing and other artifacts which he wears. To what extent do women use the relationship between clothing and success to judge a man's attractiveness? According to Wilder, such judgments are made consistently and worldwide. Tribesmen from New Guinea who are highly adorned are seen as being more desirable than those with a better physique but no decorations. In our society, men are judged to be successful if they are wearing an expensive three-piece suit (p. 1051).

As a result of this emphasis on the relationship between clothing and success, the media and advertising agencies take advantage of this point. They sell the latest "reflections of success"—for both men and women—and we buy them. For example, most people are interested in any product advertised that will make them look ten years younger. How often have you heard of a product advertised that would make you look ten years older? And if there were such products, would you buy them? How others perceive us is the main selling point used by advertisers in the clothing business.

Status, Authority, and Age

Three additional variables about which our clothing choices make a statement are status, authority, and age. In fact, a perusal of the recent nonverbal communication literature concerning clothing reveals a strong relationship between initial perceptions of authority and wearing apparel. For example, to document this relationship, Bushman (1984) dressed a forty-seven-year-old, male confederate in three different sets of clothing. He then placed him on a major street in downtown Salt Lake City, Utah. The confederate, dressed at different times as a bum, a business executive, and a firefighter, asked pedestrians to give a dime to the experimenter, who was standing beside a parked car at an expired parking meter. In each case, the experimenter was busily searching for a dime in his pocket as the confederate made the request. Results of the study revealed a significant relationship between the clothing worn by the confederate and the number of pedestrians who complied with the request. Of those pedestrians who were asked, 45 percent responded to the "bum's" request, and 50 percent responded to the "executive's" request. Interestingly enough, over 80 percent of the subjects obeyed the "firefighter's" request. Bushman concluded that perceived status and authority, indeed, are reflected in clothing choices and that all three are important variables influencing compliance. In addition, he concluded "that those holding authoritative positions have a great responsibility, especially when making requests of others" (p. 508).

As we stated earlier, age is also reflected in the clothing we wear. In fact, this relationship is so strong that we need look no further than the average American family to see its significance. (How many arguments between parents and children have escalated into out-and-out war over choices of clothing which "that crazy child" of theirs has made?) To make our point, read the following descriptions from an article entitled "Giveaways in Age Can be Found in Clothing" (*New Woman Magazine,* 1976, pp. 54–55), and see if you can identify who is the older and who is the younger woman.

> Lynda is wearing several strands of pearls cascading down the front of her blouse. Her eyes are outlined by simple wire-rim frames. A sporty navy suit jacket with a pleated skirt is her attire, complete with a scarf in her hair and . . . a wraparound coat.
> Mindy is wearing an elegant strand of graduated pearls. Her eyes are outlined by discreet blue eyeglasses. A sporty royal blue suit jacket with a straight skirt is her attire. The outfit is completed with a sensible coat with a ranch mink collar and a matching hat.

Based on the above descriptions, who is the "older" woman? If you picked Mindy, you were right. The telltale signs, according to *New Woman Magazine,* can be found in the clothing and artifacts worn. Everything Mindy is wearing communicates "age"—the color, the style, the design, and the fabric.

As you can see, both status and authority—as well as age—are communicated by clothing choices. However, additional information is also communicated by the clothes that we wear. For example, recent research has indicated that clothing sends messages concerning the degree to which we are sexy and likable. In addition, it may send messages concerning how "businesslike" we are in our jobs. In the following section, we will explore each of these three variables more completely. After completing your reading, see if you can determine the degree to which your clothing communicates these messages. Our bet is that they communicate more often than we would like to think.

Sexiness and Likability

Recently there has been a great deal of speculation about what type of clothing communicates sexiness or a businesslike attitude. Molloy (1977), America's self-acclaimed wardrobe engineer, states rather succinctly that clothes determine whether an individual is headed for the "bedroom" or the "boardroom." In a study that attempted to determine whether sexy clothing and likability go hand in hand, Williamson (1977) gathered twenty-four paired photographs of male and female models. Each set of models was dressed conservatively in one photograph and suggestively in the other. For example, in one pair of photographs the male model had on tight trousers, then baggy trousers; in another pair the male model wore a skimpy bathing suit, then a traditional one. Or a female model might be wearing regular shorts with her shirt buttoned up, then short shorts with her shirt tied above her midriff.

The models were rated for sexiness, attractiveness, and likability. As expected, the students had no difficulty in agreeing on the sexier costume in each pair of photographs. This, however, was the only area of agreement. Students found the women without a bra more sexually suggestive but not more attractive or likable. An explanation suggested by Williamson was that the braless women appeared to be too threatening. Men reported that the woman who had her shirt buttoned up was slightly less attractive than the woman who left her shirt buttons undone, but they liked her more anyway. Both males and females found men more attractive and likable in tight trousers when compared with baggy trousers. Women rejected men with tight-fitting bathing suits and unbuttoned shirts. Another interesting finding was that women rated all models less likable in sexy clothes. Williamson speculates that women look upon females who dress in sexy costumes as "engaging in unfair competition." Since the men did not seem to dislike sexually suggestive male models, Williamson speculates that perhaps males see sexy clothes as a normal part of *machismo* and therefore do not react competitively (p. 90).

In her book *I'd Love to, But What'll I Wear?* (1977) Polly Bergen claims, like Molloy, that what you're wearing will tell people whether you mean *business* or *monkey business*. Should so-called sexy clothes be worn in business settings? And if they are, how are they perceived by subordinates, equals, and superiors? Molloy (1977) presents some very definite opinions on this subject. Although he claims his comments are based on nine years of research, he fails to describe the methodology or analysis used in the studies, thereby making it impossible to assess their validity. However, the ideas presented by Molloy are interesting and important in pointing up the stereotypes that exist about clothing in business.

Stereotypes in Business

Over the last twenty years, the number of women who have entered the work force has increased dramatically. However, the proportion of women who occupy executive and managerial positions has remained relatively low. One suggestion made by researchers in the area of organizational behavior is that the lack of women in management still stems from the traditional perception that women are less qualified for executive positions. Yet others have concluded that sex-role stereotypes may be limiting employment opportunities (Forsythe, Drake, and Cox, 1985).

To improve employment opportunities, female candidates for executive positions can do a number of things, ranging from increasing their knowledge of the organization to maximizing their personal stress-management abilities. However, upwardly mobile women (and men) need to understand two additional, highly influential factors: the importance of dress on hiring decisions and the means by which they may improve their professional image via the clothing they wear. To document the relationship between clothing choices and upward mobility, Forsythe, Drake, and Cox (1985) conducted a study to determine the influence of dress on interviewers' hiring decisions of women for management positions. Results of their study showed that favorable hiring recommendations increased with the masculinity of the clothing the women wore. Specifically, the least favorable recommendations were given for a woman who was dressed in "a light beige dress in a soft fabric, with a small round collar, gathered skirt, and long sleeves" (p. 375). Recommendations concerning hiring were most favorable for the same woman when she wore a navy-blue tailored (skirted) suit and a white blouse with an angular collar. In short, in the male-dominated business world, men have an acceptable uniform—the suit. Likewise, as Molloy has argued, women need a comparable uniform. As Forsythe, Drake, and Cox suggest, the tailored, skirted suit may well be the appropriate "uniform." Like the business suit for men, it communicates an official look.

Stereotypes in Academia

The communicative value of clothing operates in the academic world as well as in the business world. In the same manner in which an executive must choose his or her clothing carefully, so must a teacher—that is, if the teacher is concerned with how he or she is perceived by the students. Dr. Steven A. Rollmann (1977) of Penn State University showed fifty students three photographs of the same male teacher and the same female teacher dressed in different attire. For example, in one photo the male instructor wore jeans, a sport shirt, and sneakers for casual dress. In the moderately formal condition, he wore casual slacks, a sport coat, and a turtleneck sweater. In the formal condition, he wore the classic IBM combination of dark suit, white shirt, and tie. Using a list of ten adjectives to rate the various degrees of formality in dress (i.e., fair, sympathetic, knowledgeable, enthusiastic, friendly, flexible, clear, organized, stimulating, and well prepared), Rollmann uncovered some interesting findings. Teachers who were dressed informally were seen as friendly, flexible, more sympathetic, fair, and enthusiastic when compared with the other modes of dress. The other extreme in dress, that of formal attire, communicated that the teacher was organized, knowledgeable, and better prepared.

The study also revealed some differences in the perception of male and female teachers. For the moderately dressed models, the males were seen as stimulating, while both males and females were seen as clear. In the formal attire, males were perceived as most knowledgeable while both males and females were seen as well prepared and organized. Although the findings are inconclusive, they do suggest that sex might be a variable in the perception of clothing. Perhaps conforming to societal stereotypes, a male in formal attire (when compared to a female in formal attire) was still seen as more knowledgeable.

Group Identification or Uniforms

Clothing in many cases serves as a means of **group identification,** thereby acting as a type of uniform in which the wearers are bound together. Prisons provide a good example of clothing used as a group identification. Writing on prison parlance, Popplestone (1977) observed that "inmates must tune in to a multitude of nonverbal messages to function successfully in this environment. They learn to identify guards by their footsteps and troublesome inmates by their dress" (p. 61). Based on personal observation and extensive interviews, Popplestone identified the clothing codes in prisons. New inmates, for instance, often wore the blue denim jumpsuits, while veteran jailbirds wore brown shirts and trousers. In an effort to establish that they were tough, new prisoners would often go unshaven and act extra tough. Black Muslims could be identified by stocking caps, turned-up cuffs, and short-trimmed hair. Black prisoners from a particular city sported Afro hairstyles and prison trousers deliberately cut 6 inches short. While homosexuals wore a pair of earrings, prisoners who wore one earring bore the mark of masculinity. Even guards were identified and stereotyped according to the appearance of their clothing. Tough guards had a crisp appearance; easy guards were much more casual in their dress (Popplestone, 1977).

Clothing sets our expectations for the behavior of the wearer—especially if the clothing is a uniform. Psychologist Robert Mauro, who was interested in documenting this statement, asked ninety people in shopping centers to rate photographs of police officers who were dressed in three different types of uniforms: the familiar navy uniform, the traditional khaki uniform often worn by sheriffs and/or deputies, and a gray slacks/dark-blue blazer combination revealing no exposed weapons. Results of his study showed that, while all three officers were rated as "equally friendly and warm," those who donned the traditional blue uniforms were perceived "to have better judgment" and to be "more competent, helpful, honest, fast, and active" when compared with officers who wore blue blazers and gray slacks (Mauro, 1984, cited in Bridgwater, 1985).

To further test his hypotheses, this time that traditional police uniforms reduce the number of assaults, Mauro evaluated data from the Menlo Park, California police department. This department had switched to the gray pants/blue blazer combination in 1969 and then returned to the traditional navy uniform in 1977. Results of this part of his study revealed that the rate of assault actually did not change during the eight-year experimental period. However, assaults on police officers were found to decline significantly after the navy uniforms, again, were required (Mauro, 1984, cited in Bridgwater, 1985).

Informal uniforms can also often be found among people who wish to communicate their political and social attitudes. In analyzing how political and social attitudes were communicated by clothing, Buckley and Roach (1974) collected data from ninety-six students. The subjects were asked to respond to nine questionnaires, which measured (1) each subject's own attitudes toward social and political issues, (2) each subject's perceptions of attitudes of wearers of clothing shown in the stimulus photographs, and (3) each subject's own responses to types of clothing shown in the photographs. Two types of student responses were studied—those from conservatives (i.e., people oriented toward the established American culture) and those from liberals (i.e., people oriented toward a counterculture). Findings indicated that the clothing was perceived as a symbol of people's social and political attitudes. In addition, students who represented the counterculture tended (although not significantly) to prefer clothing that they perceived as communicating attitudes similar to their own. Finally, the results showed that individuals who embraced the counterculture wore clothing that they perceived as being expressive of their political attitudes more often than those individuals who embraced the established culture (pp. 94–102).

A final example demonstrating the fact that the perceptions others have of us based on our clothing are important is the case of juvenile court judge Leodis Harris. The forty-three-year-old judge had a special blue-denim robe made in an effort to relate to the kids in his courtroom. When the juveniles came back with a good report, the judge would wear the denim robe to let them know he was proud of them. The robe was only part of the package. Before dismissing the juvenile, Harris would read the youngster the prediction for his or her astrological sign. In accordance with the researchers, Harris was acting on the fact that perceptions of one's appearance are critical in affecting communication outcomes.

Personal Artifacts

Personal artifacts also contribute a great deal to the perceptions others have of us. Glasses have created a controversy for a long time. The late humorist Dorothy Parker's famous line "Men never make passes at girls who wear glasses" has amused many people. It has also convinced a number of people to stay away from glasses. Over 6 million pairs of eyes currently see through contact lenses. And three-fourths of all contact lense wearers are female. In a recent survey, the American Optometric Association found that 48.6 percent of all teenage girls who require prescription lenses are opting for contact lenses instead of glasses. Obviously, we cannot assume that the reason for the high proportion of contact-lens wearers is the unfavorable stereotype about people who wear glasses. Or can we? In an early study by Thornton (1944) the stereotyped perceptions of people who wear glasses were examined. Subjects rated slides of people with glasses and people without glasses. Those with glasses were seen as more intelligent, industrious, and honest than the nonspectacled individuals. Live models wearing glasses were also rated as more intelligent and industrious but not more honest (Thornton, 1944, pp. 203–207).

Alfred Poll (1976), a Manhattan optician, contends that glasses communicate

Glasses may communicate something about the person who wears them—whether the person is wearing them or holding them. (Carolyn Brown)

important information, particularly in business. With a clientele that numbers more than 100,000—which has included top business people, jet-setters, and diplomats such as Billie Jean King, Leonard Bernstein, Isaac Stern, Dustin Hoffman, and Ethel Merman—this Manhattan optician points out that the way in which glasses are used can communicate important information. For example, the person who compulsively folds and unfolds his specs may be indicating boredom. Or the executive who suddenly removes her glasses and folds them into the case is indicating that the meeting, or at least the negotiations, are over. And what about the person who hurls her glasses across the desk? Poll suggests that this is an obvious show of displeasure. The boss who wags his spectacles instead of his finger at an errant subordinate is symbolically delivering a softer, more civilized reprimand. Chewing on the temple tip, according to Poll, is common among people who are tense, nervous, or under great stress. Because most people are embarrassed by this habit, Poll has a lot of clients who bring in their glasses claiming "Look what the dog did!" Propping the glasses on the brow and regarding the visitor with the naked eye demonstrates openness and honesty. Finally, the common pose of propping the spectacles on the end of the nose and peering over the frames signifies "You're putting me on!" (Poll, pp. 77–78). The obvious point that Poll is making is that glasses communicate as much off the face as they do on the face. Stereotyped perceptions follow the glasses, wherever they might be placed.

Much as "regular" glasses communicate messages about their wearers, so do sunglasses make a statement about the individual who dons them. During the 1980s, the singular message has been one of status, fashion, and style. Varying in design from the dark, clunky, street-tough shades of the fifties to signed and numbered items such as "Christina Ferrare," sunglasses have become the inevitable key to unbridled individuality. As *Time* correspondent Richard Stengel (1984) has noted, the sunshades of the eighties allow a double message to be imparted: "Concealment is coupled with conspicuousness, and the mask of self-efficacy is also a self-advertisement" (p. 88). Sunglasses both "beckon and deflect, suggesting the power of inpenetrability while subtly inviting intimacy" (p. 88). Dr. Frank Newell, professor of ophthalmology at the University of Chicago, supported Stengel's observation as follows:

> There are a lot of reasons other than eye protection that people wear sunglasses. People like to conceal their eyes and what they're looking at. (Stengel, 1984, p. 88)

Sunglasses provide one means by which protection to the eye is afforded but allow the "opportunity to pry at will" (Stengel, p. 88). Like masks, sunglasses are inpenetrable yet allow the wearer's eyes to roam and penetrate as they will.

If sunglasses allow us to send countless messages, how well do cosmetics fare? According to a number of researchers, cosmetics use, indeed, sends messages about the wearer. Depending on the situation, however, the statement that is made often is not a desirable one. As Cox and Glick (1986) have argued, although the presence of makeup may lead to stronger attributions of femininity, sexiness, and attractiveness, it may also strengthen sex-role stereotypes, particularly when cosmetics are used by women holding traditionally feminine jobs (e.g., secretary). Heavy users in these jobs may be seen more as ornaments than as performers. Surprisingly, this relationship was not found for women in non-gender-typed positions (e.g., accountants). The authors concluded that women in gender-typed roles should be sparing with makeup, particularly if they wish to be more upwardly mobile. For these women, "cosmetics use may enhance physical appearance, but it also may detract from perceived competence on the job" (p. 57).

As you can see, countless numbers of artifacts exist which could be explored. Although research concerning many of them is at best sketchy, three items deserve mention: T-shirts, pipes, and briefcases.

Most people do not need research to tell them about the impact of sayings on T-shirts. T-shirts are used as a medium for a variety of messages—some funny, some sexy, some patriotic, and some simply informative. For example, we all have T-shirts that are meant to get attention and to make those around us laugh. Two instances of T-shirt mottos that fall in this category are: "Someday when my ship comes in . . . I'll probably be at the airport" and, "Last one out of (fill-in-the-blank), turn out the lights." As stated earlier, T-shirts can reflect a wearer's level of patriotism as well. To illustrate, we have all seen T-shirts bearing the slogan, "America, love it or leave it!" Additionally, many T-shirts are used to provide information about upcoming events. For example, sororities and fraternities on

People often have very strong impressions of a person who smokes a pipe. (Carolyn Brown)

campuses all across the United States are aware of the power of T-shirts to advertise upcoming Greek events. They are also frequently used to advertise road races, triathalons, and other sporting events.

What do the above T-shirt messages convey to you about the wearer? We can assume that most T-shirt wearers are communicating information intentionally. T-shirt messages may even communicate thoughts or feelings that the wearer would never verbalize, such as "I'm #1." In cases like these, the wearer allows his or her T-shirt to speak for itself.

What does a pipe smoker communicate to others? The fact is that the pipe smoker gives off some very definite impressions. The owner of one of the largest used-car dealerships in the state of Arizona spoke to one of our nonverbal communication classes. He informed us that car dealers are told to beware of anything that starts with a "P"—prostitutes, plumbers, and pipe smokers were the examples he offered. Although a strange combination, these "P" people are perceived to be poor prospective buyers. Recently, a friend explained that his father told him to "never hire pipe smokers because they will spend all their time cleaning, filling, and emptying the pipe." In addition, other sales personnel have reported that pipe smokers take far too much time to reach a decision and they need a great deal of time to "turn over" an idea. Indeed, the very act of cleaning and filling the pipe serves as a mechanism for gaining time. Rudofsky (1974) provides a very eloquent description of the perception and effects of smoking a pipe in the following observation.

> Originally a container for burning tobacco, today it is used as a tranquilizer that induces slow gesturing and a more accentuated, though less intelligible speech. Men attach as much importance to its shape and color as women do to the right shade of lipstick. Not only does the pipe complement a man's facial features, it greatly bolsters his ego. A pipe in the secure grip of his teeth symbolizes meditative reflection, mature deliberation, and superiority in general. (p. 148)

Another artifact, the briefcase, has become a symbol for both the businessman and businesswoman. A handbag buyer at San Francisco's I. Magnin department store explained that women like to show off the fact that they are in the business world. The briefcase has become a symbol of upward mobility on the corporate ladder. Korda (1977) goes even further and suggests that the briefcase is an important investment requiring sometimes up to a thousand dollars to purchase. In addition, Korda adamantly recommends that a woman carry either a handbag or a briefcase, but never both. What is the concern? Once again, it is with images, with how others will perceive the wearer, or, in this case, the carrier. Briefcases, like many other artifacts, have a high communicative value.

Of course, as fashion changes, the impressions conveyed by various styles of clothing and by personal artifacts also change. At one time, a woman who wore pants was looked upon as "unladylike"; however, pants are now considered to be one of the fundamentals of a woman's wardrobe. Since fashion is dynamic, we must be careful not to assume that research in this area is irrefutable. As different styles and types of dress come into and out of fashion, the impressions created by these clothes will also change. So when we attempt to create a "good" impression through our dress, it is important to remember that current fashion dictates as well as the results of research done in this area. The following section will consider the effects of dress on both the observer and the wearer.

THE EFFECTS OF DRESS

When a waitress was wearing a daisy or a rose in her hair, diners tipped her an average of 26 cents extra, according to researchers Stillman and Hensley (1980). The study of flower power was done in a restaurant that primarily served businesspeople, with an average meal cost of $10.20. The six waitresses in the study were asked to wear the same jewelry, perfume, makeup, and hairstyle each night for the four nights the researchers were watching—with one exception. On one of the nights, they were asked to wear a flower.

The results showed that although men tipped more than women did, the flowers had a greater effect on women, who increased their tips an average of 39 cents, compared with the men's increase of 15 cents. The researchers speculated that women were simply more likely to notice the difference and respond to it.

We will now turn to an examination of the effects of artifacts (such as the flower in the hair) and clothing in terms of both the observer and the wearer. Although the observer and the wearer are two obviously different categories, they both deal with behavioral responses to clothing and artifacts.

Effects on the Observer

Clothing does have a persuasive value that influences the behavior of others. Once perceptions have been formed about another person, our subsequent communication will always be mediated by our attitudes. For instance, researchers have gathered substantial evidence which suggests that responses to requests for personal aid, political support, and charitable donations are affected by wearer attire (Miller and Rowold, 1980). The key, mediating attitude prevalent in this instance is usually perceived status and authority. Likewise, perceived status mediates other related receiver responses—for example, modeling behavior and attributions of credibility by observers. However, in addition to the mediating role of attitudes, expectations may also mediate responses to the clothing choices of others.

To illustrate each of the aforementioned principles, four studies will be examined in the following paragraphs. We begin with Walker, Harriman, and Costello's (1980) study concerning appearance and compliance with a request.

As stated above (as well as earlier in this chapter), perceptions of status are gleaned constantly from the clothing that we wear. These perceptions, in turn, mediate compliance to requests. Although a number of studies have demonstrated this principle, Walker, Harriman, and Costello (1980) took earlier research one step further by demonstrating that status, rather than guilt, mediates the clothing/compliance relationship. To support this hypothesis, the researchers dressed a confederate in either high- or low-status clothing and had him approach 400 male and female subjects, wearing a sling (or no sling) on his left arm. When the interviewer was well dressed, subjects generally responded to his question significantly more often than when he was poorly dressed. However, when sex was figured in, the effect of dress was found to be significant for female subjects only. As predicted, no significant effect was found to exist for the presence of the sling. The researchers concluded that guilt was not a significant mediator between clothing and compliance, but that perceived status did have a significant effect, especially for females. They also concluded that greater awareness of clothing may have contributed to the significant effect of clothing on females but not on males.

Although not as plentiful, research also has demonstrated the effect of perceptions of dress on observers' modeling behavior. One of the most dramatic examples was offered by Lefkowitz, Blake, and Mouton in 1955. In their now classic study, these researchers reported that pedestrians violated instructions given by a traffic light more often when another person violated it ahead of them. However, clothing made a difference in the modeling behavior of subjects who were observed. Significantly more violations occurred when the original violator was dressed to represent a high-status person (Lefkowitz, Blake, and Mouton, 1955, pp. 704–706). What about you? Have you ever jaywalked or violated directions from a traffic light after seeing a well-dressed person do the same? What if the violator had been barefoot, scraggly, and had worn only jeans and a battered T-shirt? Lefkowitz, Blake, and Mouton would have predicted that you did not model the other person's behavior in the latter situation.

Like modeling behavior, perceptions of credibility are also affected by clothing. However, status once again may be acting as the mediating variable. To demonstrate the relationship between perceived credibility and choice of apparel, Bassett (1979) asked subjects to rate photographs of either a male or female confederate. Each confederate was photographed wearing high- or low-status clothing. Results of the study indicated that high-status clothing produced significantly higher ratings of perceived competence than low-status clothing. However, no differences were found to exist for perceptions of the source's composure. Bassett concluded that receivers, indeed, make inferences about source credibility on the basis of dress, particularly with regard to knowledgeability and expertness factors. Bassett's findings also supported earlier studies concerning relationships between status, dress, and source credibility.

Much as perceptions of status mediate the relationship between clothing and observer effects, so, too, do expectations about the roles that the different sexes play. To demonstrate this hypothesis, Miller and Rowold (1980) predicted that "men would give more time and help to a woman in a tube top than to a woman wearing a traditional 'feminine' blouse with a bra . . . or to a woman wearing a man-tailored blouse without a bra" (p. 661). Their predictions were based on a belief that the latter woman would be perceived as a feminist, while the woman in the tube top would be viewed as more sensuous and alluring. They believed that the woman in the feminine blouse would be perceived as somewhere in between.

To complete the study, a female experimenter, wearing one of the three tops described above, approached 90 middle-aged men in downtown Indianapolis and asked directions to a very well known store. After each encounter, she recorded directions as well as subject reactions. Results of the study indicated that when the experimenter was dressed in the tube top, 70 percent of the subjects provided detailed instructions, 7 percent provided general instructions, and 23 percent provided no directions at all. The comparable figures for the masculine blouse with no bra were: 50 percent detailed instructions, 33 percent general instructions, and 17 percent no instructions. The feminine blouse produced 40 percent detailed instructions, 43 percent general instructions, and 17 percent no instructions. Compared with the latter two blouses, the tube top indeed yielded a greater number of detailed responses, with the second most detailed directions being given when the experimenter was wearing a masculine blouse with no bra. These results, indeed, seem to support the argument that sex-role expectations mediate the clothing/compliance relationship. Of even greater importance, however, we have shown that such a relationship, once again, seems to exist.

Effects on the Wearer

"Dress changes the manners," Voltaire stated a few centuries ago. Today, many researchers, convinced of the truth of this aphorism, seek to find out how dress affects the wearer. Simply stated, if you wear an outfit in which you're convinced you look "dynamite," do you feel dynamite? If you get up late one morning and don't have time to shower or wash your hair, and you grab the closest pair of jeans and yesterday's shirt, do you wish it were still yesterday? Do you perform better when taking an examination when you are "dressed up" or "dressed down"? Perhaps Bailey hoped that in her oversized clothing, Patty Hearst would feel small, insignificant, and somewhat overpowered by everything going on around her. If, indeed, she felt any of these things, it might be communicated by her slumped posture, her hanging head, and even the pitch and intensity of her voice.

Researchers in the area of clothing and nonverbal communication have argued that, indeed, the wearer is affected by the clothing that he or she wears. For example, in their essay entitled "Clothing: Self-Esteem in the Classroom," Daters and Newton (1984) argue that clothing enhances, among other important characteristics, the development of positive self-esteem. Their argument is supported by research such as that of Gordon, Tengler, and Infante (1982), who found that women who were more clothing-conscious were also more satisfied with job outcomes and more upward-bound. Likewise, Gordon and Infante (1980) discovered a significant relationship between clothing consciousness of the wearer and his or her self-esteem.

Another affect of clothing on the wearer, however, is more direct and is embodied in the phrase, "When I look good, I feel good." Do clothes pick you up? That is, clothes that make you look good? Do clothes get you down, especially when you have to look at the same closetful of old clothes that you've worn for the last two years? Researchers Dubler and Gurel (1984) say yes. Clothes do affect the way we feel. Dubler and Gurel explain the phenomenon as follows: Depression is reflected in part by lowered self-esteem and increased insecurity. Thus, "for someone who is depressed and whose confidence is low, clothing and appearance may take on greater importance than for someone who isn't depressed" (in Camer, 1985, p. 70). In fact, as Dubler and Gurel succinctly argue, "it is possible, at least on some days . . . that depressed persons use clothing as a tool to boost morale" (in Camer, 1985, p. 70). In this instance, clothing is actually used as a means to avoid depression.

As you can see, although we have generated some knowledge concerning the relationship between clothing and communication, much research remains to be done in a number of areas. In the meantime, experiment with your clothing and observe its relationship to you and your moods. And carefully observe when it affects your nonverbal communication.

SUMMARY

Clothing serves a variety of functions. According to Morris, these functions may be categorized into comfort/protection, modesty, and cultural display. With technological advancement, however, the need for clothing to give comfort and protection has become assumed. As a result, the two remaining functions, those of modesty and display, have become the predominant focus of American society.

How are messages of dress communicated? To address this question, we introduced a simple communication model. The wearer (source) encodes a message (transmitted by clothing) through a channel (usually visual although also tactile), which is then decoded by the observer (receiver). The response of the observer, both verbal and nonverbal, is referred to as feedback. The encoding and decoding processes are particularly important, since the message of dress is based on perceptions of the observer rather than on any inherent messages of the clothing itself.

In addition to this communication model, we examined the question of intentionality. Four possible combinations of intentionality include (1) messages sent and intentionally received, (2) messages unintentionally sent and intentionally received, (3) messages intentionally sent and unintentionally received, and (4) messages unintentionally sent and unintentionally received. One of the major purposes of studying the communicative value of clothing and artifacts is to reduce the number of messages that are unintentionally sent and unintentionally received. Messages like these are unconscious, and our awareness of them is either very low or nonexistent.

In discussing the personality characteristics of the wearer, we introduced several studies that attempted to demonstrate the relationship between what we wear and who we are. Included in the variables that were found to be related were dogmatism and Machiavellianism, verbal intelligence, mood shift, impression formation, aggressiveness, confidence, self-esteem, and many others.

The perception of clothing is the process by which an observer (receiver) decodes a message about the source's attire. Dress codes in schools and corporations are based on the assumption that the perceptions of the public are important. Research indicates that perceptions are made and, in most cases, represent stereotypes about particular clothing and artifacts. Additionally, social impressions of ourselves and others are created and sustained through the clothing we wear. Likewise, popularity and perceived success are related to clothing choices.

Other related variables communicated by clothing include status, authority, age, sexiness, and likability. In addition, clothing sustains stereotypes both in the business and academic worlds.

One additional function of clothing is that it fosters group identification, primarily through the ability of clothing to serve as a uniform. On both side of the bars, clothing acts in this capacity. The clothing of both inmates and the police serves this purpose.

Personal artifacts also contribute a great deal to the perceptions of others. These include glasses (both regular and tinted), cosmetics, T-shirts, briefcases, pipes, and so on. Of course, as fashion changes for the wearer, the impressions conveyed by various styles of clothing and personal artifacts also change. Since fashion is dynamic, we must be careful not to assume that research in this area is irrefutable.

In the final sections of this chapter, we reviewed the overall effects of clothing on both the observer and the wearer. In doing so, we argued that clothing affects such additional variables as compliance with a request, perceived credibility, and expectations. We also addressed, more completely, how clothing affects both self-esteem and overall mood. However, we argued that continued research is needed in each of these areas if we are to understand more completely how clothing communicates.

References

Aiken, L. (1963) Relationships of dress to selected measures of personality in undergraduate women. *Journal of Social Psychology, 59,* 121.

Anderson, D. (March 1977) Whatever happened to the corporate dress code? *TWA Ambassador,* pp. 43–45.

Bassett, R. E. (1979) Effects of source attire on judgments of credibility. *Central States Speech Journal, 30* (3), 282–285.

Bergen, P. (1977) *I'd love to, but what'll I wear?* Ridgefield, Conn.: Wyden Books.

Bridgwater, C. A. (1985) Police uniforms: Navy is good. *Psychology Today, 19,* 72.

Buckley, H. M., & Roach, M. E. (1974) Clothing as a nonverbal communicator of social and political attitudes. *Home Economics Research Journal, 3* (2), 94–102.

Bushman, B. J. (1984) Perceived symbols of authority and their influence on compliance. *Journal of Applied Social Psychology, 14* (6), 501–508.

Camer, R. (1985) Dressed for depression. *Psychology Today, 19* (1), 70.

Cox, C. L., & Glick, W. H. (1986) Resume evaluations and cosmetic use: When more is not better. *Sex Roles, 14* (1/2), 51–58.

Daters, C. M., & Newton, A. (1984) Clothing: Self-esteem in the classroom. *Illinois Teacher of Home Economics, 28,* 32–33.

Dubler, M. L. J., & Gurel, L. M. (1984) Depression: Relationships to clothing and appearance self-concept. *Home Economics Research Journal, 13* (1), 21–26.

Forsythe, S., Drake, M. F., & Cox, C. E. (1985) Influence of applicant's dress on interviewer's selection decisions. *Journal of Applied Psychology, 70* (2), 374–378.

Gordon, W. I., & Infante, D. A. (1980) System involvement for women subordinates: Relations with communication and personality variables. Paper presented at the meeting of the International Communication Association, Acapulco, Mexico.

Gordon, W. I., Tengler, C. D., & Infante, D. A. (1982) Women's clothing predispositions as predictors of dress at work, job satisfaction, and career advancement. *Southern Speech Communication Journal, 47,* 422–434.

Harris, M. B., James, J., Chavez, J., Fuller, M. L., Kent, S., Massanari, C., Moore, C., & Walsh, F. (1983) Clothing: Communication, compliance, and choice. *Journal of Applied Social Psychology, 13,* 88–97.

Knapp, M. L. (1978) *Nonverbal communication in human interaction* (2nd ed.). New York: Holt, Rinehart & Winston.

Korda, M. (1977) *Success: How every man and woman can achieve it.* New York: Random House.

Kuehne, S. H., & Creekmore, A. M. (1971) Relationships among social class, school position and clothing of adolescents. *Journal of Home Economics, 63* (7), 555–556.

Lefkowitz, M., Blake, R., & Mouton, J. (1955) Status factors in pedestrian violation of traffic signals. *Journal of Abnormal and Social Psychology, 51,* 704–706.

Miller, F. G., & Rowold, K. L. (1980) Attire, sex-roles, and responses to requests for directions. *Psychological Reports, 47,* 661–662.

Molloy, J. T. (1975) *Dress for success.* New York: Warner Books.

Molloy, J. T. (1977) *The woman's dress for success book.* Chicago: Follett Publishing.

Morris, D. (1977) *Manwatching: A field guide to human behavior.* New York: Harry N. Abrams, pp. 213–217.

New Woman Magazine. (July/August 1976) Giveaways in age can be found in clothing, pp. 54–55.

Pinaire-Reed, J. A. (1979) Personality correlates of predisposition to fashion: Dogmatism and machiavellianism. *Psychological Reports, 45* (1), 269–270.

Poll, A. (February 1976) Through a glass darkly. *Dun's Review, 107,* 77–78.

Popplestone, J. A. (April 1977) Prison parlance. *Human Behavior.*

Rocky Mountain News. (August 19, 1977) Unsavory T-shirts reflect incurable sex on the brain.

Rollmann, S. A. (November 1, 1977) How teachers' dress affects students' opinions. *National Enquirer.*

Rosencranz, M. L. (1962) Clothing symbolism. *Journal of Home Economics, 54,* 18–22.

Rosencranz, M. L. (April 6, 1976) Quoted in *Valley Times News* (Phoenix, Arizona), p. 3.

Rosenfeld, L. B., & Plax, T. G. (1977) Clothing as communication. *Journal of Communication, 27,* 23–31.

Rudofsky, B. (1974) *The unfashionable human body.* New York: Doubleday Anchor.

Solomon, M. R., & Schopler, J. (1982) Self-consciousness and clothing. *Personality and Social Psychology Bulletin, 8* (3), 508–514.

Stengel, R. (July 23, 1984) Status in the shading game. *Time,* 87–88.

Stillman, J. J., & Hensley, W. (June 1980) What tips tippers to tip. *Psychology Today,* p. 98.

Thornton, G. (1944) The effects of wearing glasses upon judgments and persons seen briefly. *Journal of Applied Psychology, 28,* 203–207.

Walker, M., Harriman, S., & Costello, S. (1980) The influence of appearance on compliance with a request. *Journal of Social Psychology, 112* (1), 159–160.

Wilder, R. (March 1982) Macho makeup: Cues used by women to assess the attractiveness of men. *Science Digest,* p. 120.

Williamson, L. (June 1977) Keep your shirt on. People will like you better. *Psychology Today,* p. 90.

CHAPTER 4

BODY MOVEMENTS AND GESTURES

The body says what words cannot.

Martha Graham, *The New York Times,* March
31, 1985

When was the last time you assessed your "muggability rating"? Who *actually* determines the probability of assault—the victim or the assailant? In a recent study, Betty Grayson and Morris Stein (1981) set out to answer these very questions and to identify those body movements that might characterize easy victims. What emerged from their study was a set of "muggability ratings" of sixty New York pedestrians from the people who may have been the most qualified to judge—prison inmates who had been convicted of assault.

To garner these results, the researchers unobtrusively videotaped pedestrians on weekdays between 10 A.M. and 12 P.M. Each pedestrian was taped for six to eight seconds, the approximate time it takes a mugger to size up an approaching person. The judges (prison inmates) rated the "assault potential" of the sixty pedestrians on a ten-point scale. A rating of one indicated that someone was "a very easy ripoff," a rating of two, "an easy dude to corner." Toward the other end of the scale, nine meant a person "would be heavy; would give you a hard time," and ten indicated that the mugger "would avoid it, too big a situation, too heavy." The results revealed several body movements that characterized easy victims. As Rubenstein (1980) summarized, "Their strides were either very long or very short; they moved awkwardly, raising their left legs with their left arms (instead of alternating them); on each step they tended to lift their whole foot up and then place it down (less muggable sorts took steps in which their feet rocked from heel to toe). Overall, the people rated most muggable walked as if they were in conflict with themselves; they seemed to make each move in the most difficult way possible" (p. 20). It appears that crime victims typically walk around in a daze, oblivious to what goes on around them, very much as you may have in the past before taking this class in nonverbal communication. This dreaminess, the study confirms, is expressed in body movements that criminals read as a clear signal to move in.

In the last few years, there has been an explosion of interest in the study of *kinesics,* popularly referred to as "body language." Authors have told us that if a woman sits with her arms crossed, it means she is cold toward other people. If she crosses her legs, it means that she is trying to block others out or is sexually frigid. Right? Well, maybe. Such labeling or stereotyping is one of the problems with current *popular* books concerning "body language." It overlooks twenty years of formal research as well as the "context" of a given situation. A woman may sit with her arms folded because she is physically cold. Similarly, she may have her legs crossed because she finds this to be a comfortable body position.

Education, social class, geographical background, and habit influence the development of our own individual body gestures and movements. In addition, we cannot forget the social, political, or economic context of a particular communication situation. It is only in the light of the event itself that we can come to determine what is being "communicated" by a certain posture, gesture, or body movement.

This chapter will focus on two major areas of kinesics research: body movement and posture. But first we would like to introduce you to two primary ways in which researchers have approached movement and posture. The first perspective comes from the research of Raymond Birdwhistell (1970), a noted authority on kinesics research. The second and more current approach is found in the work of A. T. Dittman (1971; 1977). We hope that when you finish this section, you will have a general understanding of two "state-of-the-art" ways in which kinesic research has been approached.

KINESICS: TWO MAJOR PERSPECTIVES

How many times have you heard the expression "we cannot *not* communicate?" Probably several times if you have ever taken any communication classes. As many researchers have noted, we may be able to stop talking in the vocal sense, but we cannot stop sending messages. Intentionally or unintentionally, our bodies continue to send messages through posture, lean, tension, gestures, and other body expressions.

Birdwhistell was one of the first researchers to conduct in-depth studies concerning the messages we send with our bodies. Birdwhistell believed that kinesics should be studied as a communication system, in much the same way that spoken language is studied—through the use of structural units or building blocks. Figure 4.1 provides an interesting comparison between the structural units of language and those of movement.

As Figure 4.1 illustrates, **allophones** are the smallest units of analysis in language. An example of an allophone might be the "p" sound in the word "pan." Researchers in language state that there are many ways in which this particular sound may be made. In fact, voice scientists have stated that even the same speaker usually does not pronounce a word in the same way every time. Each of these variations in the "p" sound is called an allophone. Likewise, **allokines** are

FIGURE 4.1   **Comparison of phonetic and kinesic concepts**

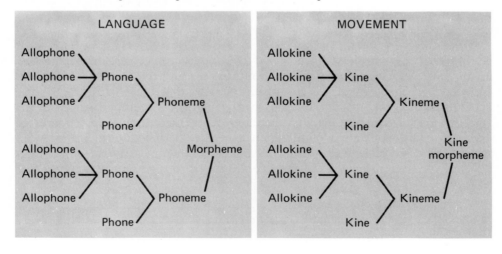

the smallest units of analysis in body language. Each individual variation in one given movement (which can be distinguished from another movement) is termed an allokine.

At this moment you might be asking yourself, "Who cares how many ways you can say the 'p' in pan or how many ways you can hold your right index finger and thumb when making the 'OK' sign for your best friend who is across the street?" In general, researchers would agree with you. These units of analysis are very minute. For that reason, a larger category is usually used in both language and body movement analysis. These units are called **phones** in language analysis and **kines** in body language analysis. More specifically, all the ways you can say the "p" sound in the word "pan," as well as the ways you can say the "p" sound in the word "tapes," are two ways of making two different "phones" of the sound. These "p" phones ultimately come together to form the **phoneme, (p)**. As you might guess, the "p" sounds are interchangeable in that any "p" sound may be used without a change in meaning. Likewise, **kinemes** consist of kines, which in turn consist of all possible variations of allokines. These kinemes, much like phonemes, can be interchanged without changes in meaning.

Thus far we have talked only about the small individual sounds and movements that are used in our two language systems. But how do these come together to form the verbal and nonverbal language we use every day? The answer is quite simple. Rarely do phonemes or kinemes occur without subsequent use of other phonemes or kinemes. Thus when phonemes are used in sequence, they form **morphemes;** likewise, sequences of kinemes are believed to form **kinemorphemes.** Does the following sequence sound familiar?

> Your friend Leigh is angry. She tosses her head, flips her hair back, clenches her fist, turns, and departs with quick, rapid steps.

Such a sequence of action, in Birdwhistell's system, constitutes the complex language of body movement.*

An Opposing Approach

Birdwhistell's system of analysis of body movement represents one perspective of the study of kinesics. There are, however, researchers who argue with his approach. A. T. Dittman, for example, contends that major differences exist between the language system and the "body language" system. Using American Sign Language (ASL) and the sign language of American Indians as the basis of his studies, Dittman concluded that body movement as a whole did not meet the criteria for spoken language, although "languages" such as ASL and Indian Sign Language were close to spoken language. More specifically, Dittman argues that

---

* For additional information concerning the study of body movement as a structural system of building blocks, see R. Birdwhistell, *Kinesics and Context* (Philadelphia: University of Pennsylvania Press, 1970).

body movements in general do not (1) form an alphabet comprised of discrete units and (2) are not governed by explicit, specific rules. On the basis of these findings, he concluded that body movements are not represented by a formalized language code. Body movements do provide valuable information, however, from which we can draw conclusions and make inferences. For this reason, the study of movement is important in the total human communication process.

We hope that at this point you understand the differences between the two major schools of thought concerning kinesics. One view of kinesics is that it is a study of the complex structure of body movements, which constitute a formalized language code. The other major perspective denies that there is a "language"; however, adherents of this viewpoint do acknowledge that body movements provide important information to the communication process. We now turn to the study of "body language" as it relates to current research and classification systems.

A KINESIC CLASSIFICATION SYSTEM

Body movements encompass an exceptionally wide range of phenomena. As Adam Kendon (1983) has noted, however, most researchers who have addressed the topic have focused on classifications of gestures. Of specific relevance to students of nonverbal communication is the functional approach posited by Paul Ekman and Wallace Friesen, two highly eminent researchers in kinesics. They divide body movement into the following five categories: emblems, illustrators, regulators, affect displays, and adaptors (or manipulators).

Emblems

Picture the following scene for a moment. A well-meaning American tourist on his first trip to northern Greece has been traveling by car for several days to get to this beautiful part of Europe. At long last he arrives, drives around the first town that he comes upon, and locates that quaint little inn that he knew would be there. As he unloads his luggage and enters to register, his excitement increases. He has always wanted to travel to this part of the world.

As he finishes registering and turns to get his bags, he gives the manager a "thumbs-up" sign. Much to his surprise, the manager begins to shout, flies around the desk to where the young man's luggage is located, and proceeds to throw his bags out the door.

What happened?

As Ekman, Friesen, and Bear (1984) have suggested, most travelers would not even think of traveling to another part of the world without a bilingual dictionary. Yet they often do not realize that the "language of gestures" can be every bit as different and can cause misunderstandings as easily as can spoken words (p. 64).

Return for a moment to our truly startled traveler. Unlike the meaning of the "thumb's-up" sign for Americans, which denotes the phrase "all right" in the

Gestures we take for granted may have very different meanings in different cultures. (Alan Carey/The Image Works)

United States and in most of western Europe, this gesture is translated to mean the insulting "up yours" in Sardinia and northern Greece (p. 67). To compound the problem for our naive tourist, things could become worse if he continues to use typical American emblems while traveling in Greece. For example, the "OK" sign (formed by placing the index finger on the tip of the thumb of the same hand) is seen as an insulting or vulgar sexual invitation in Greece (p. 67).

In short, many gestures have totally different meanings as one travels from one part of the world to another. For this reason, it may be useful to begin our focus on body movements with a discussion of those gestures that have a specific meaning for those who are either sending or receiving the message. These special kinds of gestures are called **emblems** by Ekman and his colleagues and are defined as physical acts that can fully take the place of spoken words (Ekman, Friesen, and Bear, 1984). Again, it is important to remember that the "meaning" of emblems may change as we move from group to group or culture to culture.

What distinguishes emblems from other kinds of gestures? For Ekman (1976), an emblem is an act that meets the following criteria:

1. It has a direct verbal translation, usually consisting of one or two words.
2. It is known by most or all of a group, class, subculture, or culture.
3. It is generally used with intent to send a specific message to a receiver.
4. It is received by an individual who realizes both the meaning and the intent of the emblem.

5. It has the sender taking responsibility for having sent the message.
   (p. 14)

As you can see, an emblem is a gesture that has a very precise meaning. In order to recognize the "OK" sign, one need not know who made the gesture, to whom it was sent, why it was sent, or what happened before, during, or after the sign to recognize its meaning. We must remember, however, that knowing *some* of these variables helps us to determine the more *exact* "meaning," as suggested in the illustration with which this section began.

Likewise, knowing the events that happened before, during, and after an emblem helps to establish whether a sender is serious about the message. If you ask a friend to do something for you and he or she responds with a "salute" (formed by briskly bringing a flattened hand to the right side of the forehead), he or she probably means something different than does the subordinate who elicits a similar gesture upon receiving from a superior a distasteful task to perform. (Incidentally, this particular emblem would probably have been used by our subordinate only after his or her superior had turned and walked away!) In the former case, the friend was probably responding to you affirmatively and in a friendly, joking manner. In the latter case, although the response was also affirmative, the "connotative" meaning of the gesture was probably quite different.

Before we go further, however, you should understand that emblems are made not only with the fingers or hands. Emblems can also include head nods and many other movements of the body. As an exercise, see if you can think of the "emblems" that represent the following words or phrases:

shame on you	I don't know
I promise	suicide
hitchhiking	tastes good
peace	what time is it
gossip	it's hot
whoopee	cut it out

It is interesting to note that we can also have emblematic "slips" of the tongue, much as we have verbal slips. As early as 1955, Paul Ekman discovered the phenomenon when he arranged for an interview between the director of a graduate program and one of his students. The student was subjected to several minutes of intense criticism by the director. Ekman noted that the student formed and maintained "the finger" (also known as "the bird") on one hand for a few minutes during this difficult interview (Ekman, 1976, p. 25). Perhaps this slip was due to her inability to fight back and the need for her to "maintain." Nevertheless, the study provides some interesting data concerning emblems and emblematic slips. Through our body movements, we communicate unconscious symbols for the thoughts or feeling that we are experiencing but that we are not always communicating verbally. The next time you are "under fire," it is to be hoped that you will (1) be more aware and (2) smile a little because you will remember this inside information concerning body language!

Illustrators

How would you feel if you could not use your hands when you wanted to give someone directions? What if you had to describe the action of "zigzagging" without using your hands? You probably would find yourself less able to make descriptions adequately. As many researchers have noted, language is both linked with and supported by body movement. Body movement can add to the meaning of utterances, provide feedback, and control synchronization of our everyday language. In addition, it can punctuate or display the structure of utterances, emphasize, frame (provide further information), illustrate, and signal continued interaction (Argyle, 1975, pp. 50, 254). Without the use of our hands or limbs, language would at best be less interesting, if not more difficult.

Gestures that are closely linked with language and that help to "illustrate" our spoken words are called **illustrators.** Perhaps a logical place to begin a discussion of the role of illustrators is to examine their function in the life of a child.

Jean Piaget, a noted psychologist who worked closely with children and their speech patterns, suggested that for a child under the age of seven or eight, gestures are as important as words and, in fact, may constitute the "real social language of the child."

In 1982, Thomas Pechmann and Werner Deutsch helped to substantiate this claim. Using adults and children ranging from two to nine years of age, these researchers found that pointing as a reference device steadily decreased with increasing age. In contrast, the number of adequate verbal descriptions increased with age, suggesting that children seem to employ pointing as a reference device when other means that are required in a specific context are not yet available (p. 340).

However, other researchers have found that, although we do decrease our use of simple hand gestures as we get older, we also increase our use of more complex hand movements (Jancovic, Devoe, and Wiener, 1975, pp. 922–928). There is one exception to this "rule," however. As Dalby, Gibson, Grossi, and Schneider (1980) have implied, Americans seem to use a greater number of gestures when they are excited or are communicating difficult messages. For example, they found that lecturers make twice as many gestures as people who are conversing in dyads, "due perhaps to the different communication needs in the two situations" (p. 296). In addition, we recall more information when a message is accompanied by gestures (Riseborough, 1981).

These findings suggest two functions of illustrators: (1) an encoder function, in which gestures allow us to better encode difficult material, and (2) a decoder function, in which gestures allow the decoder to benefit from use of the gestures. Research from scholars such as Marcos in 1979 and Riseborough in 1981 seems to support the encoder/decoder functions.

In a 1979 experiment, Luis Marcos found that bilingual adults who had a significant competence deficit in their nondominant language produced more illus-

Hand motions are one type of illustrator. (Carolyn Brown)

trators and groping hand movements when speaking in their nondominant language than they produced when speaking in their dominant language. This finding seems to support the existence of an encoder function (p. 940).

Likewise, using three different experiments, Riseborough (1981) found that illustrators seem to compensate for loss of auditory information, make tasks "more vivid by invoking mental images," and aid memory at the input stage of information processing (p. 182). This finding seems to suggest the existence of a decoder function of illustrators as well.

As you can see, illustrators help us to better encode and decode information. Again, we must remember that results such as these must be evaluated in the context of ethnic or cultural groups to which we belong. Italians, for instance, have been reported to have extensive gestural vocabularies and to use them more frequently in everyday interactions. In contrast, the British use gestures far less frequently and actually teach their children not to gesticulate (Walker and Nazmi, 1979, pp. 137–138).*

Regulators

Before you begin this section, try this experiment. First, put a friend in an adjoining room with the door almost closed. Then, using a monotone voice, try to have

---

* See Chapter 11 for more cultural distinctions.

an ongoing conversation with your friend. As you may assume, this particular conversation will probably be quite difficult. Without the use of your hands or of paralinguistic cues (voice raised, lowered, and so on), it may be almost impossible to speak without being interrupted. The purpose of this exercise is to show you the importance of nonverbal behaviors as **regulators** of an interaction and, in this instance, as regulators of a conversation. Although greetings and gestures that are used when arriving and departing serve as regulators, our discussion will not center on these body movements. Rather, we hope to provide you with some important information on how we use nonverbal behavior to regulate conversation.

Regulators are body movements that help us to interact with another individual. They include head nods, hand gestures, shifts in posture, and many other forms of body movement that allow us to signal the beginning and ending of interactions, as well as when to speak or to shift topics. This **turn system,** as it may be called, acknowledges the importance of signals between a speaker and a listener. The following discussion focuses on the roles of the sender and receiver with regard to nonverbal cues.

The turn system, according to Duncan and Fiske (1977), requires that each participant in the conversation see himself or herself as either a **speaker** or an **auditor** during each second of a conversation. As a result, there are four possible interactions (p. 178):

1. Speaker–auditor
2. Auditor–speaker
3. Speaker–speaker
4. Auditor–auditor

The first two states are considered "normal" states of interaction. If Cindy asks Jim a question, Jim is the auditor and Cindy is the speaker. When Jim makes a response, he becomes the speaker, and Cindy is the auditor. The second two states listed above, however, represent a "breakdown" in the interaction. For example, maybe Jim has not read Cindy's cues well enough and begins while Cindy is still talking. This miscommunication would exemplify state number three. In the fourth state, neither individual takes a speaking turn. Again, there has been a breakdown.

Let us explain further. Mark Knapp (1978) summarized a number of sources and came up with the following breakdown of cues used in the turn system. The first two types are used by a speaker. The second two are used by the auditor.

Using Jim and Cindy again, let's look at these four cues. The first is the **turn-yielding cue.** Jim has finished speaking and has told Cindy what it was that he wanted to say. By asking a question, decreasing loudness, slowing tempo, or simply by using silence, Jim could cue Cindy that it is her turn to speak. Another way that Jim could cue Cindy to speak would be to terminate or decrease gestures and to relax his posture. Gaze also serves a prominent function in turn-yielding by signaling to the listener that the speaker no longer wishes to speak (Craig and Gallagher, 1982). Thus, Jim could cue Cindy to respond by deliberately increasing eye contact. Finally, if Cindy still did not realize that it was her turn to speak, Jim could touch her on the arm or simply say, "Well?"

If Jim hasn't finished saying what he wishes to say, the way for him to continue is to use **turn-maintaining cues.** Jim could, according to Knapp, increase loudness, decrease silent pauses, fill pauses with gestures, and avoid allowing his gestures to terminate at the end of phrases or sentences. Knapp also would advise Jim to lightly touch or use a patting motion that says, "Just a few more minutes and you can talk."

If Cindy is ready to speak and Jim hasn't finished saying what he wishes to say, Cindy will use what Knapp terms **turn-requesting cues** to adopt the speaker's state instead of the auditor's state. To do this, Cindy could use rapid head nods or say "yeah," "uh-huh," or "I agree" more frequently. She also could raise her index finger, take an audible breath, or straighten or tense her posture to show Jim she is ready to speak. Knapp adds that if Jim continues speaking, Cindy can simply begin to talk. This would constitute the speaker-speaker state. You probably never realized that turn-taking behaviors in conversations were so complicated!

Another important type of turn-related behavior is **turn denying.** Using our previous example, turn denying would be used if Jim or Cindy did not wish to talk. To remain in the role of the auditor, one simply needs to maintain silence and a relaxed posture. An intent gaze at the environment, smiles and nods, or even some "um-hums" thrown in at the appropriate times will show the speaker you would rather remain silent.

It is clear that we use gestures and other nonverbal behaviors to regulate our interactions. One of the purposes of this section is to make you more aware of how we interact with others. Before your next class meeting, take some time to observe how people converse. See how many "regulators" you can discover in a conversation between two friends or between two strangers or perhaps at the checkout counter at the grocery store. Increased awareness of nonverbal communication can help us to become better communicators.

Affect Displays

When was the last time you felt really sad or depressed? Now quickly sketch a cartoon of how you felt, or visualize yourself in your mind, using posture to convey your feelings. Now draw a sketch that represents how you feel when you are happy or excited, again using posture and body parts to represent your feelings. Your sketches might look something like this:

If you drew your pictures in some way similar to these, you probably "know" something about the role of **affect displays** and nonverbal communication. Affect displays are those behaviors that reflect the intensity with which we feel an emotion; in addition, they usually can be "measured" by the amount of body tension we are feeling. Think for example, of the football player who is about to play his first game. Ninety-nine percent of the time you probably would not find this young man slumped over with bowed head. Most of the time he probably would have a rigid and erect posture, with every muscle taut. An increase in muscular tension, in fact, is usually a function of an increase in the emotion being displayed.

Posture is not the only reflection of emotional states. Shifts in body posture,

Feeling Good

Feeling Bad

clenching and unclenching our hands, and shuffling or quick movements of the feet also reveal more intensely felt emotions. Have you ever noticed, for example, the person who sits with legs crossed and makes quick, jiggling movements with the foot? What about the person who constantly crosses and uncrosses the legs, shifts around, and moves the body forward and backward? Usually this person is feeling some intensity of an emotion—contempt, disgust, anger, restlessness, or the desire to flee from the situation. However, as we discussed previously, the context of the situation is important in determining the "meaning" of such movements or body language. Without this knowledge, such "meaning" cannot be derived from body movements alone.

In addition to revealing the intensity of an emotion, body cues allow us to distinguish between certain emotions which other people may be experiencing. For example, Edelmann and Hampson (1981) report that, without the aid of body cues to distinguish them, amusement and embarrassment are often confused. The problem is that *both* emotions may elicit facial expressions signaling amusement. However, when an amused expression is accompanied by downcast eyes and nervous hand and leg movements, the two distinctly different emotions become distinguishable.

It is interesting to note that movements of the body can also be used to determine whether deception is being used. In the last few years, there has been a growing interest in deception research in the field of communication. As Eakins and Eakins (1978) have noted, the gestures we make with our hands and feet more than those we make with other parts of the body resemble the states we are feeling (p. 163). Research by other people also seems to support the idea that deception cues are often revealed in the lower part of the body.

In addition, when lying was involved in the concealment of emotions, researchers have found that observers were more accurate when they observed *only* the body of a person who was lying than when they observed that person's head and facial expressions (Hocking, Bauchner, Kaminski, and Miller, 1979). This current finding supports earlier research.

For example, Ekman, Friesen, and Scherer (1976) have hypothesized that a sender has better control over facial expression than over movements of the body or tone of voice. Bugenthal, Henker, and Whalen (1976) found similar results and concluded that when deception is involved, the body and voice send more accurate information than does facial expression with regard to deceptive cues. (Note: These studies were reported in Rosenthal, 1979, p. 222.)

As you can see, the body sends important information about the intensity of emotion as well as about deception. Try this experiment: Find a friend who hasn't had this course (or one like it) and tell him/her you are going to tell a story (which may or may not be true). Before you begin, ask your friend to watch you closely to see if you are lying. At the end of the story, ask him/her if you were lying or not. See if your friends can tell you exactly why he/she thought you were lying. You might be surprised by the results.

Adaptors

When was the last time you noted a friend's hands move to her throat as she told you something that you knew she didn't really believe? When did you last catch yourself twisting your hair or puffing a cigarette as if you had two seconds left to live? If you can picture any of these scenes in your mind, you probably are "seeing" body movements that psychiatrists and researchers in kinesics have labeled **adaptors** (or manipulators).

Although research concerning adaptors currently is not extensive, several theories and ideas have been tested by researchers. For example, Donaghy in 1980 reported that adaptors are behaviors that we at one time used for our own personal convenience or comfort but that now have become an unconscious habit (p. 14). For example, Jeff constantly adjusts his glasses when in a tense situation; Rosemary incessantly flips her hair over her shoulder when in the same kind of situation. At one time these behaviors may have been necessary (perhaps Jeff's glasses were loose or Rosemary's hair was in her eyes). However, the behaviors now have become a part of their repertoire of body movements.

Other researchers generally have agreed that adaptors are linked with negative feelings, particularly during emotional situations and in relation to depression and anxiety. For example, Ruggieri, Celli, and Crescenzi (1982) have noted that, as frustration or anxiety increases, self-contact with the body also increases. Interestingly enough, however, these researchers discovered that we touch the left and right sides of our bodies at different times. When disclosing information about internal states (e.g., when sharing information about embarrassing experiences with another person), we tend to touch the left side of our body most often. However, if we experience anxiety as a function of social contact with others, we touch the right side of the body more often (p. 695).

It should be noted that adaptors are not usually exhibited intentionally, however. They are most often performed in private, and when observed in public they usually take an abbreviated form. For example, although a person may squeeze or pick a pimple in private, when in public he or she will only rub the infection. Since the adaptor appears in an altered or shortened form in public, it is often more difficult to recognize and analyze adaptors and the purposes behind them in a communicative interaction.

Although adaptors are not usually exhibited intentionally, they do communicate to the individual who is receiving the messages. Overall, speech is accompanied by two major types of hand movements: those movements that take place away from the body and those movements that take place on the body, with the clothing, or with its "adornments." The first category of movements have been labeled object-focused and the movements that occur on some part of the body, body-focused (Barroso, Freedman, Grand, and Van Meel, 1978, p. 321). For example, scratching the blackboard with your fingernails is an object-focused movement, but scratching your head is a body-focused movement. In addition, data from a series of videotapes made by Barroso, Freedman, Grand, and Van Meel (1978) suggest that body-focused movements are linked with a cognitive state different from that linked with object-focused movements (movements away from the body). The research team explains the differences in this way:

> Object-focused movements appear to be related to processes involved in representing in spoken language internal experiences as well as external events. . . . Body-focused movements seem to be connected to attentional focusing during distraction or interference. In work with different populations, the continuous motions of the hands on the body emerged as signs of attentional disruption and as accomplishments of verbal activity during distracting conditions. (pp. 321–322)

Research by Sousa-Posa and Rohrberg in 1977 also found body-focused movements to be a reflection of uncertainty on the part of a speaker, or encoder. In contrast, object-focused movements were found to occur in relation to the type of information and listener availability (pp. 19–29).

As we have discussed, body movement functions have been divided into five categories: emblems, illustrators, regulators, affect displays, and adaptors. The following section will discuss an additional aspect of kinesics in which researchers have been interested, namely, posture and locomotion. Although some aspects of posture have been included in previous sections, we believe its study is important enough to warrant its own discussion. Included in the discussion are six major topics: (1) an introduction to posture; (2) posture as a reflection of immediacy, (3) posture and status, (4) gender differences in posture, (5) posture and locomotion, and (6) posture and emotions. This discussion will assist you in becoming more aware of the communicative nature of posture, bearing, and locomotion.

POSTURE: AN INTRODUCTION

When telling a friend or loved one that some shocking event (negative *or* positive) has just occurred, the first thing that we usually ask them to do is to sit down.

Generally, we make this request to ensure their comfort—as well as to guard against injury should the news overwhelm them to the point of faintness. (Remember the time that you had to tell your parents, mate, or spouse about the "little dent" in their brand new car? Five dollars and an "A" in your nonverbal communication class says you ensured that they were first sitting down before you told them the news!)

However, did you ever think of making sure that a friend was sitting down before asking him or her for a favor? What about ensuring this same body position before attempting to persuade someone to switch to your position on a controversial topic? According to researchers, you actually may be more persuasive if recipients of your message are sitting or lying down rather than standing. Additionally, when reclining, they will tend to analyze your message more carefully and can more easily discriminate strong from weak persuasive arguments (Petty, Wells, Heesacker, Brock, and Cacioppo, 1983). (Note: posture is no guarantee of success; however, research says it may be one factor.)

As you can see, posture is more than the ways that we stand or sit. It subtly and surely affects our everyday lives. Given the effects of posture on persuasion—and on so many other variables, as you will discover in the following pages—we invite you to stop for a moment and observe the posture you are now maintaining. What does it say about your mental and emotional state? Your status? Your attitudes in general? Given that posture may communicate all of these messages, we now turn to a more complete discussion of posture and its effects on your life.

Good posture is more than standing at attention. It applies to the way you move every moment of your life—whether walking, sitting, lifting, or pushing. Long before researchers and scientists began to study body movements and their implication for communication, dancers and artists of mime were aware of the range of communications that could be expressed by body movement and stance alone. Key (1975) has composed a list of terms that gives some idea of the variety of postural stances that we use. We can crouch, sprawl, perch, slump, lounge, repose, loll, stretch out, rest, recline, lean, and stand at attention. Can you think of others? If so, see how long you can make the list! It is interesting to note, however, that no matter how long the list, researchers can place every posture or stance you can think of into one of three categories: (1) standing; (2) bent-knee positions, such as sitting, squatting, and kneeling; and (3) lying. In addition, posture may be placed on a type of continuum between gestures and spatial behavior. For this reason, changes in posture may be seen as an extension of gestures or as a method of altering the distance between yourself and another person or object. An example is the light-footed boxer who "dances" from his opponent's powerful blows. At the same time that he springs from side to side, he himself levels deadly and accurate punches to his opponent's brow. The boxer's dancing movements are his way of changing the spatial distance between himself and his opponent; the blows he delivers are a form of gesturing. By maneuvering, he will have a better chance of ending the match victoriously.

Although researchers have divided postures into three major categories, the overall range of postures is exceptionally large. Gordon Hewes, a noted anthropologist, has studied postures in many different cultures. According to his work, there are approximately 1000 different human postures. In primitive cultures, for example, he found almost one hundred common postures, most of which are not used in more advanced cultures. The major factors that influenced posture in these primitive societies were the nature of the ground (whether it was cold or wet) and the clothes that were worn.

Another interesting fact is that the culture, as well as subgroups within that given culture, determines both the styles of posture and the situations in which we observe these specific body stances. For instance, Kudoh and Matsumoto (1985) suggest that not all cultures use the same postures in a given situation nor are they interpreted in identical ways. Whereas people of Western cultures use a number of postural indices to determine interpersonal positiveness (e.g., openness of the body, forward leans, mutual gaze, and so on), the Japanese, who use far fewer body movements in general, label substantially fewer postural expressions as characterizing interpersonal positiveness. These findings support those of an earlier study by McGinley, Blau, and Takai (1983), which found that subjects from Japan rated a female model more interpersonally attractive when she smiled infrequently and expressed closed body positions and less attractive when she smiled frequently and expressed open body positions. In contrast, U.S. college men and women rated the same model as the most interpersonally attractive when she smiled frequently and used open body positions and the least attractive when she smiled infrequently and exhibited closed body positions (p. 915).

It seems reasonable to say that culture affects both our postures as well as the situations in which we use them. Although we each have our own idiosyncratic body stance, postures, and walks (which are also a function of our body shape), culture dictates the ways in which we will use them. One of the most interesting areas of posture is its relation to immediacy and its impact on interaction, which form the subject of the following pages.

Posture and Immediacy

Picture yourself, for a moment, at a party talking with someone you have just met but would like to get to know better. This person leans forward, gazes into your eyes, and smiles as he or she talks with you. Based on this information, do you (1) think the person likes you, (2) know you must have bad breath, (3) wonder what you said to offend him or her, (4) feel like running and putting on more deodorant? Chances are you figure he or she likes you, right? You're also fairly certain that this very interesting person wants to continue the conversation as much as you do, right? But how do you know this, since this person has not actually verbalized it?

Although you believe it was your stunning personality and wonderfully good looks, researchers would probably disagree—in general. The posture and body movements of the person with whom you interact usually will encourage you to continue or terminate the conversation. Albert Mehrabian, a noted researcher in the area of kinesics, contends that posture communicates our attitudes through two main dimensions: immediacy and relaxation. **Immediacy,** the first dimension, consists of forward leans and other related nonpostural variables such as touching, gaze proximity, and direct body orientation. **Relaxation,** on the other hand, consists of such variables as asymmetrical leg position, hand relaxation, and backward lean. In addition, openness of limbs usually suggests a more positive attitude on the part of two individuals engaging in conversation. Basically, all positions that reduce proximity or improve visibility between two people suggest a more positive and open attitude. So even if you do have a stunning personality and very good looks (which we know you do), observe body positions closely. They reveal important information about you and others.

Posture and Status

Before you read any further, picture the following scene. It's your first day on the job, and you are about to walk into your boss's office. Although you met her during the interview for the job, you still feel somewhat apprehensive about talking with her. Now freeze. Before you enter the office, which of the following stances would you use: (1) relaxed and open, (2) upright and attentive, or (3) casual and friendly? Most researchers would claim that postures other than an upright stance

Postural style may communicate a great deal. What can you infer about the relative status of these two people from their nonverbal cues? (Alan Carey/ The Image Works)

will probably send a negative message, depending upon the attitudes and personality of your boss. Generally, a relaxed postural style is used by individuals of higher status, while a more upright and tense postural style is reserved for members of lower status. Behavior in the animal kingdom provides interesting support for status- and posture-related behaviors. Weisfeld and Beresford (1982) describe the following dominance roles of animals:

> Dominant primates tend to stand taller than subordinates. . . . This is true not only of nonsexual mounting behavior but also of noncontact displays: Subordinate monkeys characteristically crouch quadripedally in the presence of a dominant individual, as do chimpanzees . . . and gorillas. . . . Dominant or threatening apes sometimes assume a particular bipedal gait. [Likewise] dominant monkeys [are described] as strutting and subordinates as slinking. (pp. 116–117)

Goffman (1961), in observing staff meetings at a psychiatric hospital, found that high-status individuals put their feet on the table, slumped in their seats, and in general maintained a relaxed, nontense body position. Lower-status individuals, reported Goffman, maintained a more formal body position and sat straight in their chairs. It is generally accepted that when two strangers meet, the more relaxed one enjoys the higher status. According to Mehrabian (1971, p. 28) the "one who is powerful, that is, of higher status, can afford to relax, whereas the weak must remain watchful and tense."

Another interesting finding regarding posture and status is that an individual of equal status will usually assume a posture similar to that of the person with whom he or she is interacting. Sharing a similar posture with another person is referred to as a **congruent body position,** while dissimilar posture is considered to be an **incongruent body position.** Congruent posture between two persons generally signifies liking and equality. Incongruent posture generally signifies that some difference in status exists (for example, a secretary sitting upright and the employer reclining in a large chair).

Examples of postural congruence versus incongruence also emerge when viewing group behavior. When one group is in the presence of a competing group, less intergroup mirroring (or postural congruence) emerges. In contrast, increases in postural congruence are associated with cooperation across groups in the same communication setting (LaFrance, 1985). Additionally, group behavior may even display postural changes when an argument occurs. In such cases, postures may shift between arguing parties to reflect differences in opinion, while a leader may adopt the postures of both parties to indicate his/her refusal to take sides.

Psychotherapists and counselors are aware of the significance of congruent postures or what they refer to as the "postural echo." To document this relationship between postural congruence and perceived counselor empathy, Maurer and Tindall (1983) set up fifteen-minute interviews between eighty high school juniors and either a male or female career counselor. During the session, the counselor used either congruent or incongruent postural shifts. Results of the study indicated that counselors who used congruent postural movements were rated as significantly more empathetic than those who used incongruent postural shifts, despite the sex of the counselor. This study supports the argument that echoing a client's posture may promote rapport.

As we have discussed, the relaxation dimension of posture usually expresses status and dominance, while the immediacy dimension relates to liking and degree of trust. As early as 1972, Scheflen suggested that we tend to imitate the postural styles of peers during peer interaction. In addition, a relaxed postural style is used more by females than by males, and more by persons of the opposite sex than of the same sex. We can infer certain status messages from both our own posture and that of others. Observe your posture during the next several days and see how you change when talking with a friend, a professor, or an employer. Also examine your telephone posture and see if you change your posture while talking on the phone to another person, even though that person cannot see you.

Posture and Gender Differences

Take a look at the following two lists and place the term "males" over the column that best represents stereotypical male characteristics and "females" over the column that best categorizes stereotypical female behaviors.

staring	lowering eyes
pointing	smiling
taking more space	cocking head
initiating touch	yielding
head erect	cuddling
upright stance	overting gaze
legs apart	stop talking
hands on hips	blinking

If you know your "stereotypes" you placed "males" over the first column and "females" over the second column. Interestingly enough, these "stereotypes" are somewhat accurate in description for they tend to be consistent with gender differences and, in some instances, actually influence these differences. Eakins and Eakins (1978) support this notion when they state:

> It is considered unfeminine or unladylike for a woman to "use her body too forcefully, to sprawl, to stand with her legs widely spread, to sit with her feet up . . . to cross the ankle of one leg over the knee of the other." And depending on the type of clothing she wears, "she may be expected to sit with her knees together, not to sit cross-legged, or not even to bend over." Although restrictions on women have relaxed recently, these prescriptions of propriety are not fully accepted. (pp. 160–161)

Both parents and teachers reward and punish children for appropriate and inappropriate gender behaviors. Thus, through cultural learning, female-submissive and male-dominance behaviors have emerged. In turn, "these gender displays [represent] female shrinking and male spatial expansion," claims Henley (1977, p. 136). Other nonverbal behaviors that express femininity through shrinkage are described by Rita Brown:

> Lowering a shoulder in the presence of a man, pulling the body in (literally to take up less space so he can move more), turning the head upward or tilting it to the side, often with persistent eyebrow signals, are motions most non-feminists perform. Such gestures elicit favorable response. (1974, pp. 61–62)

Nonverbal behavioral differences in posture are representative of both individual and societal attitudes about the differences between the sexes. In addition to the influence of stereotypical classifications, posture is also defined by such factors as context, style, the person involved, clothing, and other artifacts. Your own experimentation will reveal how your posture changes depending on the type of clothing you are wearing, from a business suit to blue jeans and a T-shirt.

Posture and Locomotion

Think for a moment of the many "diet cola" commercials that have bombarded us recently on television. You know—those commercials featuring some absolutely gorgeous model who floats across the screen like a dream and truly persuades us to drink her brand of cola. Indeed, when she walks across that screen, all long legs and swinging arms, you and every other person is supposed to know she's there. (Whatever she drinks!) She doesn't need to say a word. That look and her walk seem to say, "I have arrived."

According to author Gerald Donaldson (1979) our walk, indeed, communicates a great deal of information about us. Particularly, "our gait is closely integrated with our personality . . . (thus, a 'gaitologist' should be able to cure personality defects by altering the manner of walking" (in Morris, 1979, p. 141). Psychologist Joyce Brothers agrees: "You can change the way you perceive yourself, the way other people perceive you by changing your walk. Assume the posture and walk of someone you'd like to be: self-confident, alert. If you stride out purposefully, people will assume you know where you're going" (Morris, p. 141).

The average walking pace is two steps per second or about 3 miles an hour. When you walk at an average clip, you have a stride of about 24 inches, which stretches as you pick up speed. When was the last time you thought about the way you walk? Today? Last week? Two years ago? If you are not aware of your gait, pace, and posture, you may be missing out on one of the most interesting aspects of body language: the study of **locomotion.**

As you might guess, locomotion is the way we get from one place to another. We can walk, run, skip, jump, hop, dance, trot, crawl, mosey, slide, "make tracks," boogie, or "book it." Each of us has a distinct walk, one that allows our friends (and enemies) to recognize us and that reflects our height, weight, and body structure. In addition, our walk reflects our outlook on life, our attitudes, our emotional states, as well as our cultural or ethnic background.

One researcher who has studied locomotion in humans found that the way we walk tends to place us in one of the three categories: the "pusher," the "puller," and the "balancer" (Birdwhistell, in Key, 1975, p. 92). Our individual walks, however, reflect both variety and style. See if you can find your own special walk from the following list that Birdwhistell compiled. Can you place your friends' walks into any of these categories?

_____ the bent-knee type	_____ the trudger
_____ the straight-knee type	_____ the toe pointer
_____ the bouncer	_____ the flat footer
_____ the glider	_____ the pigeon-toed
_____ the high stepper	_____ the practicer of the duck walk
_____ the foot dragger	_____ the practicer of the Indian walk
_____ the shuffler	_____ the foot stutterer

(adapted from Key, 1975, p. 92)

Not only do our walks reflect our real selves, but our walks also reflect our genders. Although the idea probably does not surprise you, see if you can pinpoint the specific differences in walks between the sexes. Eakins and Eakins (1978) state that the main differences with regard to locomotion between American males and females is that females, when moving, present the entire body as "a moving whole"—from neck to ankle. In contrast, American males "move the arms independently from the trunk, and may subtly sway the hips with a slight right and left movement involving a twist at the rib cage." In short, American males seem to be the more relaxed of the two (p. 159).

Another difference in the way American males and females walk is that the male tends to walk with his legs at a 10- to 15-degree angle and with his arms 5 to 10 degrees away from his trunk. In contrast, American females walk with their legs close together and their arms close by their sides (Eakins and Eakins, 1978, p. 160). This research is based on observations of American males and females and does not extend to males and females of other cultures. It would be interesting to compare the walks of individuals from the Soviet Union, Egypt, Australia, Great Britain, and the many other countries of the world. Perhaps such information could help us to determine more about attitudes and personalities, which, in turn, would allow us to maximize communication efficiency on the international level.

Locomotion plays an important part in the image we portray to others.

Although we cannot provide a prescriptive approach to interpreting postures and movement, we can find empirical support to suggest that such behaviors are related to our perceptions of ourselves and to the perceptions others have of us. Your walk is the crowning glory of human body locomotion. "It is an action we all take so much for granted and yet," explains Morris (1977), "when analyzed as a mechanical operation, it emerges as an immensely complex process—so complicated, in fact, that muscle experts are still arguing today over the finer points of how it operates and how we manage to stride along so successfully" (p. 288).

Posture and Emotion

"First you notice the deference people pay her—how humble her colleagues are. Then her large soft eyes look straight at you—almost through you, it seems. Her voice is low and firm. Her white hair is coiled at the crown of her head and is pinned with a fresh flower. Then you might notice her hands resting quietly in her lap. They are large, with massive knuckles, testimony to the work she does. Her cat lies on the floor nearby. Her glasses, hanging by a chain, rest on her bosom. Her hearing is weak, so conversations with her are in raised tones" (Connolly, 1977, p. 17). This is a description of Ida P. Rolf, the well-known and internationally respected founder of the body therapy of structural integration, more commonly referred to as rolfing. This area of therapeutic work is based on the premise that "the body never lies." Rolfers believe that posture, body positions, and areas holding tension say things about one's emotional history, deepest feelings, character, and personality.

What is it that rolfers do? The rolfing practitioner uses his or her fingers, elbows, and knuckles to stretch the connective tissue surrounding those muscles that need lengthening and to separate muscle bundles. When the muscle is not used properly, as a result of trauma and habit, the fascia (the tissue that surrounds the muscle) becomes shorter and thicker and adheres to neighboring fascia (Kurtz and Prestera, 1976, p. 139). The rolfer restores the body to its natural, freeflowing state, thus allowing the person to experience spontaneity of movement, release of deeply embedded emotions, and lengthening of the body. Many people enjoy this aspect of rolfing because it gives them a taller, thinner appearance.

Although somewhat lacking in empirical and laboratory-demonstrated support, body therapies are quickly gaining the attention and respect of the scholarly community. These therapies represent a significant contribution in assisting people with their posture, proper balance, coordination, freedom of movement, and psychological problems. There are six primary body-oriented approaches developed in the West. Structural integration (rolfing) is the first, developed by Ida Rolf as a body-centered approach. Reichian therapy and bioenergetics, developed primarily by Wilhelm Reich and Alexander Lowen, use a psychoanalytic approach and represent the second and third systems. Patterning, the fourth system, grew out of the same theoretical perspective as rolfing and utilized Rolf's concept of line, symmetry, and gravity. This system was developed by Judith Aston in collaboration with Ida Rolf. The fifth and sixth systems were developed by F. Matthias Alexander and Moshe Feldenkrais and are methods that focus on the functions and movement of the body rather than on the structure.

Most of these body therapies view the body as having fixed muscular patterns that connect with attitudes and predispositions about life. Structural integration, according to certified rolfer Owen Marcus, is "based on a belief that the body is plastic, rather than a fixed unit and that by ordered manipulation of the fascia, the body can resume the anatomically ordered assemblage it's supposed to have. The primary goal is to align the body with gravity" (Johnson, 1980, C-2).

Try an experiment with yourself. Assume various body postures and see what you feel like in each one. Each position will allow you to experience different emotions, ranging from confidence to insecurity and from elation to depression. As Riskind (1984) has noted, "slumped (depressed) or upright physical postures are not just passive indicators of mental states but can reciprocally affect (our) mental states . . . " and our behavior as a whole (p. 479).

SUMMARY

The study of kinesics or body movements has been a major concern of researchers in psychology, communication, and many other areas.

Birdwhistell and Dittmann offer two perspectives for viewing the structural units of kinesic behavior. Birdwhistell contends that body language should be studied as a communication system, in much the same way that spoken language is studied—through the use of structural units or building blocks. Dittmann, on the other hand, contends that major differences exist between the verbal language system and the body language system. Specifically, Dittmann argues that body movements in general (1) do not form an alphabet comprised of discrete units and (2) are not governed by explicit, specific rules. Both perspectives offer important information and views concerning the study of kinesics and the future research in this area.

The classification of kinesic behaviors assists us in understanding their functional purpose in interaction settings. Researchers Ekman and Friesen divide body movement into the following five categories: emblems, illustrators, regulators, affect displays, and adaptors. Emblems are nonverbal acts that have direct verbal translations usually consisting of one or two words, such as the popular sign of a hand wave. Illustrators are closely linked with language and help to "illustrate" our spoken words, such as saying "head north" and pointing in that direction at the same time. Body movements that help us to interact with others are referred to as regulators. Specifically, they include such behaviors as head nods, hand gestures, and shifts in posture. Affect displays are those behaviors that reflect the intensity with which we feel an emotion. And finally, adaptors are nonverbal behaviors that are not as easily defined. Some researchers claim that adaptors are linked with negative feelings toward oneself or another person. Other researchers claim that adaptors are behaviors that we used at one time for our own personal convenience or comfort but that now have become an unconscious habit. In either case, adaptive behaviors represent a different class of movements, which is drawing increasing attention as an area of study.

If you want to look ten years younger and ten pounds thinner, stand up straighter. This simple advice appears in many magazines and books claiming that posture makes an important difference in external appearance and internal functioning of body organs. The discussion of posture in this chapter focused on (1) posture and immediacy, (2) posture and status, (3) gender differences in posture, (4) posture and locomotion, and (5) posture and emotions.

Posture reveals aspects of immediacy and hence our feelings toward a person and/or a situation. Various displays of immediacy include forward lean, touching, gaze, proximity to another person, and direct body orientation. Status is often expressed through posture, particularly the status of relationships between a superior and a subordinate. Generally, a relaxed postural style is used by individuals of higher status, while a more upright and tense postural style is reserved for members of lower status.

Another interesting study of postural behaviors relates to gender differences. Stereotypically, males exhibit dominant behaviors (e.g., staring, pointing, taking up more space) while females exhibit submissive behaviors (e.g., cocking head, blinking, smiling). In the area of posture and locomotion (the way we get from one place to another), we noted how a person's distinct walk reflects that person's attitudes, emotional states, and cultural or ethnic background.

Finally, the study of posture and emotion raises the question of whether our posture induces particular emotional states or whether certain emotional states trigger a postural behavior. This chicken-or-the-egg phenomenon remains unanswered, but many serious practitioners of body therapies view the body as having fixed muscular patterns that connect with attitudes and predispositions about life. These body therapies include rolfing, Reichian therapy, bioenergetics, patterning, the Alexander method, and Feldenkrais's work. Bernard Gunther shares his insight into the literal and symbolic meanings revealed in our body movement behavior:

> *Body language is literal.*
> *To be depressed is, in fact,*
> *to press against yourself.*
> *To be closed off*
> *is to hold your muscles rigid*
> *against the world. Being open*
> *is being soft.*
> *Hardness is being up tight*
> *cold separate,*
> *giving yourself and other people*
> *a hard time. Softness*
> *is synonymous with pleasure*
> *warmth, flow, being*
> *alive.*

*Are you itching to get at
someone? Is your boss*
a pain in the neck?
*Are you sore about something?
What is your* aching back
*trying to tell you?
Is there someone on your back?
What about your ulcer?
Is there someone or thing
you can't* stomach?

*What is it that you'd like to
get off your* chest?
*Your body speaks to you
all the time, telling you
what your own needs are:
LISTEN here.**

References

Argyle, M. (1975) *Bodily communication.* New York: International Universities Press.

Barroso, F., Freedman, N., Grand, S., & Van Meel, J. (1978) Evocation of two types of hand movements in information processing. *Journal of Experimental Psychology: Human Perception and Performance, 4* (2), 321–329.

Birdwhistell, R. (1970) *Kinesics and context.* Philadelphia: University of Pennsylvania Press.

Birdwhistell, R. (1971) *Kinesics and context.* London: Allen Lane/Penguin.

Brown, R. M. (1974) The good fairy. *Quest, 1* (1).

Connolly, L. (May 1977) I. Rolf. *Human Behavior,* pp. 17–23.

Craig, H. K., & Gallagher, T. M. (1982) Gaze and proximity as turn regulators within three-party and two-party child conversations. *Journal of Speech and Hearing Research, 25,* 65–75.

Dalby, J. T., Gibson, D., Grossi, V., & Schneider, R. D. (1980) Lateralized hand gesture during speech. *Journal of Motor Behavior, 12* (4), 292–297.

Dittman, A. T. (1971) Review of kinesics and context. *Psychiatry, 34,* 334–342.

Dittman, A. T. (1977) The role of body movement in communication. In A. W. Siegman & S. Feldstein (Eds.), *Nonverbal behavior and communication.* Potomac, Md.: Lawrence Erlbaum.

Donaghy, W. C. (1980) *Our silent language: An introduction to nonverbal communication.* Dubuque, Iowa: Gorsuch Scarisbrick.

Duncan, S., Jr., & Fiske, D. C. (1977) *Face-to-face interaction: Research methods and theory.* New York: Lawrence Erlbaum/Halsted Press.

---

* Reprinted with permission of Macmillan Publishing Co., Inc. from *Sense Relaxation below your Mind* by Bernard Gunther. Copyright © 1968 by Bernard Gunther.

Eakins, B. W., & Eakins, R. G. (1978) *Sex differences in human communication.* Boston: Houghton Mifflin.

Edelmann, R. J., & Hampson, S. E. (198!) The recognition of embarrassment. *Personality and Social Psychology Bulletin, 7* (1), 109–116.

Ekman, P. (1976) Movements with precise meanings. *Journal of Communication, 26* (3), 14–26.

Ekman, P., Friesen, W. V., & Bear, J. (1984) The international language of gestures. *Psychology Today, 18* (5), 64–69.

Ekman, P., Friesen, W. V., & Scherer, K. R. (1976) Body movement and voice pitch in deceptive interaction. *Semiotica, 16,* 23–27.

Goffman, E. (1961) *Encounters: Two studies in the sociology of interaction.* Indianapolis, Ind.: Bobbs-Merrill.

Grayson, B., & Stein, M. I. (1981) Attracting assault: Victims' nonverbal cues. *Journal of Communication, 31,* 68–75.

Henley, N. M. (1977) *Body politics.* Englewood Cliffs, N.J.: Prentice-Hall.

Hocking, J. E., Bauchner, J., Kaminski, E. P., & Miller, G. R. (1979) Detecting deceptive communication from verbal, visual, and paralinguistic cues. *Human Communication Research, 6* (1), 33–46.

Jancovic, M., Devoe, S., & Wiener, M. (1975) Age related changes in hand and arm movements on nonverbal communication: Some conceptualizations and an empirical exploration. *Child Development, 46,* 922–928.

Johnson, A. (December 2, 1980) Rolfing: A new twist to the school of hard knocks. *The Phoenix Gazette,* p. C-2.

Kendon, A. (1983) Gesture and speech: How they interact. In J. M. Wiemann & R. P. Harrison (Eds.), *Nonverbal interaction.* Beverly Hills, Calif.: Sage Publications.

Key, M. R. (1975) *Paralanguage and kinesics (Nonverbal communication).* Metuchen, N.J.: Scarecrow Press.

Knapp, M. (1978) *Nonverbal communication in human interaction* (2nd ed.). New York: Holt, Rinehart, and Winston.

Kudoh, T., & Matsumoto, D. (1985) Cross-cultural examination of the semantic dimensions of body postures. *Journal of Personality and Social Psychology, 48* (6), 1440–1446.

Kurtz, R., & Prestera, H. (1976) *The body reveals.* New York: Harper & Row/ Quicksilver Books.

LaFrance, M. (1985) Postural mirroring and intergroup relations. *Personality and Social Psychology Bulletin, 11* (2), 207–217.

McGinley, H., Blau, G. L., & Takai, M. (1984) Attraction effects of smiling and body position: A cultural comparison. *Perceptual and Motor Skills, 58* (3), 915–922.

Marcos, L. R. (1979) Nonverbal behavior and thought processing. *Archives of General Psychiatry, 36* (9), 940–943.

Maurer, R. E., & Tindall, J. H. (1983) Effect of postural congruence on client's perception of counselor empathy. *Journal of Counseling Psychology, 30* (2), 158–163.

Mehrabian, A. (1971) *Silent messages.* Belmont, Calif.: Wadsworth.

Morris, D. (July 1979) What your walk says about the way you think, work, love. *Mademoiselle,* pp. 141–143.

Pechmann, T., & Deutsch, W. (1982) The development of verbal and nonverbal devices for reference. *Journal of Experimental Child Psychology, 34* (2), 330–341.

Petty, R. E., Wells, G. L., Heesacker, M., Brock, T. C., & Cacioppo, J. T. (1983) Effects of recipient posture on persuasion: A cognitive response analysis. *Personality and Social Psychology Bulletin, 9* (2), 209–222.

Riseborough, M. G. (1981) Physiographic gestures as decoding facilitators: Three experiments exploring a neglected facet of communication. *Journal of Nonverbal Behavior, 5* (3), 172–183.

Riskind, J. H. (1984) They stoop to conquer: Guiding and self-regulatory functions of physical posture after success and failure. *Journal of Personality and Social Psychology, 47* (3), 479–493.

Rosenthal, R. (1979) *Skill in nonverbal communication: Individual differences.* Cambridge, England: Oelgeschlager, Gunn, & Hain.

Rubenstein, C. (August 1980) Body language that speaks to muggers. *Psychology Today,* p. 20.

Ruggieri, V., Celli, C., & Crescenzi, A. (1982) Gesturing and self contact of right and left halves of the body: Relationship with eye contact. *Perceptual and Motor Skills, 55* (3.1), 695–698.

Scheflen, A. E. (1972) *Body language and the social order: Communication as behavioral control.* Englewood Cliffs, N.J.: Prentice-Hall.

Sousa-Poza, J. F., & Rohrberg, R. (1977) Body movement in relation to type of information (person- and nonperson-oriented) and cognitive style (field independence). *Human Communication Research, 4* (1), 19–29.

Walker, M. B., & Nazmi, M. K. (1979) Communicating shapes by words and gestures. *Australian Journal of Psychology, 31* (2), 137–143.

Weisfeld, G. E., & Beresford, J. M. (1982) Erectness of posture as an indicator of dominance or success in humans. *Motivation and Emotion, 6* (2), 113–131.

CHAPTER 5

FACIAL EXPRESSION AND EYE BEHAVIOR

*There is such a thing as looking through a
person's eyes into the heart, and learning more
of the height, and breadth, and depth of another's
soul in one hour than it might take a lifetime to
discover.*

Anne Bronte, *The Tenant of Wildfell Hall,* 1848

Whether staring is constitutional or not, it is a violation of a social norm and upsets people. Don't stare; people hate it. Your eyes and face communicate important messages. Is your face the *you* that you want to communicate? Many of us don't think so, and we spend millions of dollars each year to alter our facial appearance. In everyday conversation we hear, "I've got to put my face on," "I'm going to cover this mess," and "I can't go out with my face like this." To put our best face forward we buy cosmetics, use medications, apply ointments and creams, and undergo plastic surgery.

You may ask, "Why is so much emphasis placed on the appearance of the face?" Our society stresses the importance of "beautiful people," and often beauty is associated with the physical characteristics of the face. Every time we turn on a television or open a magazine we see beautiful people. These people may be selling a new scented shampoo or modeling the latest three-piece suit. By using people with attractive faces, advertisers imply that if we use the shampoo or wear the suit, we, too, will be beautiful.

Faces provide us with a wealth of information. Through facial observation we make predictions about the race, nationality, sex, and age of people we meet. Have you ever known identical twins? If you had difficulty in telling the twins apart, imagine each of us with identical facial features. Think of the problems we would have in recognizing each other.

Differences in human faces are limitless, and the differences allow us to recognize each other. Often one facial characteristic helps us to recognize others and acts as a trademark, for example, Liz Taylor's violet eyes or Barbra Streisand's nose.

From facial characteristics we also make predictions about the type of person someone is or the personality someone may have. For example, when selecting actresses and actors for roles, directors have to take facial features into consideration. Facial features help us to identify the so-called "good guys" and "bad guys." Audiences usually picture hardened criminals with dark, beady, closely set eyes, sunken cheeks, small, thin lips, and heavy beards, while damsels in distress typically have large, blue eyes with long lashes, fair complexions, small, well-defined noses, and small, full mouths. Although many performers indeed are selected for their natural facial characteristics, makeup helps build stereotypes.

Some areas of the face give us more cues about the context of a situation and the person's personality than others. One aspect of facial communication that spans different cultures is a form of sign language called tongue showing. Tongue showing usually occurs when tasks or interactions are difficult or undesirable. Notice yourself and others around you the next time you play a game of concentration such as pickup sticks or bridge.

Tongue display is common in all age groups. While observing children in a nursery school, Smith, Chase, and Lieblich (1974) found that children show their tongues during difficult tasks such as putting a puzzle together and in awkward social settings such as being scolded or embarrassed. Another study observed pool players and found that the poor players displayed their tongues more than the better players. This study also found that all players displayed their tongues twice as much on difficult shots as on easy ones (*Saturday Review of Education,* 1973).

Facial features also affect interpersonal relationships and judgments in interaction. Can you remember your last blind date and how you rated her or him? Was your first impression based on clothing, body shape, or personality? Probably not. Although we do notice clothing, body shapes, and so on, when forming impressions about others, most of us first judge others by facial features. We respond more favorably to those we find attractive. As you have seen in an earlier chapter, physical attractiveness affects our judgments of personality, marital competence, social and professional adjustment, and happiness. In addition, physical attractiveness increases perceived honesty and sincerity. According to research, women with beautiful facial features are less often convicted of crimes than are men or unattractive women.

However, through continued social interaction we begin to accept and reject others based on characteristics other than facial features. For example, many of us now have close friends whom we disliked at first sight. Although we do form first impressions based on a person's facial features, we also look to the face to provide other types of information about the communication situation and the individual.

The face is a primary nonverbal communicator of feelings and emotion (see chapter sections on emotion). Phrases like "His face was an open book," "It was all over her face," and "His face said it all" give us an indication of how much faces are capable of communication. According to Ekman and Friesen (1967), facial expressions usually communciate the quality and nature of emotions, while body cues tell more about the intensity of emotions. The following discussion will examine theoretical aspects of facial expression and facial expression of emotion.

DEVELOPMENT OF FACIAL EXPRESSION

The variety of facial expressions in everyday interactions is limitless. In a matter of seconds we see everything from sympathetic looks on a person's face on learning some sad news to amused expressions on another's face on hearing a good joke. This section will present theories of acquisition, development, and universality in facial expression.

Acquisition

One of the first researchers to take an interest in the types and influences of facial expression was Charles Darwin (1872). Darwin led the way in describing facial expressions of infants by producing accurate eyewitness accounts and photographs of facial, vocal, and gestural signs of emotion. He used this evidence to support his belief that facial expressions were universal and innate (Trevarthen, 1984, p. 130) and were acquired primarily to establish successful interaction. Primitive peoples, for example, communicated friendliness, dissatisfaction, and other emotions by facial expression when unable to do so verbally. Darwin suggests that as humans found other methods of communicating (i.e., language), facial expressions developed into a secondary method of communication.

Other theorists such as Birdwhistell (1970) and Mead (1975) identify facial expression as a learned skill connected to language within each culture. They believe facial expressions are used to reinforce verbal messages. Say your friend Ann asked your opinion of her new curly hairstyle. You decide you don't like it. However, to avoid hurting her feelings, you probably would say that you did like it or that you had to get used to it. According to theorists, Ann would doubt you unless your facial expression supported your verbal message. Although some researchers believe in the universality of facial expression, many others believe that similarities are only coincidental.

Tomkins (1984) suggests that facial expressions are innate but may have certain learned qualities. He believes that there are primary facial expressions that are universal and innate but that there are also cultural variations in their display. For example, young children laugh spontaneously when adults make faces for them, but as they grow up, they learn to look ashamed when they have been caught doing something wrong.

Evidence that blind and sighted children have similar facial expressions contributes to the idea that facial expressions are not entirely based on imitative learning. Eibl-Eibesfeldt has shown that children born blind and deaf—or blind, deaf, and retarded, or even blind, deaf, and without arms—smile, laugh, cry, and frown much like normal children. Blind children will also hide their faces with their hands when they are embarrassed and will "stare" in the general direction of a familiar voice (Collier, 1985, p. 72). Eibl-Eibesfeldt's contributions support research indicating that facial expresions are only partially based on imitative learning. The following section will explain the developmental processes of facial expressions and how facial expressions can be both innate and learned.

Developmental Processes

Facial expressions of parents, relatives, and friends are an important source of information for a developing child. The exact time that infants begin to respond to facial expressions of others is uncertain. However, according to Gorsen, Sarty, and Wu (1975), newborns (average age, nine minutes) will track a moving face more than they will track three other similar stimuli. By eight weeks, they develop special meaning for the face and begin to scan it visually in search of the eyes (Carey, 1981, p. 11). Since the infant is helpless, eye contact serves a crucial role in establishing and bonding the relationship between the caretaker and the infant. (For a more complete discussion, see section on eye contact in the following pages.)

Research also indicates that children begin to perceive meanings behind facial expression before they can demonstrate the facial behaviors themselves (Odom and Lemond, 1972). Babies receive cues about moods of those around them, and this may explain why babies are fussy when there is emotional conflict in their home.

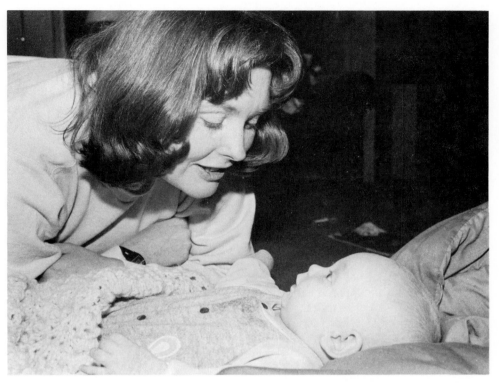

Even very young infants respond to facial expressions. (Michael Weisbrot and Family)

According to Sroufe (1978), infants begin to express laughter by the fourth month of age. By six months, they manifest a capacity to protest and can act with aggressive self-assertion (Trevarthen, 1984, p. 149). However, this ability to express anger acts as a necessary defense mechanism for children. For example, it allows them to signal to others that they are hungry, need their diapers changed, are sick, and so on.

By the end of their first year, normal children usually have recognizable facial expressions. From ages three to ten, the ability to recognize, discriminate, and imitate facial expressions of others significantly increases. For example, by the age of five, children can satisfactorily pose expressions of anger, fear, and sadness (Ekman and Oster, 1982, p. 158). From ages six to ten, they begin to develop rules for managing emotional expression (Saarni, 1978).

According to Hamilton (1973), children also learn to inhibit spontaneous productions of emotion. Society teaches children which expressions of emotion are acceptable and unacceptable. At early ages, children are admonished with such expressions as "Big boys don't cry" or "If you don't stop pouting, your face will grow like that" (Hamilton, p. 138).

Sometimes children are punished for displays of inappropriate emotions. For example, if little Laura pouts when her mother tells her to come inside to clean up her room, her mother may spank her. If Laura gets spanked each time she pouts, eventually she'll learn to hide the felt emotion to avoid another spanking.

Although they learn to inhibit their expressions of emotion at an early age, children take quite a while to distinguish between contradictory nonverbal messages. Children take negative messages very seriously, even when accompanied by smiles. If Jason's teacher smiles at him while telling him he did poorly on a reading assignment, Jason will usually focus on the negative verbal message. Children usually believe the worst. A teenager can understand that his parents love him even if they yell at him for coming in late; a small child, however, has difficulty in believing that she is loved when a parent yells at her for breaking a lamp.

The previous sections explained how facial expressions are both innate and learned. The following section will discuss cultural differences in facial expression.

Universality

Some nonverbal behaviors differ across cultures (such as those mentioned in Chapter 11), but most facial expressions are now universally associated with particular emotions. For example, try to remember the times you have seen children's faces on posters for such organizations as CARE, Project Uplift, or HUNGER. Was it difficult for you to translate the message, even though the child's home was in India, China, or Mexico? Researchers have found that observers from the United States, England, Germany, Spain, France, Switzerland, Greece, and Japan interpret facial expressions as showing the same kinds of emotion. Observers from different cultures are also accurate at judging the intensity of the emotion expressed (Ekman and Oster, 1982, p. 148).

Why, then, have researchers differed in their view of the universality of facial expression? One reason is that there are **culture-specific differences** in the expressions of emotion, in the acceptability of an emotion, and in the rules for the appropriate display of emotion (Ekman, 1984, p. 320). For example, children in the United States often make facial expressions disapproving of or questioning actions of their parents, while in Asian countries such questioning would be highly disrespectful. In middle-eastern countries, many men display their emotions (i.e., welcoming a friend with a kiss, excitement, and so on), while in America men are expected to act more reserved. In the United States children might be punished for frowning at requests from parents, while in some Oriental cultures the same behavior would cause the child to be disowned.

Ekman (1971) suggests that it is "likely that there is much more cultural variability in blends of facial expression than in facial expressions of primary emotions" (p. 223). When observing differing cultures one must remember that cultural differences depend on the circumstances that elicit an emotion, the consequences of an emotion, and the display rules that govern the use of facial behavior in particular social settings.

By now you should have gained a better understanding of the development of facial expression. The next sections of the chapter will examine differences in facial expression of emotion.

EXPRESSION OF EMOTION

Our faces communicate feelings and emotions to others. Spontaneous facial reactions and responses come from environmental stimuli. If you open the door to your apartment, and a group of friends shouts "Happy Birthday!" your face will unconsciously express surprise. On the other hand, if you were to open the door to your apartment and find a burglar going through your drawers, your face would probably show fear or apprehensive surprise.

Early research suggested that facial expressions were involuntary reactions, which were thought to be good indicators of emotional states. Since that time further research has revealed that facial cues are only partially reliable or accurate. We have learned to protect ourselves by concealing our true feelings (Zuckerman, Larrance, Spiegel, and Klorman, 1981). By controlling our facial muscles, we hide inappropriate or unacceptable responses; such manipulations of facial expressions are known as **facial management techniques.** In the next few sections we will examine facial management, expressions of emotion and their effects, measurement of facial expression, and differences in expression of emotion.

Facial Management

According to Ekman, Friesen, and Ellsworth (1982a), four basic facial management techniques may be incorporated in most social settings. When controlling our facial behavior, we can (1) intensify a felt emotion, (2) deintensify a felt emotion, (3) neutralize a felt emotion, or (4) mask a felt emotion (p. 17).

Intensifying.   Often societal pressures cause us to respond to the expectations of others, and at times such as these we usually exaggerate our facial behaviors to meet these expectations. Special occasions such as Christmas or birthdays encourage us to intensify felt emotions. We have all had the experience of receiving a gift in the presence of the giver; as we open the gift we express joy, surprise, and excitement even if we have three bottles of the same cologne, hate the color, or do not know what the gift is. The same would be true if you overheard someone mentioning a going-away party for you. Although you now knew about the party in advance, you would probably still show surprise and pleasure so that you wouldn't disappoint your friends. We exaggerate our facial responses to maintain positive social interactions.

Deintensifying.   In most social situations individuals also learn to deemphasize facial behaviors to maintain favorable interpersonal relationships; in other words, we monitor normal reactions to respond more appropriately to others. For example, Larry and his best friend Harry both applied for basketball scholarships at a large southern university. After a few weeks, Harry was notified that he had received a full scholarship, while Larry received none. Being sensitive to Larry's feelings, Harry deintensified his normal excitement around Larry by saying he was only lucky. We also try to deintensify feelings of anger. An employee who is angry at the boss might express the anger, but usually without yelling or using language that he or she might use with someone who is powerless.

Neutralizing.   In some situations we avoid showing any emotion. Men and women differ in the emotional displays they neutralize because of cultural norms. Men in the United States, for example, are expected to be strong and brave. Because facial displays of fear or sadness are considered feminine, men may try to neutralize them, even if they are experiencing the emotion at the time. Sometimes, however, covering natural emotions can be detrimental. At the death of his mother, Mike withheld normal expressions of sadness and grief in order to be strong for other family members. Weeks later, doctors diagnosed the cause of his nervous breakdown as the inability to accept or express normal emotions. We neutralize emotions at times when we are unsure of the outcomes.

Masking.   We frequently replace felt emotions with emotions thought to be more appropriate. Through masking we try to conceal such emotions as jealousy and disappointment. Girls running for positions in a Homecoming Court eagerly await the decision. As the announcer calls the name of the new Queen, the other girls, though bitterly disappointed, display wide smiles of approval. If you were to surprise someone you were dating with an unexpected visit and found that person having a party in his or her apartment, you might be jealous because you weren't invited. However, you probably would hide this emotion until a later time when the other people were not around.

Some people are better at controlling emotions with management techniques than others. **Affect rules** are culturally learned habits, but rarely do individuals pause to think about which rule to follow (Ekman, 1971, p. 216). The hesitation would destroy the purpose of using facial management techniques. The situation and the people involved determine which display rules will be used. It is important to remember that when facial management techniques are used appropriately they are unnoticeable; only when the rules are violated do others become aware of them. If you were to laugh at a funeral, cry when hearing a joke, or smile when someone falls down and gets hurt, others near you would probably give you looks of disapproval or concern.

From this discussion you can see that we manipulate our facial features constantly to achieve desired results. However, it should be noted that we are often unaware of what we are doing. Although we do control emotions on our face there are some emotions that are universally recognized. The following section will discuss different types of emotion and their effects.

Facial Movements to Express Emotion

Two of the best-known researchers who have developed a procedure for locating and classifying specific facial movements are Paul Ekman and Wallace Friesen

(1982). Their technique, the Facial Action Coding System (FACS), has produced a catalogue of all perceptible "action units" (AUs) which the face can present as well as the muscular changes which elicit each AU. Scorers are trained to break down any given facial movement into a set of single AU scores. From this starting point, they can classify and analyze any facial movement into its component parts.

From previous research with photographs by Ekman and his colleagues, seven basic emotions have been found to be judged fairly consistently. These emotions include happiness, sadness, surprise, fear, anger, disgust/contempt, and interest.

No one area of the face best reveals emotion. According to Boucher and Ekman (1975), the "value of the different facial areas in distinguishing emotions depends upon the emotion being judged." They pinpoint anger as the most ambiguous expression of emotion because, unlike the other emotions, anger must be registered in at least two areas of the face, namely, the eyes and the mouth, in order for it to be recognized accurately.

Measurement of Facial Expression

Although emotions can usually be judged accurately, we seldom display pure emotional states. Sometimes we use only one part of the face to show emotion. Such expressions are known as **partials** (Burgoon and Saine, 1978). To illustrate, a kidnap victim who is trying to remain calm might show fear in the eyes but not in any other area of the face.

In everyday interactions we can also express a mixture of the primary emotions. These mixtures are most often labeled **affect blends** (Ekman, Friesen, and Ellsworth, 1982a, p. 19). If you open your door and see a friend whom you have not seen in five years, you may show surprise in your eye area and happiness in the area of your mouth.

Affect blends occur often in interpersonal relationships. Specifically, they are thought to occur when (1) an emotion-producing circumstance, by its very nature, produces more than one feeling, or (2) habitual facial responses to one emotion become linked with a different response to a second emotion (Ekman, Friesen, and Ellsworth, 1982a, p. 19). For example, if you were listening with some of your more conservative friends to your favorite comedienne telling an off-color joke, your face might show several emotions at once, resulting in a blend.

Sometimes emotions expressed on the face are unobservable in normal conversatons. For example, in a classic study conducted in 1966, Haggard and Isaacs noticed, while analyzing nonverbal communication between a therapist and patient on a slow-motion film, that facial expressions could change drastically within a few seconds of film. These brief facial expressions have been labeled **micromomentary facial expressions.**

Micromomentary facial expressions often reveal actual emotional states unidentifiable unless played in slow motion. The slow-motion film reveals many expressions that are incompatible with the person's verbal message and perceived facial expressions. Psychologists and counselors are tremendously interested in micromomentary facial expressions of clients because they enable them to detect expressions of emotion that they formerly would have missed. If a young woman, observed on slow-motion film, had brief expressions of anger while telling a counselor that she loved her mother, the counselor would probably try to discover what caused the display of anger.

Facial expressions communicate many emotions spontaneously; however, observers must be careful because many factors can influence their interpretation. We have identified emotions that are universally accepted, but now let's look at sex and situational differences.

Sex and Situational Differences

The functions and types of facial expressions are similar for males and females, but differences do occur in interaction behaviors. As mentioned earlier, societal pressures often inhibit a man's expression of emotion. Women usually reveal their emotions more often than men, while men may feel emotions of happiness or sadness very strongly without displaying emotion on the face.

Moreover, males are more often **internalizers** than females. Internalizers are persons who inhibit overt expression of their own feelings. Generally, this phenomenon is believed to be a function of the overall socialization process, or the means by which we acquire cultural rules (Buck, 1984, pp. 222–223). For example, American males are taught not to cry or show emotion in public. However, in learning this rule, they also (indirectly) learn to internalize their feelings.

Many of us have probably seen the slogan "Smile—and they'll wonder what you've been up to." Often we do wonder if people are smiling because they are happy, covering something, or nervous; however, one reason we smile is to seek approval. When seeking approval, both sexes smile more often. Research also indicates that women smile more than men, whether or not they are happy. We've all known people who smiled constantly, and we usually questioned their sincerity until we knew them better. For example, the movie, "Animal House" well exemplified the stereotype of "plastic smiles" at sorority and fraternity rush parties (Rosenfeld, 1966).

In making judgments about facial expressions, we may be accurate or inaccurate. For example, infants expressing negative emotions are more likely to be judged boys and infants expressing positive emotions are more likely to be judged girls (Haviland, 1977). The inference, obviously, may not be correct.

Children respond differently to male and female smiles. Even though females smile more often than males, children attribute greater friendliness to male smiles. One reason may be that children interpret a male's smile as being more sincere because males usually smile only when happy or amused. Females, unlike males, are found to smile more often when giving negative messages (Bugental, Love, and Gianetto, 1971, p. 317).

Women are slightly more accurate and adept in judging facial expressions than are men, particularly when they are attempting to decode facial expressions of emotion. To test this hypothesis, Kirouac and Dore (1983) asked male and female subjects to identify the emotions being displayed in a series of photo slides.

Results of their study supported the hypothesis that women do perform slightly better in decoding facial expressions.

Along with sex differences in facial expression, we must also consider the situational differences that affect our perceptions. Our faces communicate independent information about us and our actions in a given situation. Studies examining whether the context or the facial expressions have greater influence in determining perception are inconclusive. However, it is believed that both the face and the context in which it is viewed combine directly to form our judgments of a given emotional display (Spignesi and Shor, 1981).

Now that we have discussed the effects of sex and situation on judgments of emotion in facial expressions, we turn to how facial expressions are judged and how their interpretations affect social interaction.

Judgments and Interpretations

For years researchers have tried to determine the number of emotions the face is capable of displaying. Seven basic emotions are judged accurately in most social situations, and studies utilize three basic methodologies to identify these facial expressions of emotion: photographs, videotapes, or real-life situations. The use of photographs is the most objective and controlled method of studying facial expression. However, recent attempts to document facial expressions have relied more heavily on videotaped and real-life interactions.

External factors cause difficulty in interpreting facial expressions of emotion. Factors that complicate judgments include prior exposure to the faces, contextual cues, emotional states of the judges, the methods by which the faces are presented to the judges (videotapes, photographs, and so on), and characteristics of the faces being judged. For the best results, judges should be trained in evaluation of facial expressions, have prior exposure to the faces, know the context, evaluate simple tasks, and have sufficient time to make the evaluation. If photos are used, the facial expressions should be made by skilled actors and should include the entire face (Knapp, 1978, p. 283)

Taking precautions when studying facial expression is important, but understanding the effects that facial expressions have on social situations is equally important, because facial expressions affect the emotional states of others. If you want someone to empathize with you, you must have the appropriate facial expression. For example, after dinner, Claire's date, John, drove to a motel; obviously, he had planned that the two of them would spend the evening there. Claire told him with a smile on her face that she was not that kind of girl and wanted to go home. John failed to believe her until her facial expression reinforced her verbal message.

Decisions are also affected by facial expressions. Emotional displays are powerful interpersonal tools in judicial decision making. According to Savitsky and Sim (1974), the emotional state displayed on the defendant's face helps determine the perceived severity of the crime, the likelihood of recurrent criminal behavior, and the disposition of the defender. These factors may be one reason why more and more trial lawyers are training their defendants in appropriate nonverbal behaviors, i.e., facial expressions, body movement, clothing, and so on.

Facial muscles can be consciously controlled in all areas of the face except the eyes. Because the eye muscles are not as readily controlled, the ocular response reveals not only the truth but also much about a person's individual personality structure. Libby and Yaklevich state: "The lower face may follow culturally transmitted display rules while the eyes may reveal the spontaneous or naked response" (Libby and Yaklevich, 1973, p. 203).

EYE BEHAVIOR

The eyes and eye behaviors have been a source of intense fascination since earliest times. The ancient Greeks believed eyes had special powers; the "evil eye" or fixed stare was believed to have the power to cause physical harm or death. Even today certain eye behaviors disturb some people. In one study, a supermarket placed large, frowning eyes in corners of the building and found that shoplifting was drastically reduced (Coss, 1974, p. 21).

Women, sensing the eye's intriguing power, began to find methods of eye adornment. As early as Cleopatra's time, belladonna was used to dilate the pupils, thereby darkening the eyes and increasing attractiveness. Other cultures fastened jewels around the eyes to accentuate them. Today, especially in Western cultures, women spend hours each day applying false eyelashes, putting on mascara, pluck-

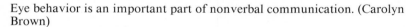

Eye behavior is an important part of nonverbal communication. (Carolyn Brown)

ing their eyebrows, and applying eye shadow to bring focus to the all-powerful eye!

Many of us have special interest in our eyes because of poor vision. Over half of the people of the United States have had their vision corrected with the aid of eyeglasses or contact lenses. If you think eyeglasses serve only a functional purpose, millions of people would disagree with you. Eyeglasses reveal much about the people who wear them. A Dun's survey of spectacled businessmen found that businessmen believed that the impression made by their glasses was as important as the suit they wore (Levy, 1976, pp. 77–78).

Americans spend over $2.4 billion a year for millions of pairs of corrective lenses. Fashion giants such as Yves St. Laurent and Oleg Cassini are designing glasses to bring eyes into a more fashionable focus. According to Alfred Poll, a noted optician in New York City, "many people are less concerned with seeing better than with how others see them" (in Levy, 1976, p. 77). More and more ophthalmic prescriptions include a facial analysis to correct physical peculiarities such as protruding eyes and long noses.

The practice of wearing or not wearing eyeglasses can be used as a protective device. Some people wear sunglasses because they can look at others without revealing interest. Myopic people with eyeglasses report that it is easier to sustain eye contact without wearing glasses. Eye contact becomes less disturbing to them because the images of the eyes are blurred (Coss, 1974, pp. 21–22).

According to *Playboy* magazine, one of the first physical characteristics noticed by both males and females is the eyes. This claim was later supported by Janik, Wellens, Goldberg, and Dell'Osso (1978), who discovered that we spend approximately 45 percent of our time looking at others' eyes. A close second focus of interest was the mouth. We have a tendency to gaze at others' mouths, which happens approximately 15 percent of the time. No other region was found to attract even 1 percent of our attention.

Recently, even more attention has been given to eyes with respect to medical diagnoses. For years medical authorities have diagnosed diabetes, brain disorders, and some metabolic diseases through examinations of the retina (Dobson, 1978, pp. 10–19), and now iridology has gained respect. This diagnostic technique, used by the Germans for decades, involves a detailed examination of the iris. Over 2,000 proponents in the United States claim that "the iris is virtually an anatomical Etch-a-Sketch, capable of revealing through coloration, fiber structure, and tint, the present, past, and future functioning conditions of every organ in the body, including any inherited genetic weaknesses and strengths" (Dobson, 1978, p. 18). Analysis of the eye cannot uncover specific diseases, but it does help pinpoint potential weaknesses in the body by matching flaws in the iris. Iridology could have a profound impact on medical diagnosis and treatment; however, most traditional physicians are reserving comment until further research is completed.

With increased interest in eye behavior, principles have been established through a variety of investigations. The remainder of this chapter will examine the functions of eye behavior, the types of eye movement, differences in eye behavior, and pupil dilation and constriction.

Functions of Eye Behavior

A primary function of eye contact is to establish relationships with others. In everyday interactions we notice the eye contact of speakers, share mutual glances with friends, become nervous when confronted with a penetrating stare, and scan rooms for familiar faces. We communicate by sharing visual interaction, whether it is labeled eye contact, gaze, or glance.

We all know how uncomfortable we feel if eye contact is different from that of our expectations. Think back to situations when a friend wouldn't look at you, when you were uncomfortable speaking to someone with a glass eye or to someone who was blind, or when you had problems in communicating over the phone. We all like to be able to see the other person and to have the other person see us so that we can receive feedback, whether that feedback is positive or negative. Eye contact is an aid to social interaction. In most interpersonal relationships eye contact signals to others that the looker is interested, attentive, and/or willing to listen to develop a relationship (Jellison and Ickes, 1974).

For the sake of clarity, it may be useful to differentiate among the concepts of "gaze," "mutual gaze," and "eye contact" at this point. Sometimes, this terminology can seem both artificial and confusing. Following the lead of Collier (1985), the term **gaze** will be defined as simply looking at another person or object. The term **mutual gaze** will be used to delineate those times when that someone looks back but does not necessarily make eye contact. (Note: Two people can look at one another without making eye contact—for example, when they are "sizing one another up.") Although the distinction is seldom made in the literature, we will reserve the term **eye contact** for those occasions in which two people look directly into one another's eyes. As Collier (1985) has argued, the time spent in eye contact is always identical for each person involved (p. 92).

Over time, researchers have examined the functions of eye behavior in human interaction. However, such examinations have been difficult, due to the extreme overlap that exists among its functions. Despite the difficulties in examining eye behavior, Kendon (1967) and Knapp (1978) have identified four major functions of eye contact. We will follow a similar format by examining how eye behavior serves (1) to establish and define relationships, (2) to control channels of communication, (3) to display emotion, and (4) to reduce distractions.

Establishing and defining relationships.   Eye contact determines the type of interaction that will take place and how the interaction will develop. Merely looking at another person is an indication of interest. Eye contact shows a willingness on your part to admit interest in others and allows others to gain information about you.

The desire to establish relationships through eye contact starts at an early age. Vulnerable infants have an innate survival instinct to search out their mother's eyes in order to have their needs taken care of. At a disco, establishing eye contact can communicate that you want to dance, be left alone, or are with someone else. For example, as Sam enters the nightclub he scans the room, looking for available females. Glancing at the bar, he catches the eyes of a hefty, middle-aged woman and quickly averts his gaze. Finally, he spots an attractive redhead and begins to stare at her. At first she avoids his gaze, but later she acknowledges his eye contact by glancing at the seat next to her. This brief glance signals Sam to join her.

When you make eye contact with someone with whom you want to establish interest or approval, eye contact will increase. Exline (1971) found that we look at a person less often when we dislike the person with whom we are talking, because looking is a signal of liking. When we want approval and attention, we look at the other person more often. For example, during a job interview, college graduates (graduating seniors) should try to maintain good eye contact to show the interviewer they are interested and alert.

As relationships develop, expectations of eye contact are established. If someone fails to accept or meet the expected standards, conflict may occur. When a female at a laundromat observes a strange male watching her intently, she will avoid his gaze to reduce the possibility of interaction. Increased eye contact is a signal of increased intimacy. If one person looks too often and for too long a time at another, the other person will feel uncomfortable with the height of the intimacy level being established (Coss, 1974, p. 18).

Reactions to differing amounts of eye contact depend on the situation. Research has revealed that love is positively related to mutual glances. One study found that eye contact causes more physiological arousal than nonmutual gaze (Mazur, Rosa, Faupel, Heller, Leen, and Thurman, 1980). In turn, prolonged looks have been found to create and heighten intimacy. Once a relationship is established (for both close friends and lovers), even brief moments of eye contact can be emotionally satisfying as long as the facial expressions are appropriate (Beier, 1974, pp. 53–56).

A study by Exline, Ellyson, and Long (1975) examined the effects of power and status on eye contact. They found that people of greater status have less direct eye contact than those of lower status, though the former may break gaze last. Another set of studies found that people look more at high-status persons (Juni and Hershkowitz-Freidman, 1981), and that couples who belong to a higher socioeconomic class have more eye contact than couples from a lower socioeconomic class (Levine and Sutton-Smith, 1973). Research also indicates that those individuals who need higher levels of affection look more often at and require more eye contact from their associates.

Just as remembering that eye contact helps to establish relationships is important, so is remembering that eye contact is essential in analyzing and monitoring feedback. Through others' visual responses we learn whether to seek out someone at a disco, to keep talking, to look more, or to avoid others' glances.

Channel control.   Eye contact often determines the type of interaction that will take place. How many times have you glanced at your watch when you were late for an appointment, looked down or away when you were embarrassed, or glared at someone who took your seat? These behaviors send messages to others and control the communication channels during interaction. Common methods of controlling the communication channel are turn-taking, power displays, and gaze aversion.

You probably have been in a situation in which everyone seemed to be talking at once; one person spoke while another chimed in. These situations are not regular occurrences, but when they do happen interaction can be very frustrating. To avoid this frustration humans have an eye behavior system of signalling to each other when to speak. These eye behavior signals are known as **turn-taking.**

You may ask where and when in the communication process visual interaction takes place. Research indicates that listeners steadily increase speaker-directed gaze and head nods as a role-change strategy. Wiemann and Knapp found that eye contact increased from 61 percent in the first third of the conversation to 83 percent in the last third of the conversation. When speakers acknowledge the turn-taking cues, they briefly look away from the listener (Wiemann and Knapp, 1975). An earlier study by Kendon (1967) also indicated that speakers increase the time spent looking at their auditors as their speaking turn approaches completion, and that speakers are less likely to break eye contact before the end of a question.

The purpose of turn-taking behavior is to help define relationships. For turn-taking cues to be successful both of the interactants must make eye contact at or

Eye contact—and avoidance of eye contact—serves a variety of functions in communication. (Carolyn Brown)

near the exchange point. These cues help us to know when to yield conversation, to obtain and check feedback, or to continue the interaction.

Channels of communication are also used as **power displays.** Have you ever felt someone's stare or felt eyes that could look straight through you? How did you feel? Most people become uncomfortable and want to avoid steady, direct gazes. These gazes are often power displays, and we react to this power with another stare or gaze aversion.

Uninterrupted gaze (a stare) is not necessarily threatening but is usually interpreted as a gesture of assertiveness or display of dominance (Mazur, Rosa, Faupel, Heller, Leen, & Thurman, 1980). In addition, such "stares" usually indicate that a response is desired. However, researchers have documented a more positive function of steady gaze as well. For example, a steady gaze from someone whom we love can give us a sense of interpersonal involvement and can also serve as a sign of close, personal bonding. Additionally, a steady gaze can be a request for aid (Mazur, Rosa, Faupel, Heller, Leen, and Thurman, 1980).

When we feel uncomfortable, we usually avoid direct eye contact. This response has been labeled by researchers as **gaze aversion,** and is usually defined as a biological response to high levels of arousal (Hutt and Ounsted, 1966). Gaze aversion begins at an early age but is generally "perfected" by the time a child reaches the age range of five to nine (Scheman and Lockard, 1979). As they mature, children practice gaze aversion by turning their entire heads and bodies. Adults also avert gaze by glancing to one side or the other when wishing to disengage an interaction.

In summary, there are several methods of controlling channels of communication through eye contact. We engage in turn-taking, power displays, and gaze aversion to control interpersonal interactions. An additional eye function, however, is to be found in the actual display of emotion.

Displaying emotion.   Some say that inner emotions are revealed only through the eyes. Even though true emotions may be revealed only through the eye area, most studies measure emotions of the face holistically rather than by focusing only on the eyes. In an early attempt to learn more about the function of eyes in displaying emotion, Ekman (1971) conducted a study and found extreme changes in the eye area for the emotions of surprise and fear but little change for the emotions of disgust and happiness. The study also indicated a difficulty in labeling shame/humiliation through eye behaviors. More recent research by Ekman and his colleagues has helped to locate and define the configurations of the eye areas while displaying emotion. (For a more complete discussion, see Ekman, 1982; and Scherer and Ekman, 1984.)

Measurement of eye behavior is difficult. For accurate judgments, we must remember to include all facial features and situational cues. Photographs are often used to analyze eye behavior, but they do not allow for changes over time (see the section on measurement of facial expression). Current theorists suggest a need for more realistic situations to get a better indication of how eyes display emotion.

As with facial expression, individuals try to mask inner feelings with their eye behaviors. As we mentioned earlier, it is difficult, although not impossible, to control eye behaviors, and observers must be trained to recognize microexpressions that give away emotions. When we open an unwanted gift at Christmas or are unsuccessful in attaining public office, we cover looks of dislike or disappointment with microexpressions (see earlier section in this chapter on facial management). These microexpressions are of an involuntary nature and often indicate conflict, repression and/or efforts to conceal emotions (Ekman, Friesen, and Ellsworth, 1982b, p. 24).

Just as eyes give us information about the inner emotions of others, they can also serve as a barrier to effective communication. Although eye contact is used to establish relationships, to control channels of communication, and to display emotions, our eyes can be easily distracted by visual stimuli.

Reducing distractions.   Individuals find it difficult to concentrate when bombarded by too many visual stimuli. Since we need to keep our thoughts on the right track, we must find ways to avoid or reduce these distractions.

The social stimulation of eye contact can be a powerful distraction during interaction. Think of the times that you have looked upward to remember an idea in a speech or looked away to recall an important fact on a test. While looking away or upward we are involved in the nonvisual function of reducing distractions.

Furthermore, we usually avoid eye contact prior to speaking. This gaze avoidance helps us concentrate on what we want to say without visual distraction. Research also suggests that we briefly avert our eyes when asked questions that require reflection. The pause from looking at others helps us to organize our thoughts.

Throughout the preceding discussion we have examined the functions of eye behavior. We have found that eye contact serves to establish and define relationships, to control channels of communication, to display emotions, and to reduce distractions. In the next section we will discuss different types of eye movement.

Eye Movement

When we are asked questions like "Who is your favorite comedian?" or "What is your favorite television program?" we usually move our eyes to the left or the right before answering. Research suggests that these eye movements may be indicators of the mode of information processing we are using (Galin and Ornstein, 1974).

According to psychological research, the direction of eye movement and the asymmetry of the brain are related. People have two processing hemispheres. The left hemisphere is the rational lobe, concerned with linguistic, mathematical, and reasoning tasks. The right hemisphere is the intuitive lobe, used to process spatial, imagistic, and gestalt tasks. For example, if you are right-handed, balancing your checkbook will be a task for the left hemisphere of your brain, while the process of listening to your favorite record album will be a task for the right hemisphere.

Most people can be classified as left- or right-eye movers. The joint movement of eyes to the right or left is known as **conjugatelateral eye movement** (CLEM). People who shift their eyes to the left would be using the right hemisphere to process information. Research indicates that about 75 percent of all lateral eye movement occurs in one direction. To determine whether someone is a left- or right-eye mover, a simple test may be given. Simply ask a question that will cause your listener to reflect on the answer and watch the direction of his or her eye movement. Possible questions include "How many letters are there in the word Mississippi?" or "How much is 12 times 34?" Besides learning whether a person is a left- or right-eye mover, recent research suggests personality differences between the two (Bakan, 1971, p. 96).

Another interesting area of eye movement is concerned with **blinking behavior.** Observe someone who is trying to solve a problem or who is daydreaming. How often does the person blink? Research suggests that people cannot think and blink at the same time. Indeed, one study found that when subjects' blinking is slowed, information is processed from memory more easily. Some theorists suggest that the process of retrieving information from our memory banks is affected by vision (Science Digest, 1976). Thus as we scan our brain for mental pictures, our blinking is slowed.

Slowed blinking is positively correlated to doing well in school. A study by Breed and Colarita (1974) observed that those students who blinked less and looked around less during a lecture scored considerably better on tests. Observations also reveal that people tend to blink at the end of sentences when reading and after completing a thought (Science Digest, 1976). If this statement is true, you should be blinking about now.

Differences in Eye Behavior

In examining the functions and types of eye movement and behavior, we have made no mention of individual differences. This section will attempt to give insight into the effects of sex, personality, culture, and context on eye behavior.

Sex differences.   The functions and types of eye behavior are similar for males and females, but one must consider sexual differences in terms of the frequency, distance, and duration of eye contact. Sex differences in human interaction are unapparent until about the fourth grade; at approximately this age, society's influences begin to affect visual interaction. Because little boys are reprimanded more often and are given more negative sanctions than little girls, boys may be more likely to interpret an adult's gaze as one of disapproval. In contrast, girls may interpret an adult's gaze as more approving, which may relate to their tendency to look more at adults (Vlietstra and Manske, 1981, pp. 32–33).

Environmental influences train women to be more aware of visual cues than men. Women are usually taught to give special attention to dress, color, spatial arrangements, and so on. The eye contact of many women becomes an emotional expression of striving to build social relationships (Rubin, 1970). Women strive to build social relationships by looking more often, by holding gazes longer, and by looking more while speaking and being spoken to (Libby, 1970).

Research also suggests that females look more at people they like but less when giving false impressions to the person in question. When males increase eye contact while talking they are seen to be more active than females with the same amount of eye contact (Argyle, Lebebure, and Cook, 1974). Apparently, both males and females look more at each other as the physical distance increases between them. Argyle and Ingham (1972) found that large distances are more comfortable for women than for men. Although there are sex differences that distinguish between men's and women's eye behavior, research has also found personality differences.

Personality differences.　　The eyes help to communicate social roles, individual desires, intentions, and spontaneous reactions in social interactions. As the eyes express themselves, much is revealed about an individual's personality structure.

Personality affects the degree to which people return the gaze of another person. Think about those people around you who look you straight in the eye and of those who do not. Do they have any personality similarities? Research indicates that extroverts have greater eye contact and look more frequently than introverts (Rutter, Morley, and Graham, 1972). Individuals with greater eye contact are seen as attractive and described with favorable adjectives such as friendly, confident, sincere, and mature, while those subjects showing little eye contact are described as cold, pessimistic, defensive, and immature (Kleck and Nuessle, 1968).

Although eye contact is not always an indication of our personalities, we need to be sensitive to what we may be communicating. We must remember that we are seen more positively, whether telling favorable or unfavorable information, when we use greater amounts of eye contact (Argyle, Lebebure, and Cook, 1974, p. 126). In learning to become aware of the effects of our eye contact, we should also learn about cultural differences in eye behavior.

Cultural differences.　　Cross-cultural differences in patterns of eye behavior are a potential problem in social interaction. Misunderstandings and conflicts are often caused by too much or too little eye contact. Effective communication depends upon a shared understanding of behavioral cues.

LaFrance and Mayo (1976) compared the eye behavior between black and white Americans and found a tendency for many blacks to avoid looking others directly in the eyes. They also found that whites in the study judged listeners who did avoid looking them in the eyes as uninterested and withholding. Awkwardness occurs because of dissimilar visual cues. Many visual turn-taking behaviors are different for blacks and whites. For example, in one situation in the study, white listeners were cued to speak when the black speakers paused with a sustained gaze. When the whites did speak they found themselves speaking while the blacks were speaking because of different interpretations of turn-taking cues (LaFrance and Mayo, 1976).

Some cultures give more emphasis to the observance of eye behaviors than others. Koreans are especially concerned with expressions communicated by the eyes. Koreans call the awareness of eye behavior *nuichee.* Because of status differences and customs most Koreans look to the eyes for real answers of the heart so they will not be embarrassed by unexpected answers to questions they ask. For example, a Korean farmer rented land from a neighbor. His rent was due, but he was unable to pay until he sold his crop. Before the farmer asked for a delay in payment, he searched the eyes of his neighbor for acceptance and approval, for if the neighbor refused his request the farmer would lose face. Finally, the farmer did ask his neighbor for a delay, which he received, but only after reading his neighbor's eye behavior correctly. But besides cultural differences in eye behavior, one must also consider topic and task differences.

Contextual differences.   Eye contact varies according to contextual and situational cues. Some situations create expectations of increased visual interaction while others decrease visual interaction. Think about the gaze behaviors of a small boy caught with the cookie jar in his hands, a group of friends sharing the latest gossip, or a newly engaged couple discussing marriage plans. Eye contact usually increases when people are comfortable, interested, or happy and decreases when people are embarrassed, guilty, or sad. Since eye contact is a sign of openness, looking away or avoiding eye contact during uncomfortable situations protects the individual.

Gaze also affects how information is received by listeners. Speakers who have greater degrees of eye contact are seen as more skilled, informed, experienced, and friendly. A study by Mehrabian and Williams (1969) found that people trying to persuade others gaze more often at their listeners. Studies also reveal that students learn more when their instructors gaze at them more often (Breed and Colarita, 1974, p. 76). Instructors reported that students who rated high on eye contact also scored higher on tests.

Eye behavior is affected by sex, personality, cultural, and contextual differences in human interaction. Another aspect of the eye that affects human interaction is the role of pupil dilation and constriction in interpersonal eye contact.

Pupil Dilation and Constriction

Many of you have stood before a mirror and observed the effects of varying amounts of light on your pupil size, but have you ever noticed differences in your pupil size in other situations? We can control the size of our pupils with light, but we are unable to consciously control pupil dilation and constriction. For this reason true feelings and emotions usually reveal themselves in the depths of a person's eyes.

One of the first people to study the process of pupil dilation and constriction was Eckhard Hess. In one of his preliminary studies (Hess and Polt, 1960), he presented five photographs to male and female subjects. The results indicated that pupils enlarged when the subjects were presented a positive stimulus (muscle man and baby for women; nude females for men). Further research also supported Hess's findings that dilation occurs with positive stimuli or things of interest (Borlow, 1969; and Hays and Plax, 1971).

Along with research concerning positive stimuli, other studies suggest that pupils dilate when we are involved in tasks that are mentally or emotionally difficult (Krinsky and Nelson, 1981). While taking an exam, telling someone that you love him or her, or working on a favorite craft, your pupil size may enlarge. Even the anticipation of a difficult problem or an emotional situation can increase pupil size.

Hess (1975) believes that pupillary research is valuable in indicating the degree of individual interest and attention. He also believes that "pupil response in combination with other physiological measures can be a powerful tool in discriminating attitudes which may be relatively hidden even to the consciousness of the individual concerned" (p. 156).

People are more attracted to others with enlarged pupils. Research indicates that men are more attracted to females with large pupils. Most cover layouts and photographs are selected by men (Hess, 1975, p. 95), and if you notice the covers of popular magazines you'll see people with enlarged pupils. According to Andersen, Todd-Mancillas, and Clementa (1980), people with dilated pupils are more attractive both physically and socially. However, although you may prefer looking at or socializing with a person with large pupils, that does not mean you would also choose to work with that person. The Andersen study found that pupil size had no effect on a person's attractiveness as a work partner.

Interestingly, research has shown that pupil dilation has a reciprocal effect on the person observing the dilated pupils. Males looking at a photograph of a female with dilated pupils underwent greater pupil dilation than males looking at a photograph of a female with constricted pupils (Hess, 1965; Hess and Goodwin, 1973; Simms, 1967). The same effect was found when females were shown photographs of males with dilated or constricted pupils (Simms, 1967). The females who were shown the pictures of males with enlarged pupils underwent the greater amount of pupil dilation. Apparently, when we look at members of the opposite sex who have enlarged or dilated pupils, we not only perceive them as more attractive but our pupils also dilate.

There are differences in pupil size among different groups. Research has found that the younger one is, the larger the pupils are. Infants and small children have large pupils—a fact that is very advantageous, since their enlarged pupils make them more attractive to those who care for them. Experimental research also has shown that blue-eyed people have larger pupillary responses. The popular statement that men prefer blondes may be partially attributed to pupillary response, since most natural blondes have blue eyes, and their pupil changes are easier to perceive.

In the sixties, many groups were interested in measuring attitudes with pupillary research. The advertising industry was particularly interested in individual pupil responses. Much of their enthusiasm vanished when studies failed to support the theory that pupils constrict when observing negative stimuli (Rice, 1974). However, in later research, Hess (1975) attributed the contradictions to the lack of proper research applications. Today, advanced technology has increased the reliability of measurement with television pupillometers.

With advanced technology many see bright research possibilities for pupillometry. The largest potential markets will probably be in social attitudes and in clinical and therapeutic procedures. The study of the pupil may be used in all areas—so don't be surprised if your pupillary response is measured in your next job interview.

SUMMARY

Faces and eyes provide a wealth of information and influence interaction by helping you to recognize others, predict personalities, and interpret complex situations. Facial expressions are universally associated with particular emotions because they communicate the quality and nature of emotions. Although there are specific differences within cultures that cause emotions to be expressed, theories of acquisition and development suggest that facial expressions are both innate and learned.

Early research indicated that facial expressions were primarily involuntary reactions to situations, but since that time facial expressions have been viewed as only partially reliable. Through the use of facial management techniques people control facial expressions of emotion by intensifying, deintensifying, neutralizing, or masking felt emotions. Manifestations of partials, affect blends, and micromomentary expressions depend on sex and situational differences. Fear, anger, happiness, surprise, disgust, sadness, and interest are seven basic emotions that can be judged accurately.

Muscles can be controlled consciously in all areas of the face except the eyes. This is one reason why eyes and eye behavior have been a source of intense fascination for thousands of years. A primary function of eye contact is to establish and define relationships with others. Eye behavior also serves to control channels of communication, to display emotion, and to reduce distractions.

Eye movements also transmit information nonverbally. The direction of eye movement is related to brain information processing. Personality differences are associated with right- and left-eye movers. One type of eye movement, blinking, is often ignored, but research suggests that we cannot think and blink at the same time. Good students blink less than poor students. Although eye behavior serves the four different functions noted above, there are individual differences in the frequency, duration, and distance of eye contact. Eye behavior is influenced by sex differences, personality differences, cultural differences, and contextual differences.

A final area of eye behavior concerns pupil dilation and constriction. Pupils characteristically enlarge when positive stimuli are present and grow smaller when negative stimuli are present. Large-pupilled and light-eyed people seem to have an advantage over others because they are perceived as more attractive than others. Although there have been conflicting results when studying pupillometry, advanced technology has increased the reliability and accuracy of pupil dilation and constriction measurement.

References

Andersen, P. A., Todd-Mancillas, W. R., & Clementa, L. D. (1980) The effects of pupil dilation as physical, social, and task attraction. *Australian SCAN of Nonverbal Communication, 7–8,* 89–96.

Argyle, M., & Ingham, R. (1972) Gaze, mutual gaze and proximity. *Semiotica, 6,* 32–49.

Argyle, M., Lebebure, L., & Cook, M. (1974) The meanings of five patterns of gaze. *European Journal of Social Psychology, 4* (2), 125–136.

Bakan, P. (April 1971) The eyes have it. *Psychology Today,* pp. 64–67, 96.

Beier, G. (October 1974) Nonverbal communication: How we send emotional messages. *Psychology Today,* pp. 52–56.

Birdwhistell, R. L. (1970) *Kinesics and context.* Philadelphia: University of Pennsylvania Press.

Borlow, J. D. (1969) Pupillary size as an index of preference in political candidates. *Perceptual and Motor Skills, 28,* 587–590.

Boucher, J. D., & Ekman, P. (1975) Facial areas of emotional information. *Journal of Communication, 25,* 21–29.

Breed, G., & Colarita, V. (1974) Looking, blinking, and sitting. *Journal of Communication, 24* (2), 75–81.

Buck, R. (1984) *The communication of emotion.* New York: Guilford Press.

Bugental, D. E., Love, L. R., & Gianetto, R. M. (1971) Verbal–nonverbal conflict in parental messages to normal and disturbed children. *Journal of Personality and Social Psychology, 17,* 314–318.

Burgoon, J. K., & Saine, T. (1978) *The unspoken dialogue: An introduction to nonverbal communication.* Boston: Houghton Mifflin.

Carey, S. (1981) The development of face perception. In G. Davies, H. Ellis, & J. Shepherd (Eds.), *Perceiving and remembering faces.* New York: Academic Press, pp. 9–38.

Collier, G. (1985) *Emotional expression.* Hillsdale, N.J.: Lawrence Erlbaum.

Coss, R. G. (1974) Reflections on the evil eye. *Human Behavior, 18,* 16–22.

Darwin, C. (1872) *The expression of emotions in man and animals.* London: John Murray. (Reprint, Chicago: University of Chicago Press, 1972.)

Dobson, J. (July 1978) A closer look at eyes. *The Atlanta Constitution Magazine,* pp. 10–19.

Ekman, P. (1971) Universals and cultural differences in facial expressions of emotions. *Nebraska Symposium on Motivation*. Lincoln, Neb.: University of Nebraska Press, pp. 207–283.

Ekman, P. (Ed.) (1982) *Emotion in the human face*, 2nd ed. Cambridge, England: Cambridge University Press.

Ekman, P. (1984) Expression and the nature of emotion. In K. R. Scherer & P. Ekman (Eds.), *Approaches to emotion*. Hillsdale, N.J.: Lawrence Erlbaum, pp. 319–343.

Ekman, P., & Friesen, W. V. (1967) Head and body cues in the judgment of emotion: A reformation. *Perceptual and Motor Skills, 24,* 711–724.

Ekman, P., & Friesen, W. V. (1982) Measuring facial movement with the facial action coding system. In P. Ekman (Ed.), *Emotion in the human face,* 2nd ed. Cambridge, England: Cambridge University Press, pp. 178–211.

Ekman, P., Friesen, W. V., & Ellsworth, P. (1982a) Conceptual ambiguities. In P. Ekman (Ed.), *Emotion in the human face,* 2nd ed. Cambridge, England: Cambridge University Press, pp. 7–21.

Ekman, P., Friesen, W. V., & Ellsworth, P. (1982b) Methodological decisions. In P. Ekman (Ed.), *Emotion in the human face,* 2nd ed. Cambridge, England: Cambridge University Press, pp. 22–38.

Ekman, P., & Oster, H. (1982) Review and prospect. In P. Ekman (Ed.), *Emotion in the human face,* 2nd ed. Cambridge, England: Cambridge University Press, pp. 147–173.

Exline, R. V. (1971) Visual interaction: The glance of power and preference. *Nebraska Symposium on Motivation*. Lincoln, Neb.: University of Nebraska Press, pp. 163–206.

Exline, R. V., Ellyson, S. L., & Long, B. (1975) Visual behavior as an aspect of power role relationships. In P. Pliner, L. Krames, & T. Alloway (Eds.), *Nonverbal communication of aggression*. New York: Plenum Press, pp. 21–52.

Fast, J. (1975) *The pleasure book*. New York: Stein and Day.

Galin, D., & Ornstein, R. (1974) Individual differences in cognitive style—I. Reflective eye movements. *Neuropsychologia, 12,* 367–376.

Gorsen, C. C., Sarty, M., & Wu, R. W. K. (1975) Visual following and pattern discrimination of face-like stimuli by newborn infants. *Pediatrics, 56,* 544–549.

Haggard, E. A., & Isaacs, F. S. (1966) Micromomentary facial expressions as indicators of ego mechanisms in psychotherapy. In L. A. Gottschalk & A. H. Auerback (Eds.), *Methods of research in psychotherapy*. New York: Appleton-Century-Crofts.

Hamilton, M. L. (1973) Imitative behavior and expressive ability in facial expression of emotion. *Developmental Psychology, 8* (1), 138.

Haviland, J. M. (1977) Sex-related pragmatics in infants' nonverbal communication. *Journal of Communication, 27* (2), 80–84.

Hays, E. R., & Plax, T. G. (1971) Pupillary response to supportive and aversive verbal messages. *Speech Monographs, 38,* 316–320.

Hess, E. H. (1965) Attitude and pupil size. *Scientific American, 212,* 46–54.

Hess, E. H. (1975) *The tell-tale eye*. New York: Van Nostrand Reinhold.

Hess, E. H., & Goodwin, E. (1973) The present state of pupillometrics. In M. P. Janisse (Ed.), *Pupillary dynamics and behavior.* New York: Plenum Press, pp. 248–290.

Hess, E. H., & Polt, J. M. (1960) Pupil size as related to interest value of visual stimuli. *Science, 132,* 349–350.

Hutt, C., & Ounsted, C. (1966) The biological significance of gaze aversion: With special reference to childhood autism. *Behavioral Science, 11,* 346–356.

Janik, S. W., Wellens, A. R., Goldberg, J. L. & Dell'Osso, L. F. (1978) Eyes as the center of focus in the visual examination of human faces. *Perceptual and Motor Skills, 4* (3), 857–858.

Jellison, J. M., & Ickes, W. J. (1974) The power of the glance: Desire to see and be seen in cooperation and competitive situations. *Journal of Experimental Social Psychology, 10,* 444–450.

Juni, S., & Hershkowitz-Friedman, T. (1981) Interpersonal looking as a function of status, self-esteem, and sex. *Psychological Reports, 48,* 273–274.

Kendon, A. (1967) Some functions of gaze-direction in social interaction. *Acta Psychologia, 26,* 22–63.

Kirouac, G., & Dore, F. Y. (1983) Accuracy and latency of judgment of facial expressions of emotions. *Perceptual and Motor Skills, 57,* 683–686.

Kleck, R. E., & Nuessle, W. (1968) Congruence between the indicative and communicative functions of eye contact in interpersonal relations. *British Journal of Social and Clinical Psychology, 7,* 241–246.

Knapp, M. L. (1978) *Nonverbal communication in human interaction,* 2nd ed. New York: Holt, Rinehart, & Winston.

Krinsky, R., & Nelson, T. O. (1981) Task difficulty and pupillary dilation during incidental learning. *Journal of Experimental Psychology: Human Learning and Memory, 7* (4), 293–298.

LaFrance, M., & Mayo, C. (1976) Racial differences in gaze behavior during conversations: Two systematic observational studies. *Journal of Personality and Social Psychology, 33,* 547–552.

Levine, M. H., & Sutton-Smith, B. (1973) Effects of age, sex, and task on visual behavior during dyadic interaction. *Developmental Psychology, 9* (3), 400–405.

Levy, R. (1976) Through a glass darkly. *Dun's Review, 107* (2), 77–78.

Libby, W. (1970) Eye contact and direction of looking as stable individual differences. *Journal of Experimental Research in Personality, 4,* 303–312.

Libby, W. L., & Yaklevich, D. (1973) Personality determinants of eye contact and direction of gaze aversion. *Journal of Personality and Social Psychology, 27,* 197–206.

Mazur, A., Rosa, E., Faupel, M., Heller, J., Leen, R., & Thurman, B. (1980) Physiological aspects of communication via mutual gaze. *American Journal of Sociology, 86* (1), 50–74.

Mead, M. (1975) Review of Darwin and facial expression. *Journal of Communication, 25* (1), 209–213.

Mehrabian, A., & Williams, M. (1969) Nonverbal concomitants of perceived and intended persuasiveness. *Journal of Personality and Social Psychology, 13,* 37–58.

Odom, R. D., & Lemond, C. M. (1972) Developmental differences in the perception and production of facial expressions. *Child Development, 43,* 359–369.

Rice, B. (February 1974) Rattlesnakes, french fries and pupillometric oversell. *Psychology Today,* pp. 55–59.

Rosenfeld, H. (1966) Approval-seeking and approval-inducing functions of verbal and nonverbal responses in the dyad. *Journal of Personality and Social Psychology, 4,* 597–605.

Rubin, Z. (1970) Measurement of romantic love. *Journal of Personality and Social Psychology, 16,* 265–273.

Rutter, D. R., Morley, E. I., & Graham, J. C. (1972) Visual interaction in a group of introverts and extroverts. *European Journal of Social Psychology, 2,* 371–384.

Science Digest. (October 1976) Blink (blank), pp. 16–17.

Saarni, C. (1978) Acquisition of display rules for expressive behavior. Paper presented at the meeting of the Eastern Psychological Association, Washington, D.C.

Saturday Review of Education. (1973) The tongue's own language. *1,* pp. 4, 77.

Savitsky, J. C., & Sim, M. E. (1974). Trading emotions: Equity theory of reward and punishment. *Journal of Communication, 24* (3), 140–146.

Scheman, J. D., & Lockard, J. S. (1979) Development of gaze aversion in children. *Child Development, 50,* 594–596.

Scherer, K. R., & Ekman, P. (Eds.) (1984) *Approaches to emotion.* Hillsdale, N.J.: Erlbaum.

Simms, T. M. (1967) Pupillary response of male and female subjects to pupillary difference in male and female picture stimuli. *Perception and Psychophysics, 2,* 553–555.

Smith, W. J., Chase, J., & Lieblich, A. K., (1974) Tongue showing: A facial display of humans and other primate species. *Semiotica, 17,* 201–246.

Spignesi, A., & Shor, R. (1981) The judgment of emotion from facial expressions, contexts, and their combination. *Journal of General Psychology, 104,* 41–58.

Sroufe, L. A. (1978) The ontogenesis of emotion. In J. Osofsky (Ed.), *Handbook of Infancy.* New York: Wiley.

Tomkins, S. S. (1984) Affect theory. In K. R. Scherer & P. Ekman (Eds.), *Approaches to emotion.* Hillsdale, N.J.: Erlbaum, pp. 163–195.

Trevarthen, C. (1984) Emotions in infancy: Regulators of contact and relationships with persons. In K. R. Scherer & P. Ekman (Eds.), *Approaches to emotion.* Hillsdale, N.J.: Erlbaum, pp. 129–157.

Vlietstra, A. G., & Manske, S. H. (1981) Looks to adults, preferences for adult males and females, and interpretations of an adult's gaze by preschool children. *Merrill-Palmer Quarterly, 27* (1), 31–41.

Wiemann, J. M., & Knapp, M. L. (1975) Turn-taking in conversations. *Journal of Communication, 25* (2), 75–92.

Zuckerman, M., Larrance, D. T., Spiegel, N. H., & Klorman, R. (1981) Controlling nonverbal displays: Facial expressions and tone of voice. *Journal of Experimental Social Psychology, 17,* 506–524.

CHAPTER 6

ENVIRONMENT

We shape our buildings, thereafter they shape us.
Sir Winston Churchill, *Time,* 1960

Buildings are designed to produce a particular "image" or "perception" for the public, and, in turn, they affect our behavior. Las Vegas, for instance, is the archetype of the commercial strip. "The analysis of Las Vegas and its physical structure is as important to architects and urbanists today as were the studies of medieval Europe and ancient Rome and Greece to earlier generations," claim architects Robert Benturi and Denise Brown in their serious inquiry into the architecture in the land of neon dreams (Goldberger, 1978, K-2).

Las Vegas has been designed precisely for the purpose of creating an environment that produces a high arousal level and the emotional state of feeling like a "king" or "queen" entering the palace. One of the most extraordinary visual sights in the world, Las Vegas, contains many elements that exist not for any structural reason but because of the emotional associations they are designed to evoke. As a fairyland, Las Vegas is designed to make us think of palaces and fantasy castles. The wedding chapels look like miniature New England churches or tiny Gothic ones, while restaurant entrances bear a remarkable similarity to Roman temples. Nowhere is light used so fully as a means of defining space. On Fremont Street there are literally blocks of neon signs, several stories high, one running into the next, to create a solid wall of brilliant, dazzling color. In Vegas, one hardly ever knows whether it is day or night. It is one continuous plan in motion, with no time restraints. The street is in constant motion, with strips of neon sliding up and down and in and out, yet the overall visual picture, like that of a theater marquee, never really changes. Las Vegas provides an escape trip for grownups into a glittering fantasy world where everybody and everything is beautiful. The reality sets in when one leaves Las Vegas poorer than when one arrived (Goldberger, 1978, K-2).

There can be no question that our environment plays an important role in affecting our communication behavior. How we perceive structures and how we respond to environmental manipulation will be explored in the following section.

PERCEPTIONS OF ENVIRONMENT

As in the case of Las Vegas, it is clear that architectural styles may be more than the reflection of the client's and architect's creative and artistic tastes. There are obvious messages intended in the selected design. One of the most dramatic examples of "restructuring" of buildings can be seen in the banking industry. Banks were originally designed to create a solid and conservative image and to impart strength and security. In the past, the design of banks frequently included oversized marble pillars, an abundance of metal bars and doors, tile floors, institutional gray interior, and barren walls. The public saw the banks as cold and impersonal but also as solid and durable.

Imagine when banks were first introduced into society. If you had never heard of a "bank," could you see yourself driving up to a small, boxlike structure, which is now known as the stop-and-go drive-in bank or an "ugly teller," and making a deposit? Could you have confidently handed over your life savings to a woman

At one time, the architecture of a bank building would have been very formal in order to convey a feeling of great stability. More contemporary banks, however, often seem much less formal. (Carolyn Brown)

whose red-and-white-striped blouse matched the awning on the bank? It is unlikely that you or anyone else would have taken the bank seriously, let alone placed your money in it. Before savings insurance was widely available and before money became devalued by inflation, bank executives wanted to assure their customers that their money was safe in a fortresslike building that would survive longer than they would. This image during the early 1900s created the perception that banks were here to stay.

The United States government, also wishing to proclaim its permanence and resistance to overthrow, patterned the architectural designs of government buildings after classical Roman or Greek styles, as if to say the government would endure as long as those classical styles had endured. Even churches adopted a serious, solid, and foreboding presence by repeating the architectural styles of the medieval period when the church was a very dominant part of the social and political scene in Europe. Twenty years later, dramatic changes had taken place with banks, government institutions, and churches.

Dentistry and oral-surgery practice have paid increasing attention to the perceptions patients have of the environment, both in the waiting room and the operating rooms. One oral-surgery practice placed friendly overstuffed animals in the waiting room and used brightly colored, comfortable vinyl chairs. An open-room arrangement was used to reduce patient anxiety. Each operating room, where procedures involving local anesthesia were performed, was painted a light blue to help the patient relax. The operating suites, where general anesthesia was used, were a deeper blue to enhance the sedative effects of preliminary medications. The offices were specially designed to create an informal, private, familiar, and nonconstraining environment for the patients. Here the oral surgeon could relax the patients enough to talk about such personal matters as restructuring their jaws or other facial bone structures.

In another dental practice, a warm and relaxing atmosphere was created in the reception area, and a semiprivate area was created for children. The far corner, designated as the "kiddie" area, was partially enclosed with waist-high planters to serve as shelving for books and toys. A 10-gallon aquarium was placed in this area and captivated the attention of the adults as well as the children (Block, 1975).

Walking into a dental office to have a tooth pulled or filled creates initial anxiety. The attempt to manipulate the internal and external environment to produce a consistent perception of warmth and relaxation is not limited to dental practice. Environmental design is happening everywhere. The perceptions of our surroundings affect the messages communicated and ultimately our behavior. Knapp (1978) identifies six perceptual frameworks of our environment. We per-

Open space is sometimes used in a medical waiting room to make patients feel less anxious. (Tim Davis/Photo Researchers)

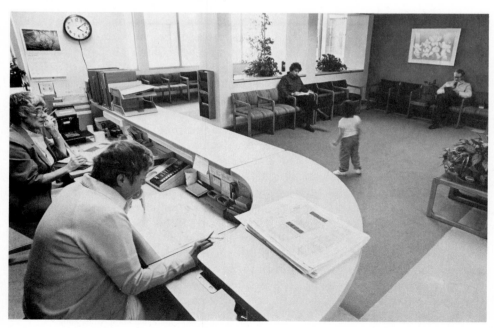

ceive the environment in terms of its (1) **formality,** (2) **warmth,** (3) **privacy,** (4) **familiarity,** (5) **constraint,** and (6) **distance.**

Formality

Is a building structure formal or informal? As we have already mentioned, early banks, government buildings, and churches represented a very formal structure. Winston Churchill's point that we shape our buildings and that later they shape us is a reality. The early formal structures of these buildings affected the communication behavior of people within them. A bank teller then was "the keeper of the keys"—very formal, stylized, and impersonal in dealing with customers. Today, with the advent of new informal structures, bank tellers undergo rigorous training programs to improve customer service. These programs teach tellers to be pleasant, use eye contact, smile, and engage in conversation beyond that of the business transaction.

Warmth

When an environment makes you feel psychologically comfortable or warm, do you have a tendency to relax or linger? Most people do. In fact, restaurants and fast-food chains faced a problem with people lingering too long. In their desire to create a "warm, comfortable, and enjoyable" environment, restaurant owners found that their patrons stayed too long and that profitable turnover and servicing of customers were greatly reduced. As a result, the Larsen chair was designed to be comfortable enough for eating the meal but not too comfortable, so that customers would be less likely to stay and converse after their meal was finished. Creating warmth in an environment includes the use of carpeting, lighting, soundproofing, and what the housing industry refers to as colorizing.

Privacy

People usually feel greater privacy in an enclosed environment that accommodates only a few people. Take a look at the cozy corner that promotes conversation. A cozy corner allows a few people to pull apart from the main conversational group at a party or office for their own tête-à-tête. Many restaurants have lost customers after expanding to a larger, more formal dining area from a smaller, more intimate one. In many cases the expansion changed the private and cozy environment so significantly that the original appeal of the restaurant was lost.

The extent to which others cannot enter or overhear the conversation creates a greater feeling of privacy. With increased privacy, the speaking distance between people is reduced and the messages are much more personal, designed and adapted for a specific person rather than "for people in general."

Familiarity

Unfamiliar environments usually produce a high arousal level because we do not know the rituals and norms; visually, the environment is new to the eye and we are hesitant to move too quickly. In a mobile society such as ours, brilliant business executives have designed "chain stereotyped structures" such as McDonald's, Dunkin' Donuts, Holiday Inn, Howard Johnson's, Taco Bell, and many others. The implication is that when the same environmental structure, external and internal, is maintained, customers will be readily familiar and comfortable with the surroundings and perceive that the service and/or product will be comparable to what they have had before in another chain. This predictability guarantees that there will be minimum demands placed on customers in terms of adjusting to the environment; the environmental structure is constant. In this way people "feel at home" in a place in which they have never been before.

Constraint

Part of our reaction to an environment is based on our perception of whether (and how easily) we can leave it. Knapp (1978) comments that "the intensity of these perceptions of constraint is closely related to the space available to us and the privacy of this space during the time we will be in the environment" (p. 88).

There is a difference between temporarily confining environments and permanently confining ones. A trip across country in a car is temporarily confining, while a trip in jail is of a much more constraining and permanent nature. Imagine yourself in a tiny room without any means of escape. The noise is endless—people shouting and talking, radio and television blaring. There is no privacy, no way to escape the spatial invasion or the gaze of others. How would you react? This is a description of the basics of jail life according to Barbara Price (1977), co-director of the National Jail Study. She believes that the average middle-class person would find the experience highly traumatic because the perception of constraint generally produces trauma.

Distance

How close or far away we are in a conversational setting with another person can affect our communication. This includes actual physical distance (such as the senior executive offices on the top floor and junior executive offices on the floor below) or psychological distance (such as an empty chair between two students working at a table in the library). As a function of distance, office location communicates a great deal about power and status, according to Michael Korda. In most cases, Korda (1975) contends, power diminishes with distance from the senior executive's office. He tells a story of Sidney, an assistant to the senior executive who worked in an airless cubbyhole beside the great man's office. No secretary would have worked in that spot, but Sidney chose to stay there because it had a door that led into the office of the executive's secretary and another opening onto the corridor, so that he could see everybody coming and going. Sidney tells his story:

> So long as I sat there, I had it made. I got to know everyone who came in; if they had to wait, they came and leaned on my desk, or used my phone to confirm lunch dates, and everybody assumed that I must know everything that was going on.
>
> When I first moved in . . . the only thing I insisted on was a telephone with several lines and an intercom to my boss. I don't think I ever used it, but when he made a call, one of the buttons would light up on my phone, and anyone in my office would have a sense of my being connected to him. It's the proximity to power that counts, not space, a carpet, or a window. (Korda, pp. 69–70)

In Sidney's case, distance served to create the perception of power and access to the head man.

RESPONSES TO ENVIRONMENT

If we grew up in sterile rooms devoid of objects, color, or movement, we would be far different creatures. Our environment stimulates curiosity and shapes our personality, communication, and performance. Our responses to the environment will be examined with regard to (1) the attractiveness of the surroundings, (2) color, (3) lighting, and (4) sound.

Attractiveness of Surroundings

When was the last time that you entered an office or classroom only to experience a very slow and subtle change in your mood? What do you think was happening at the time? Did the environment itself contribute to your mood or attitude change? Research concerning the effects of the environment on our attitudes and behaviors documents the existence of a relationship between surroundings and these variables. For example, in a classic study, Maslow and Mintz (1956) explored the impact of ugly, beautiful, and average rooms on the emotional responses of participants in their study. The ugly room was designed to look like a janitor's storeroom, with things scattered everywhere. The beautiful room had carpeting, drapes, and similar effects. Finally, the average room was designed as a professor's office. The subjects in each of the rooms were asked to rate a series of photographic negatives of faces. Given what we know about the effects of the environment, the results were not surprising. The subjects in the beautiful room gave significantly higher ratings to the faces than did the subjects in the ugly room. In addition, subjects in the ugly room engaged in various escape behaviors in an attempt to avoid the unattractive surroundings. They claimed that the room

The physical environment of a classroom can affect the performance of students. (Alan Carey/The Image Works)

produced monotony, fatigue, headaches, discontent, sleepiness, irritability, and hostility. Subjects in the beautiful room reported feelings of pleasure, importance, comfort, enjoyment, energy, and the desire to continue the activity (Maslow and Mintz, 1956; Mintz, 1956).

As you can see, environmental surroundings can influence our attitudes and moods. But can they also affect our performance level? According to Wollin and Montagne (1981), the answer is unequivocally yes. The sterility of an environment does affect individual performance. To test this hypothesis, Wollin and Montagne decorated one classroom with bright wall paint, posters, kites, rugs, softer lighting, cushions, and plants. They selected a second classroom and left it as it was—barren and sterile. The researchers then exposed two psychology classes to both of the classrooms for five weeks or half the term. Results of their study revealed that students scored significantly higher on tests while they were in the experimental classroom than when they worked and were tested in the sterile classroom. Additionally, their attitudes toward the experimental room were significantly more positive than toward the sterile control room. Finally, Wollin and Montagne discovered that the teachers' performances were rated significantly higher when teaching took place in the beautiful classroom. The researchers concluded that classroom environment not only contributes to our emotional responses but it also affects our individual performance levels.

Another important response to environment focuses on color. The following section will explore the many ways in which color affects our lives.

Color

Did you know that

- Sugar won't sell in a green package?
- Beauty aids in brown jars sit on the shelf?
- Kids want cereal in red and yellow boxes?

Advertisers are becoming increasingly selective about their use of colors in promoting products. This was not the case in the time of Henry Ford. It might be said that Henry Ford offered his customers any color automobile they desired—as long as it was black. Today, color merchandising has become big business. A major automobile manufacturer may offer 650 standard color combinations or any kind of color customizing for which the customer is willing to pay.

People react to colors emotionally and physically. One detergent manufacturer sprinkled red granules through his white soap powder, and housewives subsequently complained that the detergent was too rough on their hands. He changed the color to yellow, and women said it was easier on the hands but that the clothes were not as clean. Finally, he changed the granules to a blue color, and the women said it was just right. Nothing had changed but the color of the granules.

There are many associations with color. There are blue Mondays and various black days in history. A cowardly person is yellow; an angry person sees red. Some people are green with envy and others are in the pink. Moreover, many specific associations have been made with colors. For instance, red has been associated with more appetite appeal than any other color. Red is usually found somewhere in the decor of restaurants and on the wrappers of many food products. The red-and-white combination has probably sold more toothpaste than any other. Blue, violet, and purple have little or no appetite appeal. Green will sell vegetables in the supermarket, but a green wrapper has never been known to sell bread.

Mehrabian (1976) claims that the most pleasant hues, in order, are blue, green, red, and yellow; and that red is the most arousing hue, followed by orange, yellow, violet, blue, and green. Recent research by Nelson, Pelech, and Foster (1984) supports Mehrabian's claim, particularly regarding the arousal potential of colors. Nelson and his colleagues asked 170 eighth- to tenth-graders to complete a sensation-seeking scale and to choose which color they liked better: red or blue. Both boys and girls who sought high levels of stimulation chose red as their favorite color, while children who sought little stimulation selected the color blue. The researchers concluded that red has both stimulating and exciting properties, while blue has less stimulating and more calming properties. They also concluded that differences in characteristics of both people and colors should be taken into account in the design of optimal learning environments.

The symbolic meanings of color have a long history. Colors have been associated with moods and symbolic meanings for a long time. For example, the phrase "red-light district" suggests excitement in using the word "red" (a hot color). Burgoon and Saine (1978) have identified moods and symbolic messages associated with colors, as outlined in Table 6.1.

TABLE 6.1   Color in the Environment: Moods Created and Symbolic Meanings

Color	Moods	Symbolic Meanings
Red	Hot, affectionate, angry, defiant, contrary, hostile, full of vitality, excitement, love.	Happiness, lust, intimacy, love, restlessness, agitation, royalty, rage, sin, blood.
Blue	Cool, pleasant, leisurely, distant, infinite, secure, transcendent, calm, tender.	Dignity, sadness, tenderness, truth.
Yellow	Unpleasant, exciting, hostile, cheerful, joyful, jovial.	Superficial glamor, sun, light, wisdom, masculinity, royalty (in China), age (in Greece), prostitution (in Italy), famine (in Egypt).
Orange	Unpleasant, exciting, disturbed, distressed, upset, defiant, contrary, hostile, stimulating.	Sun, fruitfulness, harvest, thoughtfulness.
Purple	Depressed, sad, dignified, stately.	Wisdom, victory, pomp, wealth, humility, tragedy.
Green	Cool, pleasant, leisurely, in control.	Security, peace, jealousy, hate, aggressiveness, calm.
Black	Sad, intense, anxiety, fear, despondent, dejected, melancholy, unhappy.	Darkness, power, mastery, protection, decay, mystery, wisdom, death, atonement.
Brown	Sad, not tender, despondent, dejected, melancholy, unhappy, neutral.	Melancholy, protection, autumn, decay, humility, atonement.
White	Joy, lightness, neutral, cold.	Solemnity, purity, chastity, femininity, humility, joy, light, innocence, fidelity, cowardice.

Burgoon, J. K., & Saine, T. (1978) *The unspoken dialogue.* Boston: Houghton Mifflin. Reprinted by permission.

An early attempt to demonstrate the effects of color was completed by Ketcham (1958), who studied the effects of three different colors on classroom learning. One school was left unpainted, a second school was finished in the usual institutional color scheme of light buff walls and white ceilings, and the third was painted in accordance with principles of color dynamics. In the third school the corridors were painted a cheerful yellow with gray doors; classrooms facing north were done in a pale rose; classrooms facing south were done in cooler shades of blue and green; front walls were darker than side walls; the art room was a neutral gray so as to avoid interfering with the colorful work that it contained; and green chalkboards were used to reduce glare. Over a two-year period, behavior in each school was observed. The results were clear; students in the third school showed greatest improvement on several variables measured—social habits, health, safety habits, and scholastic aptitude in language, arts, arithmetic, social studies, science, and music. Those in the unpainted school showed the least improvement in these areas, and those in the traditional school fell somewhere in between.

The field of color is complex and is not subject to simple conclusions about psychological and physiological effects. The extent to which color affects emotional response is still a question of major concern to researchers.

Lighting

Lighting, like color, also has a pronounced effect on our behavior. Kowinski (1975) has observed that "Most offices are generally overlit—with often twice as much light as they need—while individuals within the office may be working in circumstances that are underlit. The results can be inefficiency, fatigue, and perhaps a sense of dislocation caused mostly by the St. Vitus dance that the pupil of the eye must do to cope" (p. 48).

Finnegan and Solomon (1981) contrasted and examined behavior in windowed versus windowless environments. The primary question of interest was how the presence or absence of natural light affected general work attitudes. To answer this question, the researchers asked 123 New York City office workers to complete a questionnaire and to indicate whether or not their offices contained a window. The attitudes of windowed (n = 81) versus windowless (n = 32) were then compared. Results indicated that the two groups did not differ significantly with regard to ability to sense the passage of time, anxiety, or feelings of isolation. However, windowless employees were significantly less positive than windowed employees regarding job satisfaction, interest value of their jobs, and physical working conditions. Windowless groups simply felt that their physical conditions were less "pleasant and stimulating" (p. 292).

Low lights tend to create a relaxed, intimate environment in which people want to linger. Extremely bright lights tend to cause fatigue and a desire to escape. Soft lighting is more flattering to a woman's makeup, so fluorescent lighting is sometimes avoided in offices where women work. Carr and Dabbs (1974) found that the combination of intimate questions and dim lighting with nonintimates caused a significant hesitancy in responding, a significant decrease in eye gaze, and a decrease in the average length of gaze.

The effects of colored lighting on performance are interesting. Birren (1975) cites evidence suggesting that human reactions are 12 percent faster than average under red lighting conditions. Green lights, on the other hand, seem to generate reactions that are slower than normal. Colored lighting also seems to influence judgments of time, length, and weight. With red lighting, these judgments tend to be overestimated, while a green or blue light appears to generate underestimation.

Fatigue rates rise in direct proportion to the dimming of the visual field. This is a fact, plain and simple. So much of a student's work depends on visual scanning and identification. Thus, lowered light levels will decrease his or her efficiency drastically, thereby decreasing the quality and quantity of his or her work (Thompson, 1973, p. 81).

The following are three guidelines for the lighting of a classroom:

1. Maintain high levels of illumination. When students must expend energy just to see, they will have little left to understand what is being said.
2. All areas of the room should be balanced in brightness. Factory and assembly-line workers should have their work well illuminated. Industry has known for a long time that eye fatigue plays havoc with production schedules. To avoid sharp contrast, the visual field around the task should be only one-third as bright as the work area. No part of the visual field should be brighter than the immediate vicinity of the task.
3. Avoid glare either from direct light sources or from reflecting surfaces.

Sound

We react emotionally to sound all the time, sometimes without conscious awareness. Since people are accustomed to background sound rather than silence, some companies use a white-noise generator. This generator creates a hum or hiss that sounds similar to an air conditioner and is generated electronically in open office surroundings to mask other background noise. In some cases, the white-sound generator, instead of creating a calm and productive environment, creates frazzled nerves. Paul Harris companies used the generator but had to shut it down because employees found it irritating. On the other hand, a senior designer in a large Philadelphia company reports an office where the generator was too successful. The designer noted that when the white sound went off, everyone thought the air conditioner had broken down. People got warmer and warmer and finally had to go home because everyone was so hot.

Remember the last time you were driving on a rather long trip and began to get a little tired? If you located some music on the radio, you probably noticed that you began to feel more alert and awake almost immediately. If you can recall an incident similar to this, then you realize that music can be a strong stimulant. Mehrabian, however, claims that music has a more immediate effect on our arousal level and pleasure than several cups of coffee. Few will deny that music has an emotional impact; for example, you must know a song that can make you feel a little sad or nostalgic, another that always lifts you up and makes you smile, or still another that makes you want to "get down" and "boogie."

Although you probably recognize the unique influence music can have upon people, it is important to realize that music is often used to evoke a particular response. For example, various types of merchants use music in an attempt to increase the desirability of their products. They use music to create an environment that will elicit a particular response from the customer. A supermarket may raise the volume of music to stimulate more purchases in a shorter period of time. A softly lit restaurant uses soothing music to match the intimate atmosphere. A disco uses flashing lights and music that is loud and has a steady beat to produce excitement. Each of these businesses uses a different type of music in order to produce a special environment—an environment that will sell their products.

SPATIAL ARRANGEMENTS AND SEATING BEHAVIOR

"Power is where you sit," claim researchers (Korda, 1975; Resnick and Jaffee, 1983). Consciously or unconsciously, people select seats to reaffirm their various roles in groups. In ancient times, seating choice was a matter of self-protection and survival. When a power figure sat at the head of a round table, for instance, it was very important where the next power figure was placed. One natural choice might be to put the next most powerful individual to the right, based on the concept of "right-hand" person. This method was not used in ancient times for the simple reason that it was easier to stab to your left with the dagger in your right hand than to stab to your right, again with the dagger in your right hand. It was therefore prudent to place a powerful guest to your immediate left, since in that position he could not stab you, while you were excellently positioned to kill him. The person on your immediate right would be someone of no risk or importance to you. Today, seating behavior requires a choice based not on physical protection but on a need for psychological protection at several levels (Korda, 1975).

The first area of seating behavior and spatial arrangements to be reviewed is the structural setting for interaction, such as the shape and size of the tables used. The following section will examine the research on seating behavior and its effect on communication and interaction.

Structural Settings for Interaction

The story of King Arthur and the Knights of the Round Table is a graphic illustration of power. Presumably, their table was round so that there could be no question of dominance and so that every knight could share equally in the honor of being seated at the table. There is only one flaw in this approach, since it makes King Arthur's seat the status marker, and status would decrease as the distance from the king increased. As a result, a knight sitting four seats away from the king would be perceived as having lower status in contrast to the knight who sat next to the king. Shapes of tables communicate important information about the nature of the interaction, dominance, power, and ultimate control before they are even occupied, as the following example indicates:

> The United States and South Vietnam wanted a seating arrangement in which only two sides were identified. They did not want to recognize the National Liberation Front as an "equal" partner in the negotiations. North Vietnam and the NLF wanted "equal" status given to all parties—represented by a four-sided table. The final arrangement was such that both parties could claim victory. The round table minus the dividing lines allowed North Vietnam and the NLF to claim all four delegations were equal. (McCroskey, Larson, and Knapp, 1971, p. 97)

The round table.   A round table without distinct edges and sides expresses unity and equality for all parties. The circle itself has become a symbol of unity and strength throughout the world. A round table, however, does reveal lines of demarcation between individuals. As in ancient times, the direction of the seated power circle reveals status. The order to power is usually clockwise, beginning with the position at 12 o'clock. Power diminishes as it moves around the positions at 3 o'clock, 6 o'clock, 9 o'clock, and so on. Therefore, the second most powerful person will sit in the 1 o'clock position, and the least prominent or powerful individual will sit at the 11 o'clock position (Koneya and Barbour, 1976, pp. 58–59).

The square table.   What types of games do you play on a square table? How about backgammon, bridge, chess, Monopoly, or any of a number of card games? The square table, with four equal sides, provides excellent corners for the separation of its participants. For a business meeting, the square table signifies equality for each business partner, since every person has equal frontage, space, and separate edges. The square table therefore signifies equality and sameness because of the equal length of each side. On the other hand, it does not signify unity because of its distinct sidedness. The square table is excellent for competition because it promotes direct eye contact in all four positions and allows for equal distance between people seated at the table.

The rectangular table.   The rectangular table has been a popular shape for boardrooms in business for some time. All types of variations of the rectangular table exist. The rectangular table has some features similar to the square table. It has four distinct sides and does not express the concept of unity because of the separation with the corners. The obvious difference from the square table is the fact that the rectangular table has two long sides and two short sides, with the long and short sides being of equal length. The short side has traditionally been viewed as the head of the table, particularly when only one short end is occupied. Who occupies the head seat in your family at Thanksgiving or Christmas? In many families, the father sits at the head (the short side of the rectangular table), with the mother sitting opposite at the other short end.

Salt River Project executives in Phoenix, Arizona, have designed an interesting variation of the rectangular table. The table has one wide short side but grows narrower and narrower toward the end of the other short side. The reasoning behind this design was to allow board participants to see the head (president) without craning their necks. This is an ingenious table design for visual ease, but it leaves something to be desired for those individuals who get the short end of the table, as it were. Not only status but also space is diminished with the distance from the head of the table.

Perceptions and Characteristics of Seating Behavior

In 1977, NBC attempted to give David Brinkley and John Chancellor a more relaxed conversational relationship with the viewers. So they moved the set around from behind the desk. After having been sprung from their imposing desks, the announcers were squeezed into identical chairs with armrests. They sometimes appeared to be as uncomfortable as oversized freshmen trying to keep their legs out of the aisle. But the point was to change the image or audience perception by manipulating the **seating arrangement** in the set (Carter, 1977a). "I've said for years that some anchor people tend to become high priests of the news," explains Chancellor. "They intone it as though they own it. I'm not trying to be a common-man Joe six-pack. But I think sharing the news this way makes it more meaningful than just sitting up there and saying this happened, that happened" (in Carter, 1977b, p. 103).

That's how it happened for NBC. The perception of the viewer was important in the station's image. Many studies have revealed that certain seating choices may be perceived as leadership positions. In addition, studies have revealed that certain types of people, such as dominant personalities, select particular seats.

Task situations.   In a now classic study, Sommer (1969) analyzed how students would sit in various task situations. The study was replicated by Cook in the United Kingdom with Oxford University students and a sample of nonstudents that included civil servants, school teachers, and secretaries. Subjects were asked to imagine themselves sitting at a table with a friend of the same sex in the following four situations.

> Conversation—sitting and talking for a few minutes before class (before work for nonstudents).

> Cooperation—sitting and studying together for the same exam (or doing a crossword puzzle together for the nonstudent).

> Coaction—sitting and studying together for the same exam (or sitting at the same table and reading for nonstudents).

> Competition—competing in order to see who would be first to solve a series of puzzles.

Most pairs who wanted to talk or work together used adjacent chairs. Sommer explains this as the need to have psychological closeness. Subjects gave such explanations as "I want to chat with my friend, not the whole cafeteria, so I sit next to her," and "More intimate, there are no physical barriers between us" (Cook, 1970). The results of the study are displayed in Tables 6.2 and 6.3.

As the tables reveal, there was a difference in response among the British non-university sample, the United States student sample, and the Oxford University sample. Almost everyone in the studies selected side-by-side choices for cooperative tasks, with the exception of the Oxford group. This might be explained by

TABLE 6.2   **Seating Preferences at Rectangular Tables**

	corner	across-adjacent	same-side	across-ends	diagonal-far	opposite-corner
Conversation						
U.S. sample (151 responses)	42%	46%	11%	0%	1%	0%
U.K. (univ.) sample (102 responses)	51	21	15	0	6	7
U.K. (nonuniv.) sample (42 responses)	42	42	9	2	5	0
Cooperation						
U.S. sample	19	25	51	0	5	0
U.K. (univ.) sample	11	11	23	20	22	13
U.K. (nonuniv.) sample	40	2	50	5	2	0
Coaction						
U.S. sample	3	3	7	13	43	33
U.K. (univ.) sample	9	8	10	31	28	14
U.K. (nonuniv.) sample	12	14	12	19	31	12
Competition						
U.S. sample	7	41	8	18	20	5
U.K. (univ.) sample	7	10	10	50	16	7
U.K. (nonuniv.) sample	4	13	3	53	20	7

Reprinted from Cook, M. (1970). Experimentation on orientation and proxemics, *Human Relations, 23,* 61–76. Used by permission of Plenum Publishing Corporation.

TABLE 6.3   **Seating Preferences at Round Tables**

	× × O	× × O	× O ×
Conversation			
U.S. sample (116 responses)	63%	17%	20%
U.K. (univ.) sample (102 responses)	58	37	5
U.K. (nonuniv.) sample (42 responses)	58	27	15
Cooperation			
U.S. sample	83	7	10
U.K. (univ.) sample	25	31	44
U.K. (nonuniv.) sample	97	0	3
Coaction			
U.S. sample	13	36	51
U.K. (univ.) sample	16	34	50
U.K. (nonuniv.) sample	24	26	50
Competition			
U.S. sample	2	25	63
U.K. (univ.) sample	15	22	63
U.K. (nonuniv.) sample	9	21	70

Reprinted from Cook, M. (1970). Experimentation on orientation and proxemics, *Human Relations, 23,* 61–76. Used by permission of Plenum Publishing Corporation.

a misinterpretation of the question by the Oxford group. Since Oxford students are encouraged to do most of their work independently, they may not have realized that the question referred to cooperation with another person. The variety of responses to the coaction question—studying for the same exam or reading at the same table as another—may be the result of the slightly different instructions for the nonuniversity sample. Finally, most persons wanted to compete in an opposite seating arrangement. The American students, however, wanted to sit closer, perhaps to have greater eye contact, body movement, or control, and in general to be more aggressive and competitive. The United Kingdom samples chose a more distant opposite position to protect their task and prevent the other person from spying.

Level of intimacy.   Cook also studied the perceptions of sex and acquaintance (level of intimacy) with regard to seating behavior. Subjects were asked in a questionnaire to select seating arrangements in two situations—a bar scene and a restaurant scene—when (1) sitting with a casual friend of the same sex, (2) sitting

TABLE 6.4   **Seating Preferences for a Bar or "Public House"**

	Corner	Opposite	Side-by-side	Other
Same-sex friend	70%	25%	45%	2%
Casual friend of opposite sex	63	37	29	7
Intimate friend	43	11	82	4

Reprinted from Cook, M. (1970). Experimentation on orientation and proxemics, *Human Relations, 23*, 61–76. Used by permission of Plenum Publishing Corporation.

with a casual friend of the opposite sex, and (3) sitting with a boyfriend or girl-friend. The results are displayed in Tables 6.4 and 6.5.

As Tables 6.4 and 6.5 indicate, the predominant patterns were as follows:

1. Corner seating was selected in the bar for same-sex friends and casual friends of the opposite sex.
2. Side-by-side seating was chosen for intimate friends in the bar setting.
3. Opposite seating in the restaurant was chosen for all three variations of sex and acquaintance.
4. Side-by-side seating occurred more with intimate friends in the restaurant.

An obvious practical reason for opposite seating in a restaurant is to avoid crowding while eating and to allow plenty of elbow room. Apparently, people do attribute certain interaction patterns and relationships to various seating arrangements. At least we know that people perceive this to be the case.

TABLE 6.5   **Seating Preferences for a Restaurant**

	Corner	Opposite	Side-by-side	Other
Same sex friend	30%	73%	34%	4%
Casual friend of opposite sex	43	64	28	4
Intimate friend	40	53	46	2

Reprinted from Cook, M. (1970). Experimentation on orientation and proxemics, *Human Relations, 23*, 71–76. Used by permission of Plenum Publishing Corporation.

Personality characteristics.   Herbert Walberg (1969) studied the relationship between seating position and student personality. He found that when a student was given a choice of where to sit, different personalities preferred different locations. For instance, students who were enthusiastic about school as well as about creative activities outside of school chose to sit close to the front in order to see and hear everything. These students, as revealed on tests, felt it was important to be creative and imaginative. They were also task-oriented and frequently thought about values and goals in life. On the other hand, students who selected seats in the back of the room were described as unhappy with school, disinterested in grades and school popularity, and not likely to be organizers or leaders. Students who preferred to sit near a window also disliked school and studying. The majority of students who did not care where they sat had similar characteristics to the group who preferred the front seats. They lacked, however, some of the extremes of enthusiasm that characterized the first group.

Dominance.   Russo (1967) found that people doing a paper-and-pencil rating of various seating arrangements stated that if one person was at the head and one on the side, there was a less equal situation in terms of status than if both persons were on the ends. This was not a surprising perception of **dominance** or **status.**

In a study conducted outside of the classroom environment, Hare and Bales (1963) found that people who scored high on a paper-and-pencil dominance test chose a seat at the head of the table or in the center of one of the long sides. Both seating areas facilitated high eye contact and visibility. Similar findings were reported by Sommer (1956) and Strodtbeck and Hook (1961). They observed that leaders are more likely to choose a position at the end of a rectangular table and that individuals who choose the corner seats of a rectangular table contribute the least.

The Strodtbeck and Hook (1961) study examined seating behavior in experimental jury settings. The researchers found that the person sitting at the head position was chosen significantly more often as the jury leader, particularly if he or she was perceived as a person from an upper economic class. If the choice was between two people sitting at each head position, the one perceived as having higher economic status was selected.

According to researchers Howells and Becker (1962), seating position also determines the flow of communication, which, in turn, determines leadership emergence. Five-person decision-making groups were examined, with three people sitting on one side of a rectangular table and two on the other side. The researchers reported that the side with two people was able to influence the other three (or at least talk more) and that they, therefore, emerged more often as group leaders.

In an analysis of talking frequency in small groups, Hare and Bales noted that people in the end or outside positions were frequent talkers. Subsequent studies revealed that these people were likely to be dominant personalities while those who avoided the central or focal positions by selecting inside seats were more anxious and actually stated that they wanted to stay out of the discussion.

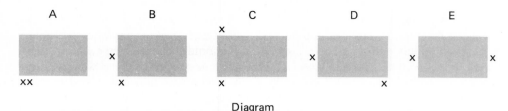

Diagram

FIGURE 6.1   **Russo's display of seating arrangements and their effect on interpersonal communication**

From Russo, N. (1967). Connotation of seating arrangement, *Cornell Journal of Social Relations, 2,* 39. Used by permission.

Friendliness.   Russo (1967) found that large distances between people generally indicate less acquaintance, less friendliness, and less talkativeness. Russo reported some interesting differences, depicted in Figure 6.1.

People who were the most friendly toward one another chose the A seating arrangement, while those who were hostile selected the E arrangement. Seating position B was viewed as more friendly and intimate than position C, C more than D, and D more than E. The same pattern applied when examining the variables of talkative versus untalkative individuals.

Introverts-extroverts.   Cook studied the relationship between the personality variable of extroversion-introversion and seating preference. He found that extroverts chose to sit opposite one another, either across the table or down the length of it. Many extroverts also chose positions that would put them in close physical proximity to the other person. Introverts, on the other hand, generally chose positions that would keep them more at a distance visually and physically from the other person (Cook, 1970).

Cook also conducted an actual observational study (as opposed to a questionnaire study) to determine interaction behavior. Actual observations of seating in a restaurant validated his questionnaire study. Cook found that most people sitting in bars showed a definite preference for side-by-side seating. The earlier questionnaire had suggested corner seating. Cook suggests that the difference may have been due to the fact that bars are equipped with many seats located against the wall. As a result, this allows persons to sit side by side and not have their backs to anyone; therefore, they have a good view of others (Cook, 1970).

Effects

Does the manipulation of objects and seating arrangements produce predictable effects on the outcome of communication events? William Agee, former president of Bendix Corporation, thought so. He banished the company's giant wooden table from the boardroom and replaced it with "nothing." The old table was brown and drab and looked like a surfboard, he declared. Besides, it was just a security blanket for directors and had little real purpose. The president believed a boardroom table is a barrier to open and frank discussions and that it exists at most corporations only because of tradition. "If you want to gesture and make a point, it's hard to do it with a table." The fact that the table was removed surprised the directors when they entered the room for a meeting. Of course, when the table was removed, the room was not left exactly bare. It was furnished with plush new velvet armchairs, which swiveled and rocked, arranged around a handsome $30,000 Oriental rug. The conclusion of the board was that the meeting was more relaxed and highly communicative in the tableless room.

In the business setting the boardroom space was arranged to produce a desired effect on behavior. The same event occurs in the educational context, where the teacher exerts behavioral control by arranging the child's environment. One educator asked the question: Why should a youngster smear slime around the classroom when she is supposed to be napping? Why does a youngster punch another child while he eyes a crowded swing set? Why does a youngster like to play near the oven? Children's learning and socialization processes are dramatically affected by the environments in which the processes occur (Johnson, 1982). Children need boundaries, occasional privacy, and controlled visual and tactile stimulation to learn effectively. The physical environment can often work against learning. For example, youngsters may forego napping for mischief because the environment is too exciting for sleep. Objects in space say "pick me up" while the teacher is saying "listen to me" (Carey, 1978, B-2).

The effects of spatial arrangements and seating behavior on interaction are significant. Whether one is in the classroom or the boardroom, spatial arrangement affects interaction. Studies have demonstrated that the formality and intimacy of communication will change with the manipulation of objects or alternative seating selection.

Classroom space. For years, teachers have made a number of assumptions about students' classroom seating preferences. Included are the assumptions that students in the front row are brighter and more interested; students in the back row are less knowledgeable and less attentive; and students on the outside aisles are concerned with quick departures. Interestingly enough, research concerning the use of classroom space actually documents many of these claims. Teachers can and do make accurate assessments based on classroom space usage.

Perhaps one of the most extensive studies of straight-row seating in classrooms was that of Adams and Biddle in 1970. Their study involved the observation of thirty-two classrooms and a variety of subject areas. Results of the study revealed that the main determinant of whether a student was actively engaged in classroom participation depended on the location of his or her seat. An **action** zone, defined as a center of activity where most activity occurs, was identified in the typical straight-row seating arrangement. The action zone extends from the front of the room directly up the center line, and interaction diminishes as one moves farther away from the instructor. This zone represents those students who engage in active communication behavior with the teacher as well as those students with whom the teacher converses.

Recently, other researchers have documented and extended early findings such as these. For example Levine, O'Neal, Garwood, and McDonald (1980) discovered that students who select seats at the front of the class perform significantly better on exams than students who choose seats in the rear. Additionally, they found that students in the front participate more than students in the rear.

To document the differences from side to side in the classroom, Stires (1980) investigated potential differences in both test scores and class evaluations. Results of his study indicated that students seated in the middle score higher on tests than students seated at the sides. Additionally, students in the middle generally rate the course and the instructor significantly higher than do students on the sides.

Spacing of desks or seats also affects communication behavior in the classroom. Heston and Garner (1972) found that, when selecting their own seats, males assume a greater seating distance from each other than do females, with distances between males and females falling between these extremes. In addition, Heston and Garner found that when spacing themselves, students take up more space. As far as preferences for particular seating arrangements, the semicircle and U-shape are highly preferred over straight rows and circles. This implies a student preference for a seating arrangement that allows the most interaction. The straight-row seating, although the traditional arrangement in the classroom, seems to be inadequate because it does not give students what they intuitively feel they need—interaction with other members of the class.

FIGURE 6.2   **Which office affords the greatest power position to its occupant? The third illustration has the desk placed well forward in the room, thus minimizing the space available for the visitor. This gives the occupant greater territorial residence and power.**
From *Power! How to Get It, How to Use It,* by Michael Korda. Copyright © 1975 by Michael Korda and Paul Gitlin, trustee for the benefit of Christopher Korda. Reprinted by permission of Random House, Inc.

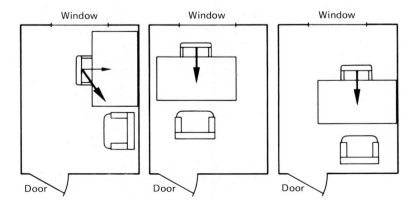

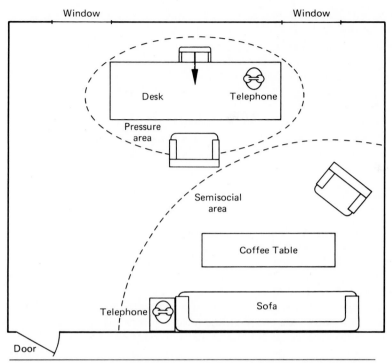

FIGURE 6.3   **Where would you sit to maintain power and control?**
From *Power! How to Get It, How to Use It,* by Michael Korda.
Copyright © 1975 by Michael Korda and Paul Gitlin, trustee for
the benefit of Christopher Korda. Reprinted by permission of
Random House, Inc.

Office space.   Desks are important objects in promoting or obstructing interpersonal communication. Gass (1984) conducted an experiment in a therapist's
office in which he manipulated both attire formality (coat and tie versus sports
shirt) and seating arrangement (behind desk versus no desk). Results of his study
revealed that the highest attractiveness ratings were given to the therapist who
wore casual attire and used no desk. Females were especially critical of the
behind-the-desk arrangement. They rated the therapist who used this arrangement significantly lower on attractiveness, expertise, and trustworthiness.

The desk also plays a significant role in student-teacher relationships. In an
earlier study conducted by Zweigenhaft (1976), faculty members were asked to
sketch the furniture arrangement in their offices. The sketches were analyzed with
other information obtained from the professors, along with a schoolwide teacher
evaluation. Not surprisingly, 24 out of 33 senior faculty members (full professors
and associate professors) put their desks between themselves and their students.

On the other hand, only 14 out of 30 junior faculty members (assistant professors and lecturers) placed the desk between themselves and their students. The most interesting findings were the students' perceptions of how this furniture arrangement affected interaction. The professors who did not use the desk were rated by students as more willing to "encourage the development of different viewpoints by students," more ready to give "individual attention to students who need it," and less likely to display "undue favoritism."

Environmental situations may discourage or facilitate interaction. Everywhere you go you can observe the effects of seating arrangements on interaction—be it in a restaurant, library, boardroom, classroom, or even a theater.

SUMMARY

During the nineteenth century, there was a common tradition of bundling (in which couples would huddle together under blankets) in New England, Wales, and the Hebrides Islands off the coast of Scotland. During cold weather, the only fire in the farmhouse was usually in the living room or kitchen. Fuel was often in short supply, and the entire family would gather in one room with a fire. This afforded warmth but did not allow for privacy for a young man and woman who were courting. In order to allow the couple to develop an intimate emotional relationship that would lead to marriage, they were given a special chance to be alone. The young couple was allowed to use the family bedroom to carry on their courtship in private. They were comfortable and warm beneath the covers. Sound good? Well, the couple was prevented from having actual intercourse by one of two methods: a wooden board placed down the center of the bed or a thong tied around the maiden's thighs and secured with a special knot. Both methods affected the interaction and intimacy of the young couple.

In less obvious ways our environment affects our communication behaviors. Low lighting, for example, increases the probability of self-disclosure, as does soft music. Desks placed between two people in an interaction can create a barrier in the conversation.

In a broader look at environment, various architectural structures produce specific perceptions and effects on our communication behavior. The perception of a bank, for instance, as a solid-form structure may determine the type of customers they will attract. Perceptions of the environment fall into six categories: formality, warmth, privacy, familiarity, constraint, and distance. Each variable reflects how the environment is perceived within the communication setting.

The more dramatic research findings reveal that the environment has a pronounced impact on (1) our emotional responses, (2) our interpersonal behavior (social interaction), and (3) our job performance and productivity. Specific elements of the environment such as color, lighting, and sound have been empirically demonstrated to create both psychological and physiological effects on others. Amos Alonzo Stagg, for instance, had his team's dressing room painted a relaxing blue to calm and rest the players during the half-time period. Last-minute pep talks, however, were a different matter. During these talks, he used an exciting, brilliant anteroom (Ketcham, 1958).

Another facet of the external environment involves furniture and seating arrangements. Spatial arrangements and seating behavior have been the subject of political and social controversy for some time. The various structural settings for interaction, specifically, the shape of a table, encourage different types of interaction. The differences, perceptual and real, between a round table, square table, and rectangular table, are significant.

Seating behavior is related to task situations, the level of intimacy between people, personality characteristics, dominance, friendliness, introversion-extroversion, and the amount of communication among interactants.

What about the effects of the manipulation of objects and seating arrangements? Once again, research findings suggest that these factors affect communication behavior both in classroom and office settings. Where a person sits may determine the extent to which that person interacts in a particular setting.

Finally, our environment, spatial arrangement, and seating behavior are significant with regard to the structural settings for interaction, the perceptions associated with certain seating locations, and the effects on behavior. Clearly, the research demonstrates that our manipulation of microspace is quite revealing.

References

Adams, R. S., & Biddle, B. (1970) *Realities of teaching: Exploration with video tape.* New York: Holt, Rinehart and Winston.

Birren, R. (1975) *Color psychology and color therapy.* New York: University Books.

Block, C. (1975) Design to dispel fear of oral surgery. *Dental Surgery: The Journal of Dental Practice, 4,* 85–89.

Burgoon, J., & Saine, T. S. (1978) *The unspoken dialogue: An introduction to nonverbal communication.* Boston: Houghton Mifflin.

Carey, S. (September 24, 1978) Educator teaches behavior control by arranging child's environment. *The Arizona Republic,* B-2.

Carr, S. J., & Dabbs, J. M. (1974) The effects of lighting, distance, and intimacy of topic on verbal and visual behavior. *Sociometry, 37,* 592–600.

Carter, M. (September 4, 1977a) NBC's news tries a copy approach. *The Arizona Republic.*

Carter, M. (September 19, 1977b) NBC's new look news. *Newsweek,* p. 103.

Cook, M. (1970) Experiments on orientation and proxemics. *Human Relations, 23,* 61–76.

Finnegan, M. C., & Solomon, L. Z. (1981) Work attitudes in windowed vs. windowless environments. *Journal of Social Psychology, 115,* 291–292.

Gass, C. S. (1984) Therapeutic influence as a function of therapist attire and the seating arrangement in an initial interview. *Journal of Clinical Psychology, 40* (1), 52–57.

Goldberger, P. (April 30, 1978) Excessive neon a purposeful ploy. *The Arizona Republic,* K-2.

Hare, A., & Bales, R. (1963) Seating position and small group interaction. *Sociometry, 26,* 480–486.

Heston, J., & Garner, P. S. (1972) *Study of personal spacing and desk arrangement in the learning environment.* Paper presented at the meeting of the International Communication Association.

Howells, L. T., & Becker, S. W. (1962) Seating arrangement and leadership emergence. *Journal of Abnormal and Social Psychology, 64,* 148–150.

Johnson, N. B. (1982) Education as environmental socialization: Classroom spatial patterns and the transmission of sociocultural norms. *Anthropology Quarterly, 55,* 31–43.

Ketcham, H. (1958) *Color planning for business and industry.* New York: Harper.

Knapp, M. (1978) *Nonverbal communication in human interaction.* New York: Holt, Rinehart & Winston.

Koneya, M., & Barbour, A. (1976) *Louder than words . . . nonverbal communication.* Columbus, Ohio: Charles E. Merrill.

Korda, M. (1975) *Power! How to get it, how to use it.* New York: Random House.

Kowinski, W. (March 7, 1975) Shedding new light. *New Times,* p. 48.

Levine, D. W., O'Neal, E. C., Garwood, S. G., & McDonald, P. J. (1980) Classroom ecology: The effects of seating position on grades and participation. *Personality and Social Psychology Bulletin, 6* (3), 409–412.

McCroskey, J. C., Larson, C. E., & Knapp, M. L. (1971) *An introduction to interpersonal communication.* Englewood Cliffs, N.J.: Prentice-Hall.

Maslow, A. H., & Mintz, N. L. (1956) Effects of esthetic surroundings: I. Initial effects of three esthetic conditions upon perceiving "energy" and "well being" in faces. *Journal of Psychology, 41,* 247–254.

Mehrabian, A. (1976) *Public places and private spaces.* New York: Basic Books.

Mintz, N. L. (1956) Effects of esthetic surroundings: II. Prolonged and repeated experience in a "beautiful" and "ugly" room. *Journal of Psychology, 41,* 459–466.

Nelson, J. G., Pelech, M. T., & Foster, S. F. (1984) Color preference and stimulation seeking. *Perceptual and Motor Skills, 59,* 913–914.

Price, B. (April 1977) A stretch in jail—how would you handle it? *Psychology Today,* pp. 27–28.

Resnick, H., & Jaffe, B. (1982) The physical environment and social welfare. *Social Casework, 63,* 354–362.

Russo, N. (1967) Connotation of seating arrangement. *Cornell Journal of Social Relations, 2,* 37–44.

Sommer, R. (1969) *Personal space: The behavioral basis of design.* Englewood Cliffs, N.J.: Prentice-Hall.

Stires, L. (1980) Classroom seating location, student grades, and attitudes: Environment or self-selection? *Environment and Behavior, 12* (2), 241–254.

Strodtbeck, F., & Hook, L. (1961) The social dimensions of a twelve man jury table. *Sociometry, 24,* 397–415.

Thompson, J. J. (1973) *Beyond words: Nonverbal communication in the classroom.* New York: Citation Press.

Walberg, H. J. (1969) Physical and psychological distance in the classroom. *School Review, 77,* 64–70.

Wollin, D. D., & Montagne, M. (1981) College classroom environment: Effects of sterility versus amiability on student and teacher performance. *Environment and Behavior, 13* (6), 707–716.

Zweigenhaft, R. (1976) Personal space in the faculty office—desk placement and the student-faculty interaction. *Journal of Applied Psychology, 61,* 529–532.

CHAPTER 7

PERSONAL SPACE, TERRITORY, AND CROWDING

Territory is not the cause of war. . . . What territory promises is the high probability that if intrusion takes place, war will follow.

Robert Ardrey, *The Territorial Imperative*, 1966

Invasion of a territory that is the "exclusive" property of others takes a variety of shapes and forms. For instance, territorial invasion may involve the movement of personal belongings by a stranger, the hijacking of a plane, or the armed invasion of a country during war. In each of these situations, the consequences may be dire, depending on the circumstances that surround it. (Note: Even in the first instance, the books that you moved may have belonged to a not-so-nice ace power lifter!) At the very least, when someone's personal territory is invaded, communication among all involved parties may become strained and tense.

To illustrate more completely the concept of invasion—and the consequences that can result—one need look no further than the year 1987 and the "breach of security" that occurred at the new American embassy in Moscow. According to top officials in the State Department, listening devices were found in the bricks and steel girders of the nearly completed office complex. The presence of the devices was attributed to a 1972 agreement allowing the new U.S. embassy to be built by Soviet workers. In addition, the agreement authorized the Soviets to assemble many of the prefabricated modules off site, away from American supervision. State Department officials argued that, as a result, the embassy could never be made secure and should be torn down and replaced at Soviet expense. In addition, U.S. officials argued that until a second new embassy was built, the Soviets should not be allowed to move into their new embassy, recently completed in Washington.

Although, at first glance, this story may reflect the concept of territorial invasion only indirectly, what obscures the perception that a *real* invasion occurred is the fact that the *potential* for future invasion was of even greater concern. The insertion of listening devices in both the bricks and steel girders of the building, indeed, constituted a real invasion of American territory. The $191 million complex had been built with American dollars and, therefore, constituted real American territory. However, because only a few residences were in use at the time that the security breach was found, the "real" invasion previously noted was *not* of primary importance. Of greater concern to American officials was the potential for an even more critical future invasion—in offices of top ranking U.S. embassy officials. Because the structure of the new building had been so completely (and thoroughly) compromised, the State Department felt that the office complex might never be completely secure. As a result, the potential for invasion was an even more overriding concern—resulting in retaliation on the part of the United States.

Although we as individuals are rarely concerned that the security of our homes or offices will be compromised, physical space has frequently become a matter of life and death in our history. World War II followed an attack on the American naval base at Pearl Harbor in 1941, while many marines lost their lives defending American embassies in the Middle East in the early 1980s.

Control of physical space often occurs much more subtly than the armed takeover of an embassy or country. Marilyn was the first to arrive at her dormitory room when school began. She looked at the two beds and immediately claimed one as "hers." Her roommate arrived twenty minutes later and accepted the division without question. For the rest of the school year, each "roomie" took care not to disturb the other's half of the room. Does this sound familiar? Concern over space in dormitories is so great that dorm rules at one southern university forbid each roommate from using the other's side of the room.

A less tangible form of space is the distance people use and control immediately around them. Hank once went out with a woman who sat and stood a little closer to him than he wanted. He liked Cindy but constantly found himself backing or turning away from her. This made her feel rejected, even though he was only trying to get some elbow room between them. Their use of space communicated different things to each other.

Space communicates, according to Edward T. Hall (1974), who coined the term **proxemics** for studies that focus on our use of space. Messages ranging from declarations of status to statements of affection are communicated through the use of space, although they may vary due to factors such as sex, age, circumstances, and other nonverbal dimensions such as eye contact, body movement, and facial expression. The purpose of this chapter is to introduce the area of proxemics as well as the many ways in which space does help us to communicate. The three primary topics to be addressed are territoriality, interpersonal space, and crowding.

TERRITORIALITY

As the opening illustration of this chapter suggests, both animals and humans stake out and defend their territories. Male dogs urinate on bushes and trees to identify them as their own; they try to chase off other dogs who enter their territory. Similarly, humans erect flags, fences, and "no trespassing" signs to define their territory. They also begin wars or call the police to discourage invaders. In each of these instances, the behaviors being described provide examples of **territoriality,** believed to be an innate characteristic in both animals and humans. For Ardrey (1966), territoriality exists when "an area of space, whether of water or earth or air [is defended by] . . . an animal or group of animals . . . as an exclusive preserve" (p. 3). As you can see, given this particular definition, both humans and animals do engage in territorial behaviors.

The importance of territoriality in animals is manifested in **homing behavior** (Ardrey, 1966), or the ability of some animals to travel hundreds or thousands of miles in order to return to a specific location, often to mate. For example, although scientists have yet to figure out how they accomplish this particular feat, sea turtles, eels, and pigeons are able to find precisely those rivers and bays that are defined as their territories. However, home is equally important to humans. In fact, the recent increase of interest in discovering our roots may provide an excellent example of our own mythical search for home.

Although territory is important for both animals and humans, as we have seen in the previous discussion, there *are* some differences in the way territoriality is manifested. As several researchers have noted, territory is not as often an "exclusive preserve" for humans, and rarely do they take up arms to defend their personal territory. In fact, humans regularly entertain visitors on their home territory without displaying any antagonism (Edney, 1976). Think of the last time you had friends over for a party, to study, or just to watch television. Did you feel hostile and threatened? Probably not. Yet if you watched very closely, your cat or dog probably did!

Another important difference between animals and humans involves the necessity of using a "defense." Animals must actively protect their territory from other animals that try to take it over. On the other hand, humans are rarely called upon to defend their rights to particular holdings. In addition, human territoriality is much more passive than that found in the animal kingdom. For example, among humans, children naturally avoid taking their father's chair at the dinner table; secretaries naturally avoid sitting behind the desks of their bosses; finally, students naturally avoid sitting at library tables that appear to be occupied, even though the "owner" is not present. In short, humans so commonly respect the territory of others that any violation rates as a media event. For example, students in the sixties and seventies captured headlines and made TV news when they took over the offices of university presidents and administrators.

Primarily because of established societal norms, human beings rarely take defensive measures to protect their territories. To support this belief, McAndrew and his colleagues (1978) conducted a study in a library to determine if students would protect their tables. A confederate lured twenty students away from their desks by asking their help in answering a questionnaire. While they were away, another confederate moved the belongings of each student to the side and put other books and a jacket in their place. When the students returned from helping the first confederate and found their belongings moved, all twenty of them withdrew to other seats. Not a single student defended his or her table! When territory is invaded, most people would rather switch than fight.

Because human territoriality typically does not involve defense, it differs from animal territoriality and, therefore, needs a different definition. As a result, territoriality in humans will be defined as the continuous association of a person or group with certain places (Edney, 1976). The place may be defended by the owner, but, more often, that place is simply avoided by others who respect the first person's claim to the given location.

Territorial rights may be strict or loose, depending on the people involved and their relationship to each other. Rosenblatt and Budd (1975) compared the territoriality of married and unmarried cohabiting couples. Among the unmarried couples, both parties were more likely to have some place in their home where they could be alone. Each individual had a special room or location that was "off limits" to the partner. Among the married couples, neither party had a place in which they could be completely alone, but they did divide up the available territory more strictly. For example, married couples were more likely to have "his closet" versus "her closet," "his chair" versus "her chair," "his drawer" versus "her drawer," and so on. Surprisingly, unmarried couples tended to intermingle their belongings more than married couples; they were less territorial. Additionally, couples who lived together and then got married had the characteristics of both groups. Like the unmarried couples, they intermingled their belongings and were less territorial; like the married couples, they did not maintain places to be alone within their homes.

Types of Territories

The United States, a library table at your college or university, a wife's bureau drawers, a father's chair, the desk you always take in chemistry class—all of these are examples of territory. They are places or locations that are or have been associated with a person or group over a period of time. Several researchers have attempted to categorize territories, identifying similarities and differences among types. Scheflen (1975) formulated a hierarchy of territories based on their size; he called the smallest territory a **spot.** A spot is a space several inches across, just large enough for a glass or an elbow. (Moviegoers stake out a spot on the armrest beside their seats and may have to jostle their neighbors to keep it in their possession.) Scheflen's hierarchy continues with a **cubit,** an 18-inch building block of space; several cubits pile up to form a **k-space,** which is the amount of territory a person generally occupies. A **location** is the space immediately around a person, while a **module** is a row of locations. (People who line up to buy tickets for a basketball game occupy a module.) Finally, a **nucleus** is at the center of a **region,** which is a room-sized territory—large enough for a number of people to occupy.

Although size is only one way to categorize territory, it is extremely relevant to the people who own or control the space. The reason is that the amount of space that a person controls is correlated with the amount of status accorded that person. Henley (1977) argued that nonverbal qualities determine and maintain power structure in society and that territory is an important nonverbal dimension. If you meet someone and learn that he or she owns several houses, property throughout the world, and a dozen classic cars, you would probably give him or her more respect than if he or she controlled less territory.

Territory is also classified according to its importance to the people who use it. Altman (1975) identified primary, secondary, and public territories. **Primary territories** are those over which a person has exclusive control. Owners of Ferrari race cars often treat them as primary territories, not allowing others to drive them. Personal belongings such as toothbrushes and clothing—also bedrooms— are generally primary territories. **Secondary territories** are not the exclusive property of the owner but are generally associated with him or her. The desk you always take in class, the table you always ask for at your favorite restaurant, and the church pew you regularly occupy on Sunday are secondary territories.

Public territories are areas open to anyone; these would include such places as a parking lot, a library, or a beach. Although these areas are "public," an individual may claim **temporary occupancy** over a piece of the territory. Claims are made by stretching out a blanket at the beach or by leaving books and personal belongings on a desk at the library. The items used to define a space as a territory in a public setting are called **markers.** Of course, a person's claim to a public territory is not legal and lasts only as long as others respect the markers.

Even in a public space, the space immediately around a person is considered to be his or her own "territory." (Carolyn Brown)

Public territories have also been identified by Lyman and Scott (1967), who have observed that they may be colonized by persons or groups. **Colonization** occurs when a public territory is taken over by a group through continuous usage or defense. Juvenile gangs claim city streets and defend them from other gangs. A fraternity group constantly sits at a certain table in a cafeteria, and others come to think of it as the fraternity's domain. Elaine's is a little restaurant in New York City that became famous because it was colonized by the rich and famous, such as Woody Allen, Ali McGraw, and Norman Mailer.

A public territory that has been colonized becomes a **home territory.** This is an area where a person has relative freedom of behavior and control over the territory. This category encompasses both the primary and secondary areas identified by Altman (1975). Lyman and Scott (1967) observed that the distinction between home and public territories is sometimes difficult to make. What is a public territory to one group may be perceived as a home territory to another. Although a restaurant in New York City may be "home" for its regular patrons, it is "public" for others who wander in. Gay bars are home territory for homosexuals but public territories for others. Likewise, a dating couple may have "their" table in a public restaurant, "their" spot on a public shady lane, or "their" niche on a secluded but public beach.

Territory is also given to groups of people who are carrying on a conversation. An invisible boundary surrounds such a group separating it from others. The space inside the boundary is called an **interactional territory** (Lyman and Scott, 1967). Svenn Lindskold and his colleagues (1976) tested the boundaries of groups who formed on a sidewalk outside a store window. Results of their study revealed that passive groups simply gazed in the window, while interacting groups carried on conversations. In addition, more people walked through the passive groups than the interacting groups. The researchers concluded that the pedestrians chose to walk around the interacting groups in order to preserve their interactional territory.

Invasion of interactional territory depends on the number and status of people who are interacting. Knowles (1973) found that fewer people walked between two people than between two wastebaskets, and still fewer walked between four people than between two people. The larger the crowd, the less likely that interactional territory will be invaded. Knowles also controlled the status of the conversationalists by changing their age and dress. Fewer subjects invaded the higher-status than the lower-status conversants.

The last category of territory which was identified by Lyman and Scott (1967) is **body territory,** which includes the human body as well as the area of space surrounding it. This accompanying area of space is classified by some as "personal space" and will be investigated more completely in a later section. The body is perhaps our most sacred territory, and access to it is strictly controlled by the owner and by social restrictions. For example, social norms dictate that a person should not invade certain parts of another person's body without explicit permission. Because the body is so important in the study of nonverbal communication, several chapters in this book introduce related topics, such as how the body is displayed (Chapter 3) and the role of touch in communication (Chapter 8).

Territorial Encroachment and Reaction

Although territorial claims are generally respected by other people, trespassing of various types does occur. Three specific forms of encroachment are violation, invasion, and contamination (Lyman and Scott, 1967).

Violation occurs when territory that belongs to someone else is used without permission. For example, when a roommate borrows your clothes or a neighbor uses your tools without first asking, he or she is said to be violating your territory. **Invasion** occurs when someone crosses boundaries and takes over another person's territory. Breaking into a line, overrunning an embassy, and hijacking a plane are examples of invasion. Third, territories may be **contaminated,** or rendered impure, through the entry or usage of others. Religious fanatics from Saudi Arabia invaded Mecca in December of 1979 to protest contamination of their country. They called for "a total rejection of Western influences in Saudi Arabia, demanding, among other things, the banning of radio, TV and even soccer" (*Newsweek,* December 3, 1979, p. 65). A growing number of Americans are concerned about the contamination of the air by cigarette smoke. Several states have either adopted or considered laws to prohibit smoking in public buildings. The Civil Aeronautics Board requires airlines to accommodate nonsmokers, much to the chagrin of smoking passengers. An Eastern Airlines flight to New York landed early in Baltimore in December of 1979 because passengers began bickering about the smoking restrictions. Smoking passengers demanded their right to smoke, while a nonsmoking passenger insisted on his right to uncontaminated air (*Newsweek,* December 17, 1979, p. 55).

When territory is violated, invaded, or contaminated, the owner may react in a variety of ways (Lyman and Scott, 1967). One alternative is **withdrawal** from the location. This type of reaction is most likely to occur when the occupancy is temporary in a public territory. People in libraries, cafeterias, and beaches withdraw when their space is attacked. A second alternative is **insulation,** which involves the erecting of boundaries and barriers. Roommates may hang a bedspread or curtain between their beds to separate their sides of a room. Family members may tightly shut and even lock doors rather than let them hang ajar, while students in the library often pile books and belongings between themselves and the people beside them. They insulate themselves by establishing barriers.

The most dramatic form of territorial protection is **turf defense,** or the active repelling of invaders. This form of defense primarily occurs when someone attempts to take over or harm what is "ours." For example, we will elicit "turf-defensive" behaviors if someone invades or contaminates our country, home or personal property. Additionally, we will defend our turf if we perceive that our family is in danger.

Not only do owners of territory react to encroachment; so do those who inadvertently invade others' space. Efran and Cheyne (1974) examined the nonverbal responses of subjects who walked down a corridor. Sometimes no one else was in the hall; sometimes two people were in the hall conversing and the subject had to walk around them; and sometimes the subject had to walk between two people carrying on a conversation. When the subjects violated the interactional territory by walking between the conversationalists, they lowered their heads, closed their eyes, lowered their gazes, tightened their lips, and pursed their mouths. Subjects who had to walk beside the people who were talking lowered their heads and gazes more than subjects who walked down an empty corridor. Invading someone else's territory may be just as annoying as having your own territory invaded.

Factors Influencing Territoriality

A number of researchers have investigated public territoriality and found that it is related to several different factors. Some of the most important of these are gender, intensity of invasion, and desirability of territory.

Gender. Feminine markers are less effective at repelling invaders than masculine markers. Shafer and Sadowski (1975) marked barroom tables with either a man's or a woman's belongings (such as a jacket and briefcase or a sweater and purse) and then observed the results. Tables with feminine markers were invaded sooner and more frequently than tables with masculine markers. Shafer and Sadowski speculated that the feminine markers were less threatening because women would be less likely to try to defend their territory.

Gender also influences invasions of library tables. In one experiment (Krail and Leventhal, 1976), male and female confederates sat down at tables already occupied by students. Students responded to the invasions by leaving, building barriers, leaning away, or challenging the confederate. Responses were fastest if the confederate was of the *same gender* as the student. (Perhaps students hoped they would get a date out of the situation when the invader was of the opposite sex!)

Intensity of invasion.   Whether or not a person withdraws from a territory depends on how significantly it is invaded. A dog may not like other dogs to enter his backyard, but he becomes even more territorial when another dog attempts to eat out of his dish. Humans also vary in their reactions according to the seriousness of an invasion. Becker and Mayo (1971) observed territorial behavior in a cafeteria. In one condition, confederates moved fifteen people's belongings and sat in their seats. All fifteen withdrew to other seats. In a second condition, confederates sat beside eighteen reserved seats; sixteen of the eighteen people left. Finally, confederates sat across from fifteen reserved seats; only one person left. In a similar study conducted in a library, Krail and Leventhal (1976) found that students responded sooner if the confederates peered over their shoulders while sitting adjacent to them than if they sat across from them. If you want to meet someone, you should probably sit across from that person rather than beside him or her!

Desirability of territory.   In the same barroom experiment that examined gender differences, Shafer and Sadowski (1975) compared territorial invasions of desirable and undesirable tables. Because bars are social locations, the desirable tables are those that promote interaction with other people, while the undesirable tables are more isolated. Consistent with predictions, the researchers found that marked desirable tables were invaded sooner and more frequently than undesirable tables.

PERSONAL SPACE

Alice and Jimmy are facing one another. As she steps backward, he steps forward. Then he takes another step forward, and she turns outward. He then turns outward, and she turns toward him and takes a step in his direction. He turns back toward her and also moves forward. They pause for a second, and each moves backward and turns slightly away from the other.

Have Alice and Jimmy learned the latest disco dance? Were they engaged in an elaborate mating ritual characterized by nonverbal maneuvers? Were they playing tennis or softball? No. Alice and Jimmy were simply carrying on a conversation about their English professor. In addition to expressing their ideas through words, they were communicating nonverbally through their use of space and personal distance. Each was attempting to maintain a certain distance from the other, although their preferred distances were not always the same. Sometimes Alice wanted more space than Jimmy, and sometimes Jimmy wanted more space than Alice. These differences led to the fancy footwork of moving backward and forward, inward and outward. Each person's preferred distance also changed throughout the conversation. When Alice disagreed with Jimmy, he wanted more space; when she flirted, he wanted less distance between them.

The distance or space that Alice and Jimmy were manipulating is called **personal space** and is the three-dimensional area of space which surrounds us. Personal space is a portable territory with invisible boundaries that expand or contract depending on the situation. Individuals carry it around with them constantly and position themselves in conversations in a way that will maintain it. Julie needs very little personal space and is constantly moving closer to people in order to reach the distance she prefers. Sandy, on the other hand, needs more personal space and frequently finds herself backed up against walls as a result of trying to move away from people. Each tries to maintain her personal space, although she may not always be successful.

Characteristics of Personal Space

The size and shape of personal space have been analyzed by several researchers. Hall (1963) initially proposed that personal space was spherical or circular. However, more recently, researchers have observed that some individuals have larger rear zones than front zones, while still others have larger front zones than rear zones. In addition, Hayduk (1978) has suggested that personal space has a vertical dimension and that the desired space around the feet may be proportionally smaller than that desired around the head. Based on the research of Hall, Hayduk and others (Haynes and Ellington, 1982; Hayduk, 1983), Figure 7.1 depicts some possible dimensions of personal space. The reader should note that larger or smaller front and rear zones would alter the size and shape of the space even more.

The purpose and function of personal space have also been analyzed. Joe stands 4 feet from his boss, 8 feet from his congressman, 2 feet from his mother, and 10 inches from his girlfriend. Why is his personal space different for each person? According to **protection theory,** space is a "body-buffer zone" used for protective purposes (Dosey and Meisels, 1969). When an individual is threatened, his or her personal space expands. The threats may be physical or emotional. According to this theory, Joe's body-buffer zone is greatest for the congressman because the congressman is very intimidating to him. On the other hand, his girlfriend is least threatening to him so he maintains the smallest distance with her.

Perhaps, the most important characteristic of personal space is that it is variable. As we previously noted in our example with Alice and Jimmy, some people need more personal space than others. Furthermore, our personal space needs vary depending on our gender, age, cultural background, and relationship to the people with whom we are interacting. For example, John's space needs are much different when he is lovingly discussing the future with his girlfriend in the back seat of a car than when he is angrily disputing a grade in his professor's office. These factors and others which affect interpersonal distancing will be discussed in greater detail in a later section.

Another important characteristic of personal space is that it interacts with other dimensions of nonverbal communication. When Hall (1963) introduced proxemics, he noted that the individual's use of space is related to several nonverbal codes. For example, our perception and use of space depends on whether people are standing, sitting, or lying down. They also depend on whether we are facing or turned away from one another (body orientation), how much touching can and does occur, how much of each other we physically can see, how loud our voices are, and whether or not body odors or heat can be detected. Sandy may feel "too close" to Paul even though she is 6 feet away from him. However, even at that distance she can smell unpleasant body odors; her ears hurt from his loud voice; and she doesn't like the fact that he is looking directly into her eyes. Lee, on the other hand, does not feel too close to Phil, even though they are only 8 inches

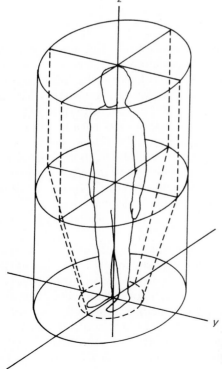

FIGURE 7.1 **Front and rear zones of personal space.**

apart. However, they are sitting back to back, cannot see one another, and are having difficulty in hearing one another. Perceptions of personal space and distance are influenced by other dimensions of nonverbal communication.

Personal appearance can also influence personal space. Caplan and Goldman (1981) asked a tall male (6'2"), a tall female (5'11"), a short male (5'5"), and a short female (5'2") confederate to stand next to the wall of a train station corridor. The researchers then recorded the number of passing pedestrians and whether they passed closer to the tall or short confederates. Results of the study indicated that commuters preferred to enter the personal space of the short rather than the tall confederate. In addition, female commuters entered the space of short confederates significantly more often than did male commuters (p. 167).

Physical attractiveness may also influence personal space. Powell and Dabbs (1976) hung pictures of beautiful and ugly male and female models on the wall and asked subjects to approach them. Females moved closer to the attractive pictures than the ugly pictures, while males moved closer only to the pictures of attractive females. The researchers also tested the effect of ugly and attractive interviewers on the personal space of pedestrians. They found that the people did not vary the distance they selected according to either gender or attractiveness. Their "real-life" experiment did not confirm the results they found when they used pictures.

Factors Influencing Personal Space

As noted earlier, several different factors are thought to influence personal-space needs. Much research has been conducted on these factors through the use of a variety of techniques for analyzing personal space. Unfortunately, the results of many studies contradict one another, probably because the investigators measured personal space in different ways (Hayduk, 1983). The technique that currently appears to be the most useful for experimental studies is called **stop distance.** Either the subject approaches the experimenter and stops when comfortable or the subject stands still while the experimenter approaches from different angles. The subject instructs the experimenter when to stop on the basis of how comfortable he or she (the subject) feels with the distance. Numerous studies have shown that the following factors influence personal space.

Gender.   Many researchers have assumed that males require more space than females and that male pairs interact at greater distances than female or mixed-sex pairs. Unfortunately, the relationship between gender and personal space is not that simple. Many researchers have found contradictory results. For example, Pederson and Heaston (1972) found that males let people approach them more closely from the front while females let people approach them more closely from the sides. On the other hand, Fisher and Byrne (1975) found that females responded more negatively when invaded from the side, while males were more negative when invaded from the front.

Our culture has taught males to take up more space, while women have been taught to use less. Males and females use space in fundamentally different ways.

Although the contradictory results have not been resolved, recent research indicates that males' and females' use of space depends on the eye contact and facial expression of the other person (Buchanan, Goldman, and Juhnke, 1977; Hughes and Goldman, 1978). Imagine that you are getting on a crowded elevator. Some of the people are looking at you while others are avoiding your glance. Where would you stand? Closer to the people looking at you or closer to those avoiding eye contact? Your answer will probably depend on whether you are male or female. Some researchers have found that when people enter elevators containing at least two other people (confederates), males choose to stand closer to the people who are not looking at them. Females behave similarly when the confederates are male but chose to violate the space of directly gazing and/or smiling female confederates rather than the space of those who avoid eye contact. Studies such as these point out that males and females use space in fundamentally different ways. However, much more research must be conducted before firm conclusions can be reached.

Age.   The effects of age on personal space have been consistently supported (Hayduk, 1978; Sarafino and Helmuth, 1981; Hayduk, 1983). By the time they are twelve years old, children have learned adult spacing, although even younger children are sensitive to the uses of space. To document the latter statement, Sarafino and Helmuth (1981) observed 101 preschoolers ranging from 25 to 62 months of age. Results of their study revealed two important developmental relationships. The 25- to 42-month-old children maintained much greater distance than 43- to 62-month-olds. Additionally, as amount of time that the children spent in day care increased, females came to maintain smaller distances than boys.

Expectations established by parents and other adults probably teach children how to use space. Additional evidence suggests that children learn spacing by imitating those around them. Bailey, Hartnett, and Glover (1973) found that fifth- and sixth-graders imitated a popular sixth-grade boy who approached another person at either a very close or a very far distance. Children who did not observe the boy stopped at an intermediate distance. Since personal space is learned by imitating the people around us, much is probably taught in the family. For instance, some families tolerate very near distances for interpersonal interaction, while others prefer larger distances.

As the aging process moves us into young adulthood, personal space gradually increases in size (Hayduk, 1983). Likewise, as we move into later life, interpersonal distance increases. To determine exact differences in interpersonal distancing between young and elderly adults, Winogrand (1981) compared the peer interactions of eighteen young white females (19 to 24 years in age), eighteen elderly white females (63 to 85), and eighteen elderly black females (53 to 86). Results of the study supported her hypothesis: the young white females used significantly closer interpersonal distances than did the elderly white adults. However, no differences emerged between the white and black elderly females' interpersonal distances. Winogrand concluded that age—not race—appears to be the significant factor. The study also supports the increase in personal space needs of adults as they move into and through adulthood.

Culture.   Although researchers have consistently agreed on the relationship between age and personal space, such a consensus does not exist regarding the role of culture outside of the normal socialization process. In fact, a number of studies addressing this particular issue have produced conflicting results. For example, Jones (1971) investigated differences in personal space among blacks, Puerto Ricans, Italians, and Chinese in New York City. He especially predicted the Chinese subjects to require greater interpersonal distances. However, the results of his study showed that none of the groups significantly differed in interactional distances. Jones concluded that cultural differences did not account for personal space needs among his subjects.

On the other hand, other researchers have discovered cultural differences in interpersonal distancing and hence in personal space needs across a number of cultures. Investigating the influence of culture, language, and gender on interpersonal distance, Sussman and Rosenfeld (1982) found that Japanese, Venezuelan, and American students, indeed, use different interpersonal distances. More specifically, when speaking their native language, Japanese students sit farther apart than Venezuelan students, and American students sit somewhere in between, or at an intermediate distance. However, when speaking English, both Japanese and

Venezuelan students approximate American distances more closely. The researchers concluded that both culture and language seem to affect interpersonal distance.

As you can see, the reviews are mixed regarding the relationship between culture and personal space. Thus, additional research must be conducted before we can determine the full impact of this factor. Until such time as conclusive results emerge, we should be aware—and wary—of the many stereotypes concerning the personal-space needs of various cultures. As we already said, the verdict is not yet in.

Relationship.   Roberto and Sandy are carrying on a conversation while standing 10 feet apart. Alice and Norman are standing only 6 inches apart. Simply by observing the distances between people, inferences can be drawn about their relationships. Most people would assume that Roberto and Sandy do not have a personal relationship, while Alice and Norman appear to be close emotionally as well as physically. Edward T. Hall identified four distinct categories of informal space associated with four different types of relationships. His observations were based on white middle-class northeasterners, so the specific distances he found may be different for other cultural groups. The categories he identified are intimate, casual-personal, socioconsultive, and public. **Intimate distance,** from zero to 18 inches, is used by people who are involved with one another on a personal level, such as Alice and Norman. Lovers interact at an intimate distance. **Casual-personal distance,** from 1½ to 4 feet, is used for personal business, such as conversations between friends and relatives. When Al and Jack discuss their plans for the evening, they stand about 3 feet apart. Impersonal business is conducted from 4 to 8 feet, or at a **socioconsultive distance.** Marilyn and Sue have a formal relationship as sales managers for a computer company and stand about 5 feet apart when discussing company policy. Finally, **public distance** ranges from 8 feet to the limits of a person's vision or hearing. Teachers communicate with students at this distance when delivering lectures.

Status is another characteristic of relationships that influences the use of personal space. As we noted in Chapter 6, people of higher rank are given more space than people of lower rank. Dean, Willis, and Hewitt (1975) investigated the role of status and rank in military personnel by observing personal-space use in 562 conversations. All of the observed interactions were informal and took place in the cafeteria, hospital, recreation center, or U.S. Navy exchange. As you can imagine, when subordinates approached superiors, they gave more space to those of higher rank than to those of lower rank. However, when superiors approached subordinates, the distance they maintained was not correlated with differences in military rank. Apparently, differences in status are more relevant when approaching superiors than when approaching subordinates.

The amount of *liking* in a relationship also influences how close people stand to one another (Mehrabian, 1969). People who like each other stand closer together than do people who dislike each other. Patty was a student who participated in a class project with several other students, including John, who missed most group meetings. In describing her group, Patty wrote:

> Our topic was relatively intimate, and we liked one another on the whole, so we sat relatively close to each other, especially when seated at a table or with our desks pulled together in a circle. John seemed to have the largest "bubble" of personal space because when he did attend meetings, he was rather alienated. Group members were less tolerant of his invasions of space and less willing to enter into his space than they were with anyone else in the group.

The group disliked John for missing group meetings and communicated with him at a greater personal distance as a result of their feelings.

Pathology and deviance.   Many researchers have studied the effects of personality on personal space. Although interesting, the findings have been inconclusive because most studies have failed to support their predictions or have contradicted the results of other studies (Hayduk, 1978). However, the research has been very conclusive in a related area. People who have been identified as deviant members of society have greater personal-space needs than usual. Deviants include people with histories of mental illness such as schizophrenia, prisoners, other individuals with criminal records, and disruptive high school students. For example, Walkey and Gilmour (1984) completed a twelve-month follow-up of seventy-three prison inmates in a New Zealand prison. The number of fights over the twelve months following the completion of a measure of preferred interpersonal distance was their unit of analysis. Results of the study revealed that those inmates who were involved in fights had a significantly greater need for interpersonal distance than inmates who were not involved in fights. Further analysis revealed that interpersonal distance scores best predicted fights in prison.

Another study demonstrating the personal space needs of incarcerated offenders took place in Ontario, Canada. Conducted by Wormith (1984), the study focused on "the attributes of offenders' personal space" (p. 824). Consistent with predictions and previous research, offenders had a larger personal space distance to the rear than in any other direction. However, contrary to previous research, the difference was not attributed to severity of offense or incarceration time. Rather, the need for greater personal space to the rear seemed to be more related to generalized anxiety.

The research related to pathology and deviance supports the notion that the boundaries of personal space represent "body-buffer zones" used to protect people from emotional and physical threats. Individuals with more serious personality problems see others as threatening and, therefore, need more space for protection. Current research suggests that most violent prisoners were abused physically as children. It appears that in response to their physical abuse as children, these prisoners developed the need for a larger personal space than most people require. As a result, their space is more likely to be invaded by others who do not need as much space, thereby causing them to feel "attacked." Thus they are more likely to respond in a pathological or deviant manner.

CROWDING

After learning that her favorite department store was having a gigantic sale, Susie stood in line for an hour waiting for the doors to open and then jostled with hundreds of other bargain hunters for the best buys. After forty-five minutes of fighting the crowd, Susie gave up, feeling anxious and closed in by the other customers. While shopping, Susie experienced the sensation of crowding. Jerry experienced the same sensation, although the circumstances were very different. He was at a quiet art museum, admiring the work, when another art lover entered the gallery. Although few people were in the museum and there were many pieces of art to enjoy, the newcomer chose to stand only 3 inches from Jerry to look at the same painting. The stranger's nearness caused Jerry to feel tense and closed in; he also experienced crowding.

Crowding is a psychological experience that occurs when a person becomes aware of spatial restrictions. Both Susie and Jerry became aware of limitations on the space around them, although for different reasons. Susie experienced crowding as a result of **stimulus overload.** So much was happening around her that she could not cope with everything. She could not process all the stimuli and consequently became fatigued and confused and escaped from the situation. City dwellers may cope with stimulus overload by becoming very aloof and isolating themselves from the people around them.

Jerry's experience of crowding resulted from **behavioral constraint.** By invading his personal space, the newcomer reduced Jerry's freedom of movement, thereby causing him to experience infringement and invasion. Although physical invasion

How would the demands of personal space affect these passengers' behavior toward each other as they walk off the airplane? (Carolyn Brown)

into personal space is a more powerful source of crowding, **surveillance** also creates behavioral constraint (Greenberg and Firestone, 1977). Have you ever felt uneasy because a stranger was watching you for no reason? Or even just because you *thought* someone was observing you? Surveillance can create a sense of crowding and motivate a person to withdraw from a situation.

The negative effects of an invasion of personal space have been well documented (Kanaga and Flynn, 1981; Zeedyk-Ryan and Smith, 1983). People whose space has been invaded display avoidance and withdrawal behaviors. They may leave the situation entirely, or they may back or turn away. Invaded individuals may also experience stress and arousal. When Jerry's space was invaded, he experienced stress and quickly moved to the next room in the museum. However, some invasions may have positive consequences. Imagine how Jerry would have reacted if the invader had been a gorgeous female and he had been looking for a date for that weekend! The violation of his personal space might have caused him to perceive her more positively.

Some researchers have found that invasions of personal space *intensify* interactions (Burgoon, 1978; Schiffenbauer and Schiavo, 1976). Rewarding invaders are perceived more *positively* than noninvaders; punishing invaders are perceived more *negatively* than noninvaders. Imagine that your boss is reprimanding you for being late to work. If she invades your space, your negative feelings for her will intensify. On the other hand, if she invades your personal space in order to compliment you for having done a superior job, your positive feelings for her will intensify. The consequences of personal-space invasions depend on the purpose of the communicators.

Density and Crowding

Crime rates in cities have led researchers to speculate about a relationship between population density and deviant behavior. **Density** is a physical condition and refers to the number of people in an area of space. Accordingly, density may lead to crowding, which may, in turn, lead to social problems. Remember that crowding is a psychological experience, while density is a physical condition. Many researchers have tried to determine if density leads to crowding; they question whether the physical condition leads to the psychological experience.

One technique (called the "sociological method") for determining a relationship has been to ascertain the density of different cities or areas and then compare their crime rates or mental-illness rates. Unfortunately, density can be measured in many different ways: the number of people per acre, per building, per city, per room in a dwelling. This is unfortunate because different measurements provide contradictory results. For example, urban areas have more people per acre, while rural areas generally have more people per room in each dwelling. Another problem with sociological studies is that dense urban areas are populated by lower socioeconomic groups. Thus higher crime rates in those neighborhoods may be caused by poverty rather than by crowding. Researchers have found that variables such as race, income, education, and parents' health are more strongly related to social problems than is density (Kirmeyer, 1978).

Although we cannot blame all social ills on density, it has been associated with some problems. For example, high in-dwelling density (the number of people living in the same quarters) is associated with both decreased socialization and reduced satisfaction. To illustrate this relationship, Rohe (1982) compared satisfaction levels of people across a number of variables, including density in residential setting, social relationship between occupants, perceived similarity, formal group structure, and previous residential experience. Results of his survey indicated that household density does affect both satisfaction and behavior. Furthermore, feelings of dissatisfaction are exacerbated when social relationships are close and when individuals have a history of high-density living conditions (p. 292). Rohe concluded that, although high density affects satisfaction, other variables contribute to perceived and actual well-being as well.

Prison researchers have also learned that high in-dwelling density creates problems. Prisoners who live in dormitory settings are less happy with their environment and have more illness complaints than prisoners who live in one- or two-person cells (Walker and Gordon, 1980; McCain, Cox, and Paulus, 1976). Density may be more likely to create crowding in prisoners than in other groups because they have larger body-buffer zones. Laboratory experiments have demonstrated that density sometimes creates stress, especially for subjects with "far personal space" (large body-buffer-zone needs). People with smaller personal-space needs are more tolerant of high-density situations (Aiello, DeRisi, Epstein, and Karlin, 1977).

Finally, the *opposite* of density may create more significant problems. Living alone is associated with a variety of problems. People who live alone use more drugs to relieve stress and have higher rates of suicide and more admissions to mental hospitals (Kirmeyer, 1978). However, for people who do find themselves in a high-density situation, whether it be rush hour in the city or going home to four roommates, perhaps an understanding of how personal space and crowding can affect communication will be helpful.

SUMMARY

The use of space, or proxemics, communicates information nonverbally to others. Territoriality, personal space, and crowding are three ways that the use of space speaks to others. Territoriality, an indication of ownership or association with a particular place, affects communication. The amount of space a person controls is associated with that person's prestige or status. By identifying similarities and differences in space usage, some researchers have categorized territories based on size, importance, and colonization.

Territorial encroachment influences interaction behaviors. When a territory is violated, invaded, or contaminated, people typically withdraw, insulate themselves, or create turf defenses. The gender of the participants, the intensity of the invasion, and the desirability of the territory are factors that influence the success of efforts to maintain your own territory or encroach on the territory of others.

Personal space, or the portable territories around people, expands and contracts, depending on the situation. The size and shape of personal spaces vary, depending on their purpose, function, and other nonverbal communication dimensions. Physical appearance and attractiveness also affect our needs. Personal space is also influenced by the gender, age, culture, relationship, status, degree of liking, and pathology or deviance of the people involved.

Crowding, a psychological experience, occurs when people become aware of spatial restrictions. Stimulus overload or behavioral constraint influences the sensation of being crowded. While crowding is a psychological experience, density, or the number of people in a given area, is a physical condition. Density and crowding are often associated with deviant behaviors and interpersonal problems. An awareness and understanding of the influence and effects of territoriality, personal space, and crowding should increase communication effectiveness.

References

Aiello, J. R., DeRisi, D. T., Epstein, Y. M., & Karlin, R. A. (1977) Crowding and the role of interpersonal distance preference. *Sociometry, 40,* 271–282.

Altman, I. (1975) *The environment and social behavior.* Monterey, Calif.: Brooks/Cole.

Ardrey, R. (1966) *The territorial imperative.* New York: Dell.

Bailey, K. G., Hartnett, J. J., & Glover, H. W. (1973) Modeling and personal space behavior in children. *The Journal of Psychology, 85,* 143–150.

Becker, F. D., & Mayo, C. (1971) Delineating personal distance and territory. *Environment and Behavior, 3,* 375–382.

Buchanan, D. R., Goldman, M., & Juhnke, R. (1977) Eye contact, sex and the violation of personal space. *Journal of Social Psychology, 103,* 19–25.

Burgoon, J. K. (1978) A communication model of personal space violations: Explication and an initial test. *Human Communication Research, 4,* 129–142.

Caplan, M. E., & Goldman, M. (1981) Personal space violations as a function of height. *The Journal of Social Psychology, 114,* 167–171.

Dean, L. M., Willis, F. N., & Hewitt, J. (1975) Initial interaction distance among individuals equal and unequal in military rank. *Journal of Personality and Social Psychology, 32,* 294–299.

Dosey, M., & Meisels, M. (1969) Personal space and self-protection. *Journal of Personality and Social Psychology, 11,* 93–97.

Edney, J. J. (1976) Human territories: Comment on functional properties. *Environment and Behavior, 8,* 31–47.

Efran, M. G., & Cheyne, J. A. (1974) Affective concomitants of the invasion of shared space: Behavioral, physiological and verbal indicators. *Journal of Personality and Social Psychology, 29,* 219–226.

Fisher, J. D., & Byrne, D. (1975) Too close for comfort: Sex differences in response to invasions of personal space. *Journal of Personality and Social Psychology, 32,* 15–21.

Greenberg, C. I., & Firestone, I. J. (1977) Compensatory responses to crowding: Effects of personal space intrusion and privacy reduction. *Journal of Personality and Social Psychology, 9,* 637–644.

Hall, E. T. (1963). A system for the notation of proxemic behavior. *American Anthropologist, 65,* 1003–1026.

Hall, E. T. (1974) *Handbook for proxemic research.* Washington, D.C.: Society for the Anthropology of Visual Communication.

Hayduk, L. A. (1978) Personal space: An evaluative and orienting overview. *Psychological Bulletin, 85,* 117–134.

Hayduk, L. A. (1983) Personal space: Where we now stand. *Psychological Bulletin, 94* (2), 293–335.

Haynes, J. R., & Ellington, J. E. (1982) Hierarchical grouping of personal space zones. *Perceptual and Motor Skills, 54,* 515–521.

Henley, N. M. (1977) *Body politics: Power, sex and nonverbal communication.* Englewood Cliffs, N.J.: Prentice-Hall.

Hughes, J., & Goldman, M. (1978) Eye contact, facial expression, sex and the violation of personal space. *Perceptual and Motor Skills, 46,* 579–584.

Jones, S. E. (1971) A comparative proxemics analysis of dyadic interaction in selected subcultures of New York City. *Journal of Social Psychology, 84,* 35–44.

Kanaga, K. R., & Flynn, M. (1981) The relationship between invasion of personal space and stress. *Human Relations, 34* (3), 239–248.

Kirmeyer, S. L. (1978) Urban density and pathology: A review of research. *Environment and Behavior, 10,* 247–269.

Knowles, E. S. (1973) Boundaries around group interaction: The effect of group size and member status on boundary permeability. *Journal of Personality and Social Psychology, 26,* 327–331.

Krail, K., & Leventhal, G. (1976) The sex variable in the intrusion of personal space. *Sociometry, 39,* 170–173.

Lindskold, S., Albert, K. P., Baer, R., & Moore, W. C. (1976) Territorial boundaries of interacting groups and passive audiences. *Sociometry, 39,* 71–76.

Lyman, S. M., & Scott, M. B. (1967) Territoriality: A neglected sociological dimension. *Social Problems, 15,* 236–249.

McAndrew, F. T., Ryckman, R. M., Horr, W., & Soloman, R. (1978) The effects of invader placement of spatial markers on territorial behavior in a college population. *Journal of Social Psychology, 104,* 149–150.

McCain, G., Cox, V. C., & Paulus, P. B. (1976) The relationship between illness complaints and degree of crowding in a prison environment. *Environment and Behavior, 8,* 283–289.

Mehrabian, A. (1969) Significance of posture and position in the communication of attitude and status relationships. *Psychological Bulletin, 71,* 359–373.

Newsweek. (December 3, 1979) The smoking war on flight 1410. p. 65.

Newsweek. (December 17, 1979) Special report. p. 55.

Pederson, D. M., & Heaston, A. B. (1972) The effects of sex of subject, of approaching person and angle of approach upon personal space. *Journal of Psychology, 82,* 277–286.

Powell, P. H., & Dabbs, J. M., Jr. (1976) Physical attractiveness and personal space. *Journal of Social Psychology, 100,* 59–64.

Rohe, W. M. (1982) The response to density in residential settings: The mediating effects of social and personal variables. *Journal of Applied Social Psychology, 12,* 292–303.

Rosenblatt, P. C., & Budd, L. G. (1975) Territoriality and privacy in married and unmarried cohabiting couples. *Journal of Social Psychology, 97,* 67–76.

Sarafino, E. P., & Helmuth, H. (1981) Development of personal space in pre-school children as a function of age and day-care experience. *Journal of Social Psychology, 115,* 59–63.

Scheflen, A. E. (1975) Micro-territories in human interaction. In A. Kendon, R. M. Harris, & M. R. Key (Eds.), *Organization of behavior in face to face interaction.* Chicago: Mouton-Aldine, pp. 159–174.

Schiffenbauer, A., & Schiavo, R. S. (1976) Physical distance and attraction: An intensification effect. *Journal of Experimental Social Psychology, 12,* 274–282.

Shafer, D. R., & Sadowski, C. (1975) An investigation of territorial invasion in a barroom environment. *Sociometry, 38,* 408–419.

Sussman, N. M., & Rosenfeld, H. M. (1982) Influence of culture, language, and sex on conversational distance. *Journal of Personality and Social Psychology, 42* (1), 66–74.

Walker, B., Jr., & Gordon, T. (March 1980) Health and high density in jails and prisons. *Federal Probation, 44,* 53–58.

Walkey, F. H., & Gilmour, D. R. (1984) The relationship between interpersonal distance and violence in imprisoned offenders. *Criminal Justice and Behavior, 11* (3), 331–340.

Winogrand, I. R. (1981) A comparison of interpersonal distancing behavior in young and elderly adults. *International Journal of Aging and Human Development, 13* (1), 53–60.

Wormith, J. S. (1984) Personal space of incarcerated offenders. *Journal of Clinical Psychology, 40* (3), 815–826.

Zeedyk-Ryan, J., & Smith, G. F. (1983) The effects of crowding on hostility, anxiety, and desire for social interaction. *Journal of Social Psychology, 120,* 245–252.

CHAPTER 8

TOUCHING BEHAVIOR

The greatest sense in our body is our sense of touch . . . we feel, we love and hate, are touchy and are touched, through the touch corpuscles of our skin.

J. Lionel Taylor, *The Stages of Human Life,* 1921

Anne was a determined toucher. Affection, cuddling, and touching were a critical part of her relationship with a man. Touch was so important in her relationships that the presence of affection prolonged an emotionally dead first marriage and the absence of affection destroyed her second one. During her first marriage, Anne had a husband who was very aggressive in the business world but a pussycat at home. In their home life, Jim gave Anne a great deal of affection, which allowed her to experience security, comfort, and contentment in their marriage, until other factors led to a divorce. After the normal cycle of loneliness following the divorce, Anne fell in love with and married a man who was her match intellectually and sexually except for one thing. Anne's new husband did not like to be touched in an affectionate manner. Whenever Anne would touch him, he would ignore the gesture and quietly find a way to move his hand, arm, or leg. Only one thing kept Anne pacified despite this absence of affection. "What kept me from feeling like some kind of ghost," Anne explains, "was that he was snuggly in the morning before he woke up (when he obviously did not know what he was doing). It wasn't much to go on, but it was enough to assuage my craving for physical affection."

Things might have been all right if Anne's second husband, Bob, had not changed his job. In his new job, Bob got up at one in the morning and rushed off to work. The result was disastrous. Anne saw him just as much, and even though he was charming and a good sexual partner, an important ingredient was missing—affection. "I saw him as often as before; he made charming and sweet speeches about how much he loved me, but—try though I might—I had no sense of his being there. When a woman thinks her husband is slipping away, she begins to clutch—to make demands for affection a secure person wouldn't need—and even if he hadn't been going anywhere originally, he's soon in full retreat" (adapted from Lee, 1978, p. 101).

And that's what ultimately happened with Bob. By the time he was back to his normal working schedule, Anne and Bob had separated. Anne claims that the lack of touch was the main cause of the breakup. "I wanted to feel loved and appreciated and he was just too cold and undemonstrative" (adapted from Lee, 1978, p. 101).

The truth is that most men and women want, crave, and long to touch each other. Because of our cultural and social tradition, feelings about being touched and desiring to be touched are confused. We even hire "licensed touchers," such as beauticians and masseurs, to take care of our need for bodily contact. Desmond Morris, author of *Intimate Behavior* (1971) and *Manwatching* (1977), claims that as a touch-starved culture we use many substitutes. Some of these substitutes include petting a dog, stroking a cat, sucking our thumbs, smoking cigarettes, hugging ourselves in distress, and drinking out of bottles that are the same shape and size as baby bottles.

The area of tactile communication has claimed the interest of many researchers during the last decade. The first part of this chapter will review the various functions of touch from a professional setting to an intimate situation and how the type of touch which is used changes in each. For instance, how would you touch a professor, a boyfriend, a girlfriend, your parents? A second area that is explored is the relationship of touch to growth and development. A great deal of research has been conducted with animals in an effort (1) to examine animal behavior and (2) to explore the parallels to human behavior. The role of touch in human growth and development will be explored to determine how touch and touch deprivation affect human development.

We live in a society in which implicit touch norms have been established. There is an acceptable amount of touch we can give others and acceptable areas of the body to touch, depending on our relationship to the other person. In the section on norms of touch, we will explore touch avoidance and factors such as gender, age, race, and religion that may affect the use of touch. In the final section we will focus on the messages of touch and the effects of touch on behavior.

FUNCTIONS OF TOUCH

We touch people in very different settings and for many different reasons. Richard Heslin has developed a taxonomy that classifies touch from a very impersonal type to full sexual contact. Touch, according to Heslin's system, falls into five categories: functional-professional, social-polite, friendship-warmth, love-intimacy, and sexual arousal (Heslin and Alper, 1983).

Functional-Professional

You have probably been touched many times for a specific purpose such as a physical examination. Remember when your physician listened to your heartbeat? He or she probably touched you on the shoulder with one hand, while placing the stethoscope on your chest. In this case, the physician used touch to do something or to perform some act. This type of touch, when used exclusively to serve a professional or functional purpose, is cold and impersonal. **Functional-professional touch** refers to an unsympathetic, cold, and businesslike touch approach. Generally speaking, when professional touch is used, the other person is treated as an object or nonperson in an attempt to keep any intimate or sexual messages from interfering.

Social-Polite

We use **social-polite touch** as a means of acknowledging another person according to the designated rules of the culture. The handshake is the most common example in the United States, while some European cultures may use kissing for acknowledgment. In all cases, social-polite touch serves to recognize the humanity of both parties. The handshake, for instance, signifies that the encounter is starting off on an equal footing. Prior to the handshake, the handclasp was used in ancient Rome for the same purpose.

Friendship-Warmth

The most misinterpreted touching behavior occurs in situations involving **friendship-warmth touch.** We use this type of touch to let other people know that we appreciate their uniqueness and special characteristics. Our society is very cautious about the differences between touching related to friendship and touching related to sex. As a result, there is usually a noticeable decrease in touch when you and your friend are alone. Imagine two friends meeting each other at an airport. Ron throws his arm around Johnny and gives him a big hug. As they walk through the terminal and crowd, they keep their arms around each other. But as soon as they reach the parking lot, they end all body contact. Why? There are no more crowds or a contextual environment to reinforce the purely friendly nature of their touching behavior. The contact situation in this more private setting becomes too immediate and too uncomfortable; it may be misinterpreted. In the area of friendship-warmth, there is a lot of cross-cultural variability. The differences among cultures reveal the various approaches to handling potentially illicit or unsanctioned sexuality.

Love-Intimacy

Love-intimacy touch includes different types of touch, such as stroking the face of another person. If you do not want to commit yourself to the responsibilities of a love-intimacy relationship, this contact will most likely make you uncomfortable. At this stage, the type of touch used is adapted to the other person, and it is more difficult to identify specific behaviors.

Sexual Arousal

Sexual arousal is the highest level of contact. To most people it is pleasurable because of the stimulation it creates. At the same time, sexual contact can also be frightening and anxiety-producing. Touch behavior in this category is viewed primarily as an expression of physical attraction.

The use of touch communicates many different types of messages, as indicated in the categories developed by Heslin. The role of touch in both animal and human growth and development is the subject of the next section.

TOUCH, GROWTH, AND DEVELOPMENT

Think back over the last twenty-four hours. How many people have you touched, hugged, patted, stroked, tickled, or kissed? And how many people have touched, hugged, patted, stroked, tickled, or kissed you? **Skin-hunger,** a common experience for most people from childhood through adulthood, is the result of not receiving enough body contact or touch for psychological well-being.

The physiological and psychological need for touch occurs at the moment of birth, both in the animal and human world. A mother cow, for instance, nudges her newborn calf to a standing position and guides the calf to her teats. A female dog's first act of mothering is to bathe the pup with her tongue. An instinctive gesture of a human mother is to reach for her baby and cuddle the baby to her breast while stroking his or her body tenderly.

These instinctive actions reaffirm the important role of touch in the growth and development of the newborn. Even certain words and phrases in our language demonstrate a preoccupation with touch—"soft touch," "rubbing the wrong way," "getting in touch," "handle with care," "handle with kid gloves," "thick-skinned," "skin-deep," and "touchy."

Touch also functions as a relationship message between people. Its importance in our lives is best understood by an examination of the role of touch in animal and human growth and development.

Animal Growth and Development

An examination of animal touching behavior provides important insights into human behavior. Ashley Montagu (1971), in his best-selling book *Touching,* raises two important questions with regard to the significance of touch in the animal and human worlds. First, what kinds of skin stimulation are necessary for the healthy development of the organism, both physically and behaviorally? Second, what are the effects, if any, of the deprivation or insufficiency of particular kinds of skin stimulation? Two specific animal behaviors, gentling and licking, will be examined in light of the questions raised by Montagu. A third area, physical contact among animals and its effect on behavior, will also be discussed.

Gentling.   **Gentling behavior** involves the stroking and touching of newborns and is essential to the growth and development of both animals and humans. For example, Hemsworth, Barnett, and Hansen (1981) found that baby female pigs grow faster (from eleven to twenty-two weeks) and interact more frequently with experimenters than identical pigs who are given either a light slap or electric shock when an experimenter enters the animals' pen. Additionally, they found that "gentled" pigs produce fewer chronic stress responses than those that are handled in an unpleasant manner. The researchers concluded that unpleasant handling of animals results in a marked withdrawal or avoidance of negative stimuli. In turn, the increased stress that results has a marked affect on animals' growth and development.

As you can see, gentling plays an important role in the productive growth and development of animals. However, licking has also been reported to have particular significance to animals.

Licking.   Have you ever wondered why a mother cat licks her young? The most common reply is that the mother cat is cleaning her kittens. **Licking,** which is used for cleanliness, also serves as a necessary physiological function for survival of newborns. If a newborn remains unlicked, for example, particularly in the perineal region (the region between the external genitalia and the anus), it is likely to die of functional failure of the genitourinary system. Breeders of chihuahua dogs are very aware of the effects on the puppies when they are not licked. Mothers in this breed of dogs make little or no attempt to lick their young. As a result, there is a high mortality rate among these puppies, caused by failure to eliminate. Unless some substitute for maternal licking such as stroking by the human hand is provided, the newborn has little chance of survival.

Lisa, a college student, had an interesting experience with a newborn and motherless kitten. The kitten had refused to eat and was not eliminating properly. Lisa had just recently heard a lecture on licking and animal behavior in her class on nonverbal communication, and she decided that the kitten needed a substitute for its mother's licking. She took a cotton swab, dipped it in warm water, and for the next few days rubbed the kitten's belly every two hours with the cotton. Soon the kitten began eating and eliminating properly. One can only speculate, but perhaps the simulated licking contributed to the kitten's regained health.

Physical contact.   **Physical contact** plays an important role in animal growth and development. In an early, highly valuable series of studies (Harlow, 1958; Harlow, Harlow, and Hansen, 1963), Harlow demonstrated the significance of physical contact between a mother monkey and her infant. The research found that the infant monkey's access to physical contact was a crucial variable in the development of normal behavior. Harlow observed laboratory-raised baby monkeys and found they showed a strong attachment to the folded gauze diapers that were used to cover the hardware-cloth floors and cages. In addition, the researcher observed that infant monkeys raised on the floor of a barred and wire-mesh cage survived with great difficulty, if at all, during the first five days of life. Based on these insights, Harlow built a terry-cloth surrogate mother with a light bulb behind her head that radiated heat. The surrogate was "soft, warm, and tender, a mother with infinite patience, a mother available twenty-four hours a day, a mother that never scolded her infant, and never struck or bit her baby in anger" (Harlow, 1958, p. 676).

A second surrogate mother was designed with wire mesh; without the terry-cloth skin, this surrogate could not provide vital contact comfort. In the initial experiment, a cloth mother and a wire mother were placed in different cubicles attached to the infant's cage. The cloth mother lactated from a concealed nursing bottle and the wire mother did not for four newborn monkeys; for another four, this condition was reversed.

The results revealed, surprisingly, that even when the wire mother provided the milk, the young monkeys spent more time with the cloth mother. Harlow concluded:

> We were not surprised to discover that contact comfort was an important basic affectional or love variable, but we did not expect it to overshadow so com-

pletely the variable of nursing; indeed, the disparity is so great as to suggest that the primary function of nursing as an affectional variable is that of ensuring frequent and intimate body contact of the infant with the mother. Certainly, man cannot live by milk alone. Love is an emotion that does not need to be bottle- or spoon-fed, and we may be sure that there is nothing to be gained by giving lip service to love. (Harlow, Harlow, and Hansen, 1963, pp. 260–261)

With the empirical and observational evidence of the significance of touch in the animal world, we may then ask: "Does touch also play an important role in human growth and development?"

Human Growth and Development

"I've had mixed feelings about going back to work," the woman explained. "It's not guilt about the children so much as a sense that something important is now missing from my life. It finally dawned on me that when I was a full-time mother, one of the kids would climb into my lap to be snuggled a dozen times a day—and I miss that. In fact, at times during the working day I get an almost irresistible urge to hug somebody, but it's not exactly office protocol. Anyway, I've begun to reserve half an hour every evening just for snuggling, and it feels marvelous—to me and to the kids, too" (Davis, 1978, p. 48).

Another person, a divorced man living some distance from his family, attended a massage workshop and found that when it was his turn to be massaged, he had to fight back tears. "It had been such a long time since anyone touched me in a

Personal services such as hair styling may provide the touch we need. (Peter Menzel)

gentle way," he said. "It brought back memories of my mother and my child-hood" (Davis, 1978, p. 48). Because touch is such a powerful symbol and signaling system and is closely related to our emotions, it is kept to a minimum in casual encounters.

These are just a few symptoms of the touch-starvation that occurs in our culture. Another sign has been the evolution of encounter groups and experiential workshops that allow limited forms of physical contact to occur. As we mentioned earlier, we use many symbolic forms of "substitute" touch; we hire licensed touchers such as beauticians and masseurs to take care of our need for bodily contact in a socially acceptable way (Morris, 1977). Why do we have such licensed touchers? Morris explains that we are a tribal species, evolved over a million years of living in small tribes. Now we live in groups, surrounded by strangers, and we tighten ourselves up. Social caution creeps into public activities and works against our natural tendency to be friendly and intimate. We button ourselves up and wear a suit of emotional armor, claims Morris.

How does touch affect human growth and development? The following section examines the evolution of touch from historical to contemporary times.

Historical background.   In the nineteenth century, more than half the infants in their first year of life regularly died from a disease called marasmus (a Greek word meaning "wasting away"), also known as infantile atrophy or debility. During the period from 1900 to 1919, the death rate among infants under one year of age in various foundling institutions in the United States was nearly 100 percent (Montagu, 1971, p. 93).

Dr. Fritz Talbot of Boston, perplexed by the high mortality rate among infants, studied the care of babies in Germany. When doctors in one hospital were unable to help a sick infant, they gave the child to a woman they called "Fat Old Anna." Talbot observed that "Fat Old Anna" would hold, rock, and cuddle the child. Somehow the tactile contact that Anna gave the infants seemed to help them recover. Talbot, after seeing the amazing effect of Anna's attentions, brought the idea back to the United States and called it "tender, loving care," which you have probably heard referred to as TLC (Talbot, 1941, p. 469).

America was influenced for a long period of time, however, by a book written by Dr. Emmett Holt, entitled *The Care and Feeding of Children.* Dr. Holt's book was first published in 1884 and was in its fifteenth edition in 1935. The book was read by millions of mothers and mothers-to-be. Holt claimed that giving the child too much attention would result in spoiling the child. Further, he claimed that sentimentality should be strictly avoided, because any show of love or close physical contact made the child too dependent on its parents (Holt, 1935).

It was not until after World War II, when studies were undertaken to discover the cause of marasmus, that it was found to occur more often among babies in the "better" homes, hospitals, and institutions than in poorer ones. This was of great interest, since it was thought that these infants were receiving the best physical attention and care. The babies in the poorer homes, however, were receiving more affectionate attention and more touch. Recognizing this fact, Dr. Brennemann in the late 1920s established the rule in his hospital that every baby should be picked up, carried around, and "mothered" several times a day. After the institution of this mothering behavior on the pediatric wards at Bellevue Hospital in New York, the mortality rates for infants under one year of age dropped from 35 to 30 percent and to less than 10 percent by 1938 (Montagu, 1971, p. 94). It is doubtful that the use of touch was the only variable in affecting mortality rates. On the other hand, the fact that touch does have some effect on physical development is more readily accepted.

Early touch: a case study.   Dr. Philip E. Durham Seitz reports a striking example of the significance of touch during an infant's first two weeks of life. The case revolves around a 2½-year-old white female who was referred for psychiatric study by a dermatologist because of a desire to continually pull out her hair.

The doctors could not find a physical reason for the problem, so additional information was collected during the psychiatric interviews. It was observed that the child cuddled herself in the arms of her mother and sucked milk from a nursing bottle. When she was sucking the nipple of the nursing bottle, which she held in her left hand, she searched for her hair with her right hand. When she found a hair or group of hairs, she would pull them out with a twisting motion of her fingers. She then carried the hairs in her fingers to her upper lip, where she rolled them against her lip and nose. She continued this pattern as long as she nursed from the bottle. The strange break in the pattern occurred when the nipple was removed from her mouth. At this point she stopped pulling her hair. The mother added that the child pulled her hair only when sucking from the bottle and that hair pulling and nose tickling always occurred together.

The psychiatrist conducted additional interviews with the parents and found that for the first two weeks, the mother nursed her baby at her breast but discontinued breast-feeding abruptly during the third week because she thought that she was not producing enough milk. During the first year and a half, the child's growth and development were normal. She was weaned from the bottle when she was one year old, after which she ate solid foods and drank liquids from a cup.

At eighteen months, a punitive program of toilet training was instituted, which involved scoldings and spankings whenever the child soiled herself. During the interviews, the mother realized that after the toilet-training program began, her daughter refused solid foods, insisted on milk from a nursing bottle, and began to pull her hair out and tickle her nose while sucking. With this information, can you analyze what was happening to the child?

Dr. Seitz concluded that the child's insistence on drinking milk from a nursing bottle revealed a wish to return to the time when she was breast-fed. As for the nose tickling, the doctor examined the mother's breasts and found a ring of long, coarse hairs surrounding each nipple. To test the hypothesis that the child was regressing to the early stage of breast-feeding, a nipple with a ring of coarse human hairs projecting around its base was constructed. This automatically tickled the child's nose whenever she held the nipple in her mouth. When the child sucked the nipple, she would slowly turn the bottle and brush the upright hairs against her nose and upper lip. This time the hair pulling did not occur. The automatic nose tickling apparently satisfied the child's need to regress to the early experience of breast-feeding.

This fascinating case demonstrates the significance of human contact during the first few weeks of life. The fact that this child, 2½ years later, tried to duplicate what she remembered of her first two weeks of life suggests that early tactile contact is critical.

The acceptability of touch in given communication situations is the subject of **touch norms** in our culture. The use of touch is regulated by implicit and sometimes explicit rules about whom you can touch, where, and how much. The touch norms that exist in our culture are discussed in the next section.

NORMS OF TOUCH

The United States is often referred to as a noncontact culture. In fact, as one newspaper reporter aptly stated, "More than other folks, pets get loving strokes" (Kaleina, 1979, p. C-2). In a survey of pet owners, a family therapist, Dr. Ann Cain, asked sixty-two persons to tell her who got the most strokes. She defined strokes as "any form of recognition such as physical touch, a look, word, a smile or gesture that conveys 'I know you're there.'" The results are interesting: 44 percent of those surveyed said their pets got the most strokes, 18 percent said their children got the most strokes, and 18 percent said family members got equal strokes (Kaleina, 1979, p. C-2). Although there is not enough research to establish the norms of how often we touch our pets, it may be that our tactile contact with animals is higher than our tactile contact with people.

In examining the norms of touch, we will review the topics of the amount and type of touch and touch avoidance in the following pages.

Amount and Type of Touch

How does the United States compare with other countries in the amount of tactile contact? Not very well, according to researcher Sidney Jourard. In a study of the rates of touch per hour for adult couples in coffee shops, the researcher reported the following frequency of contact: 180 in San Juan, Puerto Rico; 110 in Paris; 0 in London; and 2 in Gainesville, Florida (Jourard, 1968). One of the norms for adult touching behavior seems to be infrequent and limited contact.

Another set of norms for touching behavior relate to the setting in which touch is exchanged. According to research involving personal logs of college students, touch takes place in more private and public settings and across a broader range of relationship types than had previously been believed. For example, Willis and Rinck (1983) asked psychology students to keep a log of touches received and to record their relationship with the touch initiator, the body area used to touch them, the body area touched, the setting in which the touch was initiated, and their rating of the pleasantness of the touch (p. 120). Of the 1,498 touches recorded, 779 occurred in private settings, 372 in work settings, and 346 in other public settings (e.g., at stores, dances, and the university). Of the sexes, women were more likely to initiate touch than men—a marked deviation from results in past research. Also surprising were the number of different relationship types associated with received touch. Women and men in the Willis/Rinck study received sexual touches from the following people:

Women	**Men**
34 by close male friends	12 by close female friends
19 by husbands	
5 by male friends	3 by female friends
5 by other male relatives	2 by mothers
3 by male strangers	2 by female acquaintances
2 by mothers	4 by a close male friend
2 by other female relatives	
2 by female friends	
2 by male acquaintances	

Most of the sexual touches were found to be initiated at home, at friends' homes, or—for single subjects—in automobiles. However, as stated earlier, sexual touches also occurred in stores, at dances, and at the university (p. 121).

Although these "norms" for touch may be applicable only to psychology students at American universities (yet again, they may not), the study by Willis and Rinck serves to support our argument that a variety of touching norms do exist for the settings in which we interact. Despite the fact that most touch probably does occur in private settings, a great amount of touching probably occurs in other, more public settings as well.

The question, then, remains: Do norms for touch change? Does more or less touching occur as we age and grow? According to researchers Willis and Hoffman (1975), touch seems to decline from early infancy on. They report that from kindergarten through the sixth grade, the amount of touch steadily declines but still surpasses most adult touching behavior. The trend continues in junior high school, with about half as much touching as in the primary grades. In the Willis and Hoffman study, most touching occurred between same-sexed dyads and black children; females especially exhibited more touching behavior. Touching was initiated in primary grades with the hands, while in junior high school there was more shoulder-to-shoulder contact. Based on a review of studies, Knapp (1978, p. 245) concluded that "following childhood, the American child goes through a latency period in which tactile communication plays only a small role. Then, during adolescence, tactile experiences with members of the same, and then opposite, sex become increasingly important."

Despite the many types of relationships found by Willis and Rinck (1983) to be linked with touching behavior, the fact remains that many limitations do exist on touch contact in our culture. Anthropologist Paul Byers claims that senior citizens suffer the most from touch deprivation. "Perhaps," he speculates, "people are afraid that old age is contagious" (quoted in Davis, p. 48). The actual loss of physical contact must add to the older person's already increasing sense of isolation (Davis, 1978, pp. 48–50). One way that hospitals and nursing homes are helping to alleviate the problem is by allowing pets to be used as therapeutic tools. Recent research has shown that pet-facilitated therapy increases levels of social interaction, comfort, and security (Brickel, 1980–1981). Additionally, it reinforces feelings of independence.

Another common limitation on touch suggests psychological differences between males and females. Physical contact by a man with another man remains so potentially dangerous and unspeakable for many American males that, except for a contained handshake, no touch by any male (other than the dentist and the doctor) is permitted. Perhaps the involvement of women with the physical care of children—with bathing, powdering, kissing, dressing, combing, feeding, holding, and carrying—along with their own body changes and contact, results in fewer taboos against touch. The area of touch avoidance reveals many of these taboos against certain types of touch behavior.

Touch Avoidance

Are you aware that either explicitly or implicitly you ask and receive permission to touch someone else? For instance, a slow dance grants you permission to touch your partner within a limited area. A crowded elevator allows you to have body contact, as long as your arms are pulled in tightly to your sides or are crossed in front of your chest. A handshake is a legitimate means of making contact with another person, as is helping someone across the street. On the other hand, there are some norms that tell you not to touch or to limit your touch. A mother can caress her sons, but fathers are taught to avoid prolonged contact with daughters.

An interesting case of **touch avoidance** was observed on two Manhattan subway lines. Researcher David R. Maines observed that when people were forced to sit within 6 inches of each other, passengers were less likely to recoil from fellow travelers of the same race and sex than they were from "different" passengers. Significant elbow retraction occurred only between blacks and whites and between men and women. Given a little more space, however, most people relaxed their arms regardless of who was seated next to them. Maines concluded that avoidance appears to follow a predictable pattern, with those who are most like us not really considered untouchable at all (*Human Behavior*, November 1978, p. 26).

An early study by Jourard (1966) was conducted to find out which regions of the human body were permissible to touch. He divided the body into fourteen areas from the head to the foot, and he asked 300 students to indicate which regions of the body they touched. Subjects were also asked to indicate which areas of the body received touch from same-sex friends, opposite-sex friends, and parents. Jourard concluded that the greatest amount of touch occurred among opposite-sex pairs and that touch was restricted largely to the head, shoulders, and arms. Jourard also reported that the bodies of the father and mother received little intimate touching, while the mother did a good deal more intimate touching of others. The most touching occurs between friends of the opposite sex. Of the females, 76 to 100 reported that they touched all parts of their male friends' bodies, including the genital region, while only 51 to 75 percent of the males reported that they touched their female friends in the genital area. Another interesting finding was that females were more accessible to touch by all persons than were males (Jourard, 1966, pp. 221–231).

Have touch norms changed in a decade's time? Lawrence Rosenfeld and his colleagues repeated the Jourard study in 1976 with 200 new subjects and found very few changes from the earlier study. Parents, for example, continued to limit their touching of sons and daughters primarily to the head and arm regions. Fathers touched their daughters more frequently than their sons but touched them in the same general regions of the body. Mothers, on the other hand, touched both sons and daughters with about equal frequency. The major change from the earlier 1966 study was the significant increase in the percentage of touch to certain areas of the body by opposite-sex friends. The findings revealed that males now received more touch in the chest and hip areas than in the past, and females received more in the chest, stomach, hip, and thigh areas. Overall, this

---

The body is accessible not only to opposite-sex touching but to touching by members of the same gender. In male-to-male contact, touch usually takes on a "humorist"- or "buddy"-type meaning.

study found that the body is highly accessible to opposite-sex touching (Rosenfeld, Kartus, and Ray, 1976, pp. 27–30).

Gender, age, race, and religion enter into our use of and response to tactile communication. For instance, males and females agree that touch from a close friend of the opposite sex is pleasant, while touch from a same-sex person is generally unpleasant (Heslin, Nguyen, and Nguyen, 1983). However, the prevalence of sensitivity training in the seventies and eighties is slowly beginning to change negative perceptions of touch somewhat. For example, Larsen and LeRoux (1984) found that counseling students who had sensitivity training exhibited more positive attitudes toward same-sex touching than did a comparable group of science students (p. 276).

Despite changing perceptions toward the valence of touch, touch norms in our culture continue to limit both the frequency of touch and the area of the body touched. As we stated earlier, the variables that determine the frequency and area of touch include gender, age, race, religion, degree of acquaintance, and the family relationship of the interactants.

MESSAGES OF TOUCH

Physical touch always communicates some type of message. In fact, when we are unable to use physical stroking, we replace it with verbal or symbolic stroking. Our language expresses this when we use phrases such as "I was so touched by your phone call"; "That man is touched in the head"; "I feel for you"; "I felt as if he'd kicked me in the stomach"; "He rubs me the wrong way"; or "Handle with kid gloves." Symbolic or real, touch communicates strong messages to both children and adults.

According to Heslin and Alper (1983), our meanings for touch are affected by (1) the part of our body that is touched, (2) the part of our body that touches the other person, (3) the duration of the touch, (4) the amount of pressure that is applied, (5) the amount of movement after contact is made, (6) the presence or absence of another person, (7) the importance of any other person or persons who are present, (8) the situation in which the touch occurs, (9) the mood created by the situation, and (10) the relationship between the people involved (p. 50).

Of the messages communicated, at least five are of primary importance. These include status messages, emotional messages, messages of body-contact needs, messages that express our need to be held, and messages communicating our need for self-intimacy. Each of these will be addressed more completely in the following pages.

Emotional Messages

Many emotional messages are conveyed by touch, particularly in greetings and farewells. In an earlier study, Heslin and Boss (1976), observed people at an airport and found that 60 percent engaged in touching when greeting or saying goodbye to another person. An interesting difference was observed between greeting and farewell behavior—more emotional feeling was displayed in departure. Part of the reason might be that there is less embarrassment because the person is leaving. Greeting someone presupposes an additional amount of time spent together afterwards, which might become uncomfortable if there has been a very emotionally charged greeting. Another interesting finding reported by the researchers was that touching behavior was most often initiated by men.

Argyle (1975) claims that touch communicates various interpersonal attitudes, such as sexual interest, and that it is also used as a status sign. Touch behavior may even be used to regulate the flow of the conversation, or it may be accidental, as in a crowded elevator. The meaning attributed to touch behavior may also be a function of the background of the individuals involved. Researchers Nguyen, Heslin, and Nguyen (1975; 1976) examined the messages of touch in two separate studies, one with married couples and one with unmarried couples. Subjects were asked to explain what it meant to them to be touched in eleven locations on their bodies. Four different types of touch were used—the pat, the squeeze, the stroke, and the brush. Subjects were asked to view the touch as coming from an opposite-sex friend as opposed to a parent, sibling, or relative. The scales used to measure the meaning of touch included various degrees of warmth/love, playfulness, friendship/fellowship, pleasantness, and sexual desire. Interestingly, married persons associated touch more often with sexual desire than did unmarried persons, and they also tended to react more positively toward touch.

The type of touch also affected the emotional meaning of a message. Patting, for instance, was associated with play, whereas stroking was associated with warmth/love and sexual desire. Friendliness and sexuality were more closely linked to the location of the touch than the type of touch. The hands, regardless of the type of touch, were seen as pleasant, warm, and friendly; the genital area was not seen as playful, regardless of what kind of touch was being evaluated (Nguyen et al., 1975; 1976).

A universal relationship also exists between touch and attitudes. In fact, most cultural expressions of emotion seem to indicate that touch and positive attitudes go together, while touch and negative attitudes do not. To illustrate this relationship, we need look no further than instances when football and basketball players win their respective games. Generally, winning players pat the posteriors of their teammates, while losing players generally do not. To document the relationship between touching behaviors and attitudes toward winning in other competitive sports, Anderton and Heckel (1985) examined touching behaviors after 112 races in three championship swim meets (p. 289). Results of their study revealed a strong relationship between touch and the importance of winning. Winning swimmers gave and received a significantly greater number of touches than did last-place finishers.

In an earlier series of studies, Alma Smith (1970) examined the sending and receiving capacity of the skin. In a pilot study, an individual placed his hands on the hands of another individual. (The two individuals were separated by a screen to eliminate the possibility of kinesic, proxemic, artifactual, and other cues.) The sender was able to convey five different emotions—detachment, mothering, fear, anger, and playfulness.

Touch communicates many powerful emotional messages. A mother, for example, may communicate her own feelings about her body as she holds her child. Alexander Lowen (1967) writes:

> The quality of the physical intimacy between mother and child reflects the mother's feelings about the intimacy of sex. If the act of sex is viewed with disgust, all intimate body contact is tainted with this feeling. If a woman is ashamed of her body, she cannot offer it graciously to the nursing infant. If she is repelled by the lower half of her body, she will feel some revulsion in handling this part of the child's body. Each contact with the child is an opportunity for the child to experience the pleasure of intimacy or to be repulsed by the shame and fear of it. When a mother is afraid of intimacy, the child will sense the fear and interpret it as a rejection. The child of a woman who is afraid of intimacy will develop a feeling of shame about its own body. (p. 105)

Status Messages

Touch also reveals status relationships between people. Examine the following list and circle the person whom you think would initiate touch.

Boss	Employee
Nurse	Doctor
Student	Professor
Male	Female

According to Major and Heslin (1982), the person who initiates touch is generally considered to have higher status. Initiating touch increases the immediate closeness between the persons involved; therefore, bosses, doctors, and professors commonly initiate touch. In the case of the male and female, most sexual touching is initiated by males. However, in many cases, this norm is slowly but surely changing.

Additionally, the person who initiates touch generally controls the interaction. To illustrate, when was the last time that you patted a person of higher status on the back? How do you think that your touch was received by that person? Chances are good that you received an icy stare unless you and that person share a relationship outside of the one giving him or her higher status. That stare probably resulted from your perceived attempt to control the interaction.

Although previous research concerning touch initiation documents a greater number of sexual touches advanced by men, a comprehensive review by Stier and Hall (1984) revealed that women initiate touch, in general, more than do men. Reviewing over forty observational studies of touch, Stier and Hall also concluded that (1) same-sex touching among females exceeds same-sex touching among men and (2) same-sex dyads touch more often than opposite-sex dyads. (For a more complete summation of this literature, the reader is encouraged to read Stier and Hall's review. It is an excellent source of material concerning touch and gender differences).

Messages of Body-Contact Needs

Many messages of touch indicate a need for body contact. Barb strokes her cat, holds him, and cuddles him as a substitute for body contact. Steven strokes his pipe, fills it, stirs it, taps the excess tobacco out—another object-contact need. Rosemary has sex with a man in exchange for being held and touched. Mindy is recently divorced, and one lonely evening she sits and stares at the fire in the fireplace and hugs herself. These are all indications of body-contact needs expressed through different types of touch and object manipulation.

Some historians claim that the Western world was more "snuggle-prone" in the past than it is today and that group sleeping used to be the worldwide norm. In the seventeenth century, British royalty boasted of a bed that could sleep 102 people. In nineteenth-century America, before the forces of religion and hygiene took over, citizens enjoyed one last fling at cuddling known as "bundling." Snuggling in bed with a bundling board between them was a favored ritual for courting couples; others invited friends, even strangers, to bed with them during cold weather. In fact, it was considered polite to invite a guest to share your bed (Jobin, 1978, p. 174).

Body contact needs are expressed through the use of body-contact tie-signs (behaviors that indicate the need or wish to be held) and self-intimacy behaviors.

Body-contact tie-signs.   **Body-contact tie-signs** express the bond between two people in the form of physical touching. Desmond Morris identifies fourteen body-contact tie-signs: the handshake, the body guide, the pat, the arm link, the shoulder embrace, the full embrace, the hand-in-hand, the waist embrace, the kiss, the hand-to-head, the head-to-head, the caress, the body support, and the mock attack (Morris, 1977, p. 92). For the purposes of discussion, three selected body-contact tie-signs—the handshake, the body guide, and the kiss—will be discussed.

THE HANDSHAKE.   In Western culture the handshake is an expected formality, particularly when a personal bond is absent or weak or when there has been a long separation. The handshake is a modification of the primitive gesture of shaking with both hands that indicated no weapons were being concealed. Later this became a greeting—a hand-to-chest gesture—known as the Roman salute. During the time of the Roman empire, men grasped each other at the forearms instead of the hand. The modern handshake takes many different forms and serves basically as a gesture of welcome; the palms interlock, signifying openness, and the touching itself signifies oneness.

Various degrees of intimacy are expressed in the handshake. The degree of immediacy between two persons is revealed in how they shake hands (Mehrabian, 1971, p. 6). For example, does your handshake change when you contact a male, female, business associate, peer, friend, someone you like, or someone for whom you do not care?

THE BODY GUIDE.   A nonintimate way to guide someone in a particular direction is to point. The **body guide** is a more immediate behavior serving the same purpose. Remember when someone gently placed a hand on your back or when you placed your hand on someone's back to guide him or her in a particular direction? This gentle form of touch guides the person forward without the application of force.

This form of touch is an old parent-to-child behavior; therefore it is common for a superior to use it with a subordinate. This action implies an "I-am-in-control attitude." Morris (1977) explains:

> Even between spouses, it [the body guide] is an expression of momentary dominance, an act of taking charge of a situation. Used by a wife towards a husband, it presents a pseudo-motherly tie-sign to onlookers. Used deftly by a male, it imparts a masterly air to his actions. Used unwisely it can quickly become pompous and patronizing. (p. 93)

THE KISS.   Imagine all the different types of kisses you have received—the kiss on the cheek from a doting aunt, the kiss on the hand from an admirer, the kiss on the forehead from a relative, the light kiss on the mouth from a friend, or the full kiss on the mouth from a lover. The wide variety of kisses suggests that each type of kiss imparts a different message. It was not long ago that the "French kiss," in which the tongue would search out the partner's mouth, was frowned upon by adults who warned that it was a clear case of "upper persuasion for lower invasion." Kissing is a form of bonding as well as intimate contact, sometimes more intimate than the sexual act itself. As one male student commented, "When I like the woman, I will kiss her. When I make love, if it's just sex I don't want to kiss her because it's too intimate."

Morris (1971, 1977) described the messages of public kissing by observing the behavior of young lovers. These lovers, who are just beginning to form a bond, often kiss in public. It is probably safe to assume that lovers engaging in mouth-to-mouth kissing in public are not yet completely tied to one another. By comparison, older couples who have been together for a time tend not to kiss in public except at reunions, farewells, and times of significant emotional experiences such as triumphs, disasters, or even escapes from danger. At these times their emotion overcomes their usual embarrassment at kissing in public.

The cheek kiss is widely accepted as a nonsexual farewell or greeting between friends and relatives. The hand kiss reflects a lower status for the person receiving the kiss, because the hand is lower down on the body than the head. In earlier

Although nose-to-nose contact may not appear on a list of courtship behaviors, it is an affectionate sign and in some cultures a very romantic sign. (Carolyn Brown)

days, the rigid social formula was for a man to bow down and kiss the woman's hand. A dominant and important male, perceiving this as a lower-status behavior, solved the embarrassing problem of bowing down by raising the woman's hand to his mouth.

The Need or Wish to Be Held

The United States is basically a noncontact culture in which touch is legitimate only under certain conditions. One of the most obvious conditions is sex. Sometimes men and women engage in sexual relations for the sole purpose of being held. Each one of us has a **body-contact quotient**—in other words, a predictable need for a certain amount and a certain type of touch. You can get some idea of your body-contact needs by answering the following questions with "never," "almost never," "sometimes," "almost always," and "always" (Katz, 1976).

1. When you are upset, it is comforting for you to have someone to hold you.
2. If you are not held when you desire closeness, you feel hurt.

3. After sexual intercourse, you like to be held.
4. To get another person to hold you, you use sex.
5. If you have trouble falling asleep, it is helpful to have someone hold you.

The more "always" and "almost always" responses you have, the higher your body-contact score and the more you like to be cuddled. These statements are part of a questionnaire designed and administered by Dr. Marc Hollender. Cuddling, claims Hollender (1970), provides feelings of security, protection, comfort, contentment, and love. Women with a high body-contact score are comfortable with their sexuality. They like to eat and talk, and they express their feelings easily.

To date, most of Hollender's research has focused on women. Surprisingly, in the results to his questionnaire, Hollender has discovered the existence of a small group of women who have produced extremely high body-contact scores, resembling an "addiction." These women tend to be very insecure and often promiscuous because they have found that sex is an effective way to obtain the body contact they need. Deprived of tactile stimulation earlier in their lives, these women use both direct and indirect means to obtain the holding and cuddling they desire. One woman, whose need to be held was most compelling, reported:

> I would sooner have him [her husband] hold me every day—not 24 hours every day—but I would sooner have that than a Cadillac convertible, and I have told him that. . . . I was never cuddled or picked up or never had any kind of contact and affection (as a child); therefore, I believe I crave it more than the average person because of a lack of it. (Hite, 1977, p. 75)

Harris and Linn (1980) also have documented that deprivation plays a role in the need for touch. Likewise they have shown that the comforting or satisfying aspect of touch drives many to seek it out. Interestingly enough, their results also indicate that these two primary needs will drive some "to employ subterfuge, persuasion, or a direct request in order to be held" or touched by others (p. 245). In the latter instance, the need for touch has usually become extreme.

Only a handful of women express an aversion to being held. The results of Hollender's descriptive study, based on interview data obtained from twenty-seven paid volunteers and twenty-seven psychiatric patients, indicated that the need or wish to be held ranges from indifferent to intense. As one woman explained: "I require hugs, and in exchange give sex; however, I want to stress that often all I really am seeking is for a man to touch me" (Hite, 1977, p. 75).

Body contact commonly provides feelings of being loved, protected, and comforted. Both direct and indirect means are used to obtain the holding or cuddling desired. Sexual enticement and seduction are common means. Women usually separate the wish to be held from the desire for sexual gratification, and for them being held may be an end in itself. Sometimes the message communicated by the need to be held may be misunderstood. "When a man responds sexually to a woman who wants only to be held, she feels put upon. When the woman rebuffs the man's advances, he feels she has misled him. Clearly there are crossed wires in the communication system," writes Hollender (quoted in Stern, 1979, p. 90).

What about men? Originally, Hollender predicted that men would find it easier to acknowledge a need to hold rather than to be held, since American culture places a great emphasis on masculine strength. When a set of identical body-contact tests were administered to groups of male and female psychiatric patients, however, the results showed more similarities than differences between the sexes. The major differences were in the number of men and women with extremely high body-contact scores—the "cuddling addicts." Among the seventy-five people tested, there were ten women with very high body-contact scores, but only one man. "Cultural factors do influence the need to be held in men, but not in the manner originally postulated," Hollender concluded. "Men can acknowledge their longing [to be held], but its intensity either does not reach the height attained by some women or, if it does, it is not reported" (quoted in Stern, 1979, p. 90).

The *National Lampoon* commented that the need for men to touch and to be touched is so great that they go to extraordinary lengths to touch other men. According to the *Lampoon,* war, sports, and health care are the three fields of human endeavor specifically contrived to satisfy men's desire for masculine body contact. The *National Lampoon,* using its unique style of humor, suggests that men who want to maximize touching opportunities should frequent airports. Here it is possible to touch complete strangers all over by pretending to mistake them for arriving relatives.

Touching and affectionate body contact are used as part of the sex-therapy program introduced by Masters and Johnson. These well-known therapists help couples overcome problems by having them spend time together simply cuddling and enjoying the preliminary parts of lovemaking without concentrating on or worrying about what is to follow. The couple agrees they will not attempt coitus during this period of therapy. The touch practice works to the extent that it allows a couple to relax without expectations and perhaps to get to know one another in an affectionate way.

Body-contact needs express our degree of liking toward another person. As twenty-four-year-old Sandra observed, "I can have sex with someone I only like, but I can't cuddle with someone I only like" (Jobin, 1978, p. 178). Your hugs may be your most powerful medium of touch communication. By the way, have you hugged someone today?

The Need for Self-Intimacy

Picture yourself leaving your apartment or house. You've just locked the door behind you when all of a sudden you realize that you have locked the keys inside. What do you do? Before saying a word, your mouth drops open and your hand goes to your cheek or head as if to say, "Oh no, now what am I going to do?" In that brief moment, your feeling of emotional distress resulted in a self-intimacy contact with your hand. Temporarily, your hand offers you a soothing contact.

Self-contact or touching ourselves is what Desmond Morris refers to as **self-intimacy behaviors** (Morris, 1971, p. 213).

These contacts, although they are individual acts, represent the psychological need for someone else to soothe us at a critical moment, claims Morris. Remember when you were a child and a parent or adult held you or hugged you when you were hurt? Or remember when a friend reached out to comfort you when you were feeling particularly down? When these healing acts of touch are not available from other people, we simulate them ourselves to achieve a similar feeling. Do you remember feeling lonely or sad and hugging your knees—or even cold, both psychologically and physically, and putting your arms across your chest and hugging yourself? "They may appear to be one-person acts," claims Morris, "but in truth they are unconscious mimes to two-person acts, with part of the body being used to perform the contact movement of the imaginary companion" (Morris, 1971, p. 214).

Body intimacies can be classified as resulting from several situations. The first situation is when we feel depressed or nervous. At this time a loved one may give

Body-centered psychotherapists explain that when an individual is in distress the hand will touch that part of the body that is being protected—such as the heart area. (Carolyn Brown)

us a comforting hug or squeeze our hand to reassure us. In the absence of a loved one, we may turn to a specialized toucher such as a doctor, who pats our arm and tells us not to worry. If we have only a cat or dog around, we may stroke and pet its furry body. Even as we grow older, many of us exhibit behavior similar to that of Linus in the *Peanuts* comic strip; we hug a special blanket or pillow when we are sleeping. And finally, we have our own body that we hug, stroke, and touch in a variety of ways to soothe ourselves.

Self-intimacy behavior represents a message of a body-contact need. Many nonverbal gestures fall into this category. One of the most common is the **hand-to-head behavior.** One action is the hand supporting the head while the elbow is resting on some surface that offers support for the arm. Some people claim that this gesture is used as a sign of physical exhaustion. It might also be a sign of emotional exhaustion. **Mouth contact** with the hand may substitute for sucking a thumb, which, in turn, substitutes for breast-feeding. An elaborate form of this contact takes place when the finger or thumb is sometimes rubbed gently and slowly across the lips, recreating the movements of the baby's mouth on the mother's breast. During more intense emotional moments, we may succumb to nail biting. Perhaps, during tense or frustrated times, you bite your nails down so far that the nearby skin is almost chewed raw.

In severe distress, simple hand-to-head contacts are not sufficient. Instead, people use **hugging and rocking behavior,** grasping their bodies and shrinking into their own space. Almost every day we use a variation of this behavior by folding our arms across our chests, and in some cases the message we are sending is "no one allowed inside."

By holding hands with ourselves, wringing our hands, clasping our hands, and interlocking our hands, we provide a form of self-contact. In the absence of being able to interlock our hand with someone else's, we may clasp our own hands together, particularly during tense periods. At these times the clasp may be so strong that the pressure shows white on the flesh.

We use many other self-intimacy behaviors. Simply watch yourself during times of emotional crises or just when you are alone and observe the kinds of self-intimacy behaviors you use. The need for body contact and the wish to be held express themselves continually, and self-contact sometimes provides the temporary answer to this need.

Touch expresses many messages about both the sender and the receiver. The impact of touch behavior, however, does not stop at this point. There is research to suggest that touch and touch deprivation have observable effects on communication interaction. The effect of touch on human behavior and communication will be explored in the following section.

EFFECTS OF TOUCH

We know that touching behavior (or its absence) communicates specific messages of status, body-contact needs, and attitudes, but does touch behavior have an effect on our communication and on our lives? In his book *The Broken Heart,* psychologist James J. Lynch (1977) attributes many diseases, particularly cardiac diseases, to loneliness. He tells the story of a man in a coma, dying, who was still wired up to a monitoring machine that recorded his heartbeat. A nurse walked into his room and held his hand for a few moments, and his heartbeat went from rapid and erratic to slow and smooth. Perhaps his heart was literally and figuratively comforted.

A minister began to touch people more and more when he talked with them and found that he could talk much more personally and directly when he touched the other person. He found this to be especially true on sick calls. Does touch make a difference?

In terms of its effect on communication interaction, Aguilera (1967) reports some interesting observations. Nurses who touched psychotic patients were more effective in eliciting verbal responses from them than those nurses who did not touch. Blondis and Jackson (1977) discuss the importance of touch to patients in a hospital:

> In nursing, touch may be the most important of all nonverbal behaviors. Patients are touched as a part of the overall nursing procedure. You touch a patient when you take his temperature, blood pressure, give an injection or bed-bath. In fact, there is not a way to practice nursing without touching. And how you handle and touch your patient says a great deal about the way you feel toward him and his illness. The nurse who is reluctant to squeeze the hand of an aphasic patient may have no aversion to that patient, but merely an upbringing that makes touching situations difficult. Unfortunately, the patient has no way of knowing, and is only aware of her aversion. (p. 6)

Tactile contact has also been associated with positive tipping behaviors in restaurants. For example, Crusco and Wetzel (1984) examined tipping rates of customers who were touched by waitresses either on the hand or the shoulder as they (the waitresses) were returning change. "Customer tipping rate" was defined as the percentage of the bill that was given. Results of the study showed that tipping rate for the two types of touch did not differ, nor did they differ according to the gender of the customer. However tipping rates for both types of touch were significantly higher than in the "no touch" condition of the experiment (p. 512). The researchers concluded that the effects of touch can occur without knowledge or awareness, as probably occurred with those customers who inadvertently took part in the experiment. This study also supported the relationship between touch and positive affect.

Does touching behavior affect compliance to a request? Recent research in tactile contact leads us to believe so and supports a highly positive relationship between touch and our willingness to comply (for example, see Brockner, Pressman, Cabitt, and Moran, 1982; and Goldman, Kiyohara, and Pfannensteil, 1985). To support their particular hypothesis concerning this relationship, Goldman, Kiyohara, and Pfannensteil (1985) asked a confederate to approach a subject as he or she entered a university library and to ask for directions to the Education Building located nearby. In response to the subject's directions, the confederate then either thanked or rebuffed the subject and either touched or did not touch him or her as the verbal response was given. As the subject entered the library, a second confederate approached him or her and asked for a larger favor. Results of the study revealed that compliance to the second request increased significantly when both touch and a positive verbal response ("OK, thank you") were used by the first confederate. The researchers concluded that "touching an individual may increase feelings of intimacy and may enlarge that individual's self-concept of being helpful" (p. 146). Such feelings would account for the increased compliance to the second request.

SUMMARY

Research in the area of touch has become of increasing interest to such professionals as doctors, nurses, counselors, and educators. The fact that touch plays a significant role in communication and interaction is a well-accepted belief that has some empirical support.

Touch functions as a symbolic means of communication to indicate the nature of the interaction. For instance, a communication setting in which a doctor takes your blood pressure is an example of the use of functional-professional touch behavior. In this case, the touch is used specifically to perform an act. In other situations—categorized as social-polite, friendship-warmth, love-intimacy, and sexual arousal—touch communicates specific information about the relationship between the interactants. Touch may express physical attraction or an important bond of friendship. When you touch another person, consider the type of touch you are using and what you are saying about the nature of your relationship to the other person.

From a very early age we are touched, held, stroked, and rocked. This intimate form of touching also has parallels in the animal kingdom, where animals are licked and gentled to aid them in their growth and development. In fact, touch is so important to an animal at infancy that the lack of it may affect survival. Similarly, some researchers and experts claim that humans suffer from the same effects of touch deprivation. The case of Fat Old Anna in Germany is an interesting example of the use of "tender loving care" in assisting infants back to health. Your own growth and development are important in understanding how touch has affected your life. Were you breast-fed? Did you receive a great deal of touch as a child? Do you enjoy affection as an adult? Are you an affectionate person? Whether your current touch behavior reflects the touching you received early in life is still a matter of speculation. For you, however, it is an important matter for reflection.

Licensed touchers exist throughout our culture. Remember having your head massaged while the hairdresser was shampooing your hair? There are many covert means for achieving touch when we do not receive enough in our own lives. As a culture we have also developed acceptable norms of touch. In other words, we have decided how much we can touch other people and where. In our noncontact culture, you can observe the use of touch in professional and personal settings. Most importantly, you can observe your own use of touch and determine to what extent you engage in tactile communication. Touch avoidance occurs within particular restraints of the norms we have established. Elevators and subways, for example, provide us with interesting and sometimes humorous examples of how we go to extreme lengths to let another person know that we do not mean to touch them.

According to researchers, our meanings for touch are influenced by a number of factors. For instance, our meanings are affected by the part of the body that is touched, the part of the body that touches the other person, the duration of the touch, the amount of pressure that is applied, and the amount of movement after contact is made. Additionally, meanings partially result from the presence or absence of another person, the importance of any other person who is present, the situation in which the touch occurs, the mood created by the situation, and the relationship between the people involved.

A very important role that touch plays in communication is in the communication of emotional messages, status messages, messages of body-contact needs, and messages of self-intimacy. Both the sender and the receiver recognize that touch carries messages that are often more dominant than the words we speak.

Finally, there is additional evidence to suggest that touch affects communication and human behavior. More and more, we are finding that touch does make a difference. Exactly what that difference may be is not clearly understood yet. Although the empirical evidence is not available to draw conclusive results, there is testimonial evidence that causes us to reflect on the role of touch in our own lives and the lives of others. A fourteen-year-old girl tells her story of her need for touch:

> Dear Abby:
>
> I am a fourteen-year-old girl. My problem is that nobody ever touches me. My parents haven't hugged or kissed me for a long time, except when I go away for a long time. Close friends outside of the family don't touch me either.
> I am outgoing to a degree and sometimes when I really want to hug someone, I just go ahead and hug them, but they always stiffen up or back off. No one ever reaches out to me first. I need someone older to talk to. I feel like nobody cares about me or loves me. I am intelligent. I don't have a mental problem. I don't smell bad and I'm not ugly. I'm so confused—please help me.*

References

Aguilera, D. C. (1967) Relationship between physical contact and verbal interaction between nurses and patients. *Journal of Psychiatric Nursing, 5,* 5–21.

Anderton, C. H., & Heckel, R. V. (1985) Touching behaviors of winners and losers in swimming races. *Perceptual and Motor Skills, 60,* 289–290.

Argyle, M. (1975) *Bodily communication.* New York: International Universities Press.

Blondis, M. N., & Jackson, B. E. (1977) *Nonverbal communication with patients.* New York: Wiley.

Brickel, C. M. (1980–1981) A review of the roles of pet animals in psychotherapy and with the elderly. *International Journal of Aging and Human Development, 12* (2), 119–128.

Brockner, J., Pressman, B., Cabitt, J., & Moran, P. (1982) Nonverbal intimacy, sex, and compliance: A field study. *Journal of Nonverbal Behavior, 6* (4), 253–258.

Crusco, A. H., & Wetzel, C. G. (1984) The Midas touch: The effects of interpersonal touch on restaurant tipping. *Personality and Social Psychology Bulletin, 10* (4), 512–517.

Davis, F. (September 27, 1978) Skin hunger—An American disease. *Woman's Day,* pp. 48–50, 154–156.

Goldman, M., Kiyohara, O., & Pfannensteil, D. A. (1985) Interpersonal touch, social labeling, and the foot-in-the-door effect. *Journal of Social Psychology, 125* (2), 143–147.

Harlow, H. F. (1958) The nature of love. *American Psychologist, 13,* 673–685.

Harlow, H. F., Harlow, M. K., & Hansen, E. W. (1963) The maternal affectional system of rhesus monkeys. In H. L. Rheingold (Ed.), *Maternal behaviors in mammals.* New York: Wiley.

Harris, R., & Linn, M. W. (1980) Differential response of the need to be held. *British Journal of Medical Psychology, 53,* 243–248.

Hemsworth, P. H., Barnett, J. L., & Hansen, C. (1981) The influence of handling by humans on the behavior, growth, and corticosteroids in the juvenile female pig. *Hormones and Behavior, 15,* 396–403.

Heslin, R., & Alper, T. (1983) Touch: A bonding gesture. In J. M. Wiemann & R. P. Harrison (Eds.), *Nonverbal interaction.* Beverly Hills, Calif.: Sage, pp. 47–75.

Heslin, R., & Boss, D. (1976) Nonverbal intimacy on arrival and departure at an airport. Unpublished manuscript, Purdue University. Cited in Knapp, M. K. (1978) *Nonverbal communication in human interaction* (2nd ed.). New York: Holt, Rinehart, & Winston.

Heslin, R., Nguyen, T. D., & Nguyen, M. L. (1983) Meaning of touch: The case of touch from a stranger or same sex person. *Journal of Nonverbal Behavior, 7* (3), 147–157.

Hite, S. (July–August 1977) What kind of loving does a woman want? *New Woman Magazine,* p. 75.

Hollender, M. H. (1970) The wish to be held. *Archives of General Psychiatry, 22,* 445–453.

Holt, L. E. (1935) *The care and feeding of children* (15th ed.). New York: Appleton-Century.

Human Behavior. (November 1978) The untouchables, elbow-rubbing taboos, p. 26.

Jobin, J. (September 1978) How to get your husband (and other loved ones) to cuddle up a lot closer. *Redbook,* pp. 174–181.

Jourard, S. M. (1966) An exploratory study of body-accessibility. *British Journal of Social and Clinical Psychology,* pp. 221–231.

Jourard, S. M. (1968) *Disclosing man to himself.* New York: Reinhold.

Kaleina, G. (March 3, 1979) More than other folks, pets get loving strokes. *The Arizona Republic,* p. C-2.

Katz, D. (February 17, 1976) Body contact: Cuddle up with touching test. *Miami Herald.*

Knapp, M. K. (1978) *Nonverbal communication in human interaction* (2nd ed.). New York: Holt, Rinehart, & Winston.

Larsen, K. S., & LeRoux, J. (1984) A study of same sex touching attitudes: Scale development and personality predictors. *The Journal of Sex Research, 20* (3), 264–278.

Lee, A. (1978) The need for physical contact. *New Woman Magazine,* 101–108.

Lowen, A. (1967) *The betrayal of the body.* New York: Collier Books.

Lynch, J. J. (1977) *The broken heart: The medical consequences of loneliness.* New York: Basic Books.

Major, B., & Heslin, R. (1982) Perceptions of cross-sex and same-sex nonreciprocal touch: It is better to give than to receive. *Journal of Nonverbal Behavior, 6* (3), 148–162.

Mehrabian, A. (1971) *Silent messages.* Belmont, Calif.: Wadsworth.

Montagu, A. (1971) *Touching: The human significance of the skin.* New York: Harper & Row.

Morris, D. (1971) *Intimate behavior.* New York: Random House.

Morris, D. (1977) *Manwatching: A field guide to human behavior.* New York: Abrams.

Nguyen, M. L., Heslin, R., & Nguyen, T. (1976) The meaning of touch: Sex and marital status differences. *Representative Research in Social Psychology, 7,* 13–18.

Nguyen, T., Heslin, R., & Nguyen, M. L. (1975) Meanings of touch: Sex differences. *Journal of Communication, 25,* 92–103.

Rosenfeld, L. B., Kartus, S., & Ray, C. (1976) Body accessibility revisited. *Journal of Communication, 26* (3), 27–30.

Smith, A. I. (1970) Nonverbal communication through touch. Unpublished doctoral dissertation, Georgia State University, pp. 1–45.

Stern, B. L. (July 1979) You need body contact with others; It satisfies skin hunger. *Vogue,* p. 90.

Stier, D. S., & Hall, J. A. (1984) Gender differences in touch: An empirical and theoretical review. *Journal of Personality and Social Psychology, 47* (2), 440–459.

Talbot, F. (1941) Discussion. *Transactions of the American Pediatric Society, 62,* 194, 469.

Willis, F. N., & Hoffman, G. E. (1975) Development of tactile patterns in reaction to age, sex and race. *Developmental Psychology, 11,* 866.

Willis, F. N., & Rinck, C. M. (1983) A personal log method for investigating interpersonal touch. *Journal of Psychology, 113,* 119–122.

formal research in the behavioral sciences, Crystal (1978) has stated that paralinguistic phenomena are frequently the determinants of behavior in interpersonal interaction. Though the prefix "para" suggests that vocal effects are a secondary or optional consideration in communication, paralinguistic phenomena, far from being incidental or marginal, often push the verbal content of the message into a secondary role.

Traditionally, verbal language has been seen as communicating the cognitive aspects of meaning and nonverbal language, the affective aspects. For example, if I said to you, "I am going to see the play at the theater tonight," my verbal cues would give you information about the actual plans for the evening, and my nonverbal cues would give you some clues about my feelings toward those plans. In other words, I could give you the impression that going to the play was either a chore or a delight.

Expression of feeling is only one important role of paralanguage. Vocal cues also serve many other purposes. An employer may decide that a job applicant is lower middle class and has a pleasant personality on the basis of a telephone conversation. Often the voice reveals information about socioeconomic class, influences our judgments of personality, and determines whether or not we may be persuaded to a different viewpoint. We also use vocal cues to regulate conversation, to deceive, and to detect deception in others. For instance, when a person concludes a statement, she usually does so with a low pitch. This is often a cue for the other person to speak. Vocal cues are so critical that therapists and other professionals use them in assessing both mental and physical health.

Precise meanings of paralinguistic messages are difficult to determine. The contrasts in verbal language are somewhat definable and measurable; the verbal content of a message is easier to talk about than the nonverbal content. Writers often discuss paralinguistics in functional terms by trying to answer the following questions: What can vocal cues do? What do paralinguistic phenomena contribute to communication behavior? In this chapter we will explore answers to the many questions concerning the nature of paralinguistic behavior; then we will turn to the uses of vocal cues to identify emotional, demographic, and personality characteristics.

MEANING AND LISTENER JUDGMENTS

Researchers who have asked questions concerning the amount and type of meaning carried in the vocal channel have found few precise answers. For example, Mehrabian's (1972) formula, though often quoted to show the relationship between verbal and facial sources of information, is limited in interpretation by the design of his landmark experiment. Using subjects who evaluated a speaker after hearing only one spoken word, Mehrabian and Ferris (1967) concluded that total impact = 0.07 verbal + 0.38 vocal + 0.55 facial. Mehrabian later interpreted this to mean that total feeling is equal to "7% verbal feeling + 38% vocal feeling + 55% facial feeling" (Mehrabian, 1972, p. 182).

Other researchers, using statements rather than a single word, report different outcomes. For example, in an earlier study, Markel (1965) divided judgments of listeners into two categories, evaluation and strength. Evaluative judgments, based on responses to pairs of adjectives involving goodness and likability of a speaker, were found to rely primarily on verbal content rather than on vocal cues. Strength and superiority judgments were based on adjective pairs involving credibility and competence of a speaker. These judgments were often more biased for the listeners who based them on vocal cues than for listeners who based their judgments on verbal content.

Later, using different research methods, Hart and Brown (1974) found that, although some evaluative reactions to a message are related to the verbal content of that message, other evaluations such as the social attractiveness of a speaker are also related to characteristics of the voice. For example, Linda is walking across the campus and meets a guy she has seen many times before but with whom she has never taken the time to speak. When he speaks to her, he suddenly becomes more attractive to Linda. The pleasantness of his voice has made a much more positive impression than his rather ordinary appearance.

More recently, Hegstrom (1979) has attempted to determine the usefulness of research in this area. Specifically, he focused on the utility of Mehrabian's early formula. Hegstrom concluded that the formula cannot be applied generally and that the sum of verbal, vocal, and facial messages is not equal to the total impact of a message.

Although to this point we have been unable to draw firm conclusions from the differing results, these studies do serve to underscore the importance of vocal characteristics in conveying a message. In addition to the impact of vocal cues, the contributions of paralinguistic phenomena to communication behavior deserve consideration.

Paralinguistic Categories

Trager (1958), an early pioneer in paralinguistics, categorized paralinguistics into voice set, voice qualities, and vocalizations. **Voice set** is defined as prelinguistics and involves physical and psychological characteristics of the communicator and his or her circumstances. For example, a short, elderly, hunchbacked man who does not know where his next meal is coming from will have a very different voice set from a tall, handsome, successful businessman.

Voice qualities, the second category, are defined as recognizable speech characteristics that can be separated from the actual message of the speaker; these include such variables as pitch range, vocal lip control, glottis control, pitch control, articulation control, rhythm control, resonance, and tempo. When John and Kim dropped by Larry's apartment one evening, they were talking rapidly, stuttering, and using sentence fragments. Larry knew immediately that they were excited. It took longer to understand the verbal content of their speech than the nonverbal content. The nonverbal message told him their emotional state, and the verbal message explained the cause for the state.

The third category, **vocalizations,** includes the following three divisions:

1. **Vocal characterizers,** such as laughing, crying, belching, and yawning.
2. **Vocal qualifiers,** such as intensity, pitch height, and extent.
3. **Vocal segregates,** which include such vocalizations as "Uh-huh," and "Shh."

The uses of vocal cues in the identification of certain emotional, demographic, and personality characteristics is the subject of the following section. In this section we will also examine the effect of vocal cues on learning and persuasion, on turn-taking, and in deception.

VOCAL CUES AND EMOTIONAL STATES

Often when you meet a friend, your first remark is to ask, "How are you?" Before there is an answer, you may use your friend's nonverbal cues to assess her emotional state. After you hear the answer, nonverbal cues are still important, for they will strongly influence your interpretation of the information your friend conveyed verbally. The nonverbal cues that you see are not the only cues to emotional states, for if you talk with the same friend over the phone, you will probably still be able to guess your friend's mood. The voice conveys emotional cues fairly accurately. Though vocal cues may be useful in encounters with strangers, they are more useful when added to previous knowledge of an individual.

The idea that the human voice transmits cues about emotional states has been relatively easy to support; however, discovering the exact voice features that transmit an emotion is more difficult. In order to study the voice as an expresser of emotion, researchers have found various recording methods that allow them to eliminate the verbal content of speech but to preserve the vocal cues in the message. These technical methods so alter human speech that the listener can hear only the vocal cues. Studies using this **content-free speech** indicate that vocal cues alone convey information about emotional states. Reviews of studies on content-free speech indicate that judges can consistently identify the emotion expressed and can also estimate its strength. Researchers, however, have been unable to identify the exact vocal cues that convey individual emotions (Warner and Sugarman, 1986; Scherer, Koiwunaki, and Rosenthal, 1972).

Although to this point researchers have been unable to pinpoint the exact vocal cues that convey emotions, they have made a few "theoretical" assumptions. For example, some researchers believe that pitch level influences evaluative (good-bad) judgments and that volume influences perceptions about the strength of the emotion. The activity level, that is, whether a speaker seems calm or excited, is judged by the extent of change in pitch and volume. If Bob greets Anne with a fairly loud voice and with a great deal of pitch change, she will probably assume that he is experiencing a strong emotion and is feeling excited. If a smile accom-

Vocal cues convey information about emotional states. (Larry H. Mangino/The Image Works)

panies his vocal cues, she may, with some assurance of accuracy, label the emotion as a positive one. However, she may need more cues of both a verbal and nonverbal nature in order for her to identify the specific emotion that he is experiencing.

Other researchers such as Reardon (1971) have used recordings of phrases or sentences with the message content retained. For example, Reardon had six speakers present two sentences using their voices to express love, happiness, sadness, indifference, fear, or anger. The two sentences were: "There is no other answer. You've asked me that question a thousand times and my answer has always been the same; it will always be the same." He found that the listeners were more accurate in identifying negative expressions of emotion than positive ones and that anger was the most easily identified emotion.

In order to study the relationship between people's ability to observe and control their own expressions of emotion and their ability to accurately identify emotions of other people, Snyder (1974) measured the consistency of an individual's emotional expressions in different situations. He found that individuals differ in the amount of observation and control of their emotions in different situations. **High self-monitors,** that is, those subjects who watched and controlled their own emotions, were found to be especially sensitive to the emotional expressions of other people. Moreover, high self-monitors demonstrated a high level of ability to express emotion intentionally. Think about a person you like to talk to when you feel upset. That person is probably sensitive to your feelings and able to express his or her feelings intentionally.

THE VOICE AND THE IDENTIFICATION OF DEMOGRAPHIC CHARACTERISTICS

We may conclude that the voice does help to express and to identify emotions, whether or not content is an available cue. Furthermore, people who monitor their own emotions efficiently are especially capable of expressing their feelings intentionally and of judging others' emotions correctly. The voice, however, conveys a variety of other information as well. For example, research has shown that the voice emits subtle cues about our demographic status, including our average income level, height, weight, age, and sex. To more completely document this statement, we now turn to a discussion of the voice and its relationship to these particular variables. From there we will proceed to additional messages which the voice conveys.

Socioeconomic Status

Suppose that you are working on a committee to select upper-class advisers for freshmen and believe it advantageous to match advisers and students by socioeconomic status (SES). Would a telephone conversation aid in searching for this information? Researchers would say yes. Vocal cues can aid in determining demographic characteristics. For example, one graduate student informally investigated the relationship between vocal cues and SES by taping the individual voices of several people reading the same paragraph from a news magazine. The readers included a service-station attendant (working class), a businessman (upper middle class), an office worker (lower middle class), and an insurance executive from a wealthy family background (upper class). The SES of the reader was assigned on the basis of his or her parent's SES and the reader's own educational level and occupation. The tape was then played in a graduate class in speech communication. The students correctly identified each reader's SES with a high degree of accuracy.

More formal research also confirms the presence of SES indicators in speech. In an often quoted 1961 study, Harms established a clear relationship between speech and judgments of status by listeners. Speakers and listeners were classified as having high, medium, or low SES through the use of an established index that took into consideration income, education, and employment. The subjects were instructed to respond to questions printed on cards. The responses, typical of ritualistic conversations during first meetings such as "How are you?" and "I am fine," were then recorded. After the voices were evaluated, the results showed that listeners not only gave the speakers the same SES ratings already assigned them by the researchers but also assigned higher credibility ratings to high-status speakers (Harms, 1961).

Interestingly enough, when lower levels of politeness are used, higher levels of SES are attributed to male and female speakers. Conversely, as level of politeness increases, lower levels of SES are predicted. To determine these findings, Baroni and D'Urso (1984) asked forty-eight subjects at the University of Padua (in Italy) to listen to a recording of a male or female speaker, and to judge "from where the speaker was speaking, his/her educational level, his/her financial situation, his/her occupation, his/her appearance, his/her likeableness, and his/her location on a scale of social distance" (p. 68). Each recording varied in level of politeness forms used, with "politeness" defined in terms of duration of utterance, presence of hesitation pauses within words, intensity, and intonational contour. Results of the study revealed that males who used a high level of politeness were perceived to be speaking from home or a public phone booth and to work in some form of subordinate occupation. On the other hand, less polite males were perceived to be calling from their office and to hold some kind of managerial position. The profile of the female speakers who participated in the study showed even greater differences in perceptions. The more polite female speakers were perceived to be calling from home, to have financial difficulties, to be a housewife or low-level, white-collar worker, and to be less attractive. Less polite female speakers, however, were perceived to be calling from their office, to be fairly well off, to hold a managerial position, and to be more pleasant and "distinguished looking" (p. 69).

A variety of vocal cues influence opinions of a speaker's SES, although at times such perceptions may be imprecise and highly inaccurate. This potential for misjudgments occurs primarily due to the many other factors that may come into play. To illustrate we need only return to the study presented above. The judgments that were made by the Italian subjects in this experiment would be highly inaccurate if they traveled to England and conversed with people there. (The same statement would hold for English citizens visiting in Italy.) In England, politeness is both expected and desired by members of the highest socioeconomic class. Thus, differences in both cultural background and rules are two factors which influence a listener's judgments.

Dialect or nonstandard speech.   The perception of dialect or **nonstandard speech** also is related to judgments of SES. For example, in one study, teachers were found to label children as culturally disadvantaged if their speech contained a noticeable dialect or nonstandard English (Williams, 1970). In a related study, speakers of Chicano English were rated lower on success, ability, intelligence, and social awareness than speakers of standard English (Bradford, Ferror, and Bradford, 1974). Apparently, listeners often infer socioeconomic class on the basis of these vocal cues as well. However, these inferences may not always be correct, as we argued earlier. Consider the possible embarrassment if a member of a European royal family or a wealthy Mexican businessman traveling incognito was perceived as having low SES.

A related variable affecting the accuracy of SES judgments in this instance is the social situation in which an individual is placed (Tizard, Hughes, Carmichael, and Pinkerton, 1983). As both Labov (1969) and Tizard et al. (1983) point out, a black child who is interviewed by a white adult in his or her [the adult's] world will converse differently (almost monosyllabically) than when he or she is allowed to converse in his or her own world. For example, if allowed to sit on the floor, to share potato chips, to bring along another child, and to turn the interview into a party, the child will begin to talk more freely as well as more "competently" (Tizard et al., p. 533). Thus, another variable which must be taken into account in judgments of SES is the social situation. Situations affect the ways in which we interact with and, hence, perceive other people.

Height, Weight, Sex, and Age

Graddol and Swann (1983) have noted that such cues as height, weight, and sex (as well as race, educational level, and dialect region) also are available in the voice. One primary cue carrying that information is vocal pitch. If other vocal cues are used, however, information about height and weight has been found to be less reliable than information on SES. For example, in experiments that attempted to isolate the frequency of the voice as a salient cue, few links to accurate height and weight estimates have yet to be found (Graddol and Swann, 1983, p. 353).

The identification of sex (or gender) is highly accurate, however, for we carry this cue in a number of vocal channels. Likewise, a rough estimate of age is usually possible if only vocal cues are available. Consider the dorm adviser who took a telephone call for Bill from his family. Even though the person calling did not identify herself, the adviser guessed accurately that she was Bill's younger sister. Although it seems obvious that the adviser would be able to tell if Bill's caller was a male or female simply by the voice, there is research that suggests that vocal differences between the sexes may be primarily learned. Anatomically, the length and thickness of the vocal folds are in proportion to the size of the larynx, which is directly related to body size. Therefore, a larger larynx will produce a lower-pitched voice. However, social conditioning or the wish to sound as people expect us to sound may modify the results of the difference in larynx size.

One study concerning the identification of gender through vocal cues used boy and girl speakers of approximately the same size. Experimenters took measurements of height, weight, and mandible (jaw) length, and the children were instructed to speak into the telephone in normal voices. Results showed that listeners could identify the gender of the speakers accurately but that the differences in vocal characteristics resulted from socialization and not from physical size. Apparently, these children's voices were more closely related to sexual stereotypes they had observed rather than to body size (Sachs, Lieberman, and Erickson, 1973). Voice therapists observe differences in the pitch best suited to adults' physical equipment and the pitch they actually use most often. Social pressures apparently influence us to try to make our voices sound as we think they should sound.

Lass and Harvey (1976) studied ability to match pictures of people with samples of their voices. Though the subjects were of different heights and weights, the researcher found that judges were able to match voices with full-length pictures more accurately than with head-and-shoulder shots. Their study pointed out that some relationship seems to exist between height and voice and that social conditioning and/or body size may produce this relationship. A very tall or large person who speaks in a high-pitched or very soft voice is likely to be penalized socially.

To sum up, then, we may say that judgments of SES can be made with considerable accuracy on the basis of paralinguistic cues and that the gender of the speaker can also be determined reliably. Although judgments of age, height, and weight have possibilities of being correct, these judgments should be made cautiously.

THE VOICE AND JUDGMENTS OF PERSONALITY CHARACTERISTICS

When you hear the voice of another person, do you form opinions about the kind of person he or she might be? In other words, do you make judgments about personality characteristics on the basis of vocal cues? Whether we realize it or not, we do often form such opinions about people from their voices. Imagine that a friend has set up a blind date for you; during the crucial telephone call arranging the time and place at which you'll meet, you feel the urge to cancel the plans. What has happened? Probably you have quickly based some opinions about the personality of your prospective date on vocal characteristics. You may also feel a strong liking for this person only to find out that, once you meet, he or she is not what you expected. Of course, many factors about the characteristics of others enter into our conclusions, but in empirical research consistency among judges' ratings demonstrates the existence of personality stereotypes precisely related to the voice.

Benevolence and Competence

Let us go back to the question discussed earlier concerning the type of information carried by the voice. We said that evaluative information is based on verbal content and that judgments of social attractiveness and of strength are made on the basis of vocal characteristics. After reviewing research in this area, Hart and Brown (1974) more succinctly addressed these vocal phenomena. They reconceptualized the information which is carried by vocal channels as "benevolence" and "competence" information. For these researchers, **benevolence information** was conveyed primarily by verbal content, while **competence information** was transmitted via vocal characteristics. Later, Street and Brady (1982) partially supported this earlier work in a study addressing the relationships between speech rate, perceived competence, and social attractiveness. Results of the Street/Brady study revealed a strong relationship between perceived and actual speech rate and perceived speaker competence: Moderately fast and fast speaker rates produced higher judgments of competence than slower speaker rates, although perceived competence stayed about the same for moderately fast and fast rates. Additionally, Street and Brady discovered that faster speech rates had a significant impact on listeners' judgments of social attractiveness.

Another study regarding the positive and negative effects of vocal cues on personality-characteristic judgments was conducted earlier by Addington (1968), who investigated stereotyped judgments of voice qualities, rate of speech, and pitch variety. Four trained speakers were instructed to simulate seven voice qualities (breathy, tense, thin, flat, nasal, throaty, and strong); three rates of speech (normal, fast, and slow); and three pitch varieties (normal, more than normal, and less than normal). Judges listened to the tapes and rated the speakers on personality characteristics. Analysis of the results gave some interesting insights into stereotypical reactions to voice characteristics.

The ratings on voice qualities produced a complex picture. Breathiness in males was identified with artistic personalities and youthfulness, while the same trait in females elicited ratings of beauty and femininity but also shallowness. Females with thin voices were thought to be immature, but this trait in the male voice was found to be insignificant. Speakers of both genders who used a flat voice were perceived as more masculine, cool, and withdrawn. Nasality provoked ratings that indicated a wide assortment of unpleasant characteristics. Males using increased vocal tension were thought to be older and unyielding, but females speaking with tense voices were thought to be younger, more emotional, and less intelligent. Increased throatiness caused males to appear older, more mature, and more sophisticated, while "throaty-voiced" females were thought to be lazy, ugly, and careless. In general, clear, robust voices produced positive ratings. Males with this trait appeared to be enthuasiastic and healthy, while females appeared to be lively and gregarious. Females with strong, full voices were thought to be proud and humorless. Ultimately, all speakers were considered more animated and extroverted when they increased the rate of their speech and were thought to have dynamic personalities when they increased variety in their pitch. Males who varied their pitch level were thought to be more feminine and aesthetically inclined, while females using variety in pitch rated high on extroversion (Addington, 1968).

Addington's research suggested that a strong voice, varied pitch, and a lively rate of speech were associated with positive characteristics. Nasality in males and females, a tense voice in males, and a thin or throaty voice in females resulted in negative evaluations.

Anxiety

Anxiety is another personality trait that we often infer from vocal cues. In an early, classic study, Mahl (1959) found that as anxiety increases, repetitions, stuttering, omissions, and use of "ums" and "ahs" **(filled pauses)** increase. Fisher and

Apostal (1964) later found that **unfilled or silent pauses** produced no greater perception of anxiety or of genuineness but did give the impression of more willingness to talk about oneself. The tapes from which the latter judgments were made were simulated counseling sessions, with the ratings being made on the messages of the persons receiving counseling. Since self-disclosure is expected in this setting, pauses might seem more positive than those in a social conversation, and thus the judges may have chosen to rate these voices as self-disclosing rather than anxious.

A more recent survey of anxiety research also revealed some interesting results concerning pauses and their relationship to anxiety (Rochester, 1973). For example, anxiety was found to be positively related to *silent* pauses. In other words, silent pauses increase as situational anxiety increases.

The picture is relatively unclear in relation to filled pauses and their relationship to trait anxiety (being anxious or tense most of the time). **Switching pauses** (the silence within a conversation that is counted for the person who ends the silence by speaking) seems to be different for high- and low-trait-anxiety people. Switching pauses are shorter for people who are high in trait anxiety. How does this information affect everyday interactions? Suppose that you are talking with someone who pauses often, stutters, and picks up the speaking role quickly when you stop speaking. You can infer that this person is experiencing anxiety. It is Thursday evening, and Wayne and Ted are chatting about weekend plans over a drink. Ted begins to pause and stutter often. He speaks immediately when Wayne finishes a remark or even before he is finished. Wayne quickly becomes aware that Ted is experiencing anxiety about the weekend plans.

Generally, research in the area of vocal cues has been criticized on a number of fronts. First, vocal characteristics often are described unclearly by experimenters. Second, changing emotional states are not taken into account as often as they should be. Although this point is well made by researchers and textbook authors such as ourselves, we as humans continue to make stereotypical judgments on the basis of voice. These considerations are useful to remember both when thinking about traits of others and when considering the impression you make on others.

PARALINGUISTICS AND LEARNING

A student taking a vacation in the mountains notices a crude sign near his hotel that says, "Basket weaving—lessons." Since he dropped similar lessons during the school year for lack of time, he decides to investigate. He discovers that the lessons are given by a highly skilled elderly woman who speaks unclearly because she is missing some teeth. He wonders if it is worth his time and money to take the lessons. The answer is yes; he can probably benefit from the lessons in spite of the faulty speech of the teacher.

Effect of Vocal Characteristics on Learning

How do the vocal characteristics of what we hear actually affect our learning? Kibler and Barker (1972) presented three forms of a message to high school students. In the first, no words were mispronounced, in another 2 percent of the words were mispronounced, and in the third 12 percent of the words were mispronounced. Consistent with earlier studies, the findings showed that the students understood and remembered the content of the different forms of the message equally well.

In an earlier investigation by Wiener (1968) and his colleagues, positive vocal cues were shown to aid children's learning. Given positive vocal cues, the improvement in learning in the lower-class group was dramatic and in the middle-class groups slightly less so. Of course, one must remember that content factors are also involved in improving learning as well as vocal cues.

A class of fourth-graders is making maps of the town they live in. Larry asks the teacher to look at his work. The teacher inspects it and says "Mmm" in a moderately loud voice and with a high and falling pitch. A few minutes later the child sitting next to Larry, Susan, calls for the teacher. The teacher has been distracted by a phone call. With the problem from the phone message still on his mind, he looks at the work and says "Mmm" in a quiet voice with an even, low tone. Could the teacher's reactions affect the work of Larry and Susan? Common sense and research indicate that reinforcement from the teacher is important to learning.

Closely related to our earlier discussion of the effects of vocal characteristics on estimates of SES (socioeconomic status) is a consideration of the negative effect of minority students' speech on teachers' evaluation of them. Jensen and Rosenfeld (1974) had teachers rate Caucasian,* black, and Chicano students on desirable aspects of classroom behavior. The behaviors included participation, attitude, effort, attendance, courtesy, and so on. The teachers were shown tapes (audio, visual, and audiovisual) of students, all neatly dressed, in an interview situation discussing their favorite games and television programs. Results showed that Caucasian students were evaluated more favorably than blacks and Chicanos and that middle-class Caucasians received even more positive ratings when the cues were vocal rather than visual. Therefore, minority students may be receiving less reinforcement simply as a function of their vocal characteristics and other cues of ethnic background.

Time-Compressed Speech

A bright first-year law student is blinded in an automobile accident. Are there any ways to cope with the large volume of reading that must be done? Since we can comprehend at more rapid rates than we normally hear per minute, **time-compressed speech** offers some help by increasing the number of words presented per minute. Although a great deal of difference exists in people's ability to comprehend compressed speech, this method has potential as an aid to efficient learning. For example, Orr (1968) has shown that people *can* understand and learn at some degree of accelerated speech and that practice in listening at faster speeds than

---

* The study used the designation "Anglo." This term is currently used to designate those who do not fall into the black, Chicano, or Indian ethnic groups.

usual is useful. His study also showed that, although immediate retention is comparable to the retention resulting from speech at normal speed, the retention may be minimal after a few weeks. Although further investigation is needed to determine specific ways in which time-compressed speech can be used efficiently, one can see that it is an important learning tool for the blind. Try to time how long it takes you to read this page silently and how long to read it aloud. You will understand immediately the need of blind students for accelerated recordings of text material.

After considering the research reviewed here, we hope that you understand the importance of paralinguistics to learning. We have seen that we can learn even if pronunciation is less than perfect, that vocal cues are useful in classroom reinforcement, and that time-compressed speech is an important learning tool for the blind.

PARALINGUISTICS AND PERSUASION

A political rally features two speakers who take opposing views on "Star Wars" defense; both are well prepared. Before the speeches, opinion is about equally divided pro and con. Ms. James, who favors this defense plan, speaks slowly and uses the same pitch most of the time. The opposing speaker, Ms. Brannon, speaks at a lively rate with much variation in pitch. Is the audience more likely to be persuaded by one than the other? Do the rate and pitch variety of the speeches and the articulation or styles of delivery influence the credibility that the listeners assign to the speakers? Do these variables contribute to the degree to which the listeners are persuaded to a given speaker's point of view? Research indicates that these considerations are important to speakers if they want to influence the attitudes of their listeners. For instance, in our example, the audience will probably feel less favorable toward the "Star Wars" defense plan because of the superior speaking skills of Ms. Brannon.

Miller (1976) and his colleagues found that a faster rate of speech is more persuasive. Simply put, faster rates create greater attitude change in listeners. Faster rates also produce higher ratings of intelligence, knowledge, and objectivity. Miller interpreted these results to mean that greater credibility was ascribed to the faster speakers.

In another study, **conversational style** and **dynamic style** were compared by Pearce and Conklin (1971). In contrast to the dynamic style, the conversational style had a smaller range of pitch changes, more consistent rate and pitch, and less volume and lower pitch. The conversational-style speaker was rated more trustworthy, better educated, more professional, and more attractive than the dynamic speaker. His dynamic delivery was described as more tough-minded, task-oriented, self-assured, and assertive (Pearce and Conklin, 1971). How is such information useful for you? First, in giving a speech, style should be considered in terms of appropriateness to the purpose of the speech. For example, in speaking to a fraternity or sorority about poor academic performance of their pledges, an officer of the campus panhellenic council should probably choose a more con-

A speaker's paralinguistics have a significant influence on his or her persuasiveness. (Richard Wood/Taurus Photos)

versational style of delivery. Speaking in a conversational style would give the impression that he or she is trustworthy, professional, and person-oriented. In contrast, a dynamic delivery would be more useful on some occasions. For example, the president of a club for business majors must speak at their annual fund-raising rally. The funds to be raised will be used to provide convention expenses for officers and an annual social function. A dynamic delivery would be a wise choice in this case, because the advantages of impressing this audience that he is tough-minded, assertive, and so on, will aid him in achieving his purpose.

In other research, Addington (1968) studied the relationships of speaking rate, pitch variety, voice quality, and articulation to source credibility. Three dimensions of credibility were considered: competence, trustworthiness, and dynamism. The changes in vocal characteristics produced significant effects on all three dimensions; however, judgments of speaker competence were influenced most by the voice changes. (Thus, a professor who lectures in a monotone voice will not be considered competent by most students.) Credibility was also less when speakers used tense voices, nasality, or denasality.*

We can conclude, then, that a speaker should give careful attention to voice characteristics in order to have the best opportunity to influence the audience. The style of speaking should be chosen with both the audience and occasion in mind.

---

* For explanation of nasality, see section on voice improvement. Denasality is simply lack of nasality on appropriate sounds.

THE VOICE AND TURN-TAKING

In the midst of a conversation, how do you indicate that you want to say something? If you think that someone who is quiet could make an interesting contribution, can you encourage this without a verbal question? Yes, there are vocal cues and other nonverbal ways to manage turn-taking in a conversation.

Two commuters are discussing local politics during their morning train ride to downtown offices. After one has explained his views, he pauses for the other to speak. His companion nods agreement and remains silent.

A professor shows a student a report completed in the same course the previous quarter, and a moment of silence ensues. The student examines it and then says, "Oh, this is the way you want it done?"

A freshman is at home for a weekend and is making a plea for extra money for the following month. The mother begins to speak by saying, "Now, son . . . " and the father clears his throat. The student attempts "to retain the floor" and to explain by speaking faster and raising his volume.

What do the above examples have in common? Each contains examples of the use of vocal cues in conversational turn-taking.

Turn-Taking Cues

What are the types of cues for turn-taking, and how are they used? According to Duncan (1973), in conversation we use turn-yielding cues, back-channel cues, and turn-maintaining cues. Wiemann and Knapp (1975) also include turn-requesting. Let us look at each of these categories of turn-taking behavior.

Speakers use **turn-yielding cues** to let the listener know that they have finished what they want to say and that someone else may speak. Vocal cues that may serve this purpose are intonation, drawl, buffers,* changes in pitch, changes in volume, interrogative inflections, and silence. The last two—interrogative inflections (in which the pitch is raised to indicate a question) and silence—seem obvious, but the others are also frequently used effectively. For example, if someone's speech slows to a drawl and a buffer such as "Well, you know" is interspersed in the heavily content-laden speech, the listener can usually assume that he or she is being given an opportunity to contribute verbally to the conversation. Lower pitch or lower volume and change in the pattern of pitch variation can be used in a similar manner. Carol is in a professor's office to get help with a research paper. She states her opinion on how to handle the issues and finishes with a slowed pace and raised pitch followed by silence. Obviously, she is ready to hear what the professor has to say.

Back-channel cues are used by listeners to indicate that they do not wish to talk even though the speaker is displaying turn-yielding cues. That is, back-channeling

---

* Buffers are short words or phrases that are content-free and more or less stereotypical and that either precede or follow substantive statements. Examples include "but uh," "you know," or "uh-well" (Wiemann and Knapp, p. 83).

is staying in the position of listener in the conversation when there is an opportunity to become the speaker. Vocal cues appropriate for this purpose include reinforcers (e.g., "Mm," "uh-huh"), completion of a sentence by the listener, or requests for clarification. John has had a rough term and is finally home for a holiday. He is pouring out his story of a troublesome roommate and a disloyal girlfriend to his Dad. After talking about the interpersonal problems, he wonders if his Dad is bored, and so he pauses. His Dad's only reply is "Hmm." Encouraged, John continues his tale by talking about difficulties with course work. After a sentence or two his Dad interjects an "Oh" with a rising inflection. John then explains in more detail. Both "Hmm" and "Oh" in this illustration are examples of back-channeling.

Turn-maintaining cues, in which speaking-turn claims are suppressed, are used by speakers to keep their speaking turn. Although hand gestures may constitute the most important nonverbal behavior for this purpose, some vocal cues may be used alone or may accompany hand gestures. These vocal cues include increased changes in volume and rate of speech in response to turn-requesting cues from listeners. Using more filled pauses (with some form of vocalization, e.g., "Ah . . . ") than silent or unfilled pauses is a useful method of turn-maintaining. Don is telling his girlfriend about his admission to graduate school. When she tries to congratulate him, he talks a little louder and leaves no pauses unfilled. He wants to keep the speaking turn because he has more good news. He has also been awarded a fellowship.

Turn-requesting is more frequently accomplished by simultaneous talking. Buffers and reinforcers are also used. Stutter starts are similar to buffers but may reveal a stronger demand to speak than buffers. Stutter starts are also likely to be used if the speaker has had the floor for fifteen to twenty seconds or if the speaker pauses longer than usual. Tim, Sara, and Phil are discussing a proposed change in the local drinking-age law. Tim is expressing his strong opinion that the age should be lowered. Sara wants to disagree with him; therefore, when he pauses she begins with a stutter start, "B-b-but." Phil then tries to take the floor from her with the buffer "Uh . . . well."

For all of the above categories of cues, you should keep in mind that often vocal cues are used in combination with other nonverbal cues. However, the use of more than one cue is probably related to the urgency of the request being made.

Turn-Taking Cues and Social Class

Have you ever felt awkward in a conversation with a person whose background or life-style was very unlike yours? Perhaps you were unsure about the specific source of your discomfort. It may have been a difference in nonverbal behaviors, which vary for different socioeconomic statuses. Previously, we noted that vocal cues such as dialect aid listeners in determining the SES of the speaker. Another vocal cue, that of turn-taking practices, helps the listener identify the SES of the speaker. Malcolm is a graduate student in a prestigious university. His responsibility on a research project is to discuss working conditions with road construction workers. He had dressed in work clothes and remembered to use language he learned from summer work experiences. In spite of his efforts to identify with the workers he finds that he feels uneasy in his first conversation with them. Later, when he tries to analyze why he felt that way, he realizes that when they ended phrases without changing pitch and were silent at some points during the conversation, he had reacted with vague uneasiness. The difference in SES had influenced the interaction because of different habits in the use of vocal cues.

In a 1978 study, the subjects were working-class and middle-class high school students recruited from ninth-grade English classes. Each student watched a cartoon while the experimenter ostensibly prepared for the next subject in an adjoining room. After the cartoon was finished, the experimenter returned, said he had not seen it, and asked the subject to tell him about it. Unless the student ended the conversation, for example, by saying "That's all I remember," the experimenter continued to ask questions about the cartoon. The conversation between experimenter and student was videotaped, and afterward judges viewed the videotape and recorded the subjects' eye contact and changes in pitch. The study showed that working-class students used more upward changes in pitch and ended more phrases without changing their pitch than the middle-class students and that they also used more silent pauses. Middle-class students, however, used more pauses filled with some sound (e.g., "Mm") and more downward inflections of pitch. One conclusion drawn was that the upward or interrogative inflection of pitch and the silent pauses of the working class may indicate a lack of confidence and feelings of inferiority. This conclusion seems substantiated by the middle-class speakers' use of cues that are the reverse of those used by the working-class speakers; that is, the middle-class speakers used pauses filled with some sound whereas the working-class speakers used silent pauses. If silent pauses are viewed as cues for turn-taking behavior, that is, as openings where the other person can take over the conversation, then the working-class subjects displayed less resistance to yielding their turn. The predominant use of filled pauses by the middle-class speakers showed their desire to hold on to their turn. Middle-class speakers also used downward instead of upward pitch changes or no pitch change at all at the ends of sentences (Robbins, Devoe, and Wiener, 1978). This behavior is not surprising, since we would generally expect that middle-class students would have more confidence and fewer feelings of inferiority than students of lower economic status.

In conclusion, then, we may say that vocal cues are an important part of our turn-taking behavior. We make use of them when we want to keep a speaking turn, gain a turn, pass it to someone else, or pass it up. Furthermore, the specific vocal cues we use will probably be affected by our social class.

THE VOICE AND DECEPTION

Several nonverbal behaviors often accompany deception, but are there useful cues in the voice for detecting untruths? Apparently, one can gain some hints concerning truth or falsity from the voice. We must add, however, that it would be unwise to make a judgment based on voice alone.

Krauss (1975) at Columbia University has identified the following character-istics of speech associated with deception: a slow rate of speech, shifts to higher pitch, inappropriate hesitations, and many dysfluencies. Although Krauss also points out that knowing these characteristics and avoiding them can be useful in improving credibility, they are not really useful in detecting deception because they are just as often signs of nervousness as of untruthfulness.

Suppose your roommate takes a message for you while you are out. The mes-sage involves instructions for you to go to a city a couple of hours' drive away for a job interview. You read the note left by your roommate and plan to go; later, however, your roommate gives you a description of the caller's vocal character-istics (stuttering, many oral pauses, and high pitch), and you begin to doubt the wisdom of taking the message seriously. You would be wise to look into the mat-ter further, since the caller may have just been nervous or playing a practical joke.

Although vocal cues to deception that we may use in everyday activities have not been isolated, progress is being made in developing technology for lie detec-tion by voice. For example, spectrographic analysis was performed on voices of subjects replying to questions with one-word low-risk lies. The subjects chose a number and were then asked to respond with the word "No" to all questions about the number chosen. Analysis showed that false responses were shorter, thereby revealing the differences between truthful and untruthful replies. How-ever, when the tapes of the above replies were played to a group of subjects, they were unable to differentiate the true and false answers. Their accuracy was even less than we would expect by chance (Motley, 1974). Although electronic voice analysis may have possibilities for usage in lie detection, apparently the naked ear is unable to detect deception through vocal cues alone, at least in low-risk lies.

Another interesting development in mechanical voice analysis is a device called *Vopan,* which is being used by the Consumer Response Corporation in New York. It has long been apparent that consumers do not always tell the truth; for example, we hear a great deal of talk about how people detest sex and violence on television, but at the same time the programs including scenes of sex and vio-lence do well in the ratings. Surveys also show that shoppers believe that nation-ally advertised brands are superior to house brands, yet the house brands sell very well. *Vopan* is an outgrowth of technology with which the investigative agencies have experimented for a number of years; it can detect slight, inaudible shifts of pitch in the voice. General Motors Corporation marketing personnel compared accuracy in prediction of *Vopan* with attitudinal scales traditionally used to pre-dict brand usage. The attitude scales accurately predicted use of the products being considered only 43 percent of the time. *Vopan* predicted product use with 92 percent accuracy. In another experiment with *Vopan,* a group of women said that they were uninterested in reading any more magazine articles telling them how to improve their sex lives. *Vopan* analysis did confirm that they were bored with the subject (*Human Behavior,* 1978).

It is evident that cues to deception do exist in the human voice. These are unre-liably detectable, however, without the aid of modern technology. Shifts to high pitch, excessive pauses, and stutter stops or stammers may be interpreted as evi-dence of deception when they actually reflect stress. Suppose you are telling a friend about an incredible incident that you have experienced and you get stares of disbelief in return. Although your excitement is the cause of stammering, frequent pausing, and pitch changes, these behaviors are being interpreted as signs of deception. Therefore, when you hear someone whose speech is broken and you conclude that he or she is being untruthful, remember to consider that the speech pattern may be caused by stress.

THE USE OF PAUSES AND SILENCE

All activity needs to be set against a contrast; a background is needed in order for the material in the foreground to assume importance. Consider the following two situations. A yogi from India is scheduled to speak at a student government association rally on the improvement of study habits. His first statement, "I can teach you a way to improve all aspects of your life," is followed by a pause. Sylvia has had two years of basic college courses and has decided she should major in botany. She is engaged to Don, who is in the third year of an engineering program. Botany is not offered at their university. After a weekend at home to think it over, she broaches the subject with Don by saying, "It looks like I'll have to transfer to another university soon." A pause follows.

Much of the time, brief silences or pauses and longer silences assume the function of contrast or emphasis for spoken language. They serve somewhat the same purpose that the white of this paper does for the print, but they do it in a more dramatic way. Although we accept the blank part of the page without notice, silences of any duration may draw our attention, and sometimes pauses or lengthy silences may become the foreground. Silence then can become the medium for conveying a message.

Pauses

Pauses have already been discussed in connection with turn-taking, personality characteristics, and deception. However, because of their importance, it is worthwhile to give some attention to them as a separate topic.

Pauses occur at grammatical junctures

- at the end of a sentence
- preceding a conjunction (and, but, if, when, etc.)
- preceding relative and interrogative pronouns (who, which, why, whose, etc.)
- in connection with an indirect or implied question (e.g., "I'm not sure whether I will . . .")
- before adverbial clauses of time, manner, and place (e.g., "I will call you when I arrive in town.")
- at the beginning and end of parenthetical references (e.g., "It seems that those families—the ones on my block—were in favor . . .")

And there are also pauses that are not grammatical. These can occur

- in the middle or at the end of a phrase (e.g., "In all of // the sections of that course // . . .")
- in breaks between words and phrases that are repeated (e.g., "The situation with the // with the athletes in that university . . .")
- in the middle of a verbal compound (e.g., "We are // going to the convention, and then we will // stop in New York to . . .")
- when a sentence is disrupted by indecision or a false start, (e.g., "We need to remember in planning this function // I believe the important consideration here is . . .") (Goldman-Eisler, 1968, p.13)

Actually, the idea of fluent speech is an illusion. For example, Goldman-Eisler (1958a) found that the speech of her subjects was very fragmented in spontaneous speech and only somewhat less so in practiced speech. In a relaxed situation she found that almost half her subjects' speech was broken up into phrases of less than three words and that about half of their speaking time was taken up with silence. After they had practiced, there was only a slight increase in smooth, unbroken phrases.

Fluency is also associated with high predictability of words, while pauses co-occur with low predictability (Goldman-Eisler, 1958b). **Predictability** here refers to the accuracy with which others could guess which word would follow in a sequence. However, all pauses increase with an increase in the degree of abstraction and with the difficulty in encoding (Rochester, 1973). The same occasions would be characterized by low predictability and a high degree of need for encoding. For example, you will notice that if you are finding it difficult to express your thoughts in words (encoding), you will pause more often and for longer periods of time, and your listeners will find it more difficult to predict what you will say next.

For problem-solution situations, however, there may be a difference between the usefulness of filled pauses and the usefulness of silent pauses. Subjects in one study were given math problems to do while their behavior was being recorded. Those who exhibited more silent pauses solved the problems in less time than those who used more filled pauses. One researcher argues that filled pauses ("uhh . . .") serve antagonistic functions; that is, although filled pauses increase the speaker's conversational control, they also decrease the quality of production (Livant, 1963). Try asking someone to solve a problem verbally and record that person's filled and silent pauses. Consider the results in reference to this research.

Another important variable in the study of paralinguistics is the speed of speech production, which depends upon the amount of time taken up by hesitation pauses. Variations in overall speed of talking are basically variations in amount of pausing. For instance, in an early study, Chapple (1949) investigated the speech tempo of industrial workers playing different roles and found that supervisors spoke faster than the workers "under them" but that they were capable of using a slower pace when the situation demanded. One can see, then, that both the role being played and the type of work influence the speed of speech. Try to notice today whether the speed of your speech varies when you play different roles and do various types of work. Your roles as student, friend, or employee may influence the speed of your speech. Studying, doing handicrafts, and taking care of housekeeping chores will give you opportunities to observe changes in your speech rate. It seems that people who pause less are more capable of spontaneity of formulation of verbal speech; they are speakers who can "think on their feet."

Speed of speech is also an indicator of pathological states. One example of such a state is manic-depressive psychosis. In this state, speech is likely to be rapid and constant. Depression, another state, is characterized by slow speech. In both cases, however, the person is speaking to express an emotional state and is relatively unaware of the listener (Eisenson, Auer, and Irwin, 1963).

The speed of speech of a person not suffering from a pathological state follows a similar pattern. In the section on identification of emotions, we mentioned the fast rate of expression of active feelings and the slow rate of expression of passive feelings. In our discussion of the voice and personality, we learned that faster speech gives the impression of being more animated and extroverted.

Pauses serve functions that are useful for both the speaker and the listener. They delineate parts of phrases and sentences, express emotional states, aid in encoding and decoding, and provide time for problem solving.

Silence*

The day has been busy and full. A big decision looms over you. Late in the afternoon you slip away to think . . . alone . . . in silence.

A cathedral is open. Candles are burning. A lone worshiper comes in to kneel . . . to meditate . . . to pray in silence.

Demonstrators camp around the Capitol to protest an action of the Senate. For a time they are still and silent, and then they begin to chant.

A director of a social agency makes a lengthy, impassioned appeal for funds for a group that must make allocations of funds to various agencies. A period of silence follows.

Silence appears to be a concept or a process of the mind imposed by people on themselves or on others. Absolute silence does not exist. Even if a person is not talking or listening to external sounds, there may be continuous mental conversation. Bruneau (1973) believes that it is a major misconception to treat silence as the opposite of speech. Silence can be considered as an environment surrounding speech or language. Thus it is appropriate to discuss some uses of silence.

The process of putting thoughts into words is aided by the imposition of silence on the mind; that is, to encode messages the mind needs relief from other thoughts (the use of pauses in encoding was discussed earlier). Relief from all thoughts may be needed at times in order for the mental processing that occurs

---

* This section is largely adapted from Bruneau, T. (1973) Communicative silences: Forms and functions. *Journal of Communication,* 23, 17–46.

below our level of awareness to take place. The common phenomenon of going to sleep while thinking about a difficult problem and waking up with possible solutions in mind illustrates this principle.

Silence is also sometimes necessary to experience awareness of the world around us. Often you may need to go to a quiet place simply to think. If you are not in the habit of doing so, try going to a quiet, peaceful place and avoiding intentional thinking.

Silence can create interpersonal distance. Observe the intense silence of people on a crowded elevator. In other situations, silence can lessen interpersonal distance; an example of such a situation is the understanding silence between long-time friends. Closely related to the silence used to manipulate interpersonal distance is the silence that often follows an intensive sensory event. A beautiful sunset, a tremendous musical performance, or an odor that evokes childhood memories may create a need for silence. Both positive and negative emotions evoke silence, and silence is often the language of the strongest of passions—love, anger, surprise, fear.

Silence is also important for its symbolic relationship to authority. We use silence as an expression of respect and reverence in worship services. Silence, together with continuous repetition or chanting, can remove the mind from distracting peripheral stimuli. Both are often associated with meditative spiritual

Silence is often important to allow us to process ideas and problems mentally. People sometimes go to a quiet place to think. (Joel Gordon)

experiences. A person in authority can use silence to demand respect and to require subordinates to think for themselves. Think of a time when you directed a question to an expert or mentor and felt uncomfortable with the ensuing silence. Afterward, you realized that the time was allotted to give you time to think and answer the question by yourself.

Silence has an important place in psychotherapy also, in that it allows patients to recuperate and to pull themselves together, so to speak. Greater incidence of silence is often considered a sign of progress; for example, children undergoing psychotherapy seem to need periods of silence to create a field for learning new attitudes. The therapist's silence, too, is important to allow the patient time for free association.

Silence is also used to modify the behavior of others in various situations. Silence is used to punish norm violators; the Amish call this punishment "shunning." You may have experienced the coldness of silence following a blunder. Harry used slang appropriate for his campus at a formal dinner with his dad's business associates. He was treated to silence by all the people sitting near him. Silence is also a convenient way to refuse to reinforce behavior that you consider undesirable. If someone who is sitting next to you in a group continually makes remarks (asides), refusing to answer may stop this behavior. Moreover, people who are deformed or different in some way often experience the nervous silences of others, and a stranger often must bear the burden of breaking a silence or letting it remain. Finally an unexpected or unusual statement may be greeted with silence (Bruneau, 1973).

Silence, then, is useful both as a background for sound and as a means of conveying a message. On a given day, observe how many different uses you make of silence. Is silence really useful? Can you make better use of silence?

IMPROVING THE VOICE

Think about a career that interests you. Mentally list the different occasions on which it would demand oral communication. If you are interested in a career in business or education, the importance of speech is obvious. Your success in almost any career will be enhanced by effective use of your voice. Sandy Linvy (1977), who teaches speech communication to executives, emphasizes that speech is very important to success in business. Obviously, the use of the voice is a major component of the group of behaviors that determine whether one is an effective communicator.

Sarnoff (1970) gives some advice on the improvement of the most common voice problems; the most useful equipment for voice improvement is a tape recorder and a mirror. First, you can listen to your voice and decide whether you want to try to make improvements. Second, your reflection in a mirror will help you to discover tension and failure to open your mouth widely enough. If you have serious voice problems, you should see a speech therapist; however, there are some things you can do on your own.

Nasality

Nasality is a common voice problem. You can probably recall the sound of voices of people who have excessive nasality. The only legitimate nasal sounds in our language are "m," "n," and "ng." Close your nostrils with your thumb and fore-finger and talk. You should feel vibration from those three sounds only. If you feel a vibration from other sounds you are talking through your nose; opening your mouth wider and relaxing your jaw may help. If you find it difficult to relax your jaw and other parts of the speech mechanism, try to find someone who can help you with relaxation exercises.

Screeching

Screeching or shrillness in the voice is another common problem. Look in the mirror and see if your neck looks taut. Relaxation is important for this problem, too. Step into a college dining room during exam week and listen to the voices around you. They will likely be shrill and sharp. These students are very tense. Stop to look in a mirror and talk on a day when you are feeling uptight. Then do the same on a day when you are feeling relaxed and note the difference in the appearance of your face and neck.

Softness

Talking in a too-soft voice or whispering can cut off communication. Ask a friend to signal when you are speaking at too low a volume. If this simple tactic does not work, ask someone trained in speech or vocal music to help you learn to use your speech to project your voice more effectively.

Monotone

Monotonous pitch can quickly lose the attention of your listeners. Tape yourself reading aloud. Listen to the playback and concentrate on whether the pitch is varied. Decide what you need to change and then try again. Listen to the voices of those people whose speech you consider pleasant and try to imitate them.

Speed

You also may need to give some consideration to the speed of your speech. Your tape recorder and a good friend will be helpful in this, too. If you are speaking too fast, give some thought to why you are doing so. You may feel insecure or pushed for time. In the same manner, there may be underlying reasons for speaking too slowly. Exploring these reasons with a trusted friend or counselor would be helpful.

Now would be a good time to review the section on stereotypical judgments of personality characteristics in relation to voice. If you want to make changes in your voice, more extensive suggestions are available in books and articles on the subject. Remember that if you are having any serious difficulty with your voice, you should see a physician and a speech pathologist.

After reading this chapter you are probably convinced that the use of your voice is a significant component of your personal communication system. In brief, we have learned the following. Vocal cues are helpful but are inconclusive as evidence in identifying demographic and personality characteristics and emotions. They are important in planning persuasion efforts. Deception is characterized by specific vocal cues but cannot be assumed from voice alone and is often confused with anxiety. The use of the voice is an integral part of turn-taking behavior. Pauses and silences compose a large portion of our communication time and are means of communication in themselves. As with the interpretation of other forms of nonverbal communication, you should keep in mind that literal or rigid translations to verbal language are inappropriate. However, skill in observing and assessing paralinguistic cues is worth your time and effort.

SUMMARY

The study of meaning in oral speech gleaned from cues other than the content of the spoken word is known as *paralinguistics*. Vocal variations may suggest several different meanings for the same verbal message. While they answer questions concerning the nature of meaning, vocal cues also help to identify emotional, demographic, and personality characteristics of people. Vocal characteristics also affect learning, persuasion, turn-taking, and deception.

The amount and type of information carried through vocal cues vary from person to person and situation to situation. A person's "voice set," voice quality, and vocalization influence how information and people are interpreted and categorized. It is relatively simple to pick up cues about emotional states through differences in a person's voice, yet researchers have been unable to identify the exact vocal cues for individual emotions. Evaluations are often based on the volume, pitch level, and rate of the speaker. People who monitor their emotions effectively are more capable of expressing intentional feelings through their voice and more accurate at judging emotions of others. Paralinguistic cues are accurate predictors of the socioeconomic status and gender of people, but stereotypical judgments about the personalities of people are often inaccurate.

In spite of faulty speech patterns, students can learn and benefit from them. The vocal cues of teachers play an important role in student classroom reinforcement. Time-compressed speech is a useful aid and learning tool for the blind. Whether they are teachers or politicians, speakers with a persuasive purpose in mind should give careful attention to their vocal characteristics. The manner and style of speaking should be suited to both the audience and the occasion.

In conversation, vocal cues help to manage turn-taking through turn-yielding, 'back-channeling,' turn-requesting, and turn-maintaining cues. Cues are often used in combination, and the urgency is related to the number of cues used. The choice of the specific cues we use in conversation is affected by our socioeconomic class.

The voice is often used as a method of detecting deception, even though it is unreliable without the aid of modern technology. Stammering, frequent pausing, and pitch changes may be caused by factors other than deception. The uses of pause and silence convey as much information as the spoken language. Pauses help to delineate parts of phrases and sentences, express emotional states, aid in encoding and decoding, and provide time for problem solving. Silence is useful as a background for sound and as a means of conveying a message.

The use of the voice is a significant component in your personal communication system. Dissatisfaction with your vocal characteristics can be improved through training and effort.

References

Addington, D. W. (1968) The relationship of selected vocal characteristics to personality perception. *Speech Monographs, 35,* 492–503.

Baroni, M. R., & D'Urso, V. (1984) Some experimental findings about the question of politeness and women's speech (research note). *Language in Society, 13,* 67–72.

Bradford, A., Ferror, D., & Bradford, G. (1974) Evaluation reactions of college students to dialect differences in the English of Mexican-Americans. *Language and Speech, 17,* 255–270.

Bruneau, T. (1973) Communicative silences: Forms and functions. *Journal of Communication, 23,* 17–46.

Chapple, E. D. (1949) The interaction chronograph: Its evolution and present application. *Personnel, 25,* 295–307.

Crystal, D. (1978) Paralinguistics. In J. B. Pelhams & T. Pelhams (Eds.), *The body as a medium of expression.* New York: Macmillan.

Duncan, S. (1973) Toward a grammar for dyadic conversation. *Semiotica, 9,* 24–46.

Eisenson, J., Auer, J. J., & Irwin, J. V. (1963) Affective behavior (emotion) and speech. In J. J. Auer (Ed.), *The psychology of communication.* New York: Appleton-Century-Crofts.

Fisher, M. J., & Apostal, R. A. (1964) Selected vocal cues and counselors' perceptions of genuineness, self-disclosure and anxiety. *Journal of Counseling Psychology, 62,* 247–251.

Goldman-Eisler, F. G. (1968) *Psycholinguistics: Experiments in spontaneous speech.* New York: Academic Press.

Goldman-Eisler, F. G. (1958a) Speech production and the predictability of words in context. *Quarterly Journal of Speech, 10,* 96–106.

Goldman-Eisler, F. G. (1958b) The predictability of words in context and the length of pauses in speech. *Language and Speech, 1,* 226–231.

Graddol, D., & Swann, J. (1983) Speaking fundamental frequency: Some physical and social correlates. *Language and Speech, 26* (4), 351–365.

Harms, L. S. (1961) Listener judgments of status cues in speech. *Quarterly Journal of Speech, 47,* 164–168.

Hart, R. J., & Brown, B. L. (1974) Interpersonal information conveyed by the content and vocal aspects of speech. *Speech Monographs, 41,* 371–380.

Hegstrom, T. G. (1979) Message impact: What percentage is nonverbal? *Western Journal of Speech, 43,* 134–142.

Human Behavior (April 1978) Detecting consumers' fibs, p. 21.

Jensen, M., & Rosenfeld, L. B. (1974) Influence of mode of presentation, ethnicity, and social class on teachers' evaluations of students. *Journal of Educational Psychology, 66,* 540–547.

Kibler, R. J., & Barker, L. L. (1972) Effects of selected levels of misspelling and mispronunciation on comprehension and retention. *Southern Speech Communication Journal, 37,* 361–374.

Krauss, R. (January 1975) Improve your credibility. *Glamour,* p. 42.

Labov, W. (1969) The logic of non-standard English. *Georgetown Monograph of Language and Linguistics, 22,* 1–31.

Lass, N. J., & Harvey, L. A. (1976) An investigation of speaker photograph identification. *Journal of the Acoustical Society of America, 59,* 1232–1236.

Livant, W. P. (1963) Antagonistic functions of verbal pauses: Filled and unfilled pauses in the solution of additions. *Language and Speech, 6,* 1–4.

Linvy, S. (July 31, 1977) Personal performance, proper speech affects your future, her company. In C. Davis, *Business.*

Mahl, G. F. (1959) Disturbances in the patient's speech as a function of anxiety. Paper presented at the Eastern Psychological Association, Atlantic City, N.J. Reprinted in I. Pool (Ed.), *Trends in content analysis.* Urbana, Ill.: University of Illinois Press, pp. 89–130.

Markel, N. N. (1965) The reliability of coding paralanguage: Pitch, loudness and tempo. *Journal of Verbal Learning and Verbal Behavior, 4,* 306–308.

Mehrabian, A. (1972) *Nonverbal communication.* Chicago: Aldine-Atherton.

Mehrabian, A., & Ferris, S. R. (1967) Inference of attitudes from nonverbal communication in two channels. *Journal of Consulting Psychology, 31,* 248–252.

Miller, N., Maruyana, G., Beaver, R. J., & Valore, K. (1976) Speed of speech and persuasion. *Journal of Personality and Social Psychology, 34,* 615–624.

Motley, M. T. (1974) Acoustic correlates of ties. *Western Journal of Speech Communication, 38,* 81–87.

Orr, D. B. (1968) Time compressed speech—a perspective. *Journal of Communication, 18,* 288–292.

Pearce, W. B., & Conklin, F. (1971) Nonverbal vocalic communication and perception of a speaker. *Speech Monographs, 38,* 235–241.

Reardon, R. C. (1971) Individual differences and the meanings of vocal emotional expressions. *Journal of Communication, 21,* 72–82.

Robbins, O., Devoe, S., & Wiener, M. (1978) Social patterns of turn-taking: Nonverbal regulators. *Journal of Communication, 28,* 38–46.

Rochester, S. R. (1973) The significance of pauses in spontaneous speech. *Journal of Psycholinguistic Speech, 2,* 51–81.

Sachs, J., Lieberman, P., & Erickson, D. (1973) Anatomical and cultural determinants of male and female speech. In R. W. Sheely & R. W. Fasold (Eds.), *Language attitudes: Current trends and prospects.* Washington, D.C.: Georgetown Universtiy Press.

Sarnoff, D. (1970) *Speech can change your life.* Garden City, N.Y.: Doubleday.

Scherer, K. R., Koiwunaki, J., & Rosenthal, R. (1972) Minimal cues in the vocal communication of affect: Judging emotions from content-masked speech. *Journal of Psycholinguistic Speech, 1,* 269–285.

Snyder, M. (1974) Self-monitoring of expressive behavior. *Journal of Personality and Social Psychology, 30,* 526–537.

Street, R. L., Jr., & Brady, R. M. (1982) Speech rate acceptance ranges as a function of evaluative domain, listener speech rate, and communication context. *Communication Monographs, 49,* 290–308.

Tizard, B., Hughs, M., Carmichael, H., & Pinkerton, G. (1983) Language and social class: Is verbal deprivation a myth? *Journal of Child Psychology, 24* (4), 533–542.

Trager, G. L. (1958) Paralanguage: A first approximation. *Studies in Linguistics, 13,* 1–12.

Warner, R. M., & Sugarman, D. B. (1986) Attributions of personality based on physical appearance, speech, and handwriting. *Journal of Personality and Social Psychology, 50* (4), 792–799.

Wiemann, J. M., & Knapp, M. L. (1975) Turn-taking in conversations. *Journal of Communication, 25,* 75–92.

Wiener, M. (September 1968) Cited in A. Mehrabian, Communication without words. *Psychology Today,* pp. 53–55.

Williams, F. (1970) The psychological correlates of speech characteristics: On sounding disadvantaged. *Journal of Speech and Hearing Research, 13,* 472–488.

CHAPTER 10

SMELL AND TASTE

When you come down to think about it, what change in the landscape occurs when you have made a place of your own. . . . How smells rush to you, the smell of mint—could it be from the brook? Impossible—the smell of leaves green, leaves dampened by dew, but of other leaves also, old leaves, last year's fallen leaves, that sweet, soft odor of death's decomposition. And then there is the muskiness. There is an animal somewhere.

Robert Ardrey, *The Territorial Imperative*, 1966

As Mallory swayed back and forth in the breeze, suspended only by the white wicker swing that hung lazily on the porch, she closed her eyes and dreamed of what seemed like yesterday. The smell of her mother's lightly scented, rose perfume always had that effect on Mallory's senses. However, with the aroma of warm, sweet bread now emanating from her mother's kitchen, Mallory could almost hear the laughter of her playmates as they splashed and giggled in the stream that ran alongside the house.

Just then, when her body was almost completely relaxed, and the smell of fresh cinnamon had begun to evoke yet other images, Mallory was jolted into reality by the sounds of real laughter and the footsteps of tiny children running onto the porch. Although irritated at first by the interruption, Mallory stretched, then smiled, at the sight that was standing before her. Her own two small children, at last, had discovered their mother's very favorite mimosa tree and the wonderfully fragrant, pink, feathery blossoms that now adorned it.

As Mallory reached toward the outstretched hands of her youngest child and the aromatic gift clutched gently in them, she could only wonder what childhood memories would be in store for them later in their lives. She only hoped that the wonderful, pink, feathery flower's sweet aroma, as well as those smells which now emanated from their grandmother's house, would bring as many special memories to them.

As suggested in this narrative, our sense of smell can and does communicate many different messages. Although all of these messages may not be as pleasant as those described above, they do provide valuable information about our environment and impact on our emotional response to people and situations. Given the value of understanding this very subtle form of nonverbal communication, the first part of this chapter will discuss the nonverbal significance of smell, the process of olfaction, and the measurement and classification of smells.

The area of taste, closely related to smell, also deserves attention as an important area of nonverbal communication. Despite the importance of taste and smell in our lives, especially in our enjoyment of food and wine, surprisingly little information is to be found about how these senses communicate information to ourselves and others. The second part of this chapter will discuss the sense of taste, from the process of tasting to actual food preferences that we experience.

THE SENSE OF SMELL AND COMMUNICATION: AN OVERVIEW

Every day we use our sense of smell as a medium for communication. Although much taken for granted, our sense of smell tells us when our favorite people are around (Ummm . . . smell that Polo or Gloria Vanderbilt cologne!); when our favorite meal is ready and on the table (ahh . . . the aroma of a succulent roast); or when a gas stove or heater has begun to leak a deadly gas. In fact, as we shall see in a later section, natural gas does not normally have an odor in its original state. The gas industry found a way to give it an odor so that its presence could be detected.

As you can see, odors and smells do communicate very subtle nonverbal messages. If they did not, the majority of Americans would not begin each morning by using products such as soap, flavored tooth paste, and, of course, mouthwash. Likewise deodorant, scented shampoo, and cologne would be nonessentials. Finally, we would not be preoccupied with the way our clothes smell to others, and a billion-dollar detergent industry could spend far less money adding scents to its products.

Given that our sense of smell may be classified as a viable communication medium, it may be useful for you, as a budding expert on nonverbal communication, to familiarize yourself with some basic terms and definitions. For our purposes, the term **olfaction** will be used to mean the sense of smell or the act of smelling. The smells or odors around us will be referred to, in general, as **olfactory messages.** Depending on the context, the terms **smell** and **odor** will be used interchangeably. However, both terms will be used to denote an olfactory message that has been perceived.

With this understanding, we now turn to a discussion of the origins of and messages sent by body odors. Additionally, we will discuss how body odors are used in the detection and diagnosis of disease and how the sense of smell can aid in the learning process. We will conclude this opening section by addressing cultural differences regarding the sense of smell and by looking briefly at environmental olfactory communication.

Origins and Messages of Body Odors

According to Whitfield and Stoddart (1984), we all have distinct body odors. These are influenced by a number of factors, including diet, drinking water, mood, living habits, race, gender, age, reproductive state, health, exercise schedule, hygiene, and emotional state. Additionally, many environmental odors— such as cigarette smoke, and the many scented consumer products we wear—are absorbed by our skin, hair, and clothing. Consider, for example, the numerous products we apply in order to alter odor, such as after-shave lotion and perfume. The use of perfume is not a recent phenomenon. It goes back to the early periods of civilization when people worshipped their gods by offering them incense. Perfume, it was rumored, played an important role in the romances of Cleopatra with Caesar and Marc Antony. In biblical times, the Queen of Sheba supposedly used perfumes to conquer Solomon, and Catherine de Médicis was said to have had a personal alchemist who mixed exclusive potions just for her. Our preoccupation with perfumes and scents reveals our intuitive knowledge that people react to the human communication of smells.

Russell (1976) has shown that people can reliably detect their own body odors when they are presented among sets of stimuli contributed by other people. In addition, when people are asked to rate the odors on a pleasantness/unpleasantness scale, they consistently relate unpleasant odors with socially undesirable characteristics such as ugliness, obesity, and bad health. However, as Winter (1976) has noted, both our ability to detect smells and the smells our bodies emit vary with time of day and, for women, with time of month as well. Therefore, the way in which we smell and our ability to perceive smells are "strictly personal" (p. 17).

The Russell study also illustrated how odors affect our lives. Subjects in the study reliably discriminated between male and female odors and consistently described male odors as "musky" and female odors as "sweet." This sensitivity to odors begins early in life. As Filsinger and Fabes (1985) have noted, one- to two-week-old babies reliably respond to the scent of their own mothers' breasts but not to that of a strange mother's (p. 350).

Such studies have broad social implications. We know that the American preoccupation with the presence of odor is so strong that we spend billions of dollars each year to "freshen" our hair, mouths, armpits, and genital areas, as well as our laundry, kitchens, bathrooms, and carpets. As a result of this obsession with cleanliness and odorlessness, we have repressed our abilities to discriminate smells around us. This learned inability to discriminate odors is particularly unfortunate since odors have the potential to send a multitude of messages, including information about ourselves, our health, and well-being. For example, certain odors that are emitted from the human body are associated with particular diseases. In fact, many doctors use body odors in their diagnoses.

Given the relationship between our sense of smell and our overall health and well-being, the following discussion concerning olfaction and the field of medicine is offered. It is hoped that, once you have completed this section, you will be more aware of the messages received by our sense of smell and of the ways in which olfaction serves as a vital communication medium.

Smell and the Field of Medicine

The idea of diagnosis by smell seems insane in this computerized and electronically coordinated age. Yet Dr. Thomas Cone, Jr., of the Harvard Medical School, urged his fellow colleagues in 1975 to utilize their sense of smell as part of their physical examination process. He especially urged them to listen to the statements of mothers about peculiar odors of their infants, for a number of diseases reveal themselves first in the form of odors (Winter, 1976, p. 60).

The notion of diagnosis by smell is not a new one. At one time, such diseases as yellow fever, scurvy, smallpox, typhoid, and diphtheria were diagnosed by smell alone. The following table of diseases and their associated odors reveals the strong correlation between smell and the physical condition of the body.

Today, doctors still use their sense of smell to evaluate comas in patients brought into hospital emergency rooms. The doctor who smells alcohol or a poison such as cyanide can make a clear diagnosis. But if there is a sweet smell such as acetone, the doctor can deduce that the patient is probably in a diabetic coma. The use of odor in the evaluation of schizophrenic patients is perhaps the most intriguing example of this technique (the odor is especially noticeable in rooms where insulin shock therapy is being administered).

TABLE 10.1   **Diseases and Associated Odors**

Disease	Odors
Yellow fever	"Butcher-shop" odor
Scurvy	Putrid odors
Smallpox	Putrid odors
Typhoid fever	"Freshly baked bread"
Diphtheria	Very sweet odor
Plague	Odor of apples

From Winter, 1976, p. 59.

Smell and the Learning Process

As we have stated, the sense of smell aids in medical diagnosis. In addition, a link between odors and learning has also been established. In one study conducted at the Research Center for Mental Health at New York University, students were given a list of words to learn, some of which were accompanied by odors and some not. Researchers found that when words and smells were presented together and were related (for example, cheese and the odor of cheese), students retained word lists of substantial length for indefinite amounts of time (Winter, 1976, p. 124).

Because of such research, odors and smells have been used commercially to aid in student learning. For instance, both the Braille Institute of America and the Perkins School for the Blind have adopted scratch-and-sniff labels for books written in braille. Deaf and mute students have also used these learning tools. Smells not only aid in word association, but they also act as rewards (especially the smell of chocolate cake!).

Unlike animals who use their sense of smell for defense, sexual stimulation, and survival, we have made little use of our sense of smell. In general, we are conscious of smells only when they have invaded our personal space and make themselves known as either pleasant or unpleasant (Burton, 1976). We have become reliant upon our other senses, such as hearing and seeing, despite the fact that our predecessors used their sense of smell as an aid to the other senses—for example, to find food. As Burton has observed,

> The most important reason for our lack of appreciation of odours is probably that our noses are in the wrong place. The evolution of an upright posture has taken our noses away from the source of many odours. Mice, cats, and dogs walk with their noses near the ground and one can only enter their world by descending to hands and knees, as will be appreciated by a gardener grubbing weeds or a naturalist searching for specimens among the grass stems. (p. 109)

However, our sense of smell has not been entirely lost. For example, perfumers have the exceptional ability to distinguish up to 4000 basic smells—both natural and chemically produced—and to mix them in highly unique ways so that people will buy them (*The Economist,* 1985). The difference between French perfumers and "normal" people lies in their ability to step up their olfactory abilities and use them to affect the lives of others. Although recent research has shown that we are making better use of our sense of smell and that we are beginning to realize that smells affect our lives, we must strive to maintain our awareness of the messages that olfaction communicates.

Cultural Differences in Body Odor and Its Perception

In the American culture we can illustrate a broad range of attitudes when referring to our noses. As Winter (1976) states, "When we stick our noses into other people's business, we are interfering. When we stick our noses up in the air, we are snooty. If we thumb our noses at someone, we signify rejection. And, of course, if we rub our noses with someone, we demonstrate affection" (p. 23). Indeed, the nose plays an important symbolic role in American culture. But this observation also holds for other cultures. Mohammedans, for example, advise their adherents to observe a ritual washing of the nose with water each morning to expel the devils that are said to visit the body at night. Similarly, after death, the Eskimo must have their noses plugged up in order to prevent the soul from escaping and becoming restless.

The sense of smell also communicates affection in some cultures. Arabs, for example, are taught to breathe in each other's faces while speaking; to do otherwise is to deny another one's breath and is considered to be a grave insult. It is also an Arabian custom for a man's relatives to smell a woman before they select her for his bride.

In addition, in many cultures—as among the Eskimo, Maori, Samoans, and Philippine Islanders—a person may rub noses or place mouth and nose against the cheek of another person and inhale as a means of communication. Philippine lovers often exchange a piece of clothing on parting so as to remember each other by smell.

As you might suspect by now, the sense of smell *does* communicate. Yet our sense of smell communicates more than affection or cultural beliefs; it communicates racial, cultural, and family traits that help to identify us and to determine an entire range of acceptance and/or avoidance behaviors. The following table of cultural identifications shows how particular scents are associated with different cultures. As you should note, body odor is associated with the foods we consume. As Burton (1976) has argued, "the odor of Eskimos is due to a diet of fish; Mediterannean people smell of garlic and onions, and Northern Europeans have a cheesy, buttery smell. However, within these broad categories, there is much variation and people with a good sense of smell can identify individuals by odors

TABLE 10.2 Body Odor Across Cultures

Location	Diet/Odor
Central Europeans	Cabbage, turnips, radishes
Indians	Rice and spice
South Sea Islanders	Fruit and palm
Americans	Butter
Japanese	Fish

From Winter, 1976, p. 37.

alone, using true body odor and not tobacco, perfume, or other acquired odors" (p.113).

In more specific categories, some people claim that they can identify the difference between blondes, redheads, and brunettes by means of their scent. One gentleman, who travels frequently by air, tells how he will often motion a stewardess over and say, "You're a blonde, aren't you?" The stewardess is surprised because the man is blind and is also accurate about her being a blonde. Her response is usually, "Why yes, I am a blonde, but how did you know?" His answer is simply, "You smell like a blonde."

Environmental Olfactory Communication

As you begin this section, think back to the last time you walked into a hospital. How did you feel? Do you remember feeling nervous and developing sweaty palms as you breathed in the unique hospital odors? Now think of the delicious smells of popcorn you inhaled the last time you walked into a theater. Did the smell of popcorn invite you to buy? Perhaps you were flooded with brilliant memories of earlier days when, as a child, you went to the Saturday matinee.

Smells in the environment do communicate. They communicate positive messages, like the popcorn at the cinema, as well as negative messages. An example of the communication of a negative or warning message might be the smell of "gas" emitted when a tank of propane is almost empty. As we said earlier, it is not the actual gas that we are smelling but an additive, ethyl mercaptan. This additive enables humans to detect the smells of natural gas so that they may be alerted to its presence.

The addition of this odor to a harmful product is only one example of how odors can be used to communicate in the environment. Because of their chemical composition, many substances can transmit messages of potential harm to the consumer. Cain (1977) points out that people easily recognize odors from memory. In fact, even over time, sensory recognition is extremely stable.

Many people find the aroma of freshly baked donuts a difficult message to resist. (Carolyn Brown)

Based on this discussion and the experiences that you have had in the past, you can see that the environment continually communicates olfactory messages. As Wilentz (1968) concludes, "There are many smells to which we, as olfactory receivers, adapt and respond. There are school smells and army smells, laboratory smells and church smells, as well as travel smells such as the clover you smell as you ride the highways . . . , the sage smell of the far West . . . , and briny smells of seaports everywhere" (p. 111). Overall, however, Americans usually believe that their environments should remain odorless. Odors that act as warning agents and those scents generated by perfumes and foods are basically the only exceptions.

Having discussed the human and environmental olfactory messages we receive, let us now turn to an examination of how the olfactory process works.

OLFACTION: PROCESS AND PHENOMENA

As you read through the preceding pages, you may have wondered about how the nose actually "knows" when a message has been transmitted. The following section will help describe the *process* of olfaction.

In the olfactory process, the act of smelling begins with an object that emits the odor, smell, or scent. The actual "smell" consists of molecules of volatile (in other words, gaseous) substances that are carried in the air to the olfactory apparatus. This sensitive region in the nose that receives the stimuli is an area of several hundred square millimeters located on the upper surfaces of the nasal cavity. It is approximately the size of two postage stamps and contains densely packed sense cells.

The brain ultimately receives and interprets the olfactory sensations. Winter (1976) summarizes the entire process in this way:

> When you smell an after-shave lotion or the perfume someone is wearing, you smell the molecules of the scent which have drifted to your nose. The odor molecules are inhaled with the air and dissolved on the wet film of mucus in your nose, and information about the molecules is relayed by sensory cells high in each nasal passage to the olfactory bulb where it is sent along tracts . . . to the brain. You then realize within a thousandth of a second that the person is wearing a particular scent. (p. 154)

Winter informs us that when a smell or scent is pleasurable, "there is a relaxation of the facial muscles, smiling, a pleasant tone of voice, laughing, nodding, opening of the mouth, and deeper respiration" (p. 154). Conversely, when a smell or odor is unpleasant, there is

> a turning away of the head and sometimes of the entire body. The head may be jerked back, the nose wrinkled, and the upper lip raised. The individual speaks with disgust and makes characteristic sounds such as 'ugh' or 'phew.' There may be coughing, compression of the lips, rubbing of the nose, frowning, putting the hand over the mouth, actual spitting, and a waving away of the source of the smell. (p. 154)

Although our sense of smell may not measure up to that of many species of animals, our noses are still extraordinarily sensitive. They also exhibit some common olfactory phenomena, which will be discussed in the next section.

Smell Blindness, Adaptation, and Memory

Some people are insensitive to differences in smells, much as a color-blind person fails to distinguish between colors. They simply cannot detect certain smells. This phenomenon is called **smell blindness.** Smell blindness, or even variations in sensitivity to certain olfactory messages, is related to the anatomy of the nose. As Burton (1976) states, "In some people the shape of the nasal passage hinders the passage of odor-laden air into the nasal clefts" (p. 109). Thus some people may be unaware of certain smells unless they inhale (or sniff) very deeply.

Another phenomenon associated with olfaction is called **smell adaptation.** Smell adaptation occurs every time you walk into a bakery and try to retain the ability to smell freshly cooked bread. Simply stated, when an odor (here meaning any olfactory message) acts as a stimulus, that odor may have an effect on the perception of subsequent stimulations by the same or other odors. In other words, when the same odor follows itself, or when one odor follows another, the second stimulation may be perceived as less intense than the first stimulation. This effect is termed smell adaptation.

Most likely you have experienced smell adaptation on a daily basis. This phenomenon occurs frequently and acts as both a blessing and a curse. Although we would like to be able to enjoy continually the smell of the fresh bread in the bakery or to savor the aroma of an excellent wine for long periods, our ability to adapt to smells will not permit us to enjoy the odor for a long period of time. However, on the positive side, smell adaptation allows us to become less offended by unpleasant odors that we may be exposed to for a long time.

Before you read any further, imagine for a moment the smells you associate with the following environments. If you can, write down a few of these associations:

A bowling alley   _____

A drugstore   _____

A small restaurant   _____

A dentist's office   _____

A spring morning   _____

Christmas   _____

Memories can be recalled instantly if you smell a familiar odor from your childhood: the shampoo your mother used, your father's shaving lotion, your high school locker room, or your classroom. But why does the phenomenon of **smell memory** occur? How can an odor or scent set off a flood of memories?

One explanation of why "odor" or "smell" memory (the two are usually interchangeable) can create such spontaneous recall is that smells are associated with significant emotional experiences in one's personal life. In fact, smells generally have no names of their own but are associated with the names of other things. For example, think of the last time you described a scent or odor without having said "it smells like _____." Can you describe some smell now without making a comparison using "like"? Try it.

Rubin, Groth, and Goldsmith (1984) conducted two experiments that reflect the unique quality of smell memory. Overall, they concluded that, compared with memories evoked by either photographs or names, memories resulting from smells are generally thought of and talked about less. However, when memories are, in fact, evoked by smells, they are usually more pleasant and emotional than those evoked by visual or oral cues. In other words, smell memory does seem to be associated with more significant emotional experiences in our personal lives.

Other researchers have noted a similar phenomenon that may be associated with smell memory. This phenomenon resembles the "tip-of-the-tongue" phenomenon, in which people are unable to provide a label for a taste experience. In this situation, however, an individual is exposed to a very familiar smell without receiving cues from the other senses. The results of such events suggest that, although we may be able to recall a given scent, our ability to label it verbally is relatively low, especially without additional visual or aural cues. To document this statement and illustrate the effect, two of your authors completed an experiment in one of their classes in nonverbal communication. Approximately two hours before the class, we saturated approximately twenty cotton balls with a variety of familiar liquids, placed them in small paper cups with tinfoil lids, and then punched tiny holes in the foil so that the class could smell the odor-laden cotton balls inside. Included among the liquids we used were suntan lotion, baby lotion, isopropyl alcohol, olive oil, cherry juice, and a variety of perfumes and after-shave lotions. Results of our experiment revealed that the students had difficulty labeling a number of the items, although they were adamant about having recognized many of the smells. However, once the smells were accurately labeled, the students could remember a number of pleasant (or unpleasant) memories evoked by a given smell.

So far in this chapter we have discussed several aspects of olfaction, including its definition and several phenomena with which it is associated. The next section will be devoted to measurement and classification of odors.

MEASUREMENT AND CLASSIFICATION OF SMELLS

What are some of the ways in which you perceive smells in the environment? Although the answer to this question may appear obvious (just inhale . . .), it is not so simple for researchers who investigate olfaction. One of the basic problems faced by olfaction researchers is inaccessibility of the sensory apparatus that produces the smells being studied. Thus it becomes a difficult task to construct reliable techniques for presenting stimuli to subjects. In everyday life we "sniff" in order to perceive smells. This procedure is also used in the laboratory, but not without some complexity. Usually, there are two methods by which a subject may receive accurate and measurable quantities of odorous materials. The first is through the use of an **olfactometer,** which uses the "sniff" method, and the second is through the **blast-injection method.**

The olfactometer is an instrument that was first proposed and designed by Zwaardemaker, an early researcher in the field of olfaction. Mueller (1965) describes its present structure as consisting of

> a pair of concentric tubes, one of which slides inside the other much like the arm of a slide trombone. The inner surface of the outer tube is coated with the odorous material so that if we slide one of these tubes with respect to the other we change the amount of the surface of the odorous material over which air travels. One end of the inner tube is led to the nostril, so that a sniff will cause air to pass over the material on its way to the nasal cavity. (p. 73)

Although many researchers have noted that this method is crude, results can be reliably obtained when the following variables are controlled: temperature, humidity, purity of the air, and purity of the odorous materials used. With these controls, the olfactometer may be used quite accurately.

The blast-injection method attempts to eliminate some of the uncertainties of the "sniff" method. With this method the experimenter can control the volume of gas, the pressure with which the gas is applied, and the duration of the exposure. Subjects are instructed to hold their breath until the stimulus is administered. At that time they inhale passively, much the same as in normal breathing.

Although the two types of measurements differ in methodology, research has shown that these differences do not generally result in marked changes of sensitivity results. Only differences in experimental procedures lead to large differences in statements about olfactory sensitivity. Thus rigid controls should be placed on procedures in olfactory research.

Classifications of Smells

How many different smells can you name? Quickly jot down a list. How many did you think of? Four? Six? Sixty? Perhaps you can see a problem that many olfaction researchers have confronted. As you might suspect, many of the early classifications were destined to have inherent problems due to a severe lack of data. One of the earliest classifications was suggested in 1756 by the botanist Linnaeus, to whom we are indebted for the early classification of the plant kingdom. He listed seven primary smell stimuli: aromatic, fragrant, ambrosial, alliaceous, hircine, foul, and nauseous. An example of each odor is listed in Table 10.3.

Another scheme, and the one to which we most frequently refer, was proposed in 1916 (and revised in 1924) by Henning. His classification offered the following six categories: flowery, putrid, fruity, spicy, burned, and resinous. A third and more succinct classification of smells was presented by Crocker and Henderson (1927). They classified smells as fragrant, acid, burned, and coprylic.

As you can see, the three classifications reflect a difference of opinion. Even more, they reflect the amount of organization required for existing data as well as the need for further olfactory research. Until more reliable instruments are cre-

TABLE 10.3 **Linnaeus's Odor Classification**

Class	Example
Aromatic	Carnation
Fragrant	Lily
Ambrosial	Musk
Alliaceous	Garlic
Hircine	Goat
Foul	A "stink" bug
Nauseous	Putrefying flesh

Adapted from Engen, 1982, p. 8.

ated, however, valid classifications and cogent research will continue to be difficult.

In a previous section we discussed some of the aspects of the process of olfaction. At this point, we return to the study of olfactory messages as they relate to communication. In the next two sections, we will discuss olfaction and its effects on fear and sex drives as well as its powerful impact on the perfume industry.

Olfaction and the Drive States

As Cain (1977) notes, "If man does not communicate via chemical secretion, he is an exception to a very general rule. Other primates employ odourous secretions to mark territory, assert dominance, repel rivals, and attract mates. Perhaps the human primate's ability to verbalize his feelings reduced the need to communicate via olfaction" (p. 297). Yet human beings have inherited the necessary characteristics for transmitting meaningful chemical messages. For example, it is our external secretions that allow dogs to distinguish one person from another or to attack. Moreover, cowboys are said to believe that an odor of fear can be detected on humans by horses and often excites them beyond manageability (Bedichek, 1960, p. 142). Some *people* believe that they can detect fear in others through smell. Witch doctors, for example, are said to have the ability to detect the guilt of suspects. The literature reports that in order to determine the guilt of a person, the witch doctor lines up all suspects and begins a series of "divinations," which include "sniffing." Provided that the guilty person believes in the "magic," he or she will be frightened—thereby giving away guilt even though remaining outwardly controlled (Burton, 1976, pp. 109–110). There is, however, no tangible proof that aggression, fear, or friendship can be conveyed by odorants.

Before continuing this discussion of olfaction and the drive states, a definition of the term **pheromone** is necessary. The word "pheromone" was coined in 1959 from the Greek *pherein,* meaning "to carry," and *horman,* meaning "to excite" or "to stimulate." Pheromones, unlike hormones, are externally secreted substances that exert a specific effect at a distance on the behavior of another of the same species.

Although there is little evidence supporting the transmission of the message of fear, data do indicate that smells (in this case called pheromones) act as messengers in sexual relationships. The scientists who are studying these pheromones include physicists, biochemists, sociologists, entomologists, sex therapists, physicians, psychologists, and economists.

The effects of pheromones are more easily seen in the mating habits of animals rather than humans. However, in the late 1800s a phenomenon called the French Boarding House Syndrome was reported in the medical literature. The case involved girls who were living in a boarding house and who were isolated from males. Results of the report showed that these girls entered puberty later than girls who were exposed to males, even when those "exposed" had had no personal contact with the males. Researchers noted that proximity to males somehow affected the female hormones.

Another study of human pheromones was conducted by McClintock in 1971 and involved female students living in an American college dormitory. Results of his study indicated that the menstrual cycles of close friends become synchronized over time. This effect was said to have resulted solely from time spent together—not from patterns of eating, sleeping, or verbal communication. Since 1971, two additional studies (Graham and McGrew, 1980; Quadagno, Shubeita, Deck, and Francoeur, 1981) have demonstrated the McClintock effect. In each case, the only conclusion was that some subtle form of communication takes place.

In addition, the McClintock study showed that when males were present, the length of the menstrual cycles varied. The general rule seemed to be that as exposure to males increases, the average length of female menstrual cycles decreases. Unfortunately, "exposure" to males was not clearly defined but was *suggested* to be no more than physical presence. If "exposure" had included physical personal relationships, there would have been a greater possibility of pheromonal stimulation.

Is there really such a thing as "love at first sniff"? According to a recent study, men preferred the smell of women in the middle of their cycles to that of women who were menstruating. The most popular scent was that of the pregnant woman. Are pheromones responsible? No one knows for sure, but an interesting fact is that the female pheromone level is at its highest level during pregnancy (Von Driska, 1978, p. 69).

Another interesting pheromonal finding has been discovered by a British research team at the University of Warwick. These researchers have announced that they have isolated a steroid in the sweat of males. When purified, this substance smells like sandalwood oil, which is often used as an ingredient in perfumes. But that's not all. Help is on the way for men who have grown weary of Brut, English Leather, and Old Spice. These researchers claim that the steroid is a male sex pheromone, which has a scent that attracts females. Equivalent pheromones emitted by some female insects, for instance, draw males from miles around. The researchers do not claim, however, that the scent will produce wild results that will revolutionize the laws of attraction. Rather, one scientist unimaginatively notes that the isolated steroid, when refined, creates an immediate empathy between people, even strangers (*Time,* 1980). At least it's a beginning.

Although there is some documentation of the presence of pheromones in humans and also of their communicative abilities, it is still questionable whether or not males actually secrete pheromones that stimulate females. The only "evidence" of a male sex pheromone in humans is recounted as follows:

> A young man was reputed to have great success with girls. After a dance, he would wipe the perspiring brow of his partner with a handkerchief that had been carried in his armpit. Apparently his body odor acted as an aphrodisiac, and the young man claimed that his technique was highly successful. (Burton, 1976, p. 113)

Unfortunately, no attempt has been made to substantiate this technique.

Although research has not verified the existence of male sex pheromones, one cannot overlook the extraordinary interest that humans have taken in animal scents and fragrances. Since ancient times we have borrowed animal sexual-scent products such as musk, civet, and castor. Could this interest in "animal sexual scents" say something in support of the existence of the pheromone? Burton implies that this is the case when he reviews the relationship between musky smells, to which females are sensitive, and testosterone, a male hormone (Burton, pp. 111–112). The question, however, remains unanswered. We only know that human beings are extremely interested in fragrance—the essence of the perfume industry.

Olfaction and the Perfume Industry

According to British fragrance researcher Juanita Byrne Quinn, "fragrance not only has a function of its own, it also is a medium for a message. These messages may be directed to the user about the product or they may be in the product to inform other persons about the user's personality or self-image" (see Winter, 1976, p. 108). Either way, fragrances are designed to convey a highly specific message. Their primary purpose *is* communication.

Suppose a female college student wants to be considered attractive by male college students. Should she wear perfume to communicate her message? According to Baron (1981), the answer is yes and no. It depends on how she is dressed. Surprisingly, Baron found that for a woman who dresses casually (e.g., in jeans and a sweatshirt), the use of perfume enhances men's evaluations of her attractiveness and likeability. Conversely, when she dresses more formally (e.g., in a skirt, blouse, and stockings), the presence of perfume actually seems to reduce perceived attractiveness. Baron concluded that the men in his study may have reacted more positively to women who dressed in the intermediate range of formality/informality and hence most like themselves. Thus, the perfume/informal dress and no perfume/formal dress conditions produced the highest attractiveness ratings.

In what ways do results such as these hold up in other communication settings? Are similar perceptions in operation in the workplace? To test the applicability of his earlier results on evaluations in a job setting, Baron conducted a follow-up study in 1983. His primary concern was the impact of artificial scents on evaluations of job applicants. To address this concern, Baron asked male and female subjects to play the role of personnel manager and interview either a male or female job applicant for an entry-level management position. In each instance, the interviewee's dress was held constant (slacks and a blouse or shirt were worn) and she or he either wore or did not wear perfume or cologne. Results of the study indicated that male interviewers assigned lower ratings to both the male and female interviewees when they wore perfume or cologne. However, female interviewers assigned higher ratings when perfume or cologne was used. (These findings were applicable for both job-related and personal characteristics of the job applicants as perceived by the interviewers.) Baron interpreted the findings as indicating that males had greater difficulty than females in attempting to ignore extraneous aspects of the job applicants' appearance and grooming. In other words, females may perceive efforts at self-enhancement to be both positive and a given; therefore they may be able to ignore such efforts in making decisions. On the other hand, men may see such efforts as not uniformly positive; therefore they may take them into account in decision-making processes.

Perfume: a minihistory.   According to Winter (1976), the word "perfume" literally means "through smoke." Primitive people discovered that by burning certain woods and resins they could mask the smells of bloody temple sacrifices. Eventually, the Asian countries taught the Greeks the art of perfumery. In fact, Hippocrates, the famous Greek physician, was known to have prescribed scented baths and massages as well as perfumes for treatment of certain diseases.

Today, the truly talented perfumers in the industry are known as "noses." There are only about fifteen such people in the world who are considered to be great. About a hundred more people follow closely behind. These individuals push their olfactory abilities to the limits. Indeed, as we stated earlier, "noses" are said to have the ability to distinguish among 4000 different smells and to detect any given smell in a mix of a hundred or more scents (*The Economist,* 1985; Winter, 1976, p. 112).

As you can see, the perfume industry has a long history, beginning with primitive times. However, in relating its history, we have not yet mentioned *why* fragrances have been used, especially in the Western world. The original reason for adding fragrance to such items as soaps, shampoos, detergents, and plastics was to cover the odors inherent in the materials. Then in 1966 Proctor and Gamble set the precedent of adding a fragrance to give consumers the idea of a cleanser's "natural, grease-cutting ability." The product? Joy dishwashing detergent! And the idea caught on.

Since then, the use of fragrance in household products has increased more than 15 percent annually (Winter, 1976, p. 106). Today, more than $500 million per year is spent to make products smell good. In fact, marketing experts say that it is more important for a product to smell good than for it to do its job well.

Thus, smells do seem to communicate messages—messages about the environment and others around us. However, smells are not the only messages that the nose allows us to receive. Our noses allow us to receive messages concerning the foods and liquids that we daily consume. The following section will focus precisely on this issue—the sense of taste and its relation to the sense of smell.

THE SENSE OF TASTE AND COMMUNICATION: AN OVERVIEW

Recall the last time you had a cold or the flu. Did food taste different from the way it tasted when you were healthy? Were there some foods that you could not taste at all? The answer to these questions is probably yes! Without the use of our sense of smell, food generally tastes like nothing at all. Unassisted, the sense of taste is able to detect sourness, sweetness, bitterness, and saltiness. It fails utterly to encompass the full flavors of meats, fruits, butter, and coffee. These and nearly all other foods depend for their appreciation mainly on the sense of smell.

Identifying flavor involves many different sensations. Our mouths become the perceiving organs, and the substance that acts as a stimulant is generally edible, drinkable, or smokable. However, it is smell that is primarily responsible for creating flavor. Taste takes on an important secondary role. Having acknowledged, then, the debt that taste owes to olfaction, we turn to the sense of taste as a medium of communication.

Every time we place a substance in our mouths, our sense of taste communicates. Much like the sense of smell, the **sense of taste** acts as a medium that carries messages of pleasure as well as warning to the brain. Think, for example, of bitter foods that you have sampled. Did you immediately enjoy them? Probably not. We have long associated bitter flavors with poison, and only through experience do we come to enjoy bitter taste qualities.

Yet bitter qualities make up only one type of message that may be communicated to the brain. Taste is the final arbiter of all that is admitted to our bodies (Milne and Milne, 1962, p. 137). In other words, taste has the ability both to influence and reflect our own physical needs, food preferences, and cultural attitudes toward food preferences.

But what is a sense of taste? How can it "communicate"? To address these questions we offer the following sections dealing with a definition and classification of taste.

A Definition of Taste

Historically, the word "taste" was derived from the Latin verb *taxare* and/or an intensive form of the Latin verb *tangere*. *Taxare* means "to touch sharply," and *tangere* means "to touch" or "to appraise." Thus "taste" came to be defined as "a testing of the environment in an intense and intimate way" (Wilentz, 1968, pp. 131–132). In addition, the term implies both attention and coordinated activity.

Classification of Taste Qualities

Unlike the classification of smells, flavors or qualities of taste have evolved into a more formalized classification scheme: the bitter, salty, sweet, and sour taste scheme with which we are familiar. These four, however, have not always been the ones on which classifications have been based. The history of taste is said to date back to the Greek physician Alcmaeon, who lived during the middle of the sixth century B.C. However, it was not he but Aristotle who was said to have first listed the basic tastes. These taste qualities included the categories of sweet, bitter, sour, salty, astringent, pungent, and harsh. By the end of the sixteenth century, these seven evolved into nine: sweet, sour, sharp, pungent, harsh, fatty, bitter, insipid, and salty. By the end of the eighteenth century, there were additional alterations. If you followed Linnaeus, there were eleven; if you believed Haller, there were twelve. Both their lists were based on the previous sixteenth-century list, but with various changes.

Finally, in 1927 Hans Henning formalized the present classification of tastes: sweet, salty, sour, and bitter. It is interesting to note that these four had always been present in the classifications. It took the evolutionary process, however, to rule out the ones that did not utilize the sense of taste alone.

TASTE: PROCESS AND PHENOMENA

As with the sense of smell, there exist basic processes and phenomena associated with the sense of taste. Indeed, as Livingston (1978) has stated, taste is "a chemical touch system—[as such] it depends on physical contact with the object that is to be chemically appreciated" (p. 56). Because of the nature of this process, substances that are to be tasted must be soluble in water. Although a taste stimulus may initially take the form of a solid, liquid, vapor or gas, to be tasted it must be able to form a solution upon contact with saliva (Geldard, 1972, p. 480).

But what happens when the stimuli reach the receptor sites? Is a particular taste quality communicated only with the use of our tongues? These questions and others will be answered next in the discussion of the receptor mechanisms of taste.

Where Do We Taste?

As we stated earlier, learned men and women of science have proposed theories about our sense of taste since the earliest of times. Democritus of Abdera (460–360 B.C.) believed that sensations of taste were caused directly by atoms of a certain shape that fitted exactly into receptacles in the tongue. The Roman poet Lucretius (c. 90–55 B.C.) also believed this theory but stated it a bit more lyrically: particles of sweetness were smooth and caressed the palate, while bitter and sour particles were barbed and treated the palate harshly. It was not until the 1600s and the invention of the microscope that progress in the study of taste began to take place. The man who is credited with the discovery of **papillae,** the organs of taste, is Marcello Malpighi (1628–1694). Two centuries later, in 1867, Gustav Schwalbe and C. Lowen discovered and named what we now know more commonly as taste buds (Whitfield and Stoddart, 1984).

As early as 1750, the belief that the tongue alone was the center of taste was challenged by studies conducted on people without tongues. LeCat, in "A Physical Essay on the Senses" (1750), described two cases in which children without tongues were able to taste. The first child had been born without a tongue and the second had lost his tongue when gangrene, caused by smallpox, swept through his body. And yet both retained a distinct ability to taste.

And so it is that the tongue is not the only site at which stimulation takes place. We respond to taste stimuli in various regions of the mouth. These include the palate, the pharynx, the tonsils and epiglottis, the tongue, and, in some people, the mucosa of the lips and cheeks, the underside of the tongue, and the floor of the mouth. Children have additional areas of sensitivity to taste stimuli, but with maturity they eventually lose these.

Anatomy of the tongue.   Because it is so easily accessible, the tongue has been a primary target of taste research. The tongue's surface is covered with many tiny **taste buds** which are distributed fairly evenly across it. Within each taste bud is a cluster of taste cells, generally thirty to eighty in number, many of which are connected to sensitive nerve endings. The primary function of these connections is to stimulate the taste cells in each cell cluster.

Making up each cell membrane, in turn, are a number of molecules, some of which combine to form **receptor sites.** It is here, at the final level within the taste bud, that stimulation actually occurs. However, because of the structure and various locations of these molecules on a given cell membrane, many different receptor sites may be found on a given taste cell. Receptor sites, taste cells, and taste

Taste sensations are more acute in youth, but deteriorate with age as the density of taste buds on our tongues diminishes. (Carolyn Brown)

buds group together to form **papillae.** Papillae are the tiny bumps that you can see on your tongue if you stick it out at yourself in front of a mirror.

Although both papillae (and their taste buds) are distributed relatively equally over the tongue, they do not respond equally to a given stimulus. For example, at one time it was believed that the back of the tongue was more responsive to bitter tastes and that the front and sides were more sensitive to sweet and salty tastes. However, researchers have recently found that the front of the mouth and especially the palate have the lowest thresholds for bitterness. Conversely, the tip and the back of the tongue are more sensitive to sweet tastes, and the front and sides are more sensitive to salt (Coren, Porac, and Ward, 1979, p. 222).

Interestingly enough, taste cells have a relatively short life span—only a few days to be exact. This forces the composition of the taste bud into a perpetual state of change, with a number of immature cells around the outside of the bud, more mature cells near the inside, and some dying cells always present as well (Coren et al., 1979, p. 118). No one understands this phenomenon, but researchers believe that responses to certain stimuli in the mouth may damage the tiny taste cells.

Additionally, taste cells and taste buds change in number as we age. During childhood and adulthood, each of the largest gustatory papillae that we have bear from 250 to 270 taste buds. Later in life, between ages seventy-four and eighty, we lose quite a bit of sensitivity. This is due to a drop of more than 50 percent in the density of taste buds (Whitfield and Stoddart, 1984, p. 76). To illustrate the types of sensitivity that are lost, Schiffman (1977) conducted an experiment with twenty-seven college students (aged eighteen to twenty-two) and twenty-nine elderly subjects (aged sixty-seven to ninety-three). Schiffman found that college students correctly identified food stimuli (e.g., apples, bananas, pears, carrots, corn, potatoes, beef, and pork) more frequently than did the elderly subjects. As you can see, a considerable loss of food recognition and accuracy occurs as one grows into maturity.

In addition to the disintegration of taste sensitivity, there are other phenomena associated with the sense of taste. These include taste blindness and taste adaptation, both of which we will discuss in the following section.

Taste Blindness and Adaptation

Don't ever take your taste buds for granted. Every year one to two million Americans lose their ability to enjoy eating. Many common illnesses, accidents, and experiences can cause impairment of taste and smell perceptions. In fact, an estimated 30 to 50 percent of all expectant mothers suffer these problems temporarily during the first three months of pregnancy (Sobel, 1978, p. 269).

Blindness and adaptation are two phenomena associated with most senses, including the sense of taste. Think for a moment. Are there certain foods that either you or someone you know is unable to taste? When was the last time you had to resalt your food in order to retain the same level of saltiness that you encountered when you began to eat that particular dish?

Taste blindness is the inability to taste a substance that has an ordinary concentration. The common expression "that smells so good I can practically taste it" attests to the fact that the senses of taste and smell are linked very closely together. Often, an abnormality in one sense occurs simultaneously in the other. The area of taste blindness can be viewed in very specific terms. A person's sense of taste can be completely absent, diminished, distorted, or perverted. Total loss of taste is referred to as **ageusia;** a diminished sense of taste is called **hypogeusia;** a distorted sense of taste is called **dysgeusia;** and a perverted sense of taste is called **cacogeusia.** A person suffering from cacogeusia, for example, might experience pleasant-tasting food as foul or obnoxious. The best meats may suddenly taste rotten, omelets may feel like sawdust on the tongue, and even favorite foods may seem to smell like garbage. One writer relates, "While the loss of the ability to taste or smell is unpleasant, the distortion or perversion of the senses can be downright frightening" (Scott, 1977, p. 8).

Interestingly enough, people often differ extremely in their sensitivity to specific tastes. In other words, while some people experience taste blindness regarding one specific substance or set of substances, others experience "blindness" with other substances. To illustrate this phenomenon, Hall, Bartoshuk, Cain, and Stevens (1975) studied taste blindness and the effects of caffeine. They found that bitterness in caffeine was barely perceived by one group of their subjects, while a second group could perceive no bitter taste at all, even with the caffeine at the same levels of concentration.*

A second phenomenon that is associated with taste, as well as with other senses such as hearing and olfaction, is adaptation. Every time you resalt your food at the dinner table, you are displaying symptoms of **taste adaptation.** In other words, as you eat salty foods, your threshold or sensitivity to salt decreases. In order to retain that level of sensitivity you must add more salt. One way to avoid taste adaptation is simply to eat something else between bites of salty food. Recovery time is only about ten seconds; no matter what amounts of salt you have eaten, you regain your ability to taste salt at lower concentrations.

One of the most interesting effects of the relationship between taste and communication is the phenomenon of **food preferences,** or the fact that we as individuals have particular foods that we like or dislike. In the next few sections, you will learn about the origins of food preferences, the influence of food preferences on an individual's selection process, and several evaluative criteria that are applied when decisions are made about food preferences. Additionally, you will learn some interesting facts about why one has a sweet tooth and why we crave interesting and novel foods at certain times in our lives. It is taste that communicates such messages intrapersonally and that makes us aware of our body's wants and needs.

---

* At this point we want to qualify the use of the term "blindness" when speaking of the sense of taste. Unlike visual blindness, people who are taste-blind may actually taste the substance—*if* the concentration is increased enough. Visual blindness, on the other hand, is perpetual; no amount of light entering the iris will allow a blind person to see (Coren, Porac, and Ward, p. 223). Nevertheless taste blindness is a phenomenon which is considered to be a form of sense blindness.

Origins of Food Preferences

Although the exact origin of food preferences has not yet been determined, researchers believe that our likes and dislikes have both genetic and environmental influences. For instance, the preference for sweet tastes is widespread among vertebrates and invertebrates alike and seems to be innate, or genetically influenced. Likewise, aversions to bitter tastes have been demonstrated early in life across a number of species (Cowart, 1981, p. 57). For example, think of the last time that you shared a bite of either a sweet or bitter-tasting food with your favorite pet. Chances are that if the morsel was sweet, your dog or cat eagerly gobbled it up. If the food was bitter, he or she probably sniffed it unenthusiastically and walked away.

On the other hand, extensive research (Birch, Zimmerman, and Hind, 1980; Rozin, Fallon, and Mandell, 1984; Crandall, 1985) has also revealed that many taste aversions are learned. In other words, educational and cultural influences affect our food preferences as well. For example, Rozin, Fallon, and Mandell (1984) found that, although correlations between parent and child preferences are generally relatively low, considerably larger correlations exist regarding disgust or contamination sensitivity with regard to foods. In other words, although children do not always like exactly what their parents like, they do model their parents' behavior in decisions regarding what foods do *not* taste good. Additionally, they learn which evaluative criteria to apply to testing foods for contamination.

Just as educational influences affect our food preferences, so also do cultural influences. For example, preferences for specific meats, seasonings, spices, and condiments have a basic ethnic origin that is culturally linked. To support this claim, we need only think back to a time when we have traveled to a different country. For an American, the response to being offered sheep's eyes or dog meat would be similar to that of the most cultured European when offered an American cheeseburger—both would be revolted. Likewise the ways Americans season their foods is very different from the ways in which East Indians, Koreans, and Persians season their foods. In this instance, food preferences may be said to have a cultural influence.

As you can see, food preferences originate from a variety of sources, biological, educational, and cultural in nature. As you also can see, if what we have said is true, communication becomes a primary tool in the acquisition of our preferences. At this point, we now turn to a discussion of a related matter: how food preferences, in turn, communicate messages regarding our body's needs. The primary topics we will discuss are our preference for novel foods and the "sweet tooth." In both instances, our preferences act as subtle forms of nonverbal communication.

Influence of Food Preferences on the Selection Process

How do you know which foods you *should* eat? Have you ever had a craving for a certain food product or for extremely novel foods? As we know, food is needed to sustain life. More importantly, certain foods are needed for the body to function properly. But how do we know which foods to eat? One researcher, C. M. Davis, may have some answers that again reflect how the sense of taste communicates.

In a study conducted with human infants, Davis found that infants displayed innate abilities to select what was essential from a wide assortment of natural foods. In addition, he noted physiological cravings of humans with specific food deficiencies. As he stated:

> Children with a parathyroid deficiency sometimes would eat chalk or plaster as a source of calcium; (in addition,) the bizarre practices of clay- and dirt-eating that are found among the world's poorest and hungriest people (may be) derived from needs for minerals in trace elements. (in Wilentz, 1968, p. 146)

Perhaps the most dramatic case evidencing the need for specific minerals is the story of a child with an adrenal tumor who kept himself alive with excessive intakes of salt. The child did so, not knowing that he was losing great urinary amounts of salt because of the tumor. His voluntary ingestion of salts helped to keep him from dying.

Our amazing human system works to maintain physiological balance in diets. Whether we do so innately or whether we have learned to maintain this balance is, as of yet, undetermined. We only know that when we are hungry, the message is communicated, and we "increase rates of injestion, frequency of eating, and rates of bar pressing in an operant situation" (Carterette and Friedman, 1978, p. 110). In other words, we perform instrumental behavior as our needs for food and food products increase.

All of these discussions bring us back to the question we asked at the beginning of the section: Why do we sometimes find ourselves craving extremely novel foods? According to research, it may be a vitamin and/or calcium deficiency that leads us away from familiar foods and into a state called **neophilia,** or a preference for novel foods. As Rozin (1967) has shown, in need states we develop a specific aversion for the old familiar diet that led to the state of neophilia. The acceptability of a specific food is not necessarily an attribute of the food or food group itself, but rather a direct expression of our needs, our habits of eating, and our degree of hunger.

The sweet tooth.   Humans turn to foods that are both novel and beneficial when they are experiencing a physiological deficiency. Is this also what happens when we find ourselves experiencing a "sweet tooth"? Researchers say yes. However, when we crave that Hershey bar or chocolate fudge cake, it is **food deprivation** and a need for calories that is responsible. When we experience calorie deprivation, our preference threshold has been lowered and our intake of sugar solution is enhanced (Campbell, 1958). To be more specific, drag out those brownies!

Evaluative Criteria Applied in Preferences for Food

According to research conducted in the field of taste preferences, several factors influence whether we like or dislike certain foods. As we have seen, although both genetic and environmental influences are operative in our preferences for food, several evaluative criteria also are applied when decisions concerning preferences are made. These include (1) our expectations, (2) our personality, (3) the color and (4) texture of the food, and (5) frequency of ingestion. Each of these topics will be addressed more completely in the following sections.

Expectations.   How many times have you tasted what you *thought* was Pepsi but unexpectedly turned out to be Dr. Pepper or Tab? Were you surprised? Provided you like all three, did the Dr. Pepper or Tab taste as good as they normally would? Some researchers say probably not; our individual expectations do influence whether the taste experience will be pleasant, neutral, or unpleasant. In fact, as Carterette and Friedman (1978) note, classical physics suggests that tasting a sweet solution should be a pleasant experience while tasting a bitter solution should be most unpleasant, particularly at moderately high to high bitterness levels. However, in actuality, if a person expects to consume a sour fruit drink but is served a very sweet fruit drink instead, the person may find the sweet drink to be unacceptable. Often bitter tastes are preferred to sweet tastes in spite of the fact that bitter solutions are less pleasant to taste overall (p. 177).

As you can see, expectations do affect the degree to which we find a taste experience to be pleasant or unpleasant. However, several researchers have found that personality type may also affect our food preferences and selections.

Personality.   Another interesting area in food-preference research focuses on food preference and individual personalities. For example, does your preference for certain types of food reveal something about your personality? Research has shown that people who are "sensation seekers" may substitute their taste sensations to avoid boredom. These people prefer chewy foods to soft; spicy foods to bland; and bitter foods to sweet. Other people may seek love and security from their foods. Benjamin Belden, Ph.D., head of the Chicago Center for Behavior Modification, found in his clinical practice that "obese people prefer mushy foods. Eating a lot can also be a substitute for aggression. You take another bite of chewy or crunchy food, instead of turning and biting what's bothering you" (*Self,* 1980).

Taking an interest in personality and food preferences, the United States Department of Defense also conducted a study of the food preferences of soldiers. The purpose was to establish whether or not there was a relationship between diet and personality traits. The members of the test group were encouraged to select whatever they wanted to eat from a group of 150 foods. Their behavior was studied over a one-month period, and the results showed some fascinating correla-

Research has suggested some correlations between food preferences and personality. (Teri Leigh Stratford/Photo Researchers)

tions between the foods the experimental subjects preferred and their personality types (*Self,* 1980). Some of the reported findings were as follows:

- Meat eaters were enthusiastic, liked action, and enjoyed selling themselves, ideas, and products.
- Those who preferred fish, fruits, and vegetables for their meals tended to prefer books, music, and art in their recreation hours.
- Those who preferred starchy foods such as rice, mashed potatoes, and spaghetti were rather complacent and tended to avoid making hard decisions or judgments.
- Those who preferred eating salads were fast-moving types.
- Those who liked desserts above all were excellent officer-types. The study showed that dessert eaters usually liked to dominate any situation.

You can conduct your own experiment with regard to food preferences and your personality. Observe your preferences for certain types of food when you are active, unhappy, excited, bored, or experience any other emotional state. When do you like soft foods, salty foods, starchy foods, crunchy foods? The relation of food preferences to personality type raises many important but unanswered questions. In the meantime, you may have to answer these questions based on your own experiences.

Color.   How would you feel if you were offered green mashed potatoes? What about an orange filet mignon? Every day, color influences whether we choose to eat certain foods. Not only do we determine whether a food has spoiled by its color, we also use color to tell us whether a food has been cooked as necessary or as desired. Color also determines whether we like or dislike certain foods. For example, Moir (1936) conducted two early studies concerned with the color of foods. In the first study, he prepared jellies having specific flavors, but he colored them inappropriately (for example, grape jelly might be colored red). When observers were asked to identify the flavors, often they were incorrect, even when they tasted and smelled the jellies (Moir, 1936; cited in Carterette and Friedman, pp. 162–163).

Moir also conducted a second study dealing with color and perception. In this study he prepared a buffet of foods for a dinner with scientific colleagues of the Flavor Group of the Society of Chemistry and Industry in London. As you might suspect, many of the foods were colored inappropriately (for example, mashed potatoes might indeed be green!). Interestingly enough, not only did many people complain about the flavor of the dishes, some also reported feeling sick, even though only the colors of the foods were altered. The foods were perfectly wholesome and had smells, tastes, and textures intact.

Color can affect our perceptions of and preferences for food. Yet there is another evaluative criterion that we apply when determining the foods we will eat—that of texture.

Texture.   Recently, in talking with a friend about serving a Jell-O salad as part of a meal for dinner guests, the friend made a very ugly face and said that she detested Jell-O. Her aversion to that food was based primarily on her perceptions of its texture: it just simply "did not go down very well." Although at the time her response seemed humorous, many of us do decide which foods we prefer on the basis of their textures. As Milne and Milne (1962) have noted, "all of us judge foods through a delicate awareness in the realm of touch, distributed widely over lips, gums, tongue and palate" (p. 137). This awareness not only aids us in learning about specific textures but also helps us recognize any substances that require additional moisture in the mouth (p. 137).

We perceive texture, then, both orally and visually. Texture affects taste through expectation but also through the enhancement of or interference with the perception of taste stimuli. Although temperature is important, texture remains an important attribute of a food if it is to be eaten and enjoyed.

Frequency of ingestion.   How many times a week can you eat a hamburger? What about steak or pizza? Can you eat the latter two foods as often as you eat hamburgers? Data suggest that people are not only aware of how often they consume a particular food, but also tend to rate some foods as more acceptable than others on a pleasantness/unpleasantness scale. Surprisingly, higher ratings are generally given for foods that we may not be able to tolerate on a daily basis. For example, it is interesting to note that a food such as bread, which is only moderately liked, can be served more often—even daily—than steak or pizza, which are very well liked but can be tolerated only once a week by most people who are asked.

Why does this taste experience occur? For Carterette and Friedman (1978), the best explanation lies in the cyclical preference patterns that seem to occur for very distinct flavors or foods. This pattern seems to apply especially for salient foods in the meal—for example, the entree. As the researchers have noted, if foods have not been eaten for a long time, they become more preferable. Likewise, they become less preferable after they are eaten—until a sufficiently long period of time has elapsed. At that time the cyclical pattern begins again (p. 167).

Interestingly enough, food-preference surveys support this statement. In fact, the usual outcome of such surveys is that respondents prefer to eat simple, familiar foods like hamburgers and mashed potatoes rather than unfamiliar foods or those with highly unusual sauces. The latter foods seem to be "too much to handle" on a regular basis.

In conclusion, we have argued that preferences for foods originate from a number of places. They are genetically influenced, environmentally influenced, and result from evaluative criteria that we have learned to apply. We hope that the next time you enjoy your favorite meal, you will think about the messages your sense of taste communicates. It tells you which foods to eat, helps you enjoy the foods you like, signals foods that are distasteful or contaminated, and indicates specific foods needed by your body. In turn, the messages sent by our sense of taste help to communicate our needs to others (e.g., physicians) as well.

SUMMARY

We use our sense of smell to provide information about our environment and others in it. Our personal body odors are unique and are influenced by a variety of factors ranging from the food we eat to the level of sexual arousal. In American culture we tend to "cover up" body odors and replace them with artificial scents such as perfumes and deodorants. In many other cultures, natural smells are not only preferred but are considered essential for close interpersonal communication.

In the field of medicine, smells can be used to diagnose several illnesses. In addition, smells can be used to aid in learning—particularly in the case of blind students. Animals use their sense of smell for defense, sexual stimulation, and survival, but humans are usually conscious of smells only when the smells invade their personal space or environment. However, when compared across cultures, different odors and smells communicate a variety of messages.

Smells in environments communicate both positive and negative images and attitudes. Some smells make you want to stay in the environment longer, while others make you want to leave immediately.

The process of olfaction involves the smelling of an object that emits an odor or scent. This odor is interpreted by the brain, and it is labeled and evaluated. In some rare cases, people have smell blindness, a condition that allows them to smell only certain kinds of odors. Smell adaptation is a phenomenon that most of us experience. It involves the gradual inability to perceive smells when we have been exposed to them for a sustained period of time.

The measurement and classification of smells have intrigued researchers for many years. Although several smell-measuring techniques exist, many are subjective and require additional controls. Classifications of smells have been proposed by several researchers. They tend to overlap but have slight differences—a fact that again reflects the need for refined research methods.

Olfaction can have an effect on both fears and sexual drives. Some researchers suggest that substances called pheromones act as messengers in sexual relationships. These pheromones are secretions of the human body that have a scent associated with them.

In the perfume and deodorant industry, smells mean big business. Some people who work in perfume factories can actually detect subtle differences among similar smells. However, most of us know that we like or dislike certain smells, but we may have difficulty in differentiating among similar ones.

The sense of smell is also very important in the area of taste. Without smell as an aid, we can taste only four different qualities—sourness, sweetness, bitterness, and saltiness. Tastes can be classified in a variety of ways. Most classification systems include the four basic qualities noted above and add others such as pungent, spirituous, or viscous.

The taste center in the human body is, of course, the tongue. However, we also respond to taste stimuli in various other regions of the mouth such as the palate, pharynx, and tonsils.

Sensitivity to taste of different kinds changes with age. This is because the actual number and size of taste buds tend to change with age. As with the sense of smell, we can have taste blindness and taste adaptation as well. For example, the more salty foods that you eat, the more salt you will need each time you eat such foods when tasting them in the future.

Both genetic and environmental factors influence our preferences for tastes. In addition, so do biological needs, expectations, and personalities. Finally, color, texture, and frequency of ingestion affect our food preferences. Regarding each of these variables, some form of evaluative criteria are applied.

References

Baron, R. A. (1981) Olfaction and human social behavior: Effects of a pleasant scent on attraction and social perception. *Personality and Social Psychology Bulletin, 7* (4), 611–616.

Baron, R. A. (1983) "Sweet smell of success"? The impact of pleasant artificial scents on evaluations of job applicants. *Journal of Applied Psychology, 68* (4), 709–713.

Bedichek, R. (1960) *The sense of smell.* New York: Doubleday.

Birch, L. L., Zimmerman, S. I., & Hind, H. (1980) The influence of social-affective formation of children's food preferences. *Child Development, 51,* 856–861.

Burton, R. (1976) *The language of smell.* London: Routledge & Kegan Paul.

Cain, W. S. (1977) Differential sensitivity for smell: "Noise" at the nose. *Science, 195,* 796–798.

Campbell, B. A. (1958) Absolute and relative sucrose preference thresholds of the white rat for sucrose. *Journal of Comparative and Physiological Psychology, 51,* 795–800.

Carterette, E. C., & Friedman, M. P. (Eds.) (1978) *Handbook of perception,* vol. 6A. New York: Academic Press.

Coren, S., Porac, C., & Ward, L. M. (1979) *Sensation and perception.* New York: Academic Press.

Cowart, B. J. (1981) Development of taste perception in humans: Sensitivity and preference throughout the life span. *Psychological Bulletin, 90* (1), 43–73.

Crandall, C. S. (1985) The liking of foods as a result of exposure: Eating doughnuts in Alaska. *Journal of Social Psychology, 125* (2), 187–194.

Crocker, E. C., & Henderson, L. F. (1927) Analysis and classification of odors. *American Perfumer and Essential Oil Review, 22,* 325–327.

Engen, T. (1982) *The perception of odors.* New York: Academic Press.

Filsinger, E. E., & Fabes, R. A. (1985) Odor communication, pheromones, and human families. *Journal of Marriage and the Family, 47* (2), 349–359.

Geldard, F. A. (1972) *The human senses,* 2nd ed. New York: Wiley.

Graham, C. A., & McGrew, W. C. (1980) Menstrual synchrony in female undergraduates living on coeducational campuses. *Psychoneuroendocrinology, 5,* 245–252.

Hall, M. J., Bartoshuk, L. M., Cain, W. S., & Stevens, J. C. (1975) PTC taste blindness and the taste of caffeine. *Nature, 253,* 442–443.

Henning, H. (1924) *Der geruch,* rev. ed. Leipzig: Barth.

Livingston, R. B. (1978) *Sensory processing, perception, and behavior.* New York: Raven Press.

McClintock, M. K. (1971) Menstrual synchrony and suppression. *Nature, 229,* 224–225.

Milne, L., & Milne, M. (1962). *The senses of animals and men.* New York: Atheneum.

Moir, H. C. (1936) Some observations on the appreciation of flavour in foodstuffs. *Chemistry and Industry, 55,* 145–148.

Mueller, C. (1965) *Sensory psychology.* Englewood Cliffs, N.J.: Prentice-Hall.

Quadagno, D. M., Shubeita, H. E., Deck, J., & Francoeur, D. (1981) Influence of male social contacts, exercise and all-female living conditions on the menstrual cycle. *Psychoneuroendocrinology, 6,* 239–244.

Rozin, P. (1967) Thiamine specific hunger. In C. F. Code (Ed.), *Handbook of Physiology* (Volume 1). Washington, D.C.: American Physiological Society, pp. 411–431.

Rozin, P., Fallon, A., & Mandell, R. (1984) Family resemblance in attitudes to foods. *Developmental Psychology, 20* (2), 309–314.

Rubin, D. C., Groth, E., & Goldsmith, D. J. (1984) Olfactory cuing of autobiographical memory. *American Journal of Psychology, 97* (4), 493–507.

Russell, M. J. (1976) Human olfactory communication. *Nature, 260,* 520–522.

Schiffman, H. R. (Ed.) (1976) *Sensation and perception: An integrated approach.* New York: Wiley.

Schiffman, S. (1977) Food recognition by the elderly. *Journal of Gerontology, 32,* 586–592.

Scott, M. P. (May 1977) Is something wrong with your sense of taste or smell? *Better Homes and Gardens,* pp. 8–10.

Self. (February 1980) Personality and taste, pp. 22–26.

Sobel, D. (October 1978) Taste and smell: What can go wrong. *Good Housekeeping,* p. 269.

The Economist. (June 29, 1985) Why French noses are the best, p. 47.

Time. (January 14, 1980) Eau de sweat, p. 50.

Von Driska, M. B. (January 24, 1978) Love at first sniff backed by sexuality experiments. *Arizona State University State Press,* p. 69.

Whitfield, P., & Stoddart, D. M. (1984) *Hearing, taste and smell: Pathways of perception.* New York: Torstar Books.

Wilentz, J. S. (1968) *The senses of man.* New York: Crowell.

Winter, R. (1976) *The smell book: Scents, sex, and society.* Philadelphia: Lippincott.

CHAPTER 11

CULTURE AND TIME

Culture is the sum of all forms of art, of love and of thought, which, in the course of centuries, have enabled man to be less enslaved.

André Malraux

From our personalities and ways of expressing ourselves to the ways we plan our cities and organize our economic and political systems, culture molds and determines how we will live. Look for a moment at the way in which culturally based behaviors are transmitted. Parents intentionally and unintentionally teach their children the verbal and nonverbal codes of their culture. Children learn these codes by imitation and in turn transmit them to the next generation. In this way culture passes from one generation to another. And yet human beings are not the puppets of culture that we have painted them to be, for they mold culture and, in creating their world, determine the kinds of people they will be (Hall, 1976, p. 4).

But what is culture, and what role does it play in the study of communication? Individuals in every society are said to develop their own verbal and nonverbal cues and pass them down through generations. These cues may include meanings of time, body motion, physical characteristics (such as facial expressions), space and proxemics, and touching behavior, each of which helps to set one culture apart from another. In some cases the differences are great, while in others they are indistinguishable. Yet each culture, and each subculture within the culture, has its own patterns and values that help to locate that culture in its own particular time and space. In turn, these patterns and values guide individuals in that culture in the way they think, express emotions, and interact with others. Thus the ways in which individuals from different cultures and subcultures interact are important to study for many reasons. We hope that these reasons will become apparent as you read further. For now, we will limit ourselves to an overview of the chapter.

The aspects of cultural communication presented in this chapter include time, body movement, facial expression, eye behavior, proxemics, and touching behavior. More specifically, the first part of the chapter will be devoted to a study of time. Included in this section will be discussions of the variables related to time and cultural differences in conceptions and uses of time. Following these two major sections, we will present a discussion of cultural differences in body movement and facial expression; in conceptualizations and uses of space; and in tactile communication. We hope that when you finish this chapter, you will have a greater understanding of how miscommunication may occur between individuals of different cultures. It is important to remember, however, that information presented in this chapter describes behaviors that have been observed in individuals of a culture (or subculture) as a whole; therefore they should not be generalized to all individuals within a given culture. Indeed, every human being has his or her own unique identity, mannerisms, and style of communicating with others. It is the impact that culture has on the individual that makes possible the following descriptions.

CHRONEMICS: THE STUDY OF HUMAN BEINGS AND THEIR TIME SYSTEMS

In this age of advanced and modern technology, the ways we choose to spend our time are of utmost importance. Not only is time money, it is a valuable commodity. We spend it, save it, buy it, and make it, and in general treat it as tangible and divisible. For Americans, years are divided into months, weeks into days, hours into minutes, seconds into milliseconds. And yet, surprisingly enough, this American view of the uses and conceptions of time is unfamiliar to most other parts of the world. Even more surprisingly, there are people who live within the borders of the United States who are unfamiliar with what is believed to be an "American interpretation" of time. For example, the Pueblo Indians, as well as other native Americans, are taught by tradition that an event occurs only when the time is right. The Pueblo child learns at an early age to remain silent and to give information only when it is time for him or her to speak. As a result, the Pueblo Indians and other native Americans may appear more reticent than American Caucasians. However, in reality, it may be prescriptions of the culture that are influencing their interactions. And this American subculture provides only one example. Many other cultures and subcultures do not have such a frenzied, clock-bound existence.

But why do such variations in time perception exist? Do cultural differences with regard to interpretation of and relation to time create many barriers to communication between cultures and subcultures? These are only a few of the questions that exist for researchers in **chronemics,** the study of how we perceive, structure, react to, and interpret time. Perhaps a look at the three existing perceptual levels of time—the **psychological, biological,** and **cultural time orientations**—will allow you to understand why miscommunication between cultures may occur.

The Psychological Time Orientation

From the moment we are born until the time we die, our individual cultures instill in us a partly conscious, partly unconscious concept of the passage of time. Americans, for example, with their preoccupation with death, suggest by their very language the value they place on the passage of time. Many Americans perceive life as unbearably temporal; as a result, they are highly future-oriented. Think of all those "time-saving" devices that have become "essential for Americans to exist," such as dishwashers, calculators, computers, and microwave ovens. Many European cultures, on the other hand, are less conscious of time and are actually past-oriented—they look to tradition and the past for their sense of time. The point to be made is this: All cultures and societies must deal with problems of time; therefore we must make some preferential statements concerning time. Three psychological alternatives have been reflected in studies of culture and societies. These alternatives include past, present, or future orientations of time.

The **past-oriented society** or culture is one that places a strong emphasis on reliving old times and retelling old stories. These cultures have high regard or respect for their parents and elderly persons in the society. The British, for example, as characteristically close as they are to Americans, place much emphasis on tradition and on the past. The ancient Chinese culture, in which ancestor worship and family tradition play strong roles, provides another example of the past orientation of time. Likewise, most North American Indian tribes value tradition

Some cultures place strong value on traditional rituals. (John Running/Stock, Boston)

and the past. The "powwow" is only one example that reflects the importance of family and tribe to the native American. Families of a given tribe may travel across the country to some specific location—usually on tribal lands—in order to strengthen family and tribal bonds through dance, prayer, and the giving of gifts. During this time spent together, spirits and souls are rejuvenated. Like other past-oriented cultures, these people see events as circular. As Burgoon and Saine (1978) have noted, for past-oriented societies, past events perpetually recur in the present and, therefore, have relevance for either similar or new situations (p. 100).

Unlike the Americans or the British, many Spanish Americans, Filipinos, and Latin Americans place a strong emphasis on present orientations of time. For these **present-oriented societies,** pleasure is derived from events in the present, and the spontaneity and immediacy of events are viewed as most important. As Prosser (1978) has so aptly noted, "'Live for today; eat, drink, and be merry, for tomorrow you may die' perhaps best expresses the present value orientation of time" (p. 184). Although the grandfather figure may still be present, in these societies he simply does not have the authority of the grandfather in the past-oriented society.

The third orientation, and the one with which Anglo-Americans are most familiar, is that of the future orientation of time. In the **future-oriented society,** an emphasis is placed on tomorrow—a tomorrow that is bigger and brighter only if one works and saves today. According to Daltrey and Langer (1984), to have a future orientation, the members of a society must experience (1) the projection of thoughts farther ahead in time (extension), (2) some degree of organization in their future outlook (coherence), (3) an increased amount of speed with which they see themselves moving through time (directionality), (4) perceptions that the future is heavily populated with events (density), and (5) feelings or attitudes about the future (attitudes/affectivity).

To illustrate the possible differences among cultures regarding a future orientation, Bentley (1983) investigated the future time perspectives of Swazi (African) and Scottish college students. He hypothesized that, should specific issues of concern for the future differ, cultural differences in the length of future time perspectives would emerge. Results of his study revealed that when concerns about work and education were addressed, no significant differences existed in the length of the future perspectives of Swazi and Scottish subjects. However, when asked about projections concerning their personal happiness, Scottish men and women were far more concerned than Swazi men and women. As a result, the Scottish subjects placed issues of personal happiness on a more distant temporal horizon, while the Swazi subjects, who were less concerned, did not. Bentley concluded that the relative importance of this variable for both the Scottish and American cultures "reflects a concern of Western society which emphasizes individuality rather than concern for family responsibilities" (p. 228). The latter concern is generally more characteristic of societies which emphasize the importance of the extended family (e.g., the Swazi subjects in his study).

As you can see, various societies do view time differently. As a result, they also exhibit different communication behaviors and actions (e.g., if two cultures have different conceptions of tardiness, what is "late" for one culture may be "early" for the other). However, through a greater understanding of a given culture's rules, we can learn to maximize our potential for communication. Indeed, such understanding is the goal of theory and research in nonverbal communication.

The Biological Time System

Just as different cultures have different psychological time orientations, the human body has its own time orientations, which generally are based on natural rhythms. Consider for example, the differences between "owl children" and "sparrow children." "Owl children" are at their best in the late afternoon and evening, while "sparrow children" are at their best in the morning. Everything from our sleeping habits to body temperature and metabolic rate depends somewhat on natural rhythms. It is this variation in rhythms that explains the difference between people who function better at night and those who function better in the morning.

Perhaps, the best-known classification of human rhythms classifies rhythms as ultradian, circadian, or infradian in nature. Described by Sharp (1981–1982), **ultradian rhythms** span periods of less than a day and are seen in changes in human respiration, rapid eye movements during sleep, and brain and heart activity. **Circadian rhythms,** on the other hand, span a single day and are best exemplified in "sleep-wakefulness patterns, response to drugs, variations in urine content, and in metabolic processes, in general" (p. 16). Finally, **infradian rhythms** span more than one day and are reflected best in women's menstrual cycles. The underlying mechanism of each individual rhythm is believed to be a "biological clock." In turn, each clock is hypothesized to be innate and to be the underlying mechanism of all rhythmic phases (for a more complete discussion of the classification above, see Scheving, Halberg, and Pauly, 1974).

Although the three rhythms delineated above have been of concern to chronobiologists for decades, a fourth set of rhythms which has generated popular interest comprises the **biorhythms.** In its simplest form, the theory of biorhythms states that we are influenced by three internal cycles from birth to death: the physical, sensitivity, and intellectual cycles. These three cycles vary in length, with the physical cycle averaging twenty-three days, the sensitivity cycle averaging twenty-eight days, and the intellectual cycle averaging about thirty-three days. During the first half of each phase, our energy is generally high; during the second half, however, our energies wane.

Biorhythm theorists also postulate the existence of "critical days," or those days during which a given cycle crosses from positive to negative. According to proponents, a physical critical day brings greater susceptibility to fatigue, while an emotional critical day produces more deeply felt emotions and periods of great highs or lows. Conversely, an intellectual critical day means a greater chance that we will be affected by slow thinking and poor memory. Additionally, it means a decrease in analytical and logical capacity.

As we have stated, the theory of biorhythms has produced a great deal of popular interest. In turn, researchers across a number of fields have become involved in testing the theory's tenets. The primary reason for this interest is the hypothesized link between "critical days" and such events as accidents, deaths, and murders. For instance, as Sharp (1981–1982) has noted, "Ernest Hemingway, Virginia Woolf, George Sanders, and Marilyn Monroe are said to have died on critical days. [In addition, critical days coincided with the deaths of] . . . John F. Kennedy, Judy Garland, Carl Jung, William Faulkner, Robert Frost, Pope John XXIII, Douglas McArthur, Winston Churchill, Gamal Abdel Nasser, J. C. Penney, J. Edgar Hoover, the Duke of Windsor, Harry Truman, and Edward G. Robinson" (p. 20). The association of such names with biorhythm theory is only one reason for its popularity. Another positive quality is its overall intuitive appeal.

Although the theory, indeed, has generated both curiosity and interest, recent research (Prytula, Sadowski, Ellisor, Corritore, Kuhn, and Davis, 1980; Floody, 1981; Ellis and Walka, 1983; Kunz, 1983–1984) sheds some doubt on the theory's validity and viability. For example, Kunz (1983–1984) tested the theory by examining three separate data sets: 727 deaths, 319 marriages, and student diaries. Results of his study revealed that none of the relationships between the events studied and critical days were statistically significant. Likewise, in a study based on data from Grand Teton National Park, no significant relationship was found between critical days and climbing accidents specifically (Ellis and Walka, 1983). As you can see, although biorhythm theory is intuitively interesting, it is only now being subjected to rigorous scientific research. Perhaps within the next ten years, the final verdict will be in.

Cultural Time Orientations

The third time orientation is the cultural time orientation. This orientation focuses on the way in which individuals in different cultures view time, and/or the patterns that a given culture has established in using time. As you might expect, understanding time norms of different cultures is not an easy task, even for the most experienced international traveler or businessperson. The reason for the difficulty lies in the existence of three different cultural time systems: technical time, formal time, and informal time.

As researchers have noted, **technical time** is the scientific way in which time is measured and therefore deals with precise measurements of hours, minutes, seconds, and so on. Because technical time is "nonemotional" and "logical," it has the least to do with interpersonal or cultural communication processes. An example of this time system would be the tracking of time by the space program, NASA.

Formal time, on the other hand, is not scientific; it is traditional and therefore influences perceptions of individuals who are communicating across cultural boundaries. More specifically, formal time is the traditional way in which a particular culture views time. In our culture, for example, Americans break time into centuries, decades, years, seasons, months, weeks, days, hours, minutes, and seconds. Our formal calendar has 365 days, our week has 7 days, and our day has 24 hours. As we stated in the introduction to this section, however, not all cultures view our particular time system as viable. Some cultures, such as farming societies, view time according to natural events such as the phases of the moon or the different crops in a season. In addition, variations in cultural uses of formal time may often be a reflection of religious and philosophical differences among people.

The question you may be asking at this point, however, is what makes formal time different from technical or informal time? In his book *The Silent Language* (1973), Edward T. Hall discusses as many as seven isolates or components of time that distinguish formal time. These include ordering, cyclicity, valuation, tangibility, synthesisity, duration, and depth.

Ordering of events is the first isolate that Hall discusses. This component of formal time focuses on the nature of time as fixed with regard to the ordering of events. Thus "a week is a week not only because it has seven days but because they are in a fixed order" (Hall, 1973, p. 145). However, ordering of events, it must be noted, may vary from culture to culture. Different cultures may vary from lesser to greater degrees on both amount of emphasis on this isolate and ways of ordering of events.

Perhaps the most taken-for-granted isolate in the American formal time system is the cyclical element. This element focuses on our inclination to group days into weeks, months, years, and centuries and on our perception of the cycling of these units of time. As you might guess, these units of time are perceived as "cyclical" as a function of the limited nature of the units and a given culture's need to segment time.

Two additional isolates that Hall discusses are valuation and tangibility. Valuation is based on the attitude of a culture that time is valuable and therefore should not be wasted nor taken for granted. Similarly, tangibility focuses on a given culture's consideration of time as a commodity (Hall, 1973, p. 145). These two isolates are particularly synonymous with the American perception of time.

Unlike people of some cultures and their perceptions of time, Americans also view synthesisity of time as a major component or isolate of formal time. Synthesisity may be described as the perception of the time as adding up (i.e., the smaller units of time go together to form larger units). For Americans, minutes and hours add up to days and weeks. Since we as a culture begin with the assumption that there is some basic order to the universe (other cultures do *not* perceive the universe in this way), there seems to be no other way to view the basic building blocks of time. As Hall (1973) states,

> We feel it is man's job to discover the order and to create intellectual models that reflect it. We are driven by our own way of looking at things to synthesize almost everything. . . . (p. 147)

Thus, whenever we interact with other people whose culture does not emphasize this isolate of time, we often have difficulty in communicating. Should you ever experience such an interaction, the feeling of imbalance that you probably will be feeling is the absence of the synthesisity element in the other person's cultural time system.

Another element of the formal time system in which we function is duration. For most people raised in the European tradition, time is something that occurs between two points (Hall, 1973, p. 146). It is fixed; it is measurable; it is a quantity. However, as we have seen, this isolate may function to lesser or greater degrees in other cultures. For the Hopi, duration is "the natural process that takes place while a living substance acts out its life drama," says Hall. "It is what happens when the corn matures or a sheep grows up—a characteristic sequence of events" (Hall, 1973, p. 146).

The last isolate that Hall discusses is that of depth of time, or the notion that there is a past from which the present emerges. Indeed, we need look no further than the American ideal that we invest in today for a better tomorrow to see the impact that this isolate has on our formal time system.

As we can see, the American time system has several components that are shared to a greater or lesser degree by other societies. However, as Zerubavel (1982) has noted, these concepts are learned in all cultures at a very early age— and are learned as "prerequisites for participation in an adult social world" (p. 3). In fact, from the standpoint of mental health, "not knowing the day, the date, or the year is . . . regarded as indicative of . . . mental problems" across a number of cultures (Zerubavel, p. 4). This subtle realization may be the cause of our discomfort when our watches stop or we cannot recall what day of the week it is.

The third and most difficult time system to learn and understand is that of **informal time.** Because of its loose definition and its basis on day-to-day practices, informal time systems are unconscious and can only be understood within a situational context. Consequently, this time system is the most difficult for persons outside of the culture to understand.

In the American informal time system, ambiguity plays an important role. When was the last time a friend told you that he or she would be ready "in a minute" or "shortly"? Unless you knew that person, the situation, and the way in which the term was used, you would have had difficulty determining his or her meaning. Words and phrases such as "shortly" or "in a minute" are part of the eight levels of duration in the informal time system in our culture. These eight levels may be described by the following divisions of time in the informal time system in our culture: immediate, very short, short, neutral, long, very long, terribly long, and forever. As you may note, "forever" can vary from the hour you may spend in a very boring class (not this one, of course) to a lifetime and beyond, while "in a minute" or "shortly" may vary from a second to thirty minutes. As you can see, informal time frequently uses the same vocabulary as that of formal time, thus leaving many people confused over meanings. How, for instance, does one determine the nature, or criteria, of "punctuality"?

Part of the problem of determining criteria for punctuality is that there are two conflicting ways of viewing it. Hall (1972) describes these as the "displaced point pattern" and the "diffused point pattern." To explain the two patterns, the "point" itself may be defined as the time that a person might expect his or her guests to arrive at a party—say, 7 P.M. Hall's hypothesis is that some individuals will arrive at the party anywhere from 6:30 P.M. to 6:57 P.M. (the latter time would be considered as "cutting it short"), with a majority arriving around 6:55 P.M. These individuals may be said to view time as "displaced" and will arrive before the appointed point in time. "Diffused-point people," on the other hand, will arrive anywhere between 6:55 P.M. and 7:15 P.M. These individuals do not see a certain time as fixed in space but view time as scattered and probably will arrive at the party "around 7 P.M." The displacement of a point in time, however, is a function of three variables: the type of social occasion and what is being served, the status of the individual who is being met or visited, and the individual's own way of handling time. There is always the possibility that someone will intentionally use punctuality as a message. Often businesspeople will deliberately keep clients waiting to send a message of their importance or of their demanding time schedules. The two time patterns would not necessarily cause problems if everyone understood which system others were following.

Although punctuality is not considered an element of the informal time system, four elements of this time system do exist. They include **urgency, activity, variety** (variety is a factor in boredom), and **monochronism** (Hall, 1972, pp. 152–154). The timing of events, for example, may clearly signify urgency. A telephone call, for example, at two or three in the morning communicates something entirely different from a call in the early or late afternoon. Activity and variety, on the other hand, refer to whether or not we are doing something with our time and whether or not we vary the activities in which we engage. A number of other cultures—for instance, the Navajo, Trukese, eastern Mediterranean Arab cultures, Japanese, and many of those of India—include ordinary sitting as activity. For Americans, the attitude toward inactivity is much different: Without activity and variation, boredom will set in.

Perhaps the most important element in the informal time system, in terms of cultural and subcultural implications, is that of monochronism. Monochronism, which is prevalent in the North American culture, is the scheduling of only one activity at a time. Conversely, individuals in "polychronic" cultures, such as Latin America, may schedule several activities or appointments at the same time. Many Americans who have done business with either Latin Americans or Arabs have come home to the United States highly insulted. The reason is that "M-time," or **monochronic time,** emphasizes schedules, segmentation, and promptness, while "P-time," or **polychronic time,** stresses involvement of people and the completion of transactions rather than strict, preset scheduling. People in P-time cultures simply do not allow schedules to get in the way and place the job in a special category much below courtesy, consideration, and kindness to other people. In most "P-time" cultures, many people meet in one room, with the individual in charge moving from person to person.

The problem that many "outsiders" face when communicating with individuals from polychronic cultures is that one must be an insider or else have a friend in the bureaucracy in order to make any headway. People may be kept waiting because they are unknown, and unless they are willing to return repeatedly and meet their hosts outside the office, they have little chance of becoming active members in the P-time social system.* Both time orientations, however, have inherent problems. The problem with monochronic organizations often is that the M-time people are concerned only with schedules and are blind to the needs of those with whom they are interacting. The polychronic weakness is its dependence on the head person to do everything—scheduling meetings, working with many people at the same time, and simultaneously staying on top of things. If individuals of each of these time orientations are either insensitive to or unknowledgeable about the other, miscommunication can take place.

As you can see from the above discussion, time is inextricably woven into our everyday existence. We are only occasionally aware of the tremendous impact that time and our view of it have on our lives. Having looked at the different orientations and elements of time, we now turn to a discussion of time and its uses in different cultures.

CULTURAL DIFFERENCES IN CONCEPTIONS AND USES OF TIME

As we said earlier, time in our culture is considered to be a commodity—one that is cherished and bestowed as if it were tangible. As Samovar and Porter (1972)

---

* For further explanation of P-time and M-time, see Hall, 1976, pp. 14–45.

We often judge others according to their adherence to our own values about how time should be used. (Carolyn Brown)

suggest, "We place a strong emphasis on time as an aspect of history rather than as an aspect of immediate experience. We treat the present as a way-station, an intermediate point between past and future, and an immersion in the present is considered by some of us to be paganistic" (p. 15).

For Americans, a "long time" can be almost anything, from a couple of days to ten or twenty years. If a barrier to some desired goal exists, duration of time may be seen as lasting even longer (Quigley, Combs, and O'Leary, 1984). This orientation, however, does not hold true for many other cultures. A person from southern Asia, for example, often equates a "long time" with thousands of years or even an endless period. As a result, this person would probably find much humor in our stepped-up, fast-paced age of "long-term" projects lasting five to eight years.

Conversely, should an American visit a South American country, he or she might also be amused—depending on whether the trip was for business or pleasure. As Levine and Wolff (1985) note in an account of Levine's first day as a visiting professor in Brazil:

> My [first] class was scheduled from 10 until noon. Many students came late, some very late. Several arrived after 10:30. A few showed up closer to 11. Two came after that. All of the latecomers wore the relaxed smiles that I came, later, to enjoy. Each one said hello, and although a few apologized briefly, none

seemed terribly concerned about lateness. They assumed that I understood. (p. 30)

Later, in a cross-cultural experiment, Levine discovered that the average Brazilian student defines "lateness" for an event as approximately 33½ minutes after the scheduled time. Conversely, students from California consider an arrival 19 minutes after a designated time to be a "late" arrival. However, for Brazilians, to be "early" is to arrive an average of 54 minutes ahead of time; for Americans, to arrive approximately 25 minutes ahead of schedule is considered to be "early."

Another example of variations in treatment of past and future time is that of the Truk Islanders. The culture is said to treat the past as if it were the present. Because the language has no past tense, all past offenses, grudges, and personal traumas (for example, the murder of a relative many years before the present) are perpetually remembered and are treated as if they just happened. Compliments and gifts are also remembered continually.

A fourth variation in the uses and interpretations of time is one that is conceptualized by the Tiv culture. According to Hall (1972), the Tiv week varies from five to seven days and is named after the things that are being sold at the nearest market. As Hall notes,

> If we had the equivalent, Monday would be "automobiles" in Washington, D.C., "furniture" in Baltimore, and "yard goods" in New York City. Each of these might be followed by the days for appliances, liquor, and diamonds in the respective cities. This would mean that as you traveled about, the day of the week would keep changing, depending on where you were. (pp. 16–17)

Northern Europeans are perhaps the most similar to North Americans in conceptions and uses of time, although travelers may notice different values being placed on punctuality.

As you can see, conceptualizations and uses of time vary across different cultures and within cultures themselves. A better understanding of the psychological, biological, and cultural conceptions of time as well as information about different cultures can assist us in communicating with people from different cultures and understanding their nonverbal behavior cues. The cultural implications of body movements and facial expressions will be discussed in the following section.

CULTURAL DIFFERENCES IN BODY MOVEMENTS AND FACIAL EXPRESSION

Although research by Paul Ekman (1976) has focused on the existence of universals in facial expressions (we will discuss these in the latter part of the section), other forms of body movement such as emblems, greetings, body position, posture, and dance have not been viewed as universal. In fact, each culture has its own characteristic movements, body positions, and inherited meanings for interpreting them. It is important to remember that within each culture, many subcultural differences as well as individual differences exist. Thus a description of a culture only serves as a generalization and will not always apply to the individual members of that culture.

The purpose of this section is to acquaint you with some of the cultural differences of human body movement. After this section, we will introduce the notion of universality of facial expression and its relationship to culture. As we have mentioned, body movement varies from culture to culture. Perhaps a good place to begin a description of these differences is with the greetings that are used by various cultures.

Greetings and Culture

Throughout the various cultures of the world, many different kinds and types of greetings exist. Contrary to American belief, the handshake is not the only means of conveying a greeting. In fact, our handshake may seem quite out of place to some cultures such as the Polynesians, who may greet one another by embracing and rubbing each other's backs. The greeting, which some Americans use, of slapping another person on the back, however, would fit quite nicely into the Northwest Amazonian culture, whose members greet each other in precisely this way.

Another greeting in which the slapping or touching of the back is involved is the one shared by some Spanish Americans with one another. Individuals in this cultural group have almost a "stereotyped embrace"; they place their heads on the right shoulder of the other person, issue three pats on the back, and then place their heads on the left shoulder of the person and issue three more pats of greeting. To most Copper Eskimos, who greet strangers by buffeting them on the head or shoulders with their fists, this greeting would seem most out of place (LaBarre, 1972, p. 172).

Still another greeting used by many members of the Andamanese culture is perhaps the most bizarre when compared with those of the American culture:

> Andamanese greet one another by one sitting down in the lap of the other, arms around each other's necks and weeping for a while; two brothers, father and son, mother and daughter, and husband and wife, or even two friends may do this; the husband (however) sits in the lap of the wife. (LaBarre, 1972, pp. 172–173)

Thus, the greetings of various members of this culture differ vastly from those of the North American. However, other nonverbal messages differ from culture to culture as well. One such difference lies in the messages of and types of kissing behavior—a great American pastime—which you may not recognize in other cultures.

Culture and the Kissing Ritual

As described by one research team, kissing is Germanic, Graeco-Roman, and Semitic in origin. As they state,

> Greek and Roman parents kissed their children, lovers and married persons kissed one another and friends of the same or different sexes; medieval knights kissed, as modern pugilists shake hands, before the fray. Kissing relics and the hand of a superior is at least as early as the Middle Ages in Europe; kissing the feet is an old habit among various Semites; and the Alpine peasant kisses his own hand before receiving a present, and pages in the French Court kissed any article given them to carry. (LaBarre, 1972, p. 173)

Perhaps the greatest differences in **kissing behaviors,** when compared with those in the continental United States, are those of two other cultures—one with which you are probably familiar and another that you may not recognize. The one with which you are probably most familiar is the nose-rubbing behavior of the Eskimo and Polynesian cultures. The other is the kissing behaviors found in Tierra del Fuego. According to LaBarre (1972), kissing in Tierra del Fuego is performed "only between certain close relatives and young married couples or lovers; and not lip to lip, but by pressing the lips to the hand, cheek, or arm of the other, accompanied by a slight inward sucking" (p. 173). Strangely enough, this behavior is similar to most Andamanese good-byes, which, instead of the "inward sucking" motion, use a reciprocal, gentle blowing motion on the raised hand of the partner.

Finally, and most interesting, is the fact that kissing in the Orient often is considered in quite a different light. For many Oriental people, especially the Japanese, kissing is an act of private lovemaking, which arouses disgust when publicly performed. Although this fact may not seem so interesting at first glance, one need only think of the American movies that travel from the United States to Japan. Because of this sensitivity toward kissing that many Japanese feel, many of the major love scenes are often censored from these movies.

Beckoning Gestures and Gestures of Contempt

Another set of movements that may vary from culture to culture is that of **beckoning gestures** and **gestures of contempt.** As researchers have observed, simple movements elicit entirely different meanings as we move from culture to culture. Because of this fact, miscommunication between people from different cultures can occur when an emblem symbolizes different messages in two cultures. Perhaps this is especially true of beckoning gestures. In restaurants across America, for example, people often raise the forefinger to summon a waiter or waitress. Outside of these establishments, Americans may make a backward scooping motion toward the body to indicate that another person is wanted for something. In Latin America, however, beckoning gestures differ from American gestures.

Many Latin Americans will beckon other individuals with a downward arc formed by the right hand, much like the American gesture meaning "go away with you" (Ekman and Friesen, 1975, p. 175).

The Shans of Burma also have a gesture much different from the American one for summoning others. Placing the palm down, they move their fingers much as if they were playing piano arpeggios. Many individuals in the Boro and Witoto cultures would also be disconcerted by the American gesture, for these two cultural groups beckon "by moving the hand downward, not upward, as [we do] in our face-level wrist-flexing, cupped-hand 'come here' signal" (Ekman and Friesen, 1975, p. 175). It is understandable how members of one culture become confused when they visit other cultures. These kinds of problems must be dealt with in order for the cultures of the world to communicate effectively with one another.

Another set of gestures that differs from culture to culture comprises gestures of contempt. Before reading any further, think of the various ways that Americans use to communicate negative feelings such as contempt. Perhaps the two most obvious are the "social finger" (known more commonly as "the bird," performed by the upward thrust of the fist with the middle finger raised) and the slapping of the biceps with the opposite hand, resulting in an upraised fist. These two gestures differ from gestures of contempt in other cultures. Perhaps a look at some of these will help you to understand how easily individuals in given cultures miscommunicate feelings and thoughts.

One example of how a culture communicates contempt is that of the Pitta-Pitta aborigines of Australia. Many males of this culture show contempt by biting their

Hand movements may convey very specific messages, such as "hello," "good-bye," or "come here." (Carolyn Brown)

beards, while women may insult each other by protruding the abdomen, exposing themselves, and vibrating their thighs together. Another culture, the Menomini Indians, will often use the raising of a clenched fist to show contempt. The hand is placed palm downward, with the thumb and the first two fingers thrown forward (LaBarre, 1972, p. 174). Both of these gestures, however, differ from the "making of horns" or "evil eye," which is made by the extension of the first and little finger, with thumb and other fingers folded. This particular gesture is probably most familiar to Americans, for it is often found in the literature of many countries.

Interestingly enough, gestures of contempt also make use of other parts of the body and often have different meanings in different cultures and within given cultures. Hissing and spitting are two examples. Much as a Malayan Negrito may express contempt by "a sudden expiration of breath," Americans, too, have been known both to hiss and to spit. These gestures, however, may be both positive and welcomed by the Japanese, the Basuto, and the East African Masai. As LaBarre notes, hissing in Japan, by the sudden intake of air or a sudden breath, is often considered "politesse to social superiors, implying the withdrawal of the subjects' inferior breath in the presence of the superior person thus complimented" (p. 177). Likewise, an individual of the Basuto culture may applaud by hissing, and for the Masai spitting may be a sign of both affection and benediction.

Having discussed the various gestures of contempt that exist across cultures, consider the possible miscommunication that can occur when an emblem symbolizes different meanings. To sensitize yourself even more to the problem, consider the dilemma in which two world leaders, Presidents Brezhnev and Nixon, found themselves. Brezhnev, unfortunately, was unaware of American gestures of contempt and, upon entering the United States, insulted the entire nation with a seemingly innocent emblem representing the spirit of détente. What was the emblem? Upraised arms, meeting in a clasp of supposed friendship. Perceived as a symbol of victory, the gesture promoted only hostility for many Americans who watched.

As you can see, movements and emblems are culturally bound and must be dealt with if nations and cultures wish to communicate meaningfully. Posture, locomotion, and body positioning likewise play an important role in understanding nonverbal cultural variations.

According to Hewes (1972), although human postural habits have "anatomical and physiological limitations, . . . a great many choices exist, the determinates of which appear to be mostly cultural. The number of significantly different body attitudes capable of being maintained steadily is probably on the order of one thousand" (p. 193). Indeed, one need look no further than the different body positions of people in conversation to see that culture truly affects our nonverbal behaviors across cultures. Hall (1969) relates a story that clearly illustrates this point. His tale involves an Arab friend with whom he once took a walk.

> After years in the United States, (my friend) could not bring himself to stroll along, facing forward while talking. Our progress would be arrested while he

edged ahead, cutting slightly in front of me and turning sideways so we could see each other. Once in this position he would stop. His behavior was explained when I heard that for the Arabs to view the other person peripherally is regarded as impolite, and to sit or stand back-to-back is considered very rude. You must be involved when interacting with Arabs who are friends. (pp. 160–161)

Thus, the way people walk may communicate many different variables from status to how they are feeling on a particular day. Although the main purpose of the body and legs is not communication, we can receive messages from the ways in which a person walks, particularly if we are familiar with the person being observed.

Dance: A Reflection of Culture

From the beginning of time, humans have heard and felt rhythm. Their own heartbeat was the first rhythm they experienced, and then they encountered the rhythms of the ocean, the rain, and the sound of their own footsteps as they walked. Indeed, the natural development of dance, from a biological point of view, is significant in helping us to understand our human development.

Dance, like other body movements, is culturally bound and reflects natural movement patterns as well as the social and political events of the culture and times. One need look no further than the American dances of the sixties to find evidence of cries for change and revolution. The youth of the country were continually changing their dances to separate themselves from both the masses and the "older generation."

Other cultural messages, however, are also reflected in the dances that the cultures have produced. In Israel, for example, folk dances stress group unity, love of the new land, and faith in youth, and they also reflect the nation's struggle for identity and freedom. These folk dances often are done in a circle with the arms of the participants linked. In addition, each movement of the dance has its own meaning—for example, when the arms are stretched upward, the dancers are symbolizing praise to God.

Like Israel, Japan also reflects its culture through dance, and like other peoples it reflects its culture through a formally organized system of "body communication." Because the Japanese have a great affinity for the earth, the purpose of its traditional dance is to confirm the existence of the earth itself. Therefore, Japanese dance with a pressing down of the hips and with the knees slightly bent. This action makes the body appear shorter and in closer contact with the ground. The feet slide along, but with strong (foot) beats.

Many other dances could be described with regard to various cultures. The important point to remember is that dance reveals a cultural message, a philosophical view of life. For example, Western dances reflect aspirations toward the heavens, while Eastern dances reflect love for the earth.

Dance and all body movements, in whatever form they take, are bound by culture. Another set of movements involves facial expression and eye/gaze behavior.

Before discussing these, however, we will discuss a major methodological question concerning their study: Are facial expressions universal or culturally bound?

Facial Expression and Eye Contact: Universal or Culturally Bound?

As early as the year 1872, with the research of Charles Darwin, the idea of universal facial behaviors for different emotions was existent. Researchers of the twentieth century such as Allport, Asch, Tomkins, Izard, and Ekman were a few who wrote in support of Darwin's view. There were, on the other hand, researchers who argued against universal facial expressions—such investigators as Birdwhistell and LaBarre number in these ranks—and who maintained that facial expressions were "culture bound."

There is today, however, much evidence supporting both views. Facial expressions for the most part appear to be universal with regard to the expression of emotions themselves, but, as Harper, Wiens, and Matarazzo (1978) state, "specific cultural norms may dictate differently how and when they are expressed" (p. 99).* Ekman and Friesen (1975) have done considerable research that supports the contention that facial behavior is both universal and culturally bound. According to these researchers, cultural differences in facial expressions occur for the following reasons:

1. Most of the events, which through learning become established as the elicitors of particular emotions, will vary across cultures.
2. The rules for controlling facial expressions in particular social settings will also vary across cultures.
3. Some of the consequences of emotional arousal will also vary with culture (pp. 99–100)

As Ekman (1976) explains, every culture does not have to have an emblem for each emotion,

> but those cultures which do have a facial emblem for an emotion are likely to base it upon the universal facial expression of emotion. [However,] there still could be a difference. For example, in signifying fear emblematically one culture could draw upon the brow/forehead part of the universal emotion and another culture could draw upon the lips. (p. 20)

Thus, research seems to reveal some evidence of universality of facial expressions, but with the stipulation that culture defines how and when they may be

---

* Although facial expression is often treated as a separate entity in the study of body movement (Harper, Wiens, and Matarazzo, 1978), the authors have chosen to treat facial expression and eye behavior in one subsection for spatial reasons.

expressed. With this understanding, perhaps the best place to turn for a discussion of cultural differences is to **display rules,** or those "unconscious automatic habits that modify or alter facial expression in accordance with the social situation" (Harper, Wiens, and Matarazzo, 1978, p. 101).

In one study conducted by Ekman and Friesen (1975), stress-inducing films were shown in American and Japanese colleges. It was found that Japanese and Americans, when alone, had virtually identical facial expressions. However, when American and Japanese students were placed in the presence of other people (e.g., experimenters), and when cultural rules about the management of facial appearance (appropriate cultural display rules) were applied, there was little correspondence between Japanese and American facial expressions. In addition, the Japanese were found to mask or hide their facial expressions of unpleasant emotions more often than Americans.

Harper, Wiens, and Matarazzo (1978) have also noted variations in display rules across different cultures. Some Mediterraneans, for example, intensify grief and exaggerate expressions of sadness. Many British, on the other hand, are noted for their understatement of emotion; even when sad or grieving, they will show little emotion outwardly.

Americans also adhere to cultural display rules. For example, the display of sadness in the United States is often neutralized, especially in public situations. Perhaps you remember the face of Jacqueline Kennedy at the funeral of President John F. Kennedy. Her grief was very private—at no time during or after the funeral did she display her feelings to the public. But as often as many Americans neutralize facial expressions, many Japanese go one step further. Individuals in this culture may mask emotion completely; they cover anger, sorrow, and disgust with both laughing and smiling. Again, it is important to remember that not all members of a culture will choose to neutralize or mask an emotion; many will display the exact emotion that they are feeling.

Many differences exist in the display rules of cultures, even though facial expressions in themselves may remain universal. In conjunction with facial expressions, nonverbal differences in eye behavior are a very important aspect of the study of facial movements. Perhaps the most extensive study to date of cultural differences in gaze was performed by O. M. Watson in 1970. Using subject dyads of foreign students conversing in their native language, Watson observed that Arab, Latin American, and southern European subjects focused their gaze on the eyes or face of their dyadic partners. Conversely, Asian, Indian-Pakistani, and northern Europeans were found to have a tendency toward "peripheral gaze" (or an orientation toward the partner but with no direct eye contact with the face or eyes), or no gaze at all (i.e., they would look downward or stare into space). An additional finding was that no correlation existed between gaze behavior and time spent overseas, a fact that suggested that gaze patterns or behaviors may not be completely "caused" by environmental–social influences (Watson, 1970, p. 112). In addition to the Watson study, other researchers have noted cultural differences in gaze behavior. One finding, for example, is that the British do not nod their heads to let you know they understand; rather, they will blink their eyes to let you know they have heard you.

Unlike the British, however, West Africans avoid eye contact to communicate respect as well as to acknowledge being in a subordinate role. This pattern is also found in some individuals in the Japanese culture, as previously discussed.

As you can see, cultural differences exist in all forms of human movement—in emblems, gestures, postures, and movements, as well as in facial expression and gaze behaviors. However, there are additional areas of nonverbal communication that reveal cultural differences. In the next section, we will discuss another of these areas, that of proxemics.

PROXEMICS: OUR CULTURAL CONCEPTUALIZATIONS AND USES OF SPACE

Unlike the universals that appear to exist in the study of facial expressions, we have no universals for our conceptualizations and uses of space across different cultures and societies. Although we do make use of certain patterned interaction zones (the intimate, personal, social, and public distances that were discussed in another chapter), these, too, differ from culture to culture.

Engebretson and Fullmer (1972) offer one reason for the discrepancies. They state that, from infancy, the child is influenced by social associations that are characteristic for his or her social group. These associations act as a frame of reference for the individual in subsequent social interactions (p. 220). Thus, as with other nonverbal behaviors, proxemic or spatial behaviors correspond to the experiences and cultural traditions with which we have lived.

As with other nonverbal behaviors, proxemic behaviors differ from culture to culture. This statement especially holds true for intrusion distances. Hall (1969), for example, makes the following comparison between Western and Arab cultures:

> In the Western world, the person is synonymous with an individual inside a skin. And in Northern Europe, generally the skin and even the clothes may be inviolate. . . . For the Arab, the location of the person in relation to the body is quite different. The person exists somewhere down inside the body. The ego is not completely hidden, however, because it can be reached very easily with an insult. It is protected from touch but not from words. (p. 157)

For most Arab peoples, then, there can be no such thing as an intrusion in public: "Public means public." In this view, if you are standing on a street corner and someone else wants your spot, that person is within his or her rights to do whatever possible to make you uncomfortable enough to move.

In Germany, on the other hand, an individual's "space" may be invaded by as little as a gaze. To many Germans, for example, a person who is "inside" a building has been invaded when he or she can be seen from the outside. For these Germans, however, one does not have to be inside a room to be inside the zone of intrusion. Invasion may occur if one looks at another person for too long no matter how far away. The English culture is another culture that may seem to have a strange concept of "intrusion" when compared with that of most North Americans. When an English man or woman feels that he or she needs to be alone, a phone call may be considered an intrusion. In fact, to phone someone in England is often unheard of unless the situation involves business transactions or emergencies. To phone without reason is considered by many to be "pushy" or "rude." If one wishes to communicate other than in person, a letter or telegram is usually considered "less disrupting" than a telephone call (Hall, 1969, p. 140).

Thus different conceptualizations and uses exist for what is termed the **intrusion zone** in proxemic studies. However, there are also cultural differences in definitions of what is considered to be an appropriate **interaction distance.**

In one study conducted by Engebretson and Fullmer (1972), which was designed to determine the consistency of interaction distances within the Japanese culture, the researchers found that native Japanese had larger interaction distances than Hawaiian Japanese or American Caucasians. American Caucasian males and females were no different, however, than native Japanese in the distances that were maintained with authority figures such as fathers or professors (p. 225).

Many Arabs, on the other hand, have little sense of intrusion in terms of the sense of touch, and they also find an interaction distance of 2 feet or more to be equivalent to an American approximation of 5 feet. As Hall and Whyte (1966) note, to Latin Americans, we may seem "cold" and "distant," while to us they may seem intrusive and "pushy" (pp. 571–572). Likewise, we often find the Mediterranneans and eastern Europeans to be pushy, when in essence it is a natural tendency for these people to group more closely together. The definitions of interaction distances of these three peoples, along with that of individuals in the Cuban culture, who may stand only 18 inches apart when talking in quiet, all differ from American definitions of interaction distance.

On the other end of the interaction–distance continuum are British, British Americans, and black Americans, who traditionally desire large "body buffer zones." According to Scheflen and Ashcraft (1976), the Latin and eastern European Jew may find the British and British-American tendency to stand more than 36 inches apart, even in fairly intimate conversations, as a sign of both "coldness" and "detachment" (pp. 90 and 191). As we stated earlier, these latter people would find the Latins exactly the opposite—pushy and highly intrusive.

Perhaps the most extreme conceptualization of interaction distance, when compared with that of Americans, is the one that many Lebanese and Syrian villagers have adopted. Americans have a great problem when attempting to carry on a conversation across a room, but this is not the case in many of these villages, where this kind of interaction behavior may be a way of life. But as Scheflen and Ashcraft (1976) point out, adaptations within a culture are made with regard to activity, density, noise level, and so forth. These variations are, however, made from within the culture itself (p. 91).

The final question to which we now turn in this section is one concerning the different **conceptualizations and uses of office space** that exist in various cultures. The British are quite dismayed and puzzled by the American "need" for secure office space. The two cultures simply disagree on requirements of working space. For example, members of Parliament in England have no special offices in which to conduct legislative business. However, members of Congress in the United States will not tolerate a no-office situation. In their view, constituents, associates, colleagues, and lobbyists simply would not respond properly if they did not have offices (Hall, 1976, p. 53).

Another culture that varies from the American culture in its definition of office space is that of Germany, where the idea of double doors for soundproofing is important in offices and private buildings. Many Germans take the door very seriously and find American doors both flimsy and light. Additional problems that Germans find in the American use of office space include the "open-door policy" and the use of furniture arrangements. For many Germans, open doors seem "sloppy" and "disorderly" while closed doors "preserve the integrity of the room and provide a protection boundary between people" (Hall, 1969, p. 135). Similarly, many Germans feel that moving furniture about (especially to move closer to one with whom you are talking) both destroys the order of things and acts as an intrusion on personal space. To illustrate this feeling of intrusion, one German newspaper editor who moved to the United States was reported to have bolted his visitor's chair to the floor "at the proper distance" because he detested the American habit of adjusting the furniture to the occasion. Although this may sound odd, it really is not in light of German experiences. In Germany, furniture is made to be extremely heavy to act as a "deterrent" for those unfamiliar with German spatial norms (Hall, 1969, pp. 135–138).

Cultural differences exist in at least three realms of proxemics: intrusion distance, interaction distance, and the uses and conceptions of office space. As we have noted throughout this chapter, the discussion of these differences is based on generalizations, which are not necessarily indicative of all members of the given culture. In addition, we hope that you will see the potential for misinterpretations of nonverbal cues that exists in a world so diverse and rich in cultural definitions of nonverbal behavior. We now turn to a discussion of touching behaviors of various cultures in the final section of this chapter.

CULTURAL DIFFERENCES IN TACTILE COMMUNICATION

Why are some people more prone to touch other people? Most research on tactile communication says that we receive different kinds, amounts, and durations of touch from our parents as infants and that we reflect these differences as adults. Montagu shares similar views regarding tactile differences and adds that it is early tactile relationships, complemented by sound, that determine to a large extent how open, warm, and loving we will be when we reach adulthood (cited in Prosser, 1978, pp. 121–122). But what are some of the cultural differences that exist in tactile communication? This question will be addressed in the following paragraphs.

According to Montagu,

> Natural and cultural differences in tactility run the full gamut from absolute non-touchability, as among upper-class Englishmen, to what amounts to almost full expression among peoples speaking Latin-derived languages, Russians, and many nonliterate peoples. Those who speak Anglo-Saxon derived languages stand at the opposite pole in the continuum of tactility to the Latin peoples. In this continuum, Scandinavians appear to occupy an intermediate position. (cited in Prosser, p. 120)

The English occupy a position on the nontactile end of the continuum. This orientation may be attributed to the relationships between parents and their children, especially among the English upper classes. At birth, children of upper-class parents in England are usually turned over to nurses; during their early childhood years, they are reared by governesses. Once they have reached school age, they are usually sent away to school. Throughout these years, they have had a minimum of tactile experience. Thus you can see the importance of tactile experience as it relates to cultural differences. Because English upper-class children have a minimum of tactile experience, they learn to minimize their own giving and receiving of tactile communications.

Another culture that is non-touch-oriented is the Chinese culture. According to LaBarre, the Chinese people often have a strong aversion to being touched or slapped on the back; they even dislike shaking hands (p. 177). The Japanese and American cultures also may be classified as **nontactile cultures,** but perhaps not to the extent of the Chinese. Although many Japanese and Americans have certain prohibitions concerning interpersonal (tactile) contact in public, the effects of these cultural restrictions are usually restricted only to spatial separation in public (Engebretson and Fullmer, 1972, p. 221).

Even more nontactile than the English, however, are many Canadians of Anglo descent and most individuals of the German culture. Although French Canadians often are as tactilely oriented as the French from whom they have originated, Anglo Canadians are more nontactile than the English. Many Germans, too, are extremely undemonstrative, and as Montagu suggests, their "emphasis on the warrior virtues, supremacy of the hard-headed martinet father, and the complete subordination of the mother in the German family [has] made for a rigidified, unbending character which renders the average German, among other things, a not very tactile being" (cited in Prosser, p. 121).

As we stated earlier, the Latin and Russian cultures are highly tactile in nature, as is the Arab culture, with which Hall deals to a great extent in his research. As Hall (1969) has noted, "Americans and Arabs live in different sensory worlds much of the time and do not use the same senses even to establish most of the distances maintained during conversations. . . . Arabs make more use of olfaction and touch than Americans" (p. 3).

Other examples of **tactilely oriented cultures** are the Jewish and Netsilik Eskimo. The Jewish mother, for example, shows deep and unremitting care for her children. Until recently, children were breast-fed on demand, and there was much fondling of the children by the mother, father, and siblings. Interestingly, this description is akin to one that might be used to describe the Netsilik Eskimo (although not quite so extreme in terms of tactile experiences). Prosser (1978) describes this culture in the following depiction of Netsilik life:

> ... from the earliest orientations and essentially throughout their lives, the Netsilik Eskimos rely virtually upon a sense of touch, and by responding to sensations of touch or contact, learn to find their way in the environment created for the child by the mother. Later, the Eskimo male especially knows instinctively by combinations of touch how to discover a seal hidden beneath a frozen patch of ice, or how to find his way home after a long hunt in a blinding storm. (p. 123)

How different life would seem for us should we be placed in such a culture!

Having described some of the many differences in cultural displays of tactile communication, we should repeat what is perhaps our most important point: differences in nonverbal behavior often cause communication breakdowns at all levels of interaction, whether that interaction be at the interpersonal or international level. In addition, you should not forget that when you read descriptions such as these, you should avoid cross-cultural stereotyping of individuals from the cultures. These descriptions are based on cultural generalizations, which in turn are based on observation of individuals. Even if descriptions of cultural nonverbal cues are based on rigid experimentation, they cannot represent descriptions of every individual within the culture. Within every culture there are many variations. It is this variation that makes each human being a unique individual.

SUMMARY

Culture influences all aspects of our existence. Cultural interpretations and uses of time, body motion, physical characteristics, proxemics, and touch help to develop and determine behavior. Our conception and use of time has psychological, biological, and cultural influences. In some cultures psychological perceptions of time are past-oriented, that is, emphasis is placed on tradition. Other cultures perceive time as present- or future-oriented. Americans' view of time tends to be future-oriented.

Along with psychological influences, individuals experience differing biological time orientations. Three specific rhythms that we experience have been identified as ultradian, circadian, and infradian. Biorhythm theory also suggests that people are affected by physical, sensitivity, and intellectual cycles. Energy is high during the first half of each cycle and low during the second half.

Culture also helps to shape perceptions and use of formal, informal, and technical time orientations. The technical time orientation is the most universally consistent. Four elements of an informal time system include urgency, activity, variety, and monochronism. Although some cultures view time as a commodity, conceptualizations and uses of time vary across and within different cultures.

In addition, cultural factors influence differences in body movement and facial expressions. There are distinct cultural differences in manners of greeting, kissing rituals, beckoning gestures, gestures of contempt, and dance movements. Facial expressions, on the other hand, have been found to be universal for the expression of emotion. Cultural norms and expectations, however, influence how and when they are expressed. Cultural differences also tend to exist in eye behaviors.

Our cultural conceptualizations and uses of space vary across cultures and societies. The intimate, personal, social, and public patterns of interaction distances differ from culture to culture. Proxemic differences exist particularly in intrusion distance, interaction distance, and the uses and conceptions of office space.

One aspect of the use of space, that of touching behavior, also varies from culture to culture. The kinds, amounts, and durations of tactile communication are influenced by cultural norms and expectations. Differences in nonverbal behavior across cultures often cause communication breakdowns. An understanding and awareness of cultural differences should enable individuals to communicate more effectively, both interpersonally and interculturally.

References

Bentley, A. M. (1983) Personal and global futurity in Scottish and Swazi students. *Journal of Social Psychology, 121,* 223–229.

Burgoon, J., & Saine, T. (1978) *The unspoken dialogue: An introduction to nonverbal communication.* Boston: Houghton Mifflin.

Daltrey, M. H., & Langer, P. (1984) Development and evaluation of a measure of future time perspective. *Perceptual and Motor Skills, 58,* 719–725.

Ekman, P. (1976) Movements with precise meanings. *Journal of Communication, 26,* 14–26.

Ekman, P., & Friesen, W. V. (1975) *Unmasking the face: A guide to recognizing emotions from facial clues.* Englewood Cliffs, N.J.: Prentice-Hall.

Ellis, S. R., & Walka, J. J. (1983) Biorhythmic patterns of victims of mountain climbing accidents. *Psychological Reports, 53,* 612–614.

Engebretson, D., & Fullmer, D. (1972) Cross-cultural differences in territoriality: Interaction distances of native Japanese, Hawaii Japanese, and American Caucasians. In L. A. Samovar & R. E. Porter (Eds.), *Intercultural communication: A reader.* Belmont, Calif.: Wadsworth, pp. 220–226.

Floody, D. R. (1981) Further systematic research with biorhythms. *Journal of Applied Psychology, 66* (4), 520–521.

Hall, E. T. (1969) *The hidden dimension.* Garden City, N.Y.: Anchor Press/ Doubleday.

Hall, E. T. (1972) Proxemics: The study of man's spatial relations. In L. A. Samovar & R. E. Porter (Eds.), *Intercultural communication: A reader.* Belmont, Calif.: Wadsworth, pp. 205–220.

Hall, E. T. (1973) *The silent language.* Garden City, N.Y.: Anchor Press/ Doubleday.

Hall, E. T. (1976) *Beyond culture.* Garden City, N.Y.: Anchor Press/Doubleday.

Hall, E. T., & Whyte, W. F. (1966) Intercultural communication: A guide to men of action. In A. G. Smith (Ed.), *Communication and culture*. New York: Holt, Rinehart, & Winston.

Harper, R. G., Wiens, A. N., & Matarazzo, J. D. (1978) *Nonverbal communication: The state of the art*. New York: Wiley.

Hewes, W. (1972) World distribution of postural habits. In L. A. Samovar & R. E. Porter (Eds.), *Intercultural communication: A reader*. Belmont, Calif.: Wadsworth, pp. 193–200.

Kunz, P. R. (1983–1984) Biorhythms: An empirical examination. *Omega, 14* (4), 291–297.

LaBarre, W. (1972) Paralinguistics, kinesics, and cultural anthropology. In L. A. Samovar & R. E. Porter (Eds.), *Intercultural communication: A reader*. Belmont, Calif.: Wadsworth, pp. 172–180.

Levine, R., & Wolff, E. (March 1985) Social time: The heartbeat of culture. *Psychology Today,* pp. 28–30+.

Prosser, M. H. (1978). *The cultural dialogue: An introduction to intercultural communication*. Boston: Houghton Mifflin.

Prytula, R. E., Sadowski, C. J., Ellisor, J., Corritore, D., Kuhn, R., & Davis, S. F. (1980) Studies on the perceived predictive accuracy of biorhythms. *Journal of Applied Psychology, 65* (6), 723–727.

Quigley, J. J., Combs, A. L., & O'Leary, N. (1984) Sensed duration of time: Influence of time as a barrier. *Perceptual and Motor Skills, 58,* 72–74.

Samovar, L. A., & Porter, R. E. (Eds.) (1972) *Intercultural communication: A reader*. Belmont, Calif.: Wadsworth.

Scheflen, A. E., & Ashcraft, N. (1976) *Human territories: How we behave in space-time*. Englewood Cliffs, N.J.: Prentice-Hall.

Scheving, L. E., Halberg, F., & Pauly, J. E. (Eds.) (1974) *Chronobiology*. Tokyo: Igaku Shoin Limited.

Sharp, S. A. (1981–1982) Biological rhythms and the timing of death. *Omega, 12* (1), 15–23.

Watson, O. M. (1970) *Proxemic behavior: A cross-cultural study*. Hague: Mouton.

Zerubavel, E. (1982) The standardization of time: A sociohistorical perspective. *American Journal of Sociology, 88,* 1–23.

INDEX